THE

# LAW OF GOD,

AS

CONTAINED

IN THE

# TEN COMMANDMENTS,

EXPLAINED AND ENFORCED.

BY

WILLIAM S. PLUMER, D.D. LL.D.,

AUTHOR OF "THE GRACE OF CHRIST," &c., &c.

PHILADELPHIA:
PRESBYTERIAN BOARD OF PUBLICATION,
No. 821 Chestnut Street.

STEREOTYPED BY WESTCOTT & THOMSON.

# CONTENTS.

## CHAPTER XXIII.



## CHAPTER XXIV.



## CHAPTER XXV.



## CHAPTER XXVI.



## CHAPTER XXVII.



## CHAPTER XXVIII.

# THE LAW OF GOD.

---

## CHAPTER I.

### GREAT TRUTHS.

THINK not that I am come to destroy the law or the prophets; I am not come to destroy but to fulfil. . . . It is easier for heaven and earth to pass than one tittle of the law to fail.

JESUS CHRIST.

To obey is better than sacrifice, and to hearken, than the fat of rams. SAMUEL.

The law of thy mouth is better unto me than thousands of gold and silver. . . . A good understanding have all they that do his commandments.

DAVID.

The commandment is a lamp and the law is light.

SOLOMON.

He will magnify the law and make it honourable. . . . The LORD is our judge, the LORD is our lawgiver, the LORD is our king. ISAIAH.

The law is holy, and the commandment holy, and just and good. . . . Do we then make void the law through faith? God forbid: yea, we establish the law. PAUL

If thou judge the law, thou art not a doer of the law but a judge. . . . There is one lawgiver who is able to save and to destroy. JAMES.

Whosoever committeth sin, transgresseth also the law. JOHN.

If we have not the spirit of grace, the law comes only to convict and slay us. AUGUSTINE.

If even for one day I fail to compare my heart with the law of God, I am sensible of a decline in my devotional feelings. . . . If I give unto the law its proper definition, and keep it within the compass of its office and use, it is an excellent thing; but if I translate it to another use and attribute that unto it which I should not, then do I not only pervert the law, but also the whole Scripture. LUTHER.

The law is like a mirror, in which we behold, first, our impotence; secondly, our iniquity, which proceeds from it; and lastly, the consequence of both, our obnoxiousness to the curse. CALVIN.

There was never so much matter and marrow, with so much admirably holy cunning, compended, couched and conveyed in so few words, by the most laconic, concise, sententious and singularly significant spokesman in the world as we find in the *moral law*.

DURHAM.

The dignity of the name of divine laws is reserved to those which concern the duties of religion, such as the two fundamental laws [love to God and love to man] the Decalogue, and all the precepts contained in the Holy Scriptures about faith and practice.

DOMAT.

Two things there are, which, the oftener and the more steadfastly we consider, fill the mind with an ever new, an ever rising admiration and reverence; *the* STARRY HEAVENS *above, and the* MORAL LAW *within.*

KANT.

Ignorance of the nature and design of the law is at the bottom of most religious mistakes.

JOHN NEWTON.

None but rogues and felons look at a law to find out how they may evade it. HARE.

Of the law there can be no less acknowledged than that her seat is the bosom of God, her voice the harmony of the world. All things in heaven and earth do her homage, the very least as feeling her care, the greatest as not exempted from her power. Both angels, and men, and creatures of what condition soever, though each in different sort and measure, yet all with uniform consent, admitting her as the mother of their peace and joy. HOOKER.

I am confident of it, and affirm boldly there is not one man made free by Christ, that makes it his rule to be bold to commit sin because of the redemption that is in the blood of Christ; but that Christ who hath redeemed from sin and wrath, hath also redeemed from a vain conversation. All that have the pardon purchased by Christ for them, have also the power of God in them, which keeps them that they break not out licentiously. CRISP.

Though the moral law is not a Christ to justify us, yet it is a rule to instruct us. . . . The law of God is a hedge to keep us within the bounds of sobriety and piety. THOMAS WATSON.

Those only, who obey the word of the Lord's direction, shall enjoy the consolations of his love. MASON.

If a man have not spiritual and just apprehensions of the holy law, he cannot have spiritual and transforming discoveries of the glorious gospel.

COLQUHOUN.

The purity of the law appears from its forbidding sin in all its modifications, in its most refined as well as in its grossest forms; the taint of the mind as well as the pollution of the body; the secret approbation of sin, as well as the external act, the transient look of desire, the almost unperceived irregular motion.

DICK.

The divine legislator sees and knows the relations of things perfectly. He can draw no wrong deductions from them. He can make no mistake. Whatever laws have certainly emanated from him are certainly right. SHARSWOOD.

## CHAPTER II.

### LAW DEFINED.

A LAW is a rule of action. JOHNSON.

A law is a rule of action laid down or prescribed by a superior. WORCESTER.

Law as applicable to human conduct in general, may be defined a rule of moral action proceeding from a superior, having right to command, and directed to inferiors bound to obey.

EDINBURGH REVIEW.

Law is beneficence acting by rule. BURKE.

Law in its general and most comprehensive sense signifies a rule of action. BLACKSTONE.

A law is that which directs, prescribes, or controls.

STOWELL.

That which doth assign unto each thing the kind, that which doth moderate the force and power, that which doth appoint the form and measure of working, the same we term a law. HOOKER.

The law is void of desire and fear, lust and anger. It is *mens sine affectu*, mind without passion, *written reason*, retaining some measure of the divine perfection. It does not enjoin that which pleases a weak, frail man, but without any regard to persons, commands that which is good, and punishes evil in all, whether rich or poor, high or low. It is deaf, inexorable, inflexible. SIDNEY.

To every good law be required these properties: that is to say, that it be honest, righteous, possible in itself, and after the custom of the country, convenient for the place and time, necessary, profitable, and also manifest, that it be not captious by any dark sentences, or mixed with any private wealth, but all made for the commonwealth. ST. GERMAIN.

The Moral Law is a divine, unchangeable rule given to man, and accommodated to his nature, as he was created by God, obliging him to serve to God's glory as his last end. WILLARD.

The Moral Law is that which prescribes to men their religious and social duties; in other words, their duties to God and to each other. N. WEBSTER.

The Moral Law is the declaration of the will of God to mankind, directing and binding every one to personal, perfect, and perpetual conformity, and obedience thereunto, in the frame and disposition of the whole man, soul and body, and in the performance of all those duties of holiness and righteousness which he oweth to God and man: promising life upon the fulfilling, and threatening death upon the breach of it. WESTMINSTER ASSEMBLY.

A law, then, is a rule of binding force, given by a competent authority. It consists of two parts; *first*, a precept or direction given; and *secondly*, a sanction annexed, consisting of good secured to the obedient, or of evil threatened against the transgressor, or of both of these. A law without a sanction may be disregarded at pleasure. It is no law. It is mere advice. Blackstone:—"Of all the parts of a law, the most effectual is the vindicatory. . . . The main strength and force of the law consists in the penalty annexed to it." Promises of good, irrespective of law, are mere gratuities. Threatenings of evil, having no reference to law, are but arbitrary expressions of displeasure.

The Hebrew word commonly rendered *Law*, occurs more than two hundred times. It primarily signifies *instruction*, then *precept*. In a few cases it signifies a custom or manner so established as to form the rule of procedure.

The Greek word rendered *Law* occurs in the New Testament nearly two hundred times. Primarily it signifies any *thing allotted* or *apportioned*, then a *usage* or *prescription*, then a *law*.

It is not certain whether the Latin word rendered *Law* comes from a verb which signifies *to read*, because, in Rome, the laws were not binding till they were posted so that they might be read; or from a verb which signifies *to tie* or *make fast*, because law is of *binding* force.

In the Scriptures, the precise meaning of the word *Law* is varied according to the subject under consideration. In Psalms i. and xix., it is put for the whole word of God as then written. In Rom. vii. 23, it twice has the sense of a force governing our actions in our present sinful state. In Rom. ii. 14, it signi-

2

fies the law of nature. In John x. 34, and elsewhere, it signifies the Old Testament. In Gal. iii. 11, it is put for the works required by the law. In John i. 17, and elsewhere, it is a name given to the whole of the Mosaic dispensation. In popular use in Christian countries, it most commonly signifies the Moral Law containing the ten precepts or *words* as the Hebrew expresses it.

The law given from Mount Sinai consisted of three kinds of enactments:—

1. Ceremonial prescriptions and carnal ordinances. These were very numerous. All the times, and modes, and circumstances of public worship, and all the varieties of cases that could arise under a ritual the most minute are here ordained. If salvation by rites the most exact, and extensive, and Heaven-appointed had been possible, verily it had been by the Mosaic law. It far outdoes all modern devices. Yet it was powerless. It never made the comers thereunto perfect. Heb. x. 1. Indeed it was an intolerable burden. Acts xv. 10. It could not be endured. It has been wholly abolished. Acts xv. 28. And yet it had a shadow of good things to come. Heb. x. 1. Its typical representations of the Messiah were both numerous and instructive. It was abolished by being fully accomplished.

2. Another part of the law given from Sinai related to judicial proceedings. It regulated commerce between man and man. It provided for the establishment of justice, and for the punishment of crime. Some of its provisions, as the cities of refuge, had a typical reference. Some of them constitute a good part of the foundation of the municipal and judicial

rules of all Christian nations. They are not, however, of binding force on us except as they contain the principles of right and equity applicable to all men; or, unless they are incorporated into the laws of the state to which we belong. We are not living under the theocracy.

3. The third part of the code given from Sinai is the Moral Law. Very often in Scripture it is mentioned by way of excellence as *The Law.* This is the great code by which men's thoughts accuse or excuse them before God, and by which they will be finally judged.

# CHAPTER III.

## THE MORAL LAW AS GIVEN IN EXODUS XX. 1–17.

AND God spake all these words, saying, I am the LORD thy God, which have brought thee out of the land of Egypt, out of the house of bondage.

I. Thou shalt have no other gods before me.

II. Thou shalt not make unto thee any graven image, or any likeness of any thing that is in heaven above, or that is in the earth beneath, or that is in the water under the earth: thou shalt not bow down thyself to them, nor serve them: for I the LORD thy God am a jealous God, visiting the iniquity of the fathers upon the children unto the third and fourth generation of them that hate me; and shewing mercy unto thousands of them that love me, and keep my commandments.

III. Thou shalt not take the name of the LORD thy God in vain; for the LORD will not hold him guiltless that taketh his name in vain.

IV. Remember the Sabbath day, to keep it holy. Six days shalt thou labour, and do all thy work: but the seventh day is the Sabbath of the LORD thy God: in it thou shalt not do any work, thou, nor thy son, nor thy daughter, thy man-servant, nor thy maid-servant, nor thy cattle, nor thy stranger that is within thy gates: for in six days the LORD made heaven and earth, the sea, and all that in them is, and rested the seventh day: wherefore the LORD blessed the Sabbath day, and hallowed it.

V. Honour thy father and thy mother: that thy days may be long upon the land which the LORD thy God giveth thee.

VI. Thou shalt not kill.

VII. Thou shalt not commit adultery.

VIII. Thou shalt not steal.

IX. Thou shalt not bear false witness against thy neighbour.

X. Thou shalt not covet thy neighbour's house, thou shalt not covet thy neighbour's wife, nor his man-servant, nor his maid-servant, nor his ox, nor his ass, nor any thing that is thy neighbour's.

Forty years later, Moses rehearsed these commandments to Israel, with slight variations, which in no degree affect our duty to God or man.

## THE MORAL LAW AS GIVEN IN DEUTERONOMY V. 6–21.

I am the Lord thy God, which brought thee out of the land of Egypt, from the house of bondage.

I. Thou shalt have none other gods before me.

II. Thou shalt not make thee any graven image, or any likeness of any thing that is in heaven above, or that is in the earth beneath, or that is in the waters beneath the earth: thou shalt not bow down thyself unto them, nor serve them: for I the LORD thy God am a jealous God, visiting the iniquity of the fathers upon the children unto the third and fourth generation of them that hate me, and shewing mercy unto thousands of them that love me and keep my commandments.

III. Thou shalt not take the name of the LORD thy God in vain: for the LORD will not hold him guiltless that taketh his name in vain.

IV. Keep the Sabbath day to sanctify it, as the LORD thy God hath commanded thee. Six days thou shalt labour, and do all thy work: but the seventh day is the Sabbath of the LORD thy God: in it thou shalt not do any work, thou, nor thy son, nor thy daughter, nor thy man-servant, nor thy maid-servant, nor thine ox, nor thine ass, nor any of thy cattle, nor thy stranger that is within thy gates; that thy man-servant and thy maid-servant may rest as well as thou. And remember that thou wast a servant in the land of Egypt, and that the LORD thy God brought thee out thence through a mighty hand and by a stretched out arm: therefore the LORD thy God commanded thee to keep the Sabbath day.

V. Honour thy father and thy mother, as the LORD thy God hath commanded thee; that thy days may be prolonged, and that it may go well with thee, in the land which the LORD thy God giveth thee.

VI. Thou shalt not kill.

VII. Neither shalt thou commit adultery.

VIII. Neither shalt thou steal.

IX. Neither shalt thou bear false witness against thy neighbour.

X. Neither shalt thou desire thy neighbour's wife, neither shalt thou covet thy neighbour's house, his field, or his man-servant, or his maid-servant, his ox, or his ass, or any thing that is thy neighbour's.

Thus we have in two different books the whole *Moral Law*. Its precepts are of two kinds; some enjoining duties; some forbidding sins. The fourth and fifth command certain things. All the rest prohibit certain things.

## CHAPTER IV.

### THE GIVING OF THE LAW.

I. THE law was first given from Sinai two thousand five hundred and thirteen years after the creation. It is now, (1864,) three thousand three hundred and fifty-five years since this code was delivered to mankind in writing. To those living previous to the time of Moses, many of its precepts seem to have been pretty clearly taught by the light of nature, as indeed they are to all men. Paul says, "As many as have sinned without law shall also perish without law." Rom. ii. 12. Speaking of the heathen he adds, that "the work of the law is written in their hearts, their conscience also bearing witness" to it. Rom. ii. 15. Doubtless also, much of the divine will was known to eastern nations, by revelations with which they were made acquainted from time to time, before and during the existence of the theocracy. Melchisedec, Job, and the wise men who brought their gifts to the infant Saviour, are illustrations of what is here meant. It has always been true that, "in every nation, he that feareth God, and worketh righteousness, is accepted of him." Acts x. 35.

II. In giving the law, God exercised an unquestionable right. Every one's conscience says as much. Man is a creature. Surely his Creator has a right to direct him. In this very connection God claims universal sovereignty, saying, "All the earth is mine." Ex. xix. 5. Calvin: "God asserts his authority and right of giving commands, and thereby lays his chosen people under the necessity of obeying him." Man is dependent. If he, on whom he depends may not direct him, surely none else can, and man is not fit to direct himself, for he is blind, foolish and perverse. That God is fit to be a lawgiver, it is blasphemy to deny. The act of God in giving this law is therefore no usurpation, no encroachment upon our rights. It is but controlling, regulating, and asserting his own sovereignty over that which belongs to him by every conceivable tie. Weak as men are, they claim the right of doing as they please with their own. Who can deny the same to God? He is infinitely wise. None of his enactments are foolish or mischievous. In their operation they produce good only. Even the best temporal princes have err·d for lack of wisdom. To charge the same on God is atrocious wickedness. God is good. He has no evil designs. Malevolence is as far removed from him as folly. He is the most loving Being in the universe. Such a governor could not enact unrighteous laws.

III. In giving the law, God delivered it not as counsel or advice but as law. The very form of enactment indicates this—"Thou shalt," "Thou shalt not," "Honour thy father," and "Remember the Sabbath day." None but the perverse can misunderstand such language. Besides, God annexes sanctions to some of the precepts in immediate connection with them, and sanctions to the whole code in many general teachings of Scripture. These sanctions consist of rewards promised, and punishments threatened. All, therefore, which could prove any writing to be a law in the highest sense of the term, is found here. Competent authority enacts. The enactment has all the form of statute. The statute is supported by adequate sanctions. Stowell: "Obedience and blessing, disobedience and a curse, holiness and heaven, impurity and hell; these are the unalterable connections which constitute the sanctions of the law of God."

IV. In giving a law, we should expect God to enact nothing dishonourable to himself. This is just what we find in the moral law. There is no objection to the assertion that this law is a transcript of the moral character of God. He is not dishonoured by such a remark. The law is worthy of its author. The glory which Jehovah gets from the holy angels arises from their conformity to it. A great end accomplished by the gospel is the recovery of believers from sin to an agreement with the excellence of this law. In it there is nothing derogatory to the character of God. The only perfectly happy society in the universe is that of heaven, where every member is wholly conformed to the requirements of this code. The only perfectly wretched community in the universe is that of the world of darkness, where every member is entirely opposite and contrary to all the provisions of this law. On earth bodies of men are found to be either happy or miserable in proportion as they are more or less conformed to this code, so far as it regulates their intercourse with each other.

V. This law was given amidst the most extraordinary displays ever made upon earth, or ever to be made until the last day. The Jews have a tradition that there were seventy thousand angels present at the giving of the law. This may be a very incorrect enumeration; probably it is. The number may have been far greater; for "the chariots of God are twenty thousand, even thousands of angels." The number present was probably "innumerable." Heb. xii. 22. We have the best authority for stating that the law was ordained by angels in the hand of a mediator. Gal. iii. 19. The whole visible church of God on earth was also assembled around Mount Sinai on that occasion.

The greatest of all was that God himself was there—God, who is a consuming fire, whom the heaven of heavens cannot contain, whose dwelling-place is eternity, and before whom all nations are as a drop of the bucket. Yes, Jehovah was there in the brightest robes of glory and the most august and overpowering tokens of divine majesty. "So terrible was the sight, that Moses said, I exceedingly fear and quake." Heb. xii. 21. If such was the effect upon Moses, who spake to God face to face, it requires no stretch of the imagination to conceive how terror must have seized the people. Ex. xx. 19; Deut. v. 5, 23–28. Nor was God angry with them for being thus alarmed. The sight must have been terrific. The poetic description given by Moses is in these words:

> "The LORD came from Sinai,
> And rose up from Seir unto them;
> He shined forth from Mount Paran,
> And he came with ten thousands of saints:

"From his right hand went a fiery law for them.
Yea, he loved the people."

VI. The moral law was given in a way altogether peculiar. God never made to man in like manner any other communication. In the midst of the grand and awful appearances already alluded to, it was spoken by the Almighty in an audible voice from the top of Sinai, in the hearing of all the people. No other part of the law of Moses was thus uttered by Jehovah. Deut. iv. 33; v. 4, 22. Without any variation it was also twice written on tables of stone by the finger of God himself. Ex. xxxii. 15, 16; xxxiv. 1; Deut. x. 4, 5. The Lord would have it graven on a rock. These tables were long preserved in the ark of the testimony, covered with the divine glory. Ex. xxv. 16, 21; xxxvii. 1–9. Moreover, great preparations were, by divine command, made by the people for the space of two days together. They cleansed themselves and their raiment from all pollutions that they might come and stand before the Lord. Ex. xix. 10, 11. Every man seems to have been anxious to make himself ready for that great and dreadful day of hearing the law; a day more great and dreadful than ever any shall be, except that of judging men according to the law.

Besides, a strict injunction was given them to beware of touching the mount, or offering to ascend it,—a fence was placed around it, which was not to be violated on pain of death. Ex. xix. 12. "If so much as a beast touch the mountain, it was to be stoned, or thrust through with a dart." Heb. xii. 20. And even after God had descended upon the mountain, and the people had been brought out of the camp to meet with him, Moses was again called up to receive a new and more imperative prohibition of the transgression of the appointed limits. "Go down," said God, "charge the people, lest they break through unto the Lord to gaze, and many of them perish. And let the priests also, which come near to the LORD, sanctify themselves, lest the LORD break forth upon them." Ex. xix. 21, 22. No marvel that our Saviour said to the Jews, "Had ye believed Moses, ye would have believed me." John v. 46.

VII. At the giving of the moral law, it was not called by the name of the "Ten Commandments." Nor is it so denominated in any part of the Hebrew Scripture. It is more than once spoken of as the *Ten Words*. Ex. xxxiv. 28; Deut. iv. 13; x. 4. Yet the English version renders the Hebrew in these cases *Commandments;* but the original requires it should be *Words;* for we have not the word commonly rendered *Commandments*. Sometimes the Moral Law is called the *Covenant*, or the words of the covenant. Ex. xxxiv. 28; Deut. iv. 13; 1 Kings viii. 21; 2 Chron. vi. 11; Jer. xxxi. 32–34. Very often in Scripture the Decalogue has the name of *the Law* and sometimes of *the Commandments*. It is also often called the Testimony.

# CHAPTER V.

## THE GENERAL CHARACTER OF THE LAW.

I. THE law of God is *unbending*, *uncompliant.* This is the nature of all law. The law of gravitation in nature yields nothing to circumstances. The good man and the bad man alike feel its force in the prosecution of their benevolent or nefarious designs. A law that would yield to the caprices of men would be of no service either to direct them or to set forth the character of the lawgiver. The divine law may be *broken*, but it will not *bend.* We could have no confidence in the unchangeable character of God, if we found his law varying from time to time. He is a Rock, and his work is perfect. "I am the LORD, I change not." Mal. iii. 6. Domat: "There are no natural and immutable laws but those which come from God."

II. The law of God is *one* and *not many.* There is no conflict between its several precepts. The same authority enacts, the same benevolence pervades, the same sanctions attend each commandment. It is for this reason that an apostle says, "Whosoever shall keep the whole law, and yet offend in one point, he is guilty of all." James ii. 10. The law is a chain of many links. Break which link you please, and the chain is broken. Hare: "All God's commandments hang together: they are knit and woven together like a fine net, wherein you cannot loosen a single stitch without danger of unravelling the whole. . . . There is no letting any one devil into our souls, without the risk of his going and fetching seven other devils wickeder than himself." Although, by its peculiar form, the law seems to require only a few leading duties and to forbid a few atrocious sins, yet even this arrangement is found to be useful. Calvin: "Anger and hatred are not supposed to be such execrable crimes when they are mentioned under their own proper appellations; but when they are forbidden to us under the name of murder, we have a clearer perception how abominable they are in the view of God, by whose word they are classed under such a flagitious and horrible species of crime, and being influenced by his judgment, we accustom ourselves more seriously to consider the atrociousness of those offences which we previously accounted trivial."

III. The law requires compliance with its demands as *obedience to God.* It is not an accidental conformity to the letter of the law that will satisfy its claims. Men may avoid, for good reasons, the violations of its rules of temperance, honesty, and truth; but without any reference to the authority of the divine lawgiver. For their sobriety and uprightness they have their reward in health, thrift, and respectability. Men find infractions of the commandments oftentimes inconvenient and troublesome. To avoid vexation they outwardly conform, but this is not *obedience to God.* In all this they are consulting their own profit and advantage and not at all the glory of Him who made them.

Domat: "It is for God himself that God has made man. It is that he may know him, that he has given him an understanding; it is that he may love him, that he has given him a will; and it is by the ties of this knowledge, and of this love, that he would have men to unite themselves to him, that they may find in him their true life." This makes them like God.

IV. The law *comprehends all conceivable moral acts.* "Thy commandment is exceeding broad." Ps. cxix. 96. It enjoins all duties, binding on any rational creature. There is no form of sin which it does not forbid. Scott: "The breadth of the commandment shows the scantiness of man's best righteousness, and recommends the righteousness of the Redeemer, as alone commensurate with its holy and extensive requirements." All admit that the law of God extends to overt acts. The great error of many is that here they stop. Nor can it be denied that the law claims to regulate our speech. What would a rule of moral conduct be worth if it allowed all men the unbridled use of their tongues? "The tongue is a fire, a world of iniquity." James iii. 6. The law goes further. It prohibits all wicked thoughts. It is spiritual. Rom. vii. 14. Calvin: "If a king prohibits by an edict, adultery, murder, or theft, no man, I confess, will be liable to the penalty of such a law, who has only conceived in his mind a desire to commit adultery, murder, or theft, but has not perpetrated either of them; because the superintendence of a mortal legislator extends only to the external conduct, and his prohibitions are not violated unless the crimes be actually committed. But God, whose eye nothing escapes, and who esteems not so much the external appearance as the purity of the heart, in the prohibition of adultery, murder, and theft, comprises the prohibition of lust, wrath, hatred, coveting what belongs to another, fraud, and every similar vice. For, being a spiritual legislator, he addresses himself to the soul as much as to the body. . . . Human laws are satisfied, when a man abstains from external transgression. But on the contrary, the divine law being given to our minds, the proper regulation of them is the principal requisite to a righteous observance of it." The moral law enjoins all those things which are honourable to God and profitable to man. It extends to the affections and pronounces unholy desires to be sin, and all pious longings to be pleasing to God. It regulates motives. It declares David's desire to build a house for God to be pleasing to his Maker. It declares worthless all the fiery and ostentatious zeal of Jehu for the reformation of the true religion. The heart is the very centre of its dominion. The state of men's spirits no less than the actions of their lives falls under its precepts. Wickedness conceived is as truly an offence against its righteousness as wickedness acted out. "The thought of foolishness is sin." A malicious feeling, like a malicious word or deed, an unholy conception as truly as a wicked performance, infracts its principles. "Man judgeth by the outward appearance, but the LORD pondereth the heart."

V. The law is *right*. It is an unerring standard of duty. It is holy, just, and good. The Spirit of God is its author. Whoever is perfectly conformed to it knows no sin. Whoever wants conformity to it in all respects is perfectly wicked. Whoever wants conformity to it in any respect is so far a sinner. There is no moral goodness but is here enjoined. There is no moral evil but is here prohibited. Whether men's hearts and lives agree with other codes is a matter of comparatively small importance. If they agree with this, no more is required. If they disagree with this, conformity to any other can do them no good beyond this life. Every thing in the moral law is "exceedingly lovely and desirable."

VI. This law is *of perpetual obligation.* Some statutes expire by limitation. On their very face they are to be of binding force only for a term of years. But the law of God, as it has been the code of heaven ever since the creation of angels or men, so shall it be in the "dateless and irrevoluble ages of eternity." Sometimes a statute ceases to be binding, because it is repealed by a competent authority. But God has never repealed a single provision of the moral law. Christ himself declared that his mission was not to set aside any of its enactments but to fulfil them. And long after Christ's ascension the apostles repeated in various forms the precepts of the decalogue as in full force. This law is unrepealed and unrepealable. Colquhoun: "The authority and obligation of the law of nature, which is the same as the law of the Ten Commandments, being founded in the nature of God, the Almighty Creator, and Sovereign, and Ruler of men, are *necessary*, *immutable*, and *eternal.*" It is making Christ the minister of sin, and his blood the justification of licentiousness, to hold that the gospel sets aside or relaxes the moral law. Having stated with great force the doctrine of salvation by grace, Paul says, "Do we then make void the law through faith? God forbid! yea, we establish the law." Rom. iii. 31. We have never seen the Ten Commandments aright, unless we have perceived that "the obligations under which believers lie to yield obedience to them are greatly increased by the grace of the Redeemer and the mercies of redemption. If the saints are obliged as creatures, they are still more firmly bound as *new* creatures to keep those commandments. . . . The great Redeemer gives this high command to all his redeemed: "Be ye therefore perfect, even as your Father which is in heaven is perfect.''

VII. This law, like its Author, is *supreme.* It admits of no rival code—no conflicting claims. Within certain limits, father, mother, teacher, guardian, civil governments may and must be obeyed. But when they trench upon the authority of the statutes of the Lord, we can but set them aside. "We ought to obey God rather than man." Acts v. 29. Because God is greater than man, his commands override all others. God's supremacy establishes the supremacy of his laws. If He is over all, so are they. If He admits no rivals, neither do they. If any authority must yield, surely it ought not to be that of Heaven. If any claims may be deferred, those of the decalogue must not. Obedience to it may be threatened and followed by imprisonment, expatriation, confiscation, and crucifixion; but still it must be rendered. Though all other governments be disobeyed, here is a government that must not be slighted.

VIII. This law is in itself *practicable.* Man did

obey it perfectly until he fell from righteousness. His failure to obey it now is not chargeable to the law itself, but to his love of sin. A perfectly holy creature finds no difficulty in perfectly conforming to its requirements. It can be kept—it can be kept perfectly—it can be kept without weariness to its subjects. Though in the best of mere men on earth, piety is imperfect, yet the judgment of all the pious is, that the fault is their's and not God's.

Duncan: "What a strong argument for the divine origin of the system of Moses is furnished by the excellence of the moral precepts embodied in it! In science, in art, in almost every thing of a merely secular kind, the Israelites were far inferior to many nations of antiquity; yet in the writings possessed by them we find views of the character of God, and of the duty which he requires from men, immeasurably superior to those which prevailed among the most intelligent contemporary nations—nay, to those which are contained in the writings of the wisest philosophers of Greece or Rome. This fact cannot be explained on any other principle than that stated by the Psalmist: 'The Lord made known his ways unto Moses, his acts unto the children of Israel. He sheweth his word unto Jacob, his statutes and his judgments unto Israel. He hath not dealt so with any nation; and as for his judgments they have not known them.'"

## CHAPTER VI.

### CORRECT RULES OF INTERPRETING THE LAW.

EVERY document is to be explained according to its nature and design. As the law of God is spiritual, and the intention of giving it was the promotion of the divine glory, it becomes a matter of great importance that we rightly understand it. An error here may be fatal. By rules of interpretation, let no one understand so much a reference to the mere words of the law as to the general scope of the whole; and yet the sense, of course, is not to be learned without a correct grammatical construction of the words in which it is delivered. Let these rules be heeded.

I. Although no two commandments are precisely the same, yet it frequently occurs that one and the same thing, in different aspects, is required or forbidden in several commandments. Thus the eighth commandment says, "Thou shalt not steal," and the tenth says, "Thou shalt not covet." Now though there may be covetousness without actual stealing, yet there cannot be actual stealing without covetousness. So both these commandments virtually forbid us to lust after that which belongs to another. In like manner, covetousness often leads to Sabbath-breaking, and thus the fourth commandment often forbids the same sin as the tenth. And as the third commandment requires the reverent use of God's name, and as the right observance of the fourth commandment greatly promotes the fear of God, so these two commandments thus far enjoin the same thing. Colquhoun: "The first commandment is so closely connected with all the other precepts, that it is obeyed in all our obedience, and disobeyed in all our disobedience. Obedience or disobedience to it is virtually obedience or disobedience to the whole law."

II. Where a duty is commanded, the contrary sin is forbidden: and where a sin is forbidden, the contrary duty is commanded; and where a promise to the obedient is annexed, the contrary threatening to the disobedient is included; and where a threatening against the transgressor is annexed, the contrary promise to the obedient is implied. Colquhoun: "The duties required in the law cannot be performed, without abstaining from the sins forbidden in it; and the sins forbidden cannot be avoided, unless the contrary duties be performed. We must not only cease to do what the commands forbid, but do what they require; otherwise we do not obey them sincerely. A negative holiness is far from being acceptable to God. Every affirmative precept includes a negative one, and every negative command contains an affirmative." Thus the fifth commandment requires us to honour father and mother. Of course it forbids every act of disrespect to them. The eighth commandment, which forbids the sin of stealing, requires us to do all within our power to promote the temporal welfare of our fellow men. So also the promise of long life, affixed to the obeying of the fifth commandment, clearly implies the opposite curse upon those who disregard it. And the threatening annexed to the third commandment clearly implies that the opposite promise is made to the reverent and holy use of God's name. Had all sins and duties, all promises and threatenings been fully and formally expressed, the law would have become cumbrous; whereas, now it is easily remembered even by a child.

III. That which is forbidden in this law of God is never to be done, be the perils, or pains, or penalties never so great. No circumstances can excuse, much less justify transgression. Sin is always wicked. Disregard of any prohibition is always criminal. Between two natural evils we are often compelled to choose, as between the amputation of a limb and death. But between two moral evils we are never compelled to choose. He who steals may indeed be strongly tempted to lie; but the strength of the temptation does not justify falsehood. With every temptation there is a way of escape. It is not wicked to be punished for stealing, but it is wicked to lie about anything. "Let no man say when he is tempted, I am tempted of God: for God cannot be tempted with evil, neither tempteth he any man." James i. 13. There is no excuse for sinning even in the least.

IV. That which God commands is always our duty; and yet every particular duty is not to be done at all times. There is an order in our duties. Every thing is beautiful in its season. It is a duty to be tender-hearted, and to weep with those that weep; but it is not a duty to weep with those that are properly rejoicing. It is right to think upon God's name, and the habits of one's mind may be pleasing to God.

Yet our minds may be intently occupied for hours in a mathematical demonstration, so that we cannot have them turned to anything else. We are to do our duties as we have opportunity. We should always be in a right state of mind and heart to do what is required, if the occasion offers.

V. "Under one sin or duty, all of the same kind are forbidden or commanded; together with all the causes, means, occasions and appearances thereof, and provocations thereunto." Thus the prohibition to use God's name in vain forbids an irreverent use of his word. or works, or sacraments, or worship; because his name is that whereby he is known. Thus the commandment to honour father and mother obliges us to honour magistrates, who are politically our fathers; and masters and mistresses, who are domestically our parents; and teachers, who for the purposes of education are as parents to us. And as we may not kill, so we may not prepare to kill, nor indulge envy, hatred, wrath, nor any malice; nor may we use quarrelsome, abusive, or contemptuous language, nor violent and threatening gestures as these things do often lead to murder. When God forbade the use of leavened bread during the passover, he mercifully forbade the keeping of leaven in the house. "They who do always all that they lawfully may, will sometimes do more."

VI. What is forbidden or commanded to us, we are bound, according to our places, to do all that we properly can to cause to be avoided or performed by others, according to the duty of their places. In the fourth commandment, this is expressly stated to be the rule. In other parts of Scripture, the principle is applied to the whole round of our duties. What a man may not lawfully do himself, he may not lawfully aid, counsel, countenance, or encourage others in doing What a man is obliged to do himself, he ought to aid, teach, counsel and encourage others to do. We may not be partakers of other men's sins, by leaving them in ignorance of their duty, when we could teach them.

VII. The aim, scope, and tendency of this law is holiness. The sum of it is, "Be ye holy, for I am holy," saith the Lord. This holiness is not the assumption of a peculiar appearance, nor submission to a round of ceremonies, nor a mere profession of religion under any form whatever. The demand of this law is for rectitude in conduct, rectitude in speech, rectitude in thinking, rectitude in feeling. Holiness of heart alone is conformity to the law. This uprightness must be loved, and so must God the lawgiver, and man our fellow-subject. Therefore, a very important rule for interpreting any precept is to inquire what is its general scope and aim? what does God intend to prohibit? what does he design to encourage in the command? Domat: "For understanding aright the sense of a law, we ought to consider well all the words of it and its preamble, if there be any, that we may judge of the law by its motives, and by the whole tenor of what it prescribes; and not to limit its sense to what may appear different from its intention." In interpreting human laws, there is a rule, *Qui hœrit in litera, hœrit in cortice*, literally, He who sticks in the letter, sticks in the bark; that is, he does not penetrate to the heart of the tree. There is another rule of judging of the nature of a law: *Noscitur a sociis*:—It is known by its fellows. The meaning is something like this: if any of the precepts of the law are moral, they are all moral; if any of them comes to us with awful sanctions expressed, they all have awful sanctions implied. The same rule is expressed by Domat: "Laws are interpreted one by another."

VIII. This law is never to be so interpreted as to make us cruel to our fellow-men. "I will have mercy and not sacrifice." Hos. vi. 6; Matt. ix. 13; xii. 7. The law is good, and works no ill to any. It is benevolent. It abhors all cruelty. In Scripture, God often declares his preference for justice, faith and mercy, above any attention to the rites of religion, although prescribed by himself; 1 Sam. xv. 22; Ps. l. 8–15; Isa. i. 11–17.

IX. "Love is the fulfilling of the law." Rom. xiii. 10. For this there is no substitute. Compare Gal. v. 14. Jesus Christ himself taught this same doctrine. When one of the Pharisees said unto him, "Master, which is the great commandment in the law? Jesus said unto him, Thou shalt love the Lord thy God with all thy heart, and with all thy soul, and with all thy mind. This is the first and great commandment. The second is like unto it, Thou shalt love thy neigh bour as thyself. On these two commandments hang all the law and the prophets." So that no preciseness or uniformity of outward action can in the least degree take the place of heart-felt love. "Now the end of the commandment is charity out of a pure heart, and of a good conscience, and of faith unfeigned." 1 Tim. i. 5. In case our love to the creature or to life conflicts with our love to God, we must still cleave to him. So teaches the Saviour: "If any man come to me, and hate not his father, and mother, and wife, and children, and brethren, and sisters, yea, and his own life also, he cannot be my disciple." Luke xiv. 26. Of course the hatred here is *comparative* and not positive. We are to love all things less than God.

X. "The commands of the first table are not to be kept for the sake of the second; but the commands of the second are to be kept for the sake of the first. The worship and service of God are not to be performed out of respect to men; but our duty towards men is to be observed out of respect to God. For he that worships God that he might thereby recommend himself to men, is but a hypocrite and formalist; and he that performs his duty towards men without respecting God in it is but a mere civil moralist." Willard: "God and our neighbour do not stand upon even ground, so as that these must divide our love and obedience between them; but though it may seem to be a paradox, yet it is a great truth, that God must have all our love, and yet our neighbour must have some of it too. God must have our whole heart and soul, and yet our neighbour must have our hearty and undissembled love."

## CHAPTER VII.

### THE USES OF THE LAW.

THE moral law does not bear the same relation to men which it sustains to angels, and which it did sustain to man before his fall. Eternal life is no longer by our obedience to its precepts. To believers it is no more a covenant of works. By it, in the sight of God, shall no flesh be justified. Ps. cxliii. 2; Rom. iii. 20; Gal. ii. 16. To expect justification by our own works would be to supersede and render of none effect the work of our Saviour. We are not under the law but under grace. To oppose this grave fundamental heresy of salvation by works is one of the chief objects of Paul in some of his epistles, and particularly in that to the Galatians.

Seeing then that the law is not to be put in the room and stead of our Saviour, what is its use? or as Paul expresses it, "Wherefore then serveth the law?" Gal. iii. 19. The answer is,

I. The moral law is of excellent use as a rule of life. Its value in this respect is great. Its precepts are comprehensive, definite and easily understood. They cover all possible cases. They inform us with the utmost exactness what is right and wrong in action and in word. They go further. They trace sin up to its original fountain in the soul. They pronounce envy and hatred to be murder, covetousness to be theft, and forgetfulness of God to be atheism. This law is universal in its prescriptions. In all things it is holy, wise, and benevolent. None can be truly pious without consenting that it is good. Whosoever esteems any of its precepts grievous shows that his heart is still unregenerated. All pious men do sincerely and habitually desire to be conformed to this blessed code. Often and earnestly do they cry, "Oh that my ways were directed to keep thy statutes." Ps. cxix. 5, 10. "Teach me thy statutes." "Open thou mine eyes that I may behold wondrous things out of thy law." Ps. cxix. 12, 18. He who in the spirit of humility, carefulness and teachableness thus cries for divine guidance shall grow wiser than his enemies, shall have more understanding than all his teachers, and shall understand more than the ancients. Ps. cxix. 98, 99, 100; See also Micah vi. 8. The greatest grief of pious souls is not for poverty, or sickness, or slander; but because they either positively transgress or come short of keeping the holy commandments. Such is their desire to be as pure as the law requires, that there is nothing which makes them so willing to leave the body and exchange worlds as the hope that in a future state, they will be wholly conformed to its righteous demands. The superiority of this law as a rule of life is exceedingly manifest in the particulars already named as well as in others. It comes to the conscience with a sovereign authority. The heart of man when not utterly insensate recognizes God's voice in all its precepts.

Calvin: "The faithful find the law an excellent

instrument to give them from day to day a better and more certain understanding and to confirm them in the knowledge of it."

II. The moral law is of excellent use in producing conviction of sin, and thus making men sensible of their need of a Saviour. "The law entered that the offence might abound," Rom. v. 20; that is, that it might be seen by us all how many and ill-deserving our sins were. Conviction of sin is not confined to unregenerate men, nor to sinners in the earlier stages of religious impression when a *law-work* is wrought on the heart. Important as this is, the law is not then laid aside as a means of conviction. To the close of life it continues to be of use to this end. It teaches us that we are not worthy to be called God's servants; it shows that our strength to do that which is right is nothing. Colquhoun: "The children of fallen Adam are *so bent upon working for life*, that they will on no account cease from it till the Holy Spirit so convince them of their sin and misery, as to show them that Mount Sinai is wholly on fire around them, and that they cannot with safety remain a moment longer within the limits of it." "What things soever the law saith, it saith to them who are under the law: that every mouth may be stopped, and all the world may become guilty before God." Rom. iii. 19. By our early conviction of sin, we obtain some faint impression of the necessity of salvation by grace. By our subsequent convictions, we are led more and more to renounce all confidence in ourselves for righteousness; and to see more and more our need of the perfect righteousness of the Lord Jesus Christ. There is no greater mistake respecting experimental religion than that which regards the work of conviction entirely done when conversion takes place. It is true that sometimes there are certain horrors of conscience, certain pangs of remorse, certain guilty fears and awful apprehensions of the wrath to come, which in an equal degree do but seldom afflict the soul after conversion. But these horrors and fears are no necessary elements of conviction. He is truly convicted, who has a due sense that he is a sinner against a just and holy God; and that he deserves ill and only ill at the hands of the Judge of all. He may not expect to be punished. David was an experienced child of God, when he said of the commandments, "By them is thy servant warned;" and "Who can understand his errors? clease thou me from secret faults." Ps. xix. 11, 12. One may have set his hope in God through Jesus Christ; indeed, the more effectually he has despaired of helping himself, and the more completely he has cast himself on God in humble hope, the more proper and deep are his convictions. This use of the law is much insisted on in Scripture. Paul says, "By the law is the knowledge of sin." Rom. iii. 20. And when in the same epistle, he had proven the utter impossibility of salvation by the deeds of the law, he adds, "What shall we say then? Is the law sin? God forbid." Rom. vii. 7. He then goes on to say how useful it had been to him. The spirit of his declaration is, that he never would have known what a poor, lost, undone, helpless creature he was, and that he never would have felt his need of a Saviour, and never would have fled to him for refuge but for the law. His words are, "I had not known sin but by the law; for I had not known lust, except the law had said, Thou shalt not covet." Rom. vii. 7. In ancient times, schools had teachers to superintend their instruction. Besides these, there were pedagogues employed to go around and gather the children and conduct them to the school. It is probably to this latter office that Paul refers, when he says, "The law was our schoolmaster," [literally our *pedagogue*,] "to bring us to Christ." Gal. iii. 24. And as the pedagogue of old brought the child to school not only one day, but every day during the term, so the law brings us to Christ, not only when we first accept him but as often as we renew our hold on him. T. Watson: "The law is a star to lead one to Christ." The law shuts us up to the faith of Christ. It makes Christ precious to the soul. No man can esteem the redemption that is in Christ more highly than his sense of his own lost and ruined estate as a sinner shall rise. Tell me what a man thinks of himself, and I will tell you what he thinks of the Redeemer. Tell me what he thinks of the Redeemer, and I will tell you what he thinks of himself. Every believer is ready to say, "I was alive without the law once; but when the commandment came, sin revived, and I died. And the commandment which was ordained to life, I found to be unto death. For sin, taking occasion by the commandment, deceived me, and by it slew me." Rom. vii. 9–11. So that "what the law could not do in that it was weak through the flesh, God sending his own Son in the likeness of sinful flesh, and for sin, condemned [or punished] sin in the flesh; that the righteousness of the law might be fulfilled in us, who walk not after the flesh, but after the Spirit." Rom. viii.

3, 4. Why do the great mass of men feel so little interest in conversation, books and sermons which explain the way of salvation? Obviously, the reason is, they have no just view and sense of their deplorable condition. God's Spirit is indeed the Author of all true conviction of sin; but in producing it, he leads the minds of men to understand the nature of the law under which they live; and to see that their lives, words and hearts are wholly destitute of conformity to its requirements. If men saw these things as the truth demands, and as they will one day see them, the preaching of the gospel would be listened to in a manner far different, and with success far greater than we have ever witnessed in the world. Then salvation by grace through a Redeemer would be glad tidings of great joy unto all people. Listlessness would take her flight from worshipping assemblies. Eagerness would mould the features of every hearer; and the swelling solicitude of each bosom would catch every whisper of mercy from the word of God as it was pronounced by the living minister. Let then all men study the law. Let them study it candidly, carefully, solemnly. There is a great Physician, but sinners will never go to him, unless they find out that they are sick. Let regenerate men also study the law. The more they know it, the closer will they cleave to Christ; and the more profound will be their humility; and the better will they understand their indebtedness to Christ, for fulfilling its precepts and enduring its curse in their stead, and for their salvation. If a man loves God he will also love his law; and what one loves he will desire and labour to know. "Christ's promise of ease and refreshment sounds sweet after the thunderings and lightnings of Mount Sinai." Augustine: "The law gives commands, in order that, endeavouring to perform them, being wearied through our infirmity under the law, we may learn to pray for the assistance of grace. . . The utility of the law is to convince man of his own infirmity, and to compel him to pray for the gracious remedy provided in Christ. . . . . God commands what we cannot perform, that we may know for what blessings we ought to supplicate him. . . The law was given to convict you; that being convicted you might fear, that fearing you might pray for pardon, and not presume on your own strength."

III. The law is of great use to believers in restraining their corruptions, because it forbids sin and denounces the most fearful curses against those who love and practise iniquity. The very form of most of the precepts is suited to put believers on their guard. Goodwin: "Commandments in a negative form suppose the nature of man to run cross with the law." The soul says, why has God thus hedged me in, but that I may always see my peril and beware? It is true that the great and habitually influential motives of Christians in aiming at a holy life are not drawn from the terrors of the law. God's people are controlled by something more exalted. The love of Christ constrains them; that is, it bears them along. [Gr. συνεχει]. Nevertheless, it is true, *first*, that while our motives must be evangelical, yet, even in Christian obedience there is room for the entrance of the law. We are under law to Christ. We are married to him, but not to despise him. He is our husband, and, therefore, he is to be obeyed. *Secondly*, in certain states of Christian experience, when the wickedness of the heart threatens to become outrageous, and when nothing kind or tender seems to have the desired influence over us, when Satan comes as a roaring lion, when the fiery darts fly thick and fast, and our spiritual enemies become terrible, it is of eminent service to the child of God to be able to point to something far more terrible, even the wrath of Jehovah and the lake of fire. So our Lord himself taught. Compare Matt. xviii. 7–9; Matt. x. 28; Luke xii. 4, 5. It is well for the poor persecuted, tempted soul to hear the voice of salutary warning: "Fear not them which kill the body; but are not able to kill the soul; but rather fear him which is able to destroy both soul and body in hell."

And who can tell the power of the law over the hearts of men in general? Its chief aim and purpose in the world is not for this kind of power over the pious. Paul says, "The law is not made for a righteous man, but for the lawless and disobedient, for the ungodly and for sinners, for unholy and profane, for murderers of fathers, and murderers of mothers, for man-slayers, for whoremongers, for them that defile themselves with mankind, for men-stealers, for liars and for perjured persons." 1 Tim. i. 9, 10. The restraining power of the law over the wicked is very great. Bad as they are, they would be unspeakably worse, but for its terrors. Luther: "The first use of the law is to bridle the wicked."

IV. The law is eminently useful in teaching us how to regard afflictions and how to be quiet under them. Without just views of the law of God no man can have just views of his own ill-desert. Without a sense of his criminality, will he not rebel and cry out, as Cain? "My punishment is greater than I can bear." But let him see that he deserves all that has come upon him, and a thousand-fold more, and he will bow his head in profound humility, and, by the grace of God, will assent to the saying of the pious Jews returned from their seventy years' captivity: "After all that has come upon us for our evil deeds, and for our great trespass, seeing that thou our God hast punished us less than our iniquities deserve, and hast given us such deliverance as this; should we again break thy commandments, and join in affinity with the people of these abominations? wouldst not thou be angry with us till thou hadst consumed us, so that there should be no remnant nor escaping? O Lord God of Israel, thou art righteous: for we remain yet escaped, as it is this day: behold, we are before thee in our trespasses: for we cannot stand before thee because of this." Ezra ix. 13–15. Surely that must be a turbulent and unsanctified spirit which is not quiet when it remembers that our pains are lighter than our sins; that our sorrows are fewer than our crimes. Will not every pious soul be inclined carefully to avoid sin, when it sees that God is merciful and visits us not according to our deserts? Surely in such a case the ingenuous soul must hear the voice of the Redeemer, saying, "Go thy way and sin no more, lest a worse thing come upon thee."

V. The plan of salvation by grace in Christ Jesus is so arranged and ordered that obedience to the moral law sincerely rendered with evangelical motives meets a divine reward. Indeed, we know not that the spotless obedience of angels, who have never sinned, shall be any more abundantly rewarded than the obedience of the just, who have been great sinners but who have sincerely accepted the gospel and have honestly obeyed the law. O yes: in keeping the commandments there is great reward. It is true in this world. It will be true in the next. Nor will the deeply humbled soul be at all offended that the reward of his obedience is counted not of debt but of grace. He joyfully seeks the acceptance of his services in the same way that he seeks the acceptance of his person—through the mediation of Christ Jesus the Lord. The scriptural method of reasoning on this subject is this: "Wherefore we receiving a kingdom which cannot be moved, let us have grace, whereby we may serve God acceptably with reverence, and godly fear, for our God is a consuming fire." Heb. xii. 28, 29. Blessed be God! The very lowest acts of obedience rightly rendered, even a pious wish, a holy desire, a devout thought, the giving of a cup of cold water in the name of a disciple, shall not lose its reward, though that reward shall be all of grace. Nor is there any contrariety between this and the glorious doctrine of salvation by the active and passive obedience of Christ. The righteousness of the believer in his best deeds is not a justifying righteousness; but it is a righteousness accepted of God and rewarded abundantly, yet graciously. It is a righteousness secured to him and in him by the very scheme of redeeming mercy. Even the Old Testament teaches as much; "I will sprinkle clean water upon you, and ye shall be clean: from all your filthiness, and from all your idols, will I cleanse you. A new heart also will I give you, and a new spirit will I put within you:

and I will take away the stony heart out of your flesh, and I will give you a heart of flesh. And I will put my Spirit within you, and cause you to walk in my statutes, and ye shall keep my judgments, and do them. And ye shall dwell in the land that I gave to your fathers; and ye shall be my people, and I will be your God." Ezek. xxxvi. 25–28. Compare Jer. xxxi. 33. "WE KNOW THAT THE LAW IS GOOD, IF A MAN USE IT LAWFULLY."

# CHAPTER VIII.

## THE NATURE OF THE OBEDIENCE REQUIRED BY THE LAW.

PURE Christianity differs from every form of corrupt doctrine by the place it assigns to obedience to God's law. On this point the human mind loves error to such a degree that nothing but grace can cure its follies. While some teach that obedience is everything, that it is meritorious, and that by it we are justified; others assert that it is nothing; that in the gospel plan of salvation there is no room for it; that none is required, and that, if rendered, it is useless. Both of these are rank and extreme errors. Both do fundamentally oppose the truth of God. A total rejection of the law will prove as fatal as a total rejection of the gospel; while a reliance upon the law as a method of justification is both a rejection of the gospel and an abuse of the law.

Colquhoun: "Legalists teach that believers are under the law, even as it is the covenant of works: Antinomians, on the contrary, assert that believers are not only not under it as a covenant, but not under it even as a rule of duty. These two assertions are not more contrary to one another, than they both are to the *truth* as it is in Jesus."

That obedience to the law is required upon its very face, and in many parts of Scripture, is evident to any candid reader. The form of enactment has been already alluded to. The following additional passages of Scripture are here given.

"Behold, I have taught you statutes and judgments, even as the LORD my God commanded me, that ye should do so in the land whither ye go to possess it. Keep therefore and do them; for this is your wisdom and your understanding in the sight of the nations, which shall hear all these statutes, and say, Surely this great nation is a wise and understanding people. Only take heed to thyself, and keep thy soul diligently, lest thou forget the things which thine eyes have seen, and lest they depart from thy heart all the days of thy life: but teach them thy sons, and thy sons' sons." Deut. iv. 5, 6, 9. "Observe and hear all these words which I command thee, that it may go well with thee, and with thy children after thee for ever, when thou doest that which is good and right in the sight of the LORD thy God. What thing soever I command you, observe to do it: thou shalt not add thereto, nor diminish from it;" Deut. xii. 28,32, and parallel passages.

WHAT IS THE OBEDIENCE REQUIRED?

I. It is *personal.* One man cannot obey for another. "The soul that sinneth, *it* shall die." "He that doeth righteousness is righteous." Though our personal obedience to the law does not justify us in the sight of God, yet it alone can justify our profession of love to him. The obedience which the Lord Jesus Christ rendered to the precepts of the law as our substitute was intended solely for the justification of our persons, and in no wise as a substitute for our personal holiness. Scott: "The commandments are addressed in the singular number, to each person, because every one is concerned in them on his own account: and each prohibition implies a positive duty."

II. According to Scripture the obedience required is *to some command given by God.* Ames: "The matter of obedience is that very thing commanded by God." Uncommanded observances, whatever sanctity they may seem to attach to us in the eyes of man, are of no avail in the sight of God. They are all condemned in his holy word. Voluntary humility, will-worship, the dishonouring of our own bodies, the worshipping of angels, and abstaining from meats which God has created to be received with thanksgiving, are crimes in the sight of Heaven, and are marks of an apostate church. Col. ii. 18; 1 Tim. iv. 1–4. Of old we read of no worse state of the church than that in which the "fear of God is taught by the precepts of men." Isa. xxix. 13. "If ye be dead with Christ from the rudiments of the world, why, as though living in the world, are ye subject to ordinances, after the commandments and doctrines of men? Which things have indeed a show of wisdom in will-worship, and humility, and neglecting of the body; not in any honour to the satisfying of the flesh." Col. ii. 20–23.

III. The obedience required in Scripture consists not *in mere outward acts of the body, irrespective of the state of the heart.* According to Scripture no obedience is acceptable to God, unless it is rightly intended. God may accept the will for the deed, but he will never accept the deed for the will. In fact his holy word pours its heaviest curses on those who merely make clean the outside of the platter, while in their hearts they are ravening wolves, or sepulchres full of dead men's bones. Matt. xxiii. 25, 27; Luke xi. 39. This is perfectly right in God. No *man* would be willing to accept the most exact and respectful though heartless politeness of a wife or child, instead of the warm, gushing affection which was his due. There is no dispensing with godly sincerity.

IV. All obedience must flow from a principle of *love*. This is taught everywhere in Scripture. Jesus says, "If ye love me, keep my commandments. . . . . He that hath my commandments and keepeth them, he it is that loveth me: and he that loveth me shall be loved of my Father, and I will love him, and will manifest myself to him. . . . . If a man love me, he will keep my words. . . . He that loveth me not, keepeth not my sayings." John xiv. 15, 21, 23, 24. The mere legalist who trusts in salvation by his own righteousness is never the man to make great sacrifices for Christ. He has no principle of love. He is performing a task, and his task is a drudgery. On the other hand, he who trusts in the merits of Christ alone, and has any just sense of his obligations to the Redeemer, gives much, gives all, and then wishes he could give more. The legalist has the spirit of a hireling; the evangelical man has the spirit of gratitude.

V. All obedience pleasing to God is connected with godly *fear*. We will never obey unto all pleasing unless we bow to the awful authority of Jehovah. We will never keep his commandments unless we fear him. Eccl. xii. 13; Compare: Deut. vi. 2, x. 12; Ps. cxi. 10; 1 Pet. ii. 17; Rev. xix. 5. In Deut. xxviii. 58, it is expressly said that we are to "observe to do all

5 *

the words of this law that are written in this book, that we may fear this glorious and fearful name, THE LORD THY GOD."

VI. All acceptable obedience must flow from a principle of *living faith* in the divine testimony, especially respecting Christ. "Without faith it is impossible to please God: he that cometh to God must believe that he is, and that he is a rewarder of them that diligently seek him." Heb. xi. 6. "Whatsoever is not of faith is sin." Rom. xiv. 23. What made Abraham's obedience of such value as to be noted in Scripture, was the fact that he believed God even contrary to appearances.

VII. The obedience to the law required of believers under the gospel must be *evangelical;* that is, we are not to keep the commandments for the purpose of thus meriting God's favour, nor are we to render our obedience in our own strength; but by the assistance of the grace of God. All attempts to climb to heaven by the ladder of our own works must utterly fail; and all our endeavours to keep the law in the strength of our fallen nature must no less certainly overwhelm us with disgrace. Colquhoun: "Heathen morality is external obedience to the law of *nature*, and may be termed natural religion. Pharisaical righteousness is hypocritical obedience to the law as a *covenant of works*, and is usually called legal righteousness, or the works of the law. True holiness is spiritual and sincere obedience to the law as a *rule of life*, in the hand of the blessed Mediator, and is commonly styled evangelical holiness or true godliness."

VIII. All right obedience must be performed *with a just sense of our imperfections*. We must never present our obedience before God as being in itself deserving of any reward. Jesus Christ greatly insists upon this. One of his parables is on this very subject. "Which of you having a servant plowing or feeding cattle, will say unto him by and by, when he is come from the field, Go and sit down to meat? and will not rather say unto him, Make ready wherewith I may sup, and gird thyself, and serve me, till I have eaten and drunken; and afterward thou shalt eat and drink? Doth he thank that servant, because he did the things that were commanded him? I trow not. So likewise ye, when ye shall have done all those things which are commanded you, say, We are unprofitable servants: we have done that which was our duty to do." Luke xvii. 7–10. The proper spirit in which to commend our labours to God's favourable regard is beautifully exemplified in the life of that eminent young man, Nehemiah. He was the most distinguished patriot and servant of God in his day. With great intrepidity he rebuilt the holy city. His sufferings and trials were sharp. Having given a modest and truthful record of what he had endured and accomplished, he offers such prayers as these: "Remember me, O my God, for good;" "Remember me, O my God, concerning this, and wipe not out my good deeds that I have done for the house of my God, and for the offices thereof." But that we may in no case misunderstand his real temper, he has left this prayer also on record: "Remember me, O my God, concerning this also, and *spare me according to the greatness of thy mercy.*" Neh. xiii. 14, 22, 31.

IX. The obedience we render must be *universal.* God allows no eclecticism in this matter. "Then shall I not be ashamed, when I have respect unto all thy commandments." Ps. cxix. 6. "What thing soever I command you, observe to do it: thou shalt not add thereto, nor diminish from it." Deut. xii. 32.

X. Our obedience must be *perpetual.* "I will never forget thy precepts." Ps. cxix. 93. "Cursed is he that continueth not in all things written in the book of the law to do them." Stowell: "The authority of the moral law is founded in the perfection of God, and extends over all the creatures whom he has rendered capable of obeying it while that capability exists."

## CHAPTER IX.

### THE PLACE WHICH GOOD WORKS OCCUPY IN A SYSTEM OF GRACE.

I. A GREAT design of the gospel, so far as man is concerned, is his restoration to holiness. Indeed, Jesus Christ "gave himself for us, that he might redeem us from all iniquity, and purify unto himself a peculiar people, zealous of good works." God "hath chosen us in him before the foundation of the world that we should be holy and without blame before him in love." And we are expressly said to be God's "workmanship, created in Christ Jesus unto good works, which God hath before ordained that we should walk in them." Titus ii. 14; Eph. i. 4; ii. 10. So that election, redemption, and regeneration would all fail of their ends, if the subjects of them were not made holy.

II. It is only by good works manifest and open that Christians can afford to the world satisfactory evidence that their principles are better than those of other people. The world will judge of men's real characters neither solely nor chiefly by their professions, but by their practice. This is right. Words are cheap. Actions speak louder than words. That is a just challenge of the apostle when he says:

'Shew me thy faith without thy works, and I will shew thee my faith by my works." James ii. 18. Christ himself says to his disciples, "Ye are the light of the world. . . . . Let your light so shine before men, that they may see your good works, and glorify your Father which is in heaven." Matt. v. 14–16. But if their works are no better than those of carnal men, they are of course subject to the rebuke, "What do ye more than others;" and their lives can be no proof of the divine origin of their religion. In the early ages of Christianity one of the most difficult stations to fill well was that of a Christian wife, who had a heathen husband; and yet that very position afforded an opportunity of holding forth the word of life to great advantage. See 1 Pet. iii. 1–6. To such Paul says, "What knowest thou, O wife, whether thou shalt save thy husband?" 1 Cor. vii. 16.

III. Good works are in themselves pleasing to God; and for Christ's sake their imperfections are forgiven, and they are divinely rewarded. According to Scripture, our happiness hereafter will in an important sense be proportioned to our works here. Our good deeds will not be the cause, but merely the *occasions* of our receiving great and astonishing blessings. Even the penitent thief, who died on the cross, and whose public confession of Christ was one of the most illustrious acts of faith ever performed, shall not lose his reward. In accordance with these teachings speak the Scriptures. "Walk worthy of the Lord unto all pleasing, being fruitful in every good work." Col. i. 10. "He which soweth sparingly shall reap also sparingly; and he which soweth bountifully shall reap also bountifully." 2 Cor. ix. 6. "Say ye to the righteous, that it shall be well with him: for they shall eat the fruit of their doings." Isa. iii. 10. Colquhoun: "Though the law, as a rule of duty to believers, has no sanction of *judicial* rewards or punishments, yet it has a sanction of gracious rewards and paternal chastisements."

IV. God himself at the last day will determine men's characters by their works. "God shall bring every work into judgment, with every secret thing, whether it be good or whether it be evil." Eccles. xii. 14. Jesus himself said, "The hour is coming, in the which all that are in the graves shall hear his voice, and shall come forth; they that have done good, unto the resurrection of life; and they that have done evil, unto the resurrection of damnation." John v. 28, 29. So says the last book of Scripture: "The dead were judged out of those things which were written in the books, according to their works." "They were judged every man according to their works." Rev. xx. 12, 13. Compare also Dan. xii. 2, 3, and Matt. xxv. 31–46.

V. As both our Creator and our fellow men will judge us by our works, so also ought we to judge ourselves. No man has any more religion than controls his practice. He whose life is holy has a holy heart. He whose life is wicked has a wicked heart. All this is natural and fair. If the tree is not to be known by its fruits, by what shall it be known? If the fountain may not be known by the streams it sends forth, then we can determine nothing. "Be not deceived; God is not mocked; for whatsoever a man soweth, that shall he also reap. For he that soweth to his flesh shall of the flesh reap corruption:

but he that soweth to the Spirit shall of the Spirit reap life everlasting." Gal. vi. 7, 8. We ourselves lay down the same rule in judging of our fellow-men. We marvel that a man, who, without subjecting himself to penal consequences, has done all he can to injure us, should suppose himself possessed of no malignity. Those religious principles and actions which cannot bear this test are of no value. God's plan is to subject all his people to severe trials, not for the sake of giving them pain, but to illustrate his grace and their character. So says the Psalmist. "Thou, O God, hast proved us: thou hast tried us as silver is tried. Thou broughtest us into the net; thou laidest affliction upon our loins. Thou hast caused men to ride over our heads; we went through fire and through water: but thou broughtest us into a wealthy place. I will go into thy house with burnt offerings: I will pay thee my vows." Ps. lxvi. 10–13 and onwards. So to Abraham God said, "Now I know that thou fearest God, seeing that thou hast not withheld thy son, thine only son from me." Gen. xxii. 12.

VI. Good works are useful to our brethren. "These things I will that thou affirm constantly, that they which have believed in God might be careful to maintain good works. These things are good and profitable unto men. . . . Let ours also learn to maintain good works for necessary uses." Titus iii. 8, 14.

VII. The Scriptures do clearly assert the necessity of good works to prove our acceptance with God. "Be ye doers of the word, and not hearers only, deceiving your ownselves. . . . Pure religion and undefiled before God and the Father is this, To visit the fatherless and widows in their affliction, and to keep himself unspotted from the world." James i. 22, 27. "To obey is better than sacrifice, and to hearken than the fat of rams." 1 Sam. xv. 22. "Whoso hath this world's good, and seeth his brother have need, and shutteth up his bowels of compassion from him, how dwelleth the love of God in him? My little children, let us not love in word, neither in tongue; but in deed and in truth." 1 John iii. 17, 18. "Herein is my Father glorified that ye bear much fruit; so shall ye be my disciples. Ye are my friends, if ye do whatsoever I command you." John xv. 8, 14. Every Christian grace is to be judged of by the life we lead. Thus the fear of God is to be estimated not according to the secret dread which his majesty creates, but by our holiness of life. "The fear of the Lord is to hate evil." The sincerity of our benevolence can be safely tested in no other way. James ii. 15, 16. It is only thus we can manifest our gratitude in a becoming way. Thus only can we be built up in a true assurance of eternal life. 2 Pet. i. 5–10. Thus only can we put to silence the ignorance of foolish men. 1 Pet. ii. 15; Phil. i. 11.

We are bound to maintain this view of the Moral Law and its obligations at all times and under all circumstances; especially, let not the pulpit give forth a doubtful utterance on this point. There is a class of men who will accuse us of being *Legalists*, if we solemnly enforce duty. Stowell: "If by legal preaching is meant the faithful and fervid enforcements of these commands on every man's conscience as the standard by which he is to walk now, and to be judged hereafter, whence we demand, the dread of such a style of preaching? Surely not from an enlightened regard to the honour of God; we know nothing of that honour, but as we study and obey his law. Surely not from an enlightened attachment to the gospel: for we do not understand the gospel, but as it enlarges our conceptions of the divine law, and constrains us to fulfil it."

# CHAPTER X.

## SALVATION IS NOT BY OUR OBEDIENCE TO THE LAW.

THERE are two capital errors respecting the law. One maintains that we are justified by it. The other asserts that we are under no obligation to obey it. The last of these will be considered hereafter. The first now claims our attention.

The following things are made remarkably clear in God's word.

I. ALL MEN ARE SINNERS. In proof of this proposition we have the unanswered and unanswerable argument of the Apostle Paul in the first three chapters of his epistle to the Romans. In the first chapter he proves that all the Gentiles are sinners. In the second, he shows that the Jews are involved in the same condemnation. In the third, he shows that all men indiscriminately have offended God, maintaining that, "There is none righteous, no, not one." This great argument is but the summing up of irrefragable statements found in all the Scriptures, and confirmed by universal observation.

II. MAN IS UNDER A CURSE. The reason is because he is a transgressor. This was declared at the giving of the law. Moses said, "Behold, I set before you this day, a blessing and a curse; a blessing, if ye obey the commandments of the Lord your God, which I command you this day: and a curse, if ye will not obey the commandments of the Lord your God, but turn aside out of the way which I command you this day." Deut. xi. 26–28. "The curse of the Lord is in the house of the wicked." Prov. iii. 33. "The curse is poured upon us, and the oath that is written in the law of Moses the servant of God, because we have sinned against him." Dan. ix. 11. "Ye are cursed with a curse." Mal. iii. 9. "As many as are of the works of the law are under the curse." Gal. iii. 10.

III. THIS IS NOT THE FAULT OF THE LAW. The Scriptures abundantly declare that the law is good. Rom. vii. 16; 1 Tim. i. 8. "If there had been a law given which could have given life, verily righteousness should have been by the law." Gal. iii. 21. "The law was weak through the flesh;" Rom. viii. 3, not through any defect inherent in itself.

IV. YET JUSTIFICATION BY THE LAW IS IMPOSSIBLE. It is often and expressly so declared. "By the deeds of the law there shall be no flesh justified in his sight;" "The law worketh wrath;" "Now we are delivered from the law, that being dead wherein we were held;" "Ye are become dead to the law by the body of Christ;" "Israel which followed after the law of righteousness hath not attained to the law of righteousness; because they sought it not by faith, but as it were by the works of the law;" "A man is not justified by the works of the law;" "If righteousness come by the law, then Christ is dead in vain;" "That no man is justified by the law in the sight of

God, it is evident." Rom. iii. 20, iv. 15, vii. 4, 6, ix. 31, 32. Gal. ii. 16, 21, iii. 11.

V. THE SCRIPTURES REVEAL AN ALTOGETHER DIFFERENT PLAN OF JUSTIFICATION. They say, We are "justified freely by his grace, through the redemption that is in Christ Jesus." "The promise is of faith, that it might be by grace." "There is no condemnation to them who are in Christ Jesus." "A man is justified by the faith of Jesus Christ." "The life which we now live in the flesh, we live by the faith of the Son of God." "The just shall live by faith." Rom. iii. 24, iv. 16, viii. 1; Gal. ii. 16, 20; Gal. iii. 11; Hab. ii. 4; Rom. i. 17. This scheme of pardoning the guilty and accepting them as righteous through the merits of the Lord Jesus suits us exactly. Nor is this mere theory. It enters into the very life of religious experience. The Rev. Jotham Sewell says, "When I was not very far from twenty-one years of age, I read a sermon which exposed the insufficiency and folly of self-righteousness. I felt the force of the reasoning, and was convinced that I had been self-righteous. I resolved that I would be so no more, but would try to trust in Christ. I then thought that I had freed myself from this sin, though I had no idea that I was convicted. Not long after, in giving a reason for the hope that he was a Christian, I heard a man express the conviction, that, while in secret and in his family before conversion, he was hypocritical and self-righteous. I thought with myself, shall I ever have to say as much as that man says? I am not convicted; but if I should be, whatever I may have to throw away, it will not be self-righteousness; for I fancied that I was already free from that; so blind was I to my real condition! I afterwards saw that I had made a righteousness of my resolution, that I would not be self-righteous! So true it is 'that the heart is deceitful above all things and desperately wicked.'" In like manner spoke that godly minister, Owen Stockton, of Ipswich: "I find, that though in my judgment and profession, I acknowledge Christ to be my righteousness and peace; yet upon examination I observe that my heart hath done quite another thing, and that secretly I have gone about to establish my own righteousness, and have derived my comfort and peace from my own actings." Luther: "If I were able to keep the whole moral law, I would not trust to this for justification."

To the truly pious and humble child of God, however simple or youthful, there is nothing more unpleasant than the suggestion of the wicked one or of ignorant guides that we can commend ourselves to God by our own works. A lovely young female, whose memoir has been printed, though not published, has lately departed this life in the triumph of faith. One of her dying testimonies was, "I would not like to think of my sufferings having any thing to do with my going to heaven, as a *cause*. If I ever stand before God, it will be because Jesus Christ has redeemed me by his own blood—his ransom availed. God was satisfied—I am saved by him entirely." The best practical writers of all ages have warned men against seeking justification by the law. Charnock: "Affecting to stand by a righteousness of our own is natural to us. . . . Adam was to have lived upon his own righteousness, in the state of innocence; since we are fallen this relic of nature is in us to desire to rise by our own strength. We would find matter of acceptance and acquittance in ourselves. . . . What pains had the apostle to work the Romans and the Galatians from their own righteousness. A desire of a legal justification is inbred. . . . An imperfect righteousness cannot afford a perfect peace; the righteousness of a sinful nature is not the righteousness of a pure law."

John Owen: "Take heed of a degeneration into self-righteousness. . . . The way is narrow and strait that lies between the indispensable necessity of holiness and its influence into our righteousness. . . . The righteousness of Christ is utterly a strange thing to the best of unbelievers; and this puts them by all means upon the setting up of their own. Rom. x. 3."

Willard: "The fall hath utterly cut man off from ever obtaining life by the law, as a Covenant."

John Newton: "It is not a lawful use of the law to seek justification and acceptance with God by our obedience to it; because it is not appointed for this end, or capable of answering it in our circumstances. The very attempt is a daring impeachment of the goodness and wisdom of God; for if righteousness could come by the law, then Christ has died in vain; Gal. ii. 21; iii. 21; so that such a hope is not only groundless but sinful; and, when persisted in under the light of the gospel, is no less than a wilful rejection of the grace of God."

Colquhoun: "The great error of the Galatians was this: they did not believe that the righteousness of Jesus Christ *alone* was sufficient to entitle them to the justification of life; and therefore they depended for justification partly on their own obedience to the moral law, and to the ceremonial law."

VI. Salvation partly by the law, and partly by the Gospel, is impossible. Grace and works are utterly opposed to each other as schemes of acceptance with God. In two epistles, Paul says as much. He says that if salvation is "by grace, then is it no more of works: otherwise grace is no more grace. But if it be of works, then is it no more grace: otherwise work is no more work." Rom. xi. 6. Again, "Christ is become of no effect unto you, whosoever of you are justified by the law: ye are fallen from grace." Gal. v. 4.

The ways in which a self-righteous spirit gains fearful power over man are such as these:

First.—Do and live is the law of nature. "The man that doeth those things shall live by them." Rom. x. 5. Righteousness by works is the natural method of justification. Until the fall, Adam stood accepted of God on this ground. To this day the holy angels are justified by works alone. The heart of man is wedded to the law.

Secondly.—Self-righteousness requires no humility, but leaves the heart under the full control of self-complacency. Pride is natural to man; and the expectation of life by his own works feeds his self-esteem. The first and great demand of the gospel is humility. Matt. xviii. 4, xxiii. 12; Luke xiv. 11, xviii. 14; 1 Pet. v. 6.

Thirdly.—It is of the very nature of sin to blind the mind respecting all spiritual good. The sinner naturally perceives neither the holiness of the law, the sinfulness of his own heart, nor the glory of God in the gospel scheme. "The god of this world hath blinded the minds of them which believe not." 2 Cor. iv. 4.

Fourthly.—Men are often led to indulge self-righteous hopes by comparing themselves with others. 2 Cor. x. 12. This, indeed, is not wise. The rule of final judgment will not be the life of our fellow-man but the perfectly holy law of God. Yet many say, If I am lost, what will become of these sinners around me? The correct answer is, Repent and believe on the Lord Jesus Christ, or you shall all perish together. Yet how many are found full of self-righteousness, saying like the Pharisee, God, I thank thee, I am not as other men, or even as this publican.

Fifthly.—Probably not a few mistake gifts for graces; and because they are fluent in prayer, they think they have the spirit of prayer; or because they have prophesied in the name of the Lord, and in his name done many wonderful works, or commended his gospel with great earnestness to their fellow-men, they think themselves safe.

Sixthly.—Others say, "We have Abraham to our father." They expect to go to heaven because of their pious ancestry, or relations. They cannot conceive how the descendants of so good people as their parents should ever come short of heaven.

Let us, therefore, not imitate the wretched example of those, of whom Paul speaks, when he says, "They being ignorant of God's righteousness and going about to establish their own righteousness, have not submitted themselves unto the righteousness of God."

Rom. x. 3. Let us rather follow the example and utter the prayer of David when bowed down with a just sense of his heinous guilt, he cried, "Enter not into judgment with thy servant: for in thy sight shall no man living be justified." Ps. cxliii. 2.

## CHAPTER XI.

### ANTINOMIANISM.

ANTINOMIANISM is opposition to law. The word has, however, become tolerably precise in its meaning. Strictly speaking, Antinomianism is the doctrine, which asserts that under the gospel dispensation the moral law is not binding. In a more extended sense it is any system of doctrine, which, if fairly carried out, would destroy belief in the necessity of good works, or of a holy life.

The sect, called Antinomians, arose in the 16th century. Their founder was John Agricola. He reduced libertine principles to a system. His followers were at one time numerous. They were pests to society in many places. They can hardly be said to have a separate existence now.

But opposition to the law as a rule of life is coeval with the fall of man. Antinomianism has its seat in the deep depravity of the human heart. "The carnal mind is enmity against God; for it is not subject to the law of God, neither indeed can be." Rom. viii. 7. Its spirit is of the essence of sin. The Old and New Testaments, and indeed all histories, are full of records showing the deadly hostility of men to the restraints of the divine precepts. Solomon, Jeremiah, Hosea and many others tell us of men, who by anticipation were followers of Agricola. Pr. vii. 14–18; Jer. vii. 9, 10; Hos. xii. 7, 8.

The principles of Antinomians are variously stated. A thorough-paced Antinomian holds that if Christ finished his work, there is nothing left for us to do, that the moral law is no rule of duty to Christians, that the transgression of its precepts by God's people is not sinful; that the law is of no use under the gospel, and that of course it is not of binding obligation. The reasoning of Antinomians is something like this: salvation is wholly by grace; man is impotent to good himself; God's grace is sovereign, so that it is not of him that willeth nor of him that runneth; therefore we are not under law, even to Christ; all our endeavours are useless, and we may give a loose rein to all our corruptions.

Richard Baxter describes three classes of Antinomians in his day. There were the libertines, who said "The heart is the man; therefore you may deny the truth with your tongue, you may be present at false worships, (as at the mass,) you need not suffer to avoid the speaking of a word, or subscribing to an untruth or error, or doing some little thing; but, so long as you keep your hearts to God, and mean well, or have an honest mental reservation, and are forced to it by others, rather than suffer, you may say, or subscribe, or swear anything which you can yourselves put a lawful sense upon in your own minds, or you may comply with any outward actions or customs to avoid offence or save yourselves."

Then there were regular Antinomians who said that "The moral law is abrogated, and that the gospel is no law; that the elect are justified before they are born, or repent, or believe; that their sin is pardoned before it is committed; that God took them as suffering and fulfilling all the law in Christ, as if it had been they that did it in him: that we are justified by faith only in our consciences: that justifying faith is but believing that we are justified: that every man must believe that he is pardoned, that he may be pardoned in his conscience; . . . that all are forgiven that so believe: that it is legal and sinful to work or do any thing for salvation: that sin once pardoned need not be confessed and lamented, or at least we need not ask pardon of sin daily, or of one sin oft," &c., &c.

The third class described by Baxter are the Autonomians, who claimed that they were a law unto themselves. "They equally contend against Christ's government, and for their own. They fill the world with war and bloodshed, oppression and cruelty; and the ears of God with the cries of the martyrs and oppressed ones. . . . They are the scorners and persecutors of strict obedience to the laws of God, and take those that fear his judgments to be men affrighted out of their wits; and that to obey exactly is but to be hypocritical or too precise: but to question their domination, or break their laws, this must be taken for heresy, schism, or a rebellion like that of Korah and his company."

The world abounds with Antinomians. These are of three classes; 1. Speculative Antinomians. They are such as embrace some of the leading principles set forth above. They may hold but one or two of them; or they may receive the system. 2. There are Antinomians in desire. These feel the restraints of the law to be irksome. They would gladly cast off its cords and burst its bands asunder. And yet they have been too well instructed, and have too much conscience to be able to do so at once. But as the process of hardening the heart is going on rapidly, they may yet be able to say, "We will none of thy ways." 3. Then we have the Practical Antinomians. They care little about systems. They hardly avow a creed. But "the worst heresy is a wicked life." This they lead always. They practically and continually say, "Who is the Lord that we should obey him?"

In every form of Antinomianism, and especially in the systematic form it sometimes assumes, we can hardly fail to notice its utter contrariety to Scripture. Paul says, "Shall we continue in sin that grace may abound? God forbid." Rom. vi. 1, 2. He declares that it was a *slanderous report* against him and his brethren that they taught, that we may *do evil that good may come.* He says that the "*damnation*" [condemnation] of those who hold such a principle is "just." Rom. iii. 8. "Any doctrine inconsistent with the first principles of morals must be false, no matter how plausible the metaphysical argument in its favour. . . . Paul assumed, as an ultimate fact, that it is wrong to do evil that good may come."

How clearly the Scriptures testify against all Antinomian tendencies will appear by citing even a few passages. Paul says, "There are many unruly and vain talkers and deceivers, who subvert whole houses, teaching things which they ought not, for filthy lucre's sake." Titus i. 10, 11. John says, "If we say that we have fellowship with him, and walk in darkness, we lie, and do not the truth." 1 John i. 6. "He that saith, I know him, and keepeth not his commandments, is a liar, and the truth is not in him." 1 John ii. 4. "Every man that hath this hope in him, purifieth himself, even as he is pure." 1 John iii. 3. Peter also tells us of such: "Spots they are and blemishes, sporting themselves with their own deceivings while they feast with you; having eyes full of adultery, and that cannot cease from sin; beguiling unstable souls: an heart they have exercised with covetous practices; cursed children." 2 Pet. ii. 13, 14. Jude also says of such: "These are spots in your feasts of charity, when they feast with you, feeding themselves without fear: clouds they are without water, carried about with winds; trees whose fruit withereth, without fruit, twice dead, plucked up by the roots; raging waves of the sea, foaming out their own shame; wandering stars, to whom is reserved the blackness of darkness for ever." Jude 12, 13. No wonder that in the strong language of Scripture, such men are "abominable and disobedient, and to every good work reprobate." Titus i. 16.

When we open the gospel we find the most urgent calls to holiness founded on its gracious proposals: "Having therefore these promises, dearly beloved, let us cleanse ourselves from all filthiness of the flesh and spirit, perfecting holiness in the fear of God." 2 Cor. vii. 1. Indeed, Paul expressly declares that "the grace of God that bringeth salvation," that is, the gospel, "teaches us that, denying ungodliness and worldly lusts, we should live soberly, righteously, and godly in this present world." Titus ii. 11, 12. Again, "God hath not called us to uncleanness, but unto holiness." John says: "Let no man deceive you: he that doeth righteousness is righteous. . . He that committeth sin is of the devil." 1 John iii. 7, 8.

The following propositions laid down by Flavel are abundantly supported by Scripture:

1. The Scriptures "frequently discover God's anger, and tell us his castigatory rods of affliction are laid upon his people for their sins." 2 Sam. xii. 9–14; Ex. iv. 13, 14; Jer. xxx. 15; Lam. iii. 39, 40; Ps. xxxviii. 3–5; Micah vii. 9, &c., &c.

2. They "represent sin as the greatest evil; most opposite to the glory of God and good of the saints; and are therefore filled with cautions and threatenings to prevent their sinning." Jer. v. 30, xliv. 4, xviii. 13, xxiii. 14; Hosea vi. 10; Ps. xiv. 1, liii. 1; Titus i. 16; 1 Pet. iv. 3; Rom. vi. 23; Dan. v. 23; Rom. iii. 23; Heb. iv. 1, and many other places.

3. "The Scriptures call the saints frequently and earnestly, not only to mourn for their sins before the Lord, but to pray for the pardon and remission of them in the blood of Christ." Matt. vi. 12; 1 Pet. v. 6; James iv. 10, &c., &c.

4. "They earnestly and everywhere press believers to strictness and constancy in the duties of religion, as the way wherein God would have them to walk." Rom. xii., throughout, 1 Cor. xv. 58, &c., &c.

Many other Scriptures might be cited to the same effect. He, who has read thus far, and who shall read the next chapter also, can be at no loss for proof-texts.

Of all errors in religion, perhaps none is more revolting to the truly pious than the grosser forms of Antinomianism. It is hardly more shocking to deny the divine existence altogether than it is to teach that God is the patron of iniquity. Those pious men, who seem to have had most intercourse with Antinomians, regard their principles and practices with extreme abhorrence. It is impossible to read the works of those venerable servants of Christ, Thomas Scott, the Commentator, and Andrew Fuller, without perceiving that they must have witnessed the most odious exhibitions of human wickedness. They were doubtless right in expressing in many forms the belief that nothing more imperils the soul than any religious principle, which releases us from the government of God.

Perhaps the most shocking thing in Antinomianism is that ordinarily it makes Christ the minister of sin. It impudently marches up to his cross, and says, "O thou bleeding Lamb, who didst live and die for me, I will neither live nor die for thee; but I will serve divers *lusts* and please myself."

The testimony of sound and pious writers in all branches of the church of Christ against Antinomian laxity of life and doctrine has been clear and uniform. The best writers of the 17th century have lifted up their united voices in the most solemn manner against it.

Bishop Hopkins says: "Antinomianism is to be abominated, which derogates from the value and validity of the law, and contends that it is to all purposes extinct to believers, even as to its preceptive and regulating power; and that no other obligation to duty lies upon them who are in Christ Jesus, but only from the law of gratitude: that God requires not obedience from them upon so low and sordid an account as the fear of his wrath and dread severity; but all is to flow only from the principle of love and the sweet temper of a grateful and ingenuous spirit. . . . . This is a most pestilent doctrine, which plucks down the fence of the law, and opens a gap for all manner of licentiousness and libertinism to rush in upon the Christiàn world."

Leighton: "The gospel sets not men free to profaneness: no, it is a doctrine of holiness. 'We are not called unto uncleanness, but unto holiness.' 1 Thess. iv. 7. He hath indeed taken off the hardness, the iron yoke, and now, his commandments are not grievous. 1 John v. 3. His yoke is easy, and his burden light. They who are most sensible, and have most assurance of their deliverance, are ever the most active and fruitful in obedience: they feel themselves light and nimble, having the heavy chains and fetters taken off. 'Lord, I am thy servant; thou hast loosed my bonds.'" Ps. cxvi. 16.

Flavel: "God preserve all his people from the gross and vile opinions of *Antinomian libertines*, who cry up grace, and decry obedience: who under specious pretences of exalting a naked Christ upon the throne, do indeed strip him naked of a great part of his glory, and vilely dethrone him. My pen shall not English what mine eyes have read. Tell it not in Gath."

Charnock: "Libertinism and licentiousness *find no encouragement in the gospel. It was made known to all nations for the obedience of faith.* The goodness of God is published, that our enmity to him may be parted with. Christ's righteousness is not offered to us to be put on, that we may roll the more warmly in our sins. The doctrine of grace commands us to give up ourselves to Christ to be accepted through him, and to be ruled by him. Obedience is due to God, as a sovereign in his law; and it is due out of gratitude, as he is a God of grace in the gospel . . . . The gospel frees us from the curse, but not from the duty and service. '*We are delivered from the hands of our enemies, that we might serve God in holiness and righteousness.*' Luke i. 74, 75. *This is the will of God in the gospel, even our sanctification.* When a prince strikes off a malefactor's chains, though he deliver him from the punishment of his crime, he frees him not from the duty of a subject . . . Christ's righteousness gives us a title to heaven; but there must be holiness to give us a fitness for heaven."

T. Watson: "They who cast God's law behind their backs, God will cast their prayers behind his back; they who will not have the law to rule over them shall have the law to judge them . . . If God spake all these words, then we must *hear* all these words. As we would have God hear all *our* words when we pray, so we must hear all *his* words when he speaks. He that stops his ears when God cries, shall cry himself and not be heard."

Boston: "All men are obliged to keep these commandments, for God is Lord of all; but the saints especially; for besides being their Lord, he is their God and Redeemer too. So far is the state of the saints from being one of sinful liberty that there are none so strongly bound to obedience as they, and that by the strongest of all bonds, those of love and gratitude."

Nor have modern divines of high character been

more slow or less sweeping in expressing their abhorrence of this corrupt system of faith and practice. May it not rather be called a system of unbelief and of want of practice? John Newton: "It is an unlawful use of the law, that is an abuse of it, an abuse both of law and gospel, to pretend that its accomplishment by Christ releases believers from any obligation to it as a rule. Such an assertion is not only wicked, but absurd and impossible in the highest degree: for the law is founded in the relation between the Creator and the creature, and must unavoidably remain in force so long as that relation subsists."

In his lectures in divinity, George Hill speaks of Antinomianism as "this horrible doctrine," and guards his readers against the impression "that the disrepute into which Antinomian preaching has begun to fall is owing to a departure from Calvinism;" and declares that there is "no room to suppose that Calvinism is inconsistent with rational, practical preaching."

Dr. Dwight well says: "Why is the law no longer a rule of righteousness to Christians? Is it because they are no longer under its condemning sentence? For this very reason they are under increased obligations to obey its precepts. Is it because they are placed under a *better* rule or a *worse* one? A better rule cannot exist: a worse, God would not prescribe."

Robert Hall: "The principles which compose the Antinomian heresy, are as much opposed to the *grace*, as to the authority of the great head of the church."

## CHAPTER XII.

### THE GOSPEL DOES NOT SUPERSEDE THE MORAL LAW.

A GREAT desire of the adversary of souls in every age has been to effect a divorce between doctrine and practice. Probably in no other way has more harm been done. Owen: "There is no way whereby the whole rule of duty can be rendered more vain and useless unto the souls of men than by the separation of the duties of the law from the grace of the gospel." If men can be brought to believe that morality will save them without piety, the gospel is at once rendered of none effect. On the other hand, if men believe that any species of piety towards God renders unnecessary the great principles of morality towards men, they will of course turn the grace of God into lasciviousness. That the apostles saw a happy harmony existing between our duties to God and our duties to man, and that in their view doctrine and practice were not hostile is evident from their writings. The epistle to the Romans makes a near approach to a systematic body of evangelical doctrine. It consists of sixteen chapters. The first eleven assert the highest doctrines of grace. The last five contain a better code of morals than can be found in the writings of the whole heathen and infidel world. The epistle to the Ephesians is one of the sublimest ever written. It contains six chapters. One can hardly imagine how an apostle standing at the gate of heaven could utter sublimer doctrine than is found in the first three. Yet the last three give directions for the guidance of our conduct before men, which, if honestly carried out, would make a heaven upon earth.

It would indeed be very remarkable if the Son of God should have done anything against the law of which he himself was the author. This matter is made entirely clear by Stephen, in his last address to the Jews. Speaking of the great prophet promised to them like unto Moses, he says of Christ, "This is he, that was in the church in the wilderness, with the angel which spake to him in the Mount Sina, and with our fathers: who receive the lively oracles to give unto us." Acts vii. 38. See also Heb. xii. 24–26.

That the gospel does not supersede the law is explicitly taught in the word of God. Having stated the doctrine of a gratuitous justification for Jew and Gentile, Paul says, "Do we then make void the law through faith? God forbid: yea, we establish the law." Rom. iii. 31. That this is so will appear if we but remember that no one, not even an angel of heaven, ever magnified the law and made it honourable, as Christ has done in his life of obedience and suffering, and that all his genuine followers make it their great concern to walk in his footsteps. That Jesus Christ taught nothing contrary to a perfect obedience to the moral law, and made no war upon it, he expressly asserts: "It is easier for heaven and earth to pass, than one tittle of the law to fail." Luke xvi. 17. Much more at length in the sermon on the mount, the Lord says, "Think not that I am come to destroy the law, or the prophets; I am not come to destroy, but to fulfil. For verily I say unto you, Till heaven and earth pass, one jot or one tittle shall in no wise pass from the law, till all be fulfilled. Whosoever therefore shall break one of these least commandments, and shall teach men so, shall be called the least in the kingdom of heaven; but whosoever shall do and teach them, the same shall be called great in the kingdom of heaven. For I say unto you, that except your righteousness shall exceed the righteousness of the Scribes and Pharisees, ye shall in no case enter into the kingdom of heaven." Matt. v. 17–20.

Besides this explicit declaration of our Lord, it is manifest on the very face of the sermon on the mount that the great aim of much of it was to rescue the law from the glosses and false interpretations of the Scribes and Pharisees. But the object at present is, to consider somewhat at length the four verses already quoted. Stier thinks that the choice of a mountain, as a place for the delivery of Christ's great sermon, had reference to something more than merely a fitting pulpit. He says, "We involuntarily and naturally think of that mountain of the law which preached condemnation. The Old Testament placed foremost the curse; the New, being glad tidings, begins with a blessing."

The question naturally arises, how did our Lord come to introduce this subject? Was there any popular error which required this refutation? The very first words, "*Think not*" would intimate either that they had thought, or were in great danger of thinking erroneously. There was an old Rabbinical saying that, "In the days of the Messias, the unclean shall be clean, and the forbidden allowed." If no error on this point was publicly taught, our Lord knew the heart of man too well to doubt that it would endeavour to pervert the doctrines of grace, as promulged by himself, to the purposes of a wicked life. The two words, *the Law* and *the Prophets*, evidently denote the whole of the Scriptures. We have the same phrase in Matt. vii. 12, xxii. 40; Luke xvi. 16; Acts xiii. 15; Rom. iii. 21. In all these cases the phrase evidently designates the entire word of God then written. In no sense did Jesus Christ come to introduce lawlessness. Himself submitted to the rite of circumcision and to baptism also, that he might fulfil all righteousness. He had not come to release mankind from the municipal laws under which they lived; much less had he come to wage a war of destruction upon the great principles of piety and morality as taught in the moral law. The whole sense of the passage must very much turn upon the meaning of the words rendered *destroy* and *fulfil.* In giving the sense of this passage, commentators have been remarkably agreed. Luther: "I am not come to make of none effect, but to complete." *To destroy* the law and the prophets, says Diodati, is, "To derogate from their authority, to cause them to be thought false or unprofitable, to propound a doctrine contrary to them." *To fulfil* he paraphrases thus: "Observing the law in all points myself, and bringing to pass all that was foretold by the prophets, and putting in force the right of the law; namely, to require a perfect obedience, and its promise, which is to give life to them that fulfil it, and is effected in me alone for all my church." Pool thinks that by Christ's saying he came not to *destroy* the law, we are to understand that he came not to "put an end to the moral law," and by *fulfilling* it we are to understand "not that he came to fill it up, as papists and Socinians contend, adding any new precepts to it; but by yielding himself a personal obedience to it, by giving a fuller and stricter interpretation of it than the Jews formerly had, and by taking the curse of it, and giving a just satisfaction to divine justice for it." Clarke: "I am not come to make the law of none effect—to dissolve the connection which subsists between its several parts, or the obligation men are under to have their lives regulated by its moral precepts; nor am I come to *dissolve* the *connecting* reference it has to the *good things promised.* But I am come to complete—to perfect its connection and reference, to accomplish every thing shadowed forth in the Mosaic *ritual,* to fill up its great design, and to give grace to all my followers, to fill up or complete every moral duty." Scott: "Christ assured the Jews that he had not come to teach anything inconsistent with the true meaning of their sacred writings, which would still continue in force as a part of divine revelation. . . . The moral law he came to fulfil, by perfectly obeying it as the surety of his people, in his life, sufferings, death and doctrines; to establish it in its fullest honour and authority; and to make the most effectual provision for men's loving and obeying it." Tholuck: "The Saviour says, 'My coming has not a negative, but a positive end: I am come not to do away, but to fulfil.' " Stier: "Has Christ, then, in any sense, brought a new, a better, a more perfect law, than *the* law, to fulfil which he avows himself to be come? By no means, as the whole sermon on the mount, his whole word, and the virtue of that law itself in our consciences attest. . . . If ye expect a Messiah, such as the prophets fore-announced, and yet suppose that he will come as a relaxer of the law, ye do greatly err, not understanding the prophets in their central harmony with the law. If I did not fulfil the law, then would the prophets also fail of their fulfilment. . . . *Let not the world think*, even the Christian world down to this day, that he came for any other end than to establish the whole will of God, as the law and the prophets in Israel especially enforced and foretold it:—let this be declared to the world continually in the Lord's own words, both for its encouragement and warning." There is not the slightest ground for the opinion that to *fulfil* means no more than to *teach;* and that to *destroy* means no more than *not to teach* or to *teach the contrary.* The early fathers, the reformers and the best writers in the seventeenth century dwell much upon the perfection of the fulfilling of the law by Christ. Melancthon says, "In four ways has the law been fulfilled by Christ; 1. By the obedience he showed to it in his own behalf; 2. By suffering for us its penalty. 3. Inasmuch as he fulfils the law in us through the Holy Spirit; 4. Inasmuch as he has confirmed it, and given his testimony to the necessity of keeping it." Maldonatus says, "Christ fulfilled the law; 1. In his own person, and by enjoining upon his apostles also compliance with its ceremonial precepts; 2. By rightly interpreting it; 3. By giving us grace to keep it; 4. By realizing in his person the types of the law." No doubt a Jew of those days by *the law* understood the whole of the dispensation as settled in the Old Testament; but as the Decalogue constituted the centre and indeed the very heart of that system, so far as precept is concerned, the moral law is unquestionably here included.

In the eighteenth verse, our Lord reiterates in the most explicit terms what he had asserted in the seventeenth. "For verily I say unto you, Till heaven and earth pass, one jot or one tittle shall in no wise pass from the law till all be fulfilled." Diodati says, that the form of expression here used is a proverbial kind of speech, as much as to say, Never while the world lasts. He thinks it is equivalent to that phrase in Job xiv. 12, "Till the heavens be no more;" or to that in Ps. lxxii. 5, "As long as the sun and moon endure." No doubt this is the Saviour's real meaning. Augustine thinks that the jot [or iota] is the Latin *i*, and by the tittle he understands the dot over the *i*. But our Saviour was not speaking to Latins nor in the Latin language. Yet what our Saviour did say is as striking as if the Bishop of Hippo had given the correct explanation. The jot no doubt means the tenth and smallest letter of the Hebrew alphabet, or the ninth and smallest letter of the Greek alphabet, and by the *tittle* we are to understand a small stroke of the pen of no more importance in composition than our (,). Stier: "The iota is the smallest letter, the tittle, little horn or point, is the smallest part of a letter which appertains to the true and established Scripture" Tholuck: "This expression of Christ is an emphatic designation of the law in its most minute parts." Stier: "That this strong expression refers figuratively, in its special meaning, to the least important of its contents, is plainly to be understood." This verse is characterized by the solemn word, *Amen*, in English *Verily;* and by that peculiar form of speech employed by Christ, *I say unto you*—as if he had said, I, the Alpha and Omega, the infallible Teacher and final Judge of quick and dead.

The 19th verse is of somewhat difficult interpretation as to its *precise* meaning in two points. The first relates to the phrase, *one of these least commandments.* These words themselves have been taken in three senses. Some suppose they refer to the provisions of the *Ceremonial Law.* But this is not admissible, since Christ himself speaks of David as blameless, though he eat the shew-bread. And everywhere in the Old Testament, no less than in the New, acts of justice, mercy, and dutifulness to parents receive a decided commendation over any attention to religious ceremonies, though prescribed by God. And in the 15th chapter of Acts, the council of the apostles and elders did not hesitate to declare that the Mosaic ritual was not binding upon the Gentiles. Others think the reference is to the commands of our Saviour as given in the New Testament. This can hardly be its meaning, because it was not the topic of his discourse. The other opinion, which is most probably the correct one, is that by *commandments* here, we are to understand the precepts of the Decalogue. This is the usual sense of the word commandments in the New Testament. See Matt. xxii. 40;

Mark x. 19; Luke i. 6, xviii. 20; 1 Cor. xii. 19. When the peculiar precepts of our Saviour are spoken of by himself, he calls them *my commandments;* when they are spoken of by others, they are called the *commandments of the Lord*, or *his commandments.* 1 Cor. xiv. 37; 1 John ii. 4, iii. 24.

The New Testament admits that all the command ments are not of equal importance. Matt. xxii. 36, 38, 40; Mark xii. 30. The Saviour admits the same in this verse. The Scribes and Pharisees had greatly abused this principle. They had put ceremonies above moral duties. They had declared that "Whosoever after meat washeth not his hands is no better than he who hath committed a murder." By their traditions, they had in many ways made void the commandments of God. Our Saviour does not deny that one commandment may be more important than another. But he guards against the infraction of the very least, in the solemn manner now to be considered. He says, "Whosoever therefore shall break one of these least commandments, and shall teach men so, he shall *be called the least in the kingdom of heaven.*" Here is the second point of difficulty mentioned above. This is very alarming language, and should be well weighed by every man. If the evil here threatened is suited to strike terror, the blessing promised to those who do and teach these commandments is very glorious; *they shall be called great in the kingdom of heaven.* Commentators are not agreed whether by the kingdom of heaven we are to understand the visible church on earth as constituted by Christ, or the invisible kingdom of glory in heaven. But we need not perplex ourselves on this matter, inasmuch as he who is really unfit to be a member of the church on earth, is not fit to enter heaven. So we may give to the phrase the most solemn meaning. The views of commentators on the import of the phrase, *the least in the kingdom of heaven*, are such as these: Diodati: They "shall lose much of God's approbation and of the good esteem of true believers." Henry: "Those who extenuate and encourage sin, and discountenance and put contempt upon strictness in religion and serious devotion, are the dregs of the church." Doddridge: "*He shall be accounted* [*one of*] *the least* and unworthiest members in the *kingdom of heaven*, or in the church of the Messiah; and shall soon be entirely cut off from it as unfit for so holy a society." Whitby: "He shall be unworthy to be reckoned one of the members of my kingdom." Clarke: "Shall have no place in the kingdom of Christ here, nor in the kingdom of glory above." Scott: "Either no true disciple at all, or one of the most inconsistent and mean of the whole company." Pool: "Shall be accounted of the least value and esteem in the church of God, and shall never come into the kingdom of glory." Tholuck: "We are obliged to conclude that it is not exclusion, but inferiority of station, which is here spoken of." Stowell: "Christ assures his disciples that he who in the slightest degree departs from the most rigid demands of that rule, and either directly or indirectly teaches others so to do, shall scarcely be esteemed as belonging to the Christian church, or, if belonging to it, as the least worthy and consistent of its members; whilst, on the other hand, he who is obedient in all things, and by his instruction, persuasion, or example, influences others to the same obedience, shall be honoured as an enlightened, decided, and useful subject of "the kingdom of heaven." Hare: "He shall be considered a most unworthy member of Christ's kingdom even here, and therefore, I need not add, can have no chance of being admitted into Christ's glorious and everlasting kingdom hereafter." Whatever, therefore, may be the precise meaning of the phrase, *least in the kingdom of heaven*, we cannot doubt that it contains an awful warning against the error of lightly esteeming any one of the Ten Commandments.

In the 20th verse, the Lord says, "For I say unto you, that except your righteousness shall exceed the righteousness of the Scribes and Pharisees, ye shall in no case enter into the kingdom of heaven." "The righteousness of the Scribes and Pharisees," says Diodati, "was all set upon vain ceremonies, arbitrary disciplines, false shows, and dead works without God's Spirit." The Scribes and Pharisees were very highly esteemed by the people for their piety; but Jesus Christ says his disciples must exceed them, both in their principles and practice. "Their interpretation of the moral law," says Pool, "was so short and jejune, that it is manifest that their righteousness was not only a righteousness not of faith, but of works, and those works that were very imperfect, and short of what the true sense of the law required." Scott: "The zeal and strictness of the Scribes and Pharisees, both in doctrine and practice, was chiefly shown about their own traditions, by which they 'made void the law of God;' and about minute observances, by which they covered over their neglect of judgment, mercy, faith, and the love of God and man." It was always true that the letter of the law killed. It is the Spirit that maketh alive. The most exact observance of a ritual, and the most decent, though heartless conformity to the precepts of the moral law, never did meet the demands of God's word. Those, therefore, whose piety goes not beyond externals, however faultless in the eyes of men, will never secure the smiles of God. Of such the Saviour says, "they shall in no case enter into the kingdom of heaven;" that is, they shall not be accepted members of his visible church, nor reign with him in glory. Yes, verily, our obedience must vastly excel that of any formalist that ever lived. Stowell: "Your righteousness must exceed theirs in the principle from which it springs,—not like theirs, from pride and self-sufficiency, but from love;—in the motives by which it is influenced,—not the applause of mortals, but by the approbation of God, and the promotion of his glory;—in the standard by which it is regulated,—not the traditions and specious explanations of the Scribes and Pharisees themselves, but by the full and spiritual meaning of the law; in the extent to which it is carried,—not merely to the visible observance, but also to the secret thoughts and feelings;—in the effect it produces on others,—not securing their admiration of your ostentatious virtue, and forcing them to submit to your usurped authority, but leading them to admire the grace of God, to adore him in the purity and goodness of his law, and to emulate the example you have set them."

The conclusion is, nothing is said or done in the

gospel to depreciate the law; but much to honour and magnify it. The apostasy gave no license to rebellion. Sinning can never make sinning lawful or excusable. Nor does the grace of God in the gospel open a door to unholy living.

# CHAPTER XIII.

## DETACHED REMARKS.

### I. IGNORANCE OF THE LAW.

THE evils of ignorance of the law are very great. They are such as these: Where the law is not well known, there is but little knowledge of sin. Of course convictions, if any, are slight. The fallow-ground of the human heart is not well broken up. And where the law is not well known, repentance is slight. We are called upon to mourn for our sins; but if we do not know how numerous and vile they are, our sorrow will not bear any just proportion to their enormity. Besides, where there is general ignorance of the law, false confidence will abound. Multitudes will presume upon God's mercy where none is promised; and multitudes will lie in carnal security. When such ignorance becomes general, society assumes its very worst forms. Lawlessness runs riot. The animal nature of man fearfully prevails. Irreligion becomes general, and all sober men cry out, what are we coming to? The gospel itself becomes for a loathing, like the manna to the Israelites; for "without an experimental knowledge and an unfeigned faith of the law and the gospel, a man can neither venerate the authority of the one, nor esteem the grace of the other."

### II. HOW THE LAW IS MADE VOID.

The error of many ancients, and of not a few moderns, consists, not in a formal denial of the obligation of the moral law, but in inventing various devices for evading its force. The Scribes and Pharisees superadded a great mass of the traditions of the elders, which they regarded as equal and even paramount to the law of God. Against this capital error our Saviour directed much of his discourse. He charged them directly with transgressing the commandments of God by their traditions. The fifth commandment said, Honour thy father and mother. The tradition of the elders said, If a parent was suffering with hunger, and his son had an animal whose meat, when dressed, would be suitable food for the hungry, if the son wished not to relieve the distresses of his parents all that was necessary was to say, It is a gift; it is Corban; it is devoted to religious uses. Thus Christ declares, They made the commandments of God of none effect by their tradition. The worship of such is an offence to God. Jesus but expresses the tenor of the Old Testament when he says of such; "In vain do they worship me, teaching for doctrines the commandments of men." Matt. xv. 2–9. Others render null and void the law by not sufficiently discriminating between it and the gospel. Colquhoun: "To blend or confound the law and the gospel has been a fatal source of error in the Christian church; and has embarrassed many believers not a little, in their exercise of faith and practice of holiness." The church of Rome follows both these devices fully. An old commentator says:

"The Scriptures teach that there is no difference to be put between meats, in regard of holiness, but that every creature of God is good. This the Papists make void by teaching that it is matter of religion and conscience to abstain from flesh meats at certain seasons. The Scripture teacheth that we should pray to God alone. This they make void by their manifold prayers to saints departed. The Scripture teacheth Christ alone to be our Mediator, both of redemption and intercession. This they make void by making saints intercessors. The Scripture teacheth Christ to be the only head of the church. This they abrogate by the doctrine of the Pope's supremacy. The Scripture teacheth that every soul should be subject to the higher power. This they abrogate by exempting the Pope and popish clergy from subjection to the civil power of princes and magistrates. Lastly, to instance in the same kind as our Saviour here against the Pharisees, whereas the word of God commands children to honour their parents, the papists teach that if the child have vowed a monastical life, he is exempted from duty to parents."

### III. A RIGHT TEMPER.

If in any thing, surely in the study of the law, a right temper is exceedingly important. The law is not to be looked upon as the word of man, but is to be received as it is in truth the word of God, spoken in most solemn circumstances. We are as much bound to look back to the awful scenes of Sinai, as if we ourselves had been present at the giving of the law. Whoever would study the law aright, must have a docile temper. He must be willing to learn whatever

God would teach him. His language should be, "Speak, Lord, for thy servant heareth." We should know the law of God better if we would more zealously practise what we have already learned. Perhaps nothing more impedes our spiritual progress than refusing to do as well as we know how. James iv. 17. We ought also to think much on the commandments. One mark of a good man, as laid down in the First Psalm is, that "his delight is in the law of the Lord; and in his law doth he meditate day and night." Although the word *law* here includes more than the ten Commands, even all Scripture, yet the law is an excellent part of the sacred writings; so that it is not excluded. If we would study the law profitably, we must be open to conviction. We must not be scared away from beholding sad sights in our own hearts, habits and lives revealed to us by the law. We must be willing to borrow light from all proper sources. Not a book of Scripture is there but that it throws some light on the Commandments. Above all, we must ask for the illumination of the Holy Ghost. Without his teaching we shall labour in vain. Let us, therefore, cry mightily to God, asking him to quicken us in his way, and not to hide his commandments from us, to teach us the way of his statutes, and not to take his Holy Spirit from us.

### IV. HOW SHOULD THE LAW BE DIVIDED?

1. All admit that the law as at first given was upon two tables of stone written upon both sides, Ex. xxxii. 15. It is commonly thought that the first table contained all the law to the end of the requirements respecting the Sabbath day; and that the

second table contained all from the words, "Honoür thy father," &c. to the close of the Decalogue. Tradition has been so uniform in handing down this report that it is entitled to respect. The first table, therefore, enjoins duties directly owing to God; and forbids sins directly committed against him and his worship. The second, prescribes our duties to man; and forbids every species of sin against our neighbour. Calvin: "We have a reason at hand which removes all ambiguity on this subject. For God has thus divided his law into two parts, which comprise the perfection of righteousness, that we might assign the first part to the duties of religion, which peculiarly belong to the worship of his majesty; and the second to those duties of charity which respect men. The first foundation of righteousness is certainly the worship of God; and if this be destroyed, all the other branches of righteousness, like the parts of a disjointed and falling edifice, are torn asunder and scattered. . . . It is vain to boast of righteousness without religion." The precepts of both tables proceeded from the same authority, and yet sins against God are more heinous than sins directed against man. "If one man sin against another, the judge shall judge him: but if a man sin against the LORD, who shall intreat for him?" 1 Sam. ii. 25.

2. The method of numbering the commandments has not been entirely uniform. They are not in Scripture called the Ten Commandments, but the *Ten Words*. Hence some writers have felt at liberty to regard what is ordinarily called *The Preface* to the Commandments as the first WORD. Meier divides the ten words into two pentads, thus. I. (1.) I am Jehovah

thy God. (2.) Thou shalt have no other gods beside me. (3.) Thou shalt not make to thyself any graven image. (4.) Thou shalt not take the name of Jehovah thy God in vain. (5.) Remember the Sabbath day to keep it holy. II. (1.) Honour thy father and thy mother. (2.) Thou shalt not commit adultery. (3.) Thou shalt do no murder. (4.) Thou shalt not bear false witness against thy neighbour. (5.) Thou shalt not steal. This arrangement omits entirely every thing respecting covetousness, and claims to be "the original form of the Decalogue." Kurtz says, that according to Meier: "These were the entire contents; there was not a single word more or less; and this was the way in which the commandments were arranged in the two tables!!" No wonder he adds the marks of exclamation.

The words, "I am the LORD thy God, &c." clearly cannot be taken as constituting a commandment. They enjoin nothing. They prohibit nothing. They are a very fit preface to the whole code or to each commandment in it. And they have been commonly so regarded. They form, indeed, a very important sentence or *word*. The Jews and some others have put this sentence as the first *word*. They have united the prohibitions to have other gods and to make any graven image into one commandment, and made it the first; and so have thrown the numbers forward in every instance, making but nine commandments. Augustine took a different course. He united the prohibition against having other gods and the use of images into one commandment, and called it the first. He divided the law concerning covetousness into two, numbering them the ninth and the tenth. He took the copy of the law not as given in the twentieth chapter of Exodus, but as given in the fifth chapter of Deuteronomy. According to him, the ninth commandment was, "Thou shalt not desire thy neighbour's wife;" and the tenth comprehended every thing else which we are forbidden to covet. The Roman Catholic church, and at least one Protestant church, have adopted this division. It should be fatal to it, that in the twentieth chapter of Exodus, the first thing we are forbidden to covet is our neighbour's house, and not our neighbour's wife. The rehearsal of the law in Deuteronomy is evidently given by a speaker who presents the sense of the whole, but is not claiming to give an exact copy of the very words used on Mount Sinai, or of the order in which they were written. The ordinary mode of division is, that the law against having other gods is the first commandment; that against images, the second; that against profaning God's name, the third; that against profaning the Sabbath, the fourth; and so on, making the law against every kind of covetousness, the tenth. "This division," says Kurtz, "was unhesitatingly adopted by *Philo*, *Josephus*, and *Origen;* and they were followed by nearly all the Greek fathers, and by all the Latin until the time of Augustine. In the Greek church it continued to prevail, (the law against the worship of images being of course interpreted as referring to *latria* and not to *doulia*,) and the Swiss Reformers introduced it again in connection with the *Reformed* church. It has been most warmly and thoroughly defended by *Züllig* and *Geffken*, and is almost universally adopted by modern theologians." This division is followed in this work. No particular importance attaches to the numbering of the commandments, provided every word that God has spoken be faithfully delivered to the people. It is not reckoning the commandments aright, but keeping them, that is pleasing to God. And yet Roman Catholics have availed themselves of their mode of numbering the commandments entirely to omit from their short Catechisms all allusion to image worship. This is maiming and mutilating the word of God. It is pleasant to find, that of late years, in America at least, some disposition is manifested by them to give this prohibition its place in their formularies. Bishop Hopkins (of the seventeenth century) says that in his time the words, "Thou shalt not make unto thee any graven image, &c.," were generally omitted in all Roman Catholic books of devotion and of instruction for the people. Who has ever seen these words in any copy of the commandments placed near the altar in a mass house?

### V. THE PREFACE TO THE MORAL LAW.

I AM THE LORD THY GOD, WHICH HAVE BROUGHT THEE OUT OF THE LAND OF EGYPT, OUT OF THE HOUSE OF BONDAGE. The first title here claimed by God is LORD—in the Hebrew, *Jehovah*. It teaches the self-existence, independence, eternity and immutability of God. The word is commonly supposed to be derived from the Hebrew verb which signifies *to be*. Next to Elohim this is much the most usual name given to God in the Old Testament. It might have been well to transfer it into our English Bible in every case; but our translators followed those versions which had been previously made; and their authors in their turn had been guided not a little by the *Septuagint*, which rendered it by a word signifying *Lord* or *Master*. But our English translation has guarded against misapprehension on the subject, by putting in small capitals the word LORD, when it is a translation of Jehovah.

The second title here claimed by the lawgiver is *God*—in the Hebrew *Elohim*, which is in the plural form. There is no satisfactory explanation of the use of these plurals concerning God, except that they were intended to recognize a plurality of persons in the godhead. Being in the singular, *Jehovah* expresses the divine unity. Being in the plural, *Elohim* points to the trinity. The Lord says, I am thy God; by which he claims to have that people in covenant relation with himself. The residue of the preface is a direct appeal to the gratitude of those to whom the law was first given, on the score of God's amazing mercies to them personally and nationally, temporally and spiritually. It reminded them of all that God had done for their fathers as well as for themselves. It specially pointed to the deliverance from Egyptian bondage, as no mean type of the greater redemption promised to our first parents in the garden of Eden.

To us this preface teaches that "because God is the Lord, and our God and Redeemer, therefore we are bound to keep all his commandments." While claiming that these words are a preface to the whole law, we may yet admit that they have a particular relation to the first commandment.

This preface then clearly points to the authority of the Most High, as the Creator and Governor of the world, as possessed of infinite and independent excellence, as having bound all his creatures to himself by bonds which they may not innocently disregard, and holding all who profess his name truly and firmly bound to his service by a covenant which he will not break, and which they may not lightly esteem. God's sovereignty is entire and absolute; and is so declared in Scripture. Rom. ix. 20–23.

# CHAPTER XIV.

## THE FIRST COMMANDMENT.

THOU SHALT HAVE NO OTHER GODS BEFORE ME.

THE phrase *before me* in this commandment occurs nowhere else in the Decalogue. Some writers render it by the phrases, *Beside me*, or *But me.* Both of these are mistakes. The phrase, *Before me*, if rendered literally would be, *Before my face.* It specially refers to God's omnipresence and omniscience. It reminds us at the very beginning of the commandments that He, with whom we have to do, searches the heart. "If we have forgotten the name of our God, or stretched out our hands to a strange god: shall not God search this out? For he knoweth the secrets of the heart." Ps. xliv. 20, 21. He knows our down-sitting and up-rising, he understands our thought afar off. He compasseth our path and our lying down, and is acquainted with all our ways. He has beset us behind and before, and laid his hand upon us. We cannot flee from his presence. In heaven, in hell, in the uttermost parts of the sea, every where he is present. The darkness hideth not from him; the night shineth as the day; the darkness and the light are both alike to him. He possesses our reins. Every sin, therefore, and in particular every sin against this commandment, is committed in the immediate presence of God. For there is no "creature that is not manifest in his sight: but all things are naked and opened unto the eyes of him with whom we have to do." Heb. iv. 13. "God's understanding is infinite." Ps. cxlvii. 5. Concealment from him is impossible. An attempt to hide ourselves or any thing from him is itself folly and wickedness. Man judges of the heart by the deed; but God judges of the deed by the heart; and he judges the heart by itself. To him nothing is indistinct. He never makes a mistake. His omniscience is infallible. This therefore is a great aggravation of all iniquity, that it is perpetrated under the immediate eye of God, and is an affront offered him to his face. So he says, "Will ye steal, murder, and commit adultery, and swear falsely, and burn incense unto Baal and walk after other gods whom ye know not, and come and stand before me in this house, which is called by my name, and say, We are delivered to do all these abominations?" Jer. vii. 9, 10. It is considered an act of extraordinary impudence when men will lie, or steal, or commit lewdness in the very presence of those who are most wronged and insulted thereby. This principle is of easy application to God.

### WHAT THE FIRST COMMANDMENT REQUIRES.

I. *It requires us to have a God.* It is not so unnatural for man to be without hands, or feet, or hearing, or vision, as to be without the religious sentiment. If man is a creature, then it is clear to reason, that he owes all to the Creator. If man is weak and dependent to an extent, which even the heathen themselves have admitted, then it is impossible to give him adequate strength, or meet his pressing wants, except by a divinity. An attempt or desire to obliterate the religious sentiment from the mind of ourselves or of others is an appalling atrocity. If it could be successful in any case, it would but sink its victim below the devils, for they believe and tremble. James ii. 19.

II. *This precept requires us to have Jehovah for our God.* He is the Creator of the ends of the earth. He is possessed of all and infinite perfections. He is glorious in holiness, fearful in praises, doing wonders. He is over all, God blessed for ever. Cleaving to him, saints and angels rise from glory to glory. All rational creatures are elevated in their natures and conceptions by every species of divinely appointed service rendered to him. His authority is acknowledged by the whole inanimate creation. Not a particle of dust nor a solid globe, not a drop of water nor a mighty ocean, but is wholly subject to his will, as expressed in the laws of nature. All deeps, and fire, and hail, and snow, and vapour, and stormy wind fulfil his word. Yea, the dragons, and beasts and all cattle, and creeping things, and flying fowl are wholly subject to his authority. For man therefore to deny Jehovah's sovereignty over him is to make himself like the devils. From the days of Moses until this time, having Jehovah for our God has been declared fundamental in true religion, and is mighty in producing obedience to the other commandments. Ex. xv. 2; Ps. cxviii. 28.

But what is it to have Jehovah for our God? Surely this means much more than some decent public declaration that we take him as such. For in works, many deny him, being abominable, and disobedient, and unto every good work reprobate. Titus i. 16.

1. Whoever takes Jehovah for his God must *know* him. So important is the knowledge of God that often in the Scriptures it is put for the whole of religion. Prov. ii. 5; Isa. xi. 9; Ps. xxxvi. 10, xlvi. 10. If it may be truly said to us as to the Samaritans, "Ye worship ye know not what," it is not only a terrible rebuke of our ignorance, but it proves that our religion is vain. John iv. 22. "To know God and Jesus Christ whom he has sent, is eternal life." John xvii. 3. Not to know that God is, and that he is a rewarder of them that diligently seek him, is subversive of all piety. Our knowledge must extend not only to his existence, but to his character. He is "the LORD, the LORD God, merciful and gracious, long-suffering, and abundant in goodness and truth, keeping mercy for thousands, forgiving iniquity, transgression and sin, and that will by no means clear the guilty." Ex. xxxiv. 6, 7. The knowledge of God is either speculative or practical. The former we may have and be none the better, but only the more guilty. The practical knowledge of God is saving. It controls the heart and life; it brings our moral nature into a blessed conformity to the truth of God; it shows its power by humbling the soul. Job xl. 4, 5. It desires to bring others acquainted with the Most High, 1 Chron. xxviii. 9, and it is valued above all the treasures of earth. Prov. ii. 3–5.

2. We must *confess God* in all our ways. Ps. xlviii. 14; Prov. iii. 6. We must be ready to declare, "Thou art our Father, though Abraham be ignorant of us, and Israel acknowledge us not; thou, O Lord,

art our father, our redeemer." Isa. lxiii. 16. Unless we are brought to the "acknowledgment of the mystery of God, and of the Father, and of Christ, in whom are hid all the treasures of wisdom and knowledge," we cannot hope for salvation. Col. ii. 2, 3; Deut. xxvi. 17, 18.

3. We must *love* God. This duty is largely insisted on in all the Scriptures. Jesus Christ said nothing more terrible to his foes, if it be rightly considered, than this; "I know you that ye have not the love of God in you." John v. 42. Nor can any more important prayer be offered than this, "The Lord direct your hearts into the love of God." 2 Thess. iii. 5. Nor do the Scriptures enjoin on man any more weighty duty than this, "Keep yourselves in the love of God." Jude 21. This love, when genuine, is controlling. Many Scriptures require that we love God with all the heart, with all the soul, with all the mind, and with all the might. Deut. vi. 5, x. 12, xi. 1, 13, 22, xix. 9, xxx. 6; Matt. xxii. 37; Mark xii. 30.

4. The Scriptures no less clearly require us to *fear* God. Lev. xxv. 17; 1 Pet. ii. 17. Great promises are made to such as fear him. Eccles. viii. 12. The rebuke the penitent thief gave to his companion was in the words, "Dost not thou fear God?" One mark of a good man is, that he honours them that fear the Lord. Ps. xv. 4. While the servility of ignorance and unbelief may cower at the very thought of God, only they, that fear him after a godly sort, are ever ready to say, "His mercy endureth for ever." Ps. cxviii. 4. Nor may any religious teacher cease to call on the church, saying, "O fear the Lord, ye his saints: for there is no want to them that fear him."

Ps. xxxiv. 9. All claims to true piety, unsupported by holy living, are false. Calvin: "We manifest a becoming reverence for him, only when we prefer his will to our own. It follows then that there is no other legitimate worship of him, but the observance of righteousness, sanctity, and purity."

5. We must *obey God.* In the absence of hearty obedience, all other evidences of piety are deceptive. "Hath the Lord as great delight in burnt-offerings and sacrifices, as in obeying the voice of the Lord?" 1 Sam. xv. 22. Men perish because they will not be obedient. Deut. viii. 20. This test is fair. All pretences to godly fear or holy love, not accompanied by a spirit of prompt and cheerful obedience to the known will of God, will sooner or later cover us with shame. "Augustine sometimes calls obedience to God the parent and guardian, and sometimes the origin of all virtues."

6. We must *worship* God. The essentials of worship pleasing to God are first, That the service rendered be something commanded by himself. Secondly, That we adore his glorious perfections, and make prostrate obeisance of all our faculties before him, submitting our understanding to his teaching, our consciences to his guidance and all our powers to be moulded by his Spirit. Just conceptions of the greatness and majesty of God must lead all right minds to adoration. Thirdly, That we depend upon him, confide in him, and rely upon his power, wisdom, goodness, holiness, truth, and righteousness. Fourthly, That we be heartily thankful and render him our praise for all his mercies. To the truly pious mind this is a delightful part of all worship. Fifthly, That

we confess our sins before him and hide not our faults in his presence. Sixthly, That we supplicate his blessing upon ourselves and all for whom we are bound to pray, not doubting his faithfulness, nor his readiness to give us all needed aid.

All these things enter into the essence of our having Jehovah for our God. They imply that we believe in him, Heb. xi. 6; that we choose him, Josh. xxiv. 15; that we hope in him, Ps. cxxx. 7; that we honour him, Mal. i. 6; that we joyfully serve him, Ps. ii. 11; that we submit to him, James iv. 7; that we humble ourselves under his mighty hand, 1 Pet. v. 6; that we devote ourselves to him, Deut. xxvi. 17; that we are zealous in his cause and for his glory, Rom. xii. 11; Rev. iii. 19; that we make it our business to please him, 1 Thess. iv. 1; that we wait for him and wait upon him, Ps. xxv. 3, cxxx. 5; that we be sorry for our sins, Jer. xxxi. 18, 19: that we mourn the sins of our fellow-men, Neh. xiii. 8; Ps. lxxiii. 21; that we desire God above all things, Ps. lxxiii. 25; that we delight in him, Ps. xxxvii. 4; that we think upon his name, Mal. iii. 16; that we meditate upon him, Ps. lxiii. 6; that we walk with him, Gen. v. 22; and that he be supreme in all our affections, 1 Chron. xxviii. 9; Ps. xcv. 6, 7; Matt. iv. 10.

This commandment requires of us these things in perfection. It also enjoins the use of all means that may promote these things in our hearts and lives, or in the hearts and lives of others.

III. *The first commandment requires that we should take the Lord Jehovah to be* OUR *God* EXCLUSIVELY. Calvin: "The end of this precept is, that God chooses to have the sole pre-eminence, and to enjoy, undiminished, his authority among his people." All other gods are vanities. They are no gods. They can neither hear, nor help, nor see, nor save. Jehovah is God alone. There is no God beside him; there is no God with him; there is no God above him; there is no God under him. Isa. xliv. 6, 8, xlv. 5. In this matter there are two errors; one entirely disowns Jehovah and exclusively worships some false god or gods. In that case the real object of worship is Satan himself. He is the author of it, and his kingdom is built up by it. Paul says: "The things which the Gentiles sacrifice, they sacrifice to devils, and not to God; and I would not that ye should have fellowship with devils." 1 Cor. x. 20. The other error consists in mingling the worship of the true God and of false gods. So we read of some who "feared the LORD and yet served their own gods, after the manner of the nations whom they carried away thence." 2 Kings xvii. 33. Daniel's image of clay and iron had some consistence. But such worship as this has none whatever. By the prophet Zephaniah (i. 4, 5,) God declares his purpose to cut off "them that worship the host of heaven upon the housetops; and them that worship and that swear by the LORD, and by Malcham," or by *their* king, *as Malcham signifies*. Even Joseph in Egypt seems to have fallen into this sin. He swore "by the life of Pharaoh." Gen. xlii. 15. The great sin of such corrupt mixtures in worship arises from two things. One is, that God everywhere forbids it. The other is, that all such worship goes on the supposition that God is no better, or little better, than other objects to which we thus pay homage. Let every man beware lest in the day of prosperity he sacrifice unto his own net, and burn incense to his own drag. Hab. i. 16. Jehovah has as much right to be loved and worshipped as God *alone*, as to be desired and adored at all.

Let us next consider this commandment in the negative form, and see

WHAT IT FORBIDS.

I. ANTI-THEISM. The greatest error into which man can fall is the positive and affirmative conclusion that there is no God. The number, who go this fearful length, is, perhaps, very small ; but that some should be given up to believe such a lie will surprise no one, who witnesses the diligence of men in corrupting themselves, and in seeking darkness rather than light. No man is so blind as he who does not wish to see. No darkness is more impenetrable than that in which the carnal mind envelopes itself. The rashness of asserting that there is no God has no parallel. Foster: "The wonder turns upon the great process by which a man would grow to the immense intelligence that can know there is no God. What ages and what lights are requisite for this attainment! This intelligence involves the very attributes of Divinity, while a God is denied. For unless this man is omnipresent, unless he is at this moment in every place in the universe, he cannot know but that there may be in some place manifestations of a Deity, by which even he would be overpowered. If he does not absolutely know every agent in the universe, the one that he does not know may be God. If he is not himself the chief agent in the universe, and does not know what is so, that which is so may be God. If he is not in absolute possession of all the propositions that constitute universal truth, that one which he wants, may be that there is a God. If he cannot with certainty assign the cause of all that he perceives to exist, that cause may be a God. If he does not know every thing that has been done in the immeasurable ages that are past, some things may have been done by a God. Thus unless he knows all things, that is, precludes another Deity, by being one himself, he cannot know that the Being, whose existence he rejects, does not exist." So that it can never be proven to be even probable, much less certain, that there is no God. Every assertion that he does not exist but evinces unequalled rashness and pretension. Finite intelligence can never be sure that there is no infinite intelligence. A being limited to a small part of one small world cannot safely say but that in many other worlds there may be incontestable proofs of divinity. Surely no man can elevate his character, or improve the knowledge or the virtue of his race, by making bold assertions respecting a point, on which his information does not bear some just proportion to the extent of the proposition which he lays down. The mass of mankind will find it exceedingly difficult to conceive by what amazing stretch of depravity, one of their race should reach so monstrous a conclusion.

II. Pantheism. The extremes often lie nearer than the means. Anti-theism and Pantheism are not separated by any great gulf. Men easily pass from one to the other. He, who declares that there is no God, and he, who declares that everything is God, have each a theory well-suited to the most brutal knowledge and to the lowest depravity. As such a belief can spring from nothing but great wickedness of heart, it need surprise no one to find mankind generally avoiding avowed Pantheists. Yet for thousands of years there have been in the world men who believe that the sun, moon and stars, the earth, the sea and the dry land, the mountains and valleys, the lakes and rivers, they themselves, their dogs, their swine, their cats, their turnips and their onions were not proofs of a divinity, but were divinity itself. The founder of the sect of Pantheists was Orpheus. At a later time, various classes of these errorists were found in ancient Greece and Rome. The most conspicuous of modern Pantheists was Spinoza. The last development of this monstrous system is found in certain transcendentalists of Europe and America. These wrap up their dogmas in modes of expression which may well be denominated learned gibberish. But when you are able to get hold of one of their thoughts, it is found to have less claim to profundity of thinking than Spinozism, and is entirely destitute of the frankness and candour of Toland and his followers, who, during the last century, organized themselves into a body, and set forth a creed, asserting that "the ethereal fire environs all things, and is therefore supreme. The ether is a reviving fire: it rules all things, it disposes all things. In it is soul, mind, prudence. This fire is Horace's particle of divine breath, and Virgil's inwardly nourishing spirit. All things are comprised in an intelligent nature." This is obviously nonsense; but there is no serious attempt made to cover it up with high-sounding words. As to the *ether* here spoken of, there is simply no evidence of any such thing. The first trace of its existence is nowhere found.

Modern Pantheists are much addicted to contempt of all the men and literature of the world except their own. They are proud and haughty scorners, and often in a high degree malignant. They show considerable zeal, and sometimes fabricate the grossest slanders against godliness. A few of them aim at literary and scientific fame, and make high pretensions to politeness: but the mass of their disciples are found in the depths of social debasement, yet full of great swelling words of vanity. Their grand error is of course the denial of the personality of God.

III. Atheism. Atheists are of three classes: 1. Such as do not regard the existence of God sufficiently proven to make it an article of hearty, practical belief; 2. Such as cannot deny that there is considerable, perhaps satisfactory evidence, that there is a God, but in their hearts really wish there was none; and 3. Such as live and act just as they would, if they believed there was no God. The first are called speculative atheists; the second, atheists in desire; the third, practical atheists. These all agree in this, that to all good ends and purposes they are "without God in the world." Atheists in desire will probably continue in their error until regenerated by the Spirit of God. Practical atheists abound. Many of them would be shocked if charged with atheism; yet they could not live more entirely without prayer, and without the fear and love of God, if it was an article of their creed that there was no God. His laws do not bind them. His mercies do not attract them. His judgments do not correct them. They know nothing, but what they know naturally as brute beasts. It is a mournful fact in human history that men have been found ready to publish their want of belief in the divine existence, and have died for the maintenance of their speculations. So true is it that love of falsehood may be stronger than the fear of death.

Lord Bacon says, that up to his time, "atheism did never perturb states." This was true. But since his time, especially within the last century, its outbreaks have been usually accompanied by political disturbances. The conversion of speculative atheists is of rare occurrence. Yet the power of God can bend the will of the most rebellious.

The utter unprofitableness of atheism is worthy of special note. It takes away all, and makes no returns. If it could be incontestably proven to be true, it would make no man less wretched, less foolish, less vicious, less criminal than he is now; but on the contrary it would make him every way less fit to live and less fit to die. It begets no lively, solid hopes. Its moral lessons (if it taught any) would be enforced by no sanctions. It is the darkest gulf, into which the human mind ever looked. Nevins: "If atheism be true, annihilation would be the object of most earnest longing to all thinking men." Lothrop: "If it were true that there is no God, what evidence can the atheist have that he shall not live and be miserable after death? How came he to exist at all? Whatever was the cause of his existence here, may be the cause of his existence hereafter. Or, if there is no cause, he may exist in another state as well as in this. And if his corrupt heart and abominable works make him so unhappy here, that he would rather be annihilated than run the hazard of a future existence, what hinders but he may be unhappy for ever? The man then is a fool, who wishes that there was no God, hoping thus to be secure from future misery; for, admitting that there is no God, still the man may exist hereafter as well as here; and if he does exist, his corruptions and vices may render him miserable eternally as well as for the present."

Atheism is both very stupid and very wicked. The case is this. The ox knoweth his owner, and the ass his master's crib. The sheep is a silly thing, and yet it knows the voice of its shepherd, and will not heed the voice of a stranger. But men are more foolish. God feeds them daily. He opens his hand and liberally supplies their wants. He watches them with more than a shepherd's care. Yet are these men more brutish than the beasts. They know not their owner. They doubt, or even deny his existence. Not only does the Lord provide for each of us, but for every living thing. Everett: "The human race is usually estimated at about one thousand millions of individuals. . . Let, then, the thoughtful husbandman, who desires to form just ideas, reflect, when he gathers his little flock about him to partake the morning's meal, that one thousand millions of fellow-men have awakened from sleep that morning, craving their daily bread with the same appetite, which reigns at his family board; and that if, by a superior power, they could be gathered together at the same hour for the same meal, they would fill both sides of five tables, reaching all round the globe where it is broadest, seated side by side, and allowing eighteen inches to each individual; and that these tables are to be renewed twice or thrice every day." Then let him consider that the supply of food is but a small part of the care of Providence over him and his, and how can he go away and deny his Master, and refuse to know his Owner and his Shepherd?

What would be thought of a man, or company of men, who would accept an invitation to even one feast provided by a neighbour, and then go and deny not only his kindness, but even his existence? Truly inspiration is right when it says that such folly and wickedness are never found among wise men. "The fool hath said in his heart, There is no God." Ps. xiv. 1. None but a fool could be brought to say so vile a thing even in his heart.

Without going at length into the proof of the divine existence, it may be proper to suggest something of the line of argument that might be pursued on this subject.

1. A fair argument for the divine existence is drawn from the consent of mankind. This argument is based on the just axiom that the belief of all nations and of all ages must be founded in truth. The whole world has never yet received an error as truth. Nor is there one instance, in which the learned and the unlearned, the polished and the rude, the rich and the poor, the civilized, the barbarous, and the savage, have united to support a falsehood. It is not possible to find in the history of the world a notice of any people, whose language, rites, laws or customs did not evince their belief of the existence of a God. Cicero says, "There is no nation so savage or wild as not to know that there is a God." No fairer argument for a Divinity

can be found than that stated by many a heathen, yea, even by many a savage. The atheist, therefore, sets up the conclusions of his own mind against the judgments of his race. For it is as rare to find a man, who denies the existence of a God, as to find a man blind, or deaf, or dumb.

It does not weaken the force of this argument to admit that the idea of a God is given from one generation to another. Before instruction, one does not know how to spell the monosyllables of his own language; nor does he know the axioms of science, but when he is taught these things, he is a madman to deny them.

It strengthens the argument from the consent of mankind that the belief of a God is not to unsanctified men pleasing, but troublesome. It "crosses their worldly interests, contradicts their sensual desires, deranges their joys, and torments their natural consciences." And yet no nation has ever been able to persuade itself that there was no God. If the belief of a Divinity is not based in irrefragable truth, why cannot the delusion be shaken off? Mankind have clearly shown two things; *first*, that they did not like to retain God in their knowledge, and *secondly*, that when they knew him, they did not glorify him as God. How comes it to pass then that with the whole current of corrupt sentiment, and wicked desires, and unholy living against true religion, men should still believe in a God? There is no fair answer to this question, except that the truth is too obvious to admit of sober denial.

2. In every man's mind is something, which reproves him for evil actions, however secret or ap-

plauded; and commends him for right conduct, however misunderstood or condemned. In clear cases of wrong-doing, there is a sense of guilt, which is always painful, sometimes intolerable. Many a man has sought death rather than endure the sting of the scorpion in his own bosom. Caligula confessed to the Roman senate that he suffered the pains of death every day. It is common with offenders to be in torment. But where there is transgression, there must be law; and where there is law, there must be a lawgiver; and who is lord of the conscience if there be no God? If the world has no moral governor, how can this self-condemnation be accounted for? There is no fairer reasoning than this: "*There is a conscience in man; therefore, there is a God in heaven.*" So mighty is the power of conscience, that among men nothing is more dreaded than its scourgings. Nor can it be so obliterated by false doctrines or a course of crime, as not to annoy the guilty every where. Herod was a bloody man. In principle he was a Sadducee, and believed neither in angel, nor spirit, nor heaven, nor hell, nor in a resurrection of the dead. At the solicitation of a bad woman he killed one, whom he knew to be the best man of his day. By and by, Jesus began to work amazing miracles among the people. These caused much talk. Some said one thing and some another. But Herod, in the teeth of all his principles, said he knew all about it: "It is John, whom I beheaded: he is risen from the dead." Mark vi. 16. Atheists have consciences, and though they are ignorant, erroneous, and sometimes seared as with a hot iron, yet from this quarter annoyance arises to those, who deny, no less than to those who own a God. No man, however debased in principle or behaviour, can tell what moment a drop of the divine wrath may fall into his soul, and the fires of perdition flame out from his own bosom. Every effect must have an adequate cause. What is the cause of conscience if there be no God, who is the author of man's moral nature? It is evident too that the author of the moral nature of one race of men is the author of the moral nature of every race of men, for they are all alike. Whoever is the lawgiver to the conscience of an American, is the lawgiver to the conscience of the European, the Asiatic, and the African. It is a favourite idea of atheists that fear formed a God. But if there is no God, why should all men fear him? It would be much nearer the truth to say that fear formed atheists. The good fear not that there is a God, but would be dismayed if they even doubted his existence. It is the wicked who flee when no man pursueth. A dreadful sound is in his ears. Terrors take hold of him as waters. God casts upon him and does not spare. Conscience stands a great bulwark against wickedness, and no less against atheism.

3. All creation says, There is a God, a God of power, wisdom and goodness. THE BLAZING UNIVERSE ABOVE US. Is it without a cause? About a thousand years before the Christian era, lived a Hebrew king and poet. In early life he had been a shepherd-boy, and had watched the motions of the heavenly bodies. Later in life he had been a fugitive from home, being pursued to the wilderness by his cruel and jealous monarch. There too he had seen how the azure vault above was all bespangled with gems brighter than

ever had been set in earthly crowns. By and by he seized his pen and wrote: "The heavens declare the glory of God; and the firmament showeth his handy-work. Day unto day uttereth speech, and night unto night showeth knowledge. There is no speech nor language, where their voice is not heard. Their line is gone out into all the earth, and their words to the end of the world. In them hath he set a tabernacle for the sun, which is as a bridegroom coming out of his chamber, and rejoiceth as a strong man to run a race. His going forth is from the end of the heaven, and his circuit unto the ends of it: and there is nothing hid from the heat thereof." Are not such views just, pure, elevating? Do they not commend themselves to every man?

Seven hundred years later lived the great man of Stagira, whose philosophy ruled the reasonings of men almost without interruption for nineteen hundred years. He wrote on logic, on ethics, on poetry, on politics, on physics, and on metaphysics. Among all his voluminous writings there is none more deserving of commendation than that commended by Cicero as "*noble.*" Aristotle says: "If there were beings who had always lived underground, in convenient, nay, magnificent dwellings, adorned with statues and pictures, and every thing which belongs to prosperous life, but who had never come above ground,—who had heard, however, by fame and report, of the power of God,—if at a certain time, the portals of the earth being thrown open, they had been able to emerge from those hidden abodes to the regions inhabited by us; when suddenly they had seen the earth, the seas, and the sky; had perceived the vastness of the clouds and the force of the winds; had contemplated the sun, his magnitude and his beauty, and still more his effectual power, that it is he who makes the day by the diffusion of his light through the sky; and, when night had darkened the earth, should then behold the whole heavens studded and adorned with stars, and the various lights of the waxing and waning moon, the risings and the settings of all these heavenly bodies, and their courses fixed and immutable in all ages: when, I say, they should see these things, truly they would believe in a God, and that these things are his works."

The bard of Bethlehem, who had been educated in the law of Moses, and who was the father of the wisest of mere men, and the philosopher of Stagira, who had been the tutor of Alexander the Great, though differing in a thousand other things, did not fail to see alike in this, that all we see, when we lift up our eyes, by day or by night, declares that this world had a divine author.

SEEDS. Have they no maker? All kinds of grass and grain, most kinds of roots and trees, of shrubs and plants, are propagated by seeds. Some of these are large, but most of them are small. Their shape and appearance are exceedingly diverse; but each of them contains a germ, in which is the vital principle. Men can make things which look like these seeds; but all the chemical skill and physical power of men cannot produce one germ. It is as much beyond created power to form a seed with the vital principle in it as to form a solar system. Yet from the creation to this day men have beheld the wonders of divine skill and energy in the production of myriads of seeds in every acre on earth not doomed to sterility. In this matter nothing is more surprising than the amazing fecundity of plants. A few years ago a farmer saw one stool of wheat springing up in the cleft of a rock. He thought there was something remarkable about it. When it was ripe he gathered it, and at the right season sowed it again. It has produced millions of bushels already. Most seeds too have a tenacity of life that is amazing. Wheat has grown and produced its kind three thousand years after it had been stored away. Seeds have been found more than a hundred feet under ground, which seemed to have been formed many ages before, and yet when exposed to the action of moisture, air, and the light and heat of the sun, have grown vigorously.

INSECTS. Have they no Maker? If they have, he is God. Plato believed there was a God, because all the world could not make a fly. Yet he who has made the fly has made it capable of propagating its kind. The product of a common house-fly in one season is over twenty millions. Some spiders produce nearly two thousand eggs. There are six or seven generations of gnats in a season, and each one lays two hundred and fifty eggs. A single bee is said to produce in one season a hundred thousand of its own kind. The eggs of insects, in some cases, retain the vital principle for a long time. Dr. Bright informed the world of the case of an egg that produced an insect eighty years after it must have been laid. And how wondrously these creatures are formed. Spiders have four paps for spinning their webs. Each pap has a thousand holes. The fine web itself is a cord made of four thousand strands. The spinning jenny is a coarse and rude thing compared with the amazing machinery of the spider. Nor can man make any thing of such amazing elasticity and durability as are found in the spider's web. The late Dr. Mitchell showed me, as connected with the most delicate portion of the machinery of the observatory at Cincinnati, Ohio, one piece of spider's web which had been stretched three hundred and ninety-five thousand times, and yet when the tension was off, it contracted to its wonted length. The numbers of insects found even in a small space is almost incredible. A pound of cochineal contains 70,000 insects. A German naturalist has discovered in the space of ten miles square 600 species of insects injurious to the growth of grain. Captain Buford saw near Smyrna in 1841 a cloud of locusts forty-six miles long and three hundred yards deep. The least insect examined with a proper microscope shows as great wonders in its structure as are detected in creatures that can be well examined with the naked eye. Have not these little creatures a Creator? May not a wise man walk through this portion of the kingdom of nature, and be justified in exclaiming at every step, "How manifold are thy works, O Lord; in wisdom hast thou made them all?"

THE FISHES AND MONSTERS OF THE SEA. Have they no Maker? We are amazed at the fecundity of the finny tribes. The roe of a mackerel has been found to contain half a million of eggs; that of a flounder, about a million and a half; that of a codfish as many as nine millions. The whole watery world is teeming with life. Is there no presiding Deity here?

The intelligent reader can pursue like trains of thought respecting the fowls of heaven. The feathers of those which are designed to be much on the wing are remarkably light, and their bones are hollow. Is not this a display of creative wisdom?

The beasts of the field, the beasts of the mountain, and the beasts of the desert would all in their turn furnish amazing illustrations of the creative skill of Him who made all things.

The existence of man, with his varied powers, the existence of society, with its untold resources and complications, the organization of plants and minerals, in short every thing in nature, when rightly considered, show that there must be a great *First Cause*. It can be shown that the little chip of granite required a Creator as truly as a living organism. He, therefore, who denies the being of a God, flies in the face of all science, of all creation, of all the facts in the case. Nor can such monstrous folly be accounted for without the belief of great depravity. "The carnal mind is enmity against God"—reveals the first great cause of atheism. But sometimes the human mind in casting off prejudices does not distinguish between them and truths, and so rejects both the vile and the precious together. Sometimes long, unbroken health and prosperity lead to the same result. Men feel no changes, and they say all things are stable of themselves, and that there is no God.

> Health chiefly keeps an atheist in the dark;
> A fever argues better than a Clarke;
> Let but the logic in his pulse decay,
> The Grecian he'll renounce, and learn to pray. YOUNG.

Sloth is another fruitful source of atheism. "The

sluggard is wiser in his own conceit than seven men that can render a reason." It is no trifling task to arouse men from their natural torpor respecting divine things. A bold and dashing spirit of speculation misleads others. They are ruined by their self-conceit. Others affect great singularity, and wish to be distinguished from all around them. This wind has blown many into hell. Atheism will ruin any community. It dissolves all the bonds of society. A great truth is quaintly but forcibly expressed by old Arthur Golding, when he commends "true Relygion, true Godlynesse, true Vertue, wythout the whych neyther force, policie, nor friendship are of any value, neyther can any common weale, any citie, any householde, or any company bee wel gouerned, or haue any stable or long continuance." It is as true of States as of persons, that they who despise God shall be lightly esteemed. All, who rear their fabrics on unrighteousness, are but preparing for a fearful overthrow. The higher they rise, the more dreadful will be their fall.

The wickedness of atheism is truly dreadful. It subverts all religion; it makes it impossible for a man even to pray without stultifying himself. Aristotle said: "He, that does not confess a Deity, is not fit to live." Cogan: "A female atheist would to all mankind be a more hideous object than a female, whose face was covered with carbuncles." Yet the sin of atheism is not to be searched for in the sex of those who embrace it. It is found in the dreadful wickedness of heart, which can cherish such vile notions, and deny the being of a God. Shall the universe blush to own its Author? Shall a worm be ashamed to confess him who made it, and keeps it, and feeds it, and renders its existence a blessing?

Lord Bacon says, "God never wrought a miracle to convince an atheist." The reason is the best in the world. He, who believes that the whole order of nature was established without an Infinite Cause, would easily believe that the laws of nature were suspended in the same manner. So that he, who will shut his eyes against the light before him, must continue in his blindness till he perishes in his own corruption.

IV. Idolatry. Another sin forbidden in the first commandment is idolatry, which is committed when we direct religious worship to any but the true God alone, or when we ascribe to persons or things properties peculiar to God, or when we unduly set the affections of our hearts upon any creature. Idolatry may exist in men's opinions, as when they believe that some divinity is found in the creatures of God, or in creatures of their own imaginations, as when men invest the gods of the heathen, or saints, or angels, or places, or things, with properties and powers, that belong to God only. Such are in doctrine idolaters. Sometimes idolatry is merely practical, as when men set up themselves, their own elevation, their covetousness, their pleasures, their aggrandizement, or their ease, above all the obligations of religious duty. The Bible throws no covering over any species of idolatry. He, who worships the sun, the moon or stars, does as truly sin against God as he, who worships a farthing rush-light. He, who worships saints or angels, does as truly insult the Most High, as he who worships debauchees and devils. For the essence of the sin of idolatry is found in putting the creature in place of the Creator. If he shall be punished who worships a snake, shall he escape God's displeasure who worships yellow dust, called gold, or sinful pleasures, or the breath of worms, uttered in applause? It is very true that some forms of idolatry are more gross and shocking to the sensibilities of men than others. But in the gorgeous ceremony or in the secret observance of idolatrous rites, God may be as justly offended as in the most shameless and bloody practices.

There are two entirely different classes of objects, toward which we may practise idolatry, open or secret. We may desire the wages of *unrighteousness*, and be greedy of *filthy* lucre. That is all sinful from beginning to end. That, which God has absolutely forbidden, in all cases and at all times, is then lusted after. Or, we may be guilty of idolatry by an inordinate affection to *lawful* gains, and wealth obtained by means which men esteem *honourable*. An idol may, therefore, be something which we love, although we are forbidden to love it at all; or, it may be something which it is lawful to love in moderation, but which we love excessively. In either case, we set up some object before our affections in a way which draws our hearts from God. Whenever we esteem, or honour, or love, or fear, or serve, or obey, or confide in any person, or thing, or opinion, more than in God, or in any way that interferes with our duty to God, then we are guilty of idolatry. To whatever, or to whomsoever we yield obedience, we are servants unto that which we obey. Rom. vi. 16. When we put so high a value upon our ease, or houses, or lands, or husband, or wife, or children, or parents, or stations, or offices, or public favour, as that we pine away in rebellion against God at their loss, we do, by our conduct, cry out as Micah, "Ye have taken away my gods, and what have I more?" All things that perish in the using are dangerous to our souls, when, in apprehending our loss of them, we hold our remaining mercies, the promises of the gospel, and the adorable Trinity, as of little value to us. The same is true when we are ready to make use of unlawful or doubtful means for regaining what we have lost.

Much idolatry is committed by unduly setting our affections on the things of this world. The Bible is explicit in stating that the covetous man is an idolater, Eph. v. 5; and that covetousness is idolatry, Col. iii. 5. It further teaches that this love of the world cannot co-exist with true piety. "Love not the world, neither the things that are in the world. If any man love the world, the love of the Father is not in him. For all that is in the world, the lust of the flesh, and the lust of the eyes, and the pride of life, is not of the Father, but is of the world." 1 John ii. 15, 16. This love of the world sometimes breaks out in atrocious wickedness, as when it leads to theft, or forgery, or murder. So intent was Ahab on Naboth's vineyard that he would not rest till the dogs licked up his blood. Demas apostatized from Christianity, that he might secure the gains of idolatry in a heathen temple. Again, this love of the world greatly weakens our courage, and diminishes our zeal, and makes us languid in the service of God. This is the prevailing sin of multitudes in Christian countries. It often happens that even good men are not "valiant for the truth." Jer. ix. 3. Then their course of conduct concerning the interests of religion is vacillating, and they do not exert all the authority with which they are invested to put down wickedness. Thus Eli said to his sons, "It is no good report that I hear: ye make the Lord's people to transgress." 1 Sam. ii. 24. But he "restrained them not." This love of the world, uncured and unrepented of, will work the ruin of any soul. It is as true that the covetous shall not be saved, as that fornicators, idolaters, adulterers, effeminate, sodomites, thieves, drunkards, revilers, and extortioners shall be excluded from the kingdom of God. 1 Cor. vi. 9. Wealth may cause the wicked to be envied by fools, courted by sycophants, and applauded by the multitude; but all his gains will not help him in the day of wrath. They cannot cure a pain of body, nor relieve a pang of mind. In death, so far from comforting him, his wealth often adds terrors to the event. And in judgment and eternity all his earthly possessions will be but as fuel to kindle the fires of Tophet. For the riches of the wicked shall eat their flesh as it were fire. They have heaped treasure together against the last day. James v. 3. Sometimes idolatry assumes the form of *trust* in something besides God. "Some trust in chariots and some in horses," Ps. xx. 7; some make "gold their hope, or say to the fine gold, "Thou art my confidence," Job xxxi. 24; some "have pleasure in the legs of a man," Ps. cxlvii. 10; some expect to be "saved by the multitude of an host," Ps. xxxiii. 16; some in sickness "seek not to the Lord, but to the physicians," 2 Chron. xvi. 12; some expect ease and quiet and a happy life through the "much goods which they have laid up for many years," Luke xii. 19; some, despairing of help from God, betake themselves to those that have familiar spirits," 1 Sam. xxviii. 7–14. All these practise a form of idolatry. They put a creature in the place of God. They rely upon means and instruments instead of the almighty agent. Let none trust in uncertain riches, but in the living God. "Cease ye from man, whose breath is in his nostrils; for wherein is he accounted of?" Isa. ii. 22.

It is no less idolatry to be greatly *afraid* of man, or of the power of any creature. Our business is to sanctify the Lord of hosts himself, and let him be our fear, and let him be our dread. Isa. viii. 13. It is as true now, as in former days, that "the fear of man bringeth a snare." Prov. xxix. 25. We cannot expect to please God and do our duty until we can say, "I will not be afraid what man can do unto me;" "The Lord is my strength; of whom shall I be afraid?" Ps. xxvii. 1. "I will not be afraid of ten thousands of people, that have set themselves against me round about." Ps. iii. 6. So that if we suffer for righteousness' sake, we may count ourselves happy. Let us never be afraid of the terror of man, neither be troubled. 1 Pet. iii. 14. What sad work the fear of man made among some who believed on Christ, and yet did not own him, may be learned from John xii. 42, 43. Even Peter, who truly loved him, and who seems to have been habitually intrepid, was more than once led into great errors by his fear of man. Mark xiv. 66–72; Gal. ii. 11–13.

Sometimes men give themselves up to a *service*, which is practical idolatry. When we seek to please men, we are not the servants of Christ. Gal. i. 10. When we expect to be able to serve both God and mammon, we miserably deceive ourselves. Cares and engagements, which so engross our time as to leave none for God's service, which make such demands upon our exertions as to leave us unfitted for devotions public and private, which fill us with excessive solicitude and carry us away far from the paths of simple and earnest piety, do make us idolaters.

The objects of practical idolatry are many, and wholly undeserving of our warm affection. When a man goes forth, crying, "Who will show us any good? Ps. iv. 6, he is a candidate for shame, and is on the high road to idolatry. When one is devoted to his appetite, he is already an idolater. Phil. iii. 19. When a man believes that the chief end of his existence is to provide the means of gratifying the appetites of himself and his dependents, and is content with a portion in this life, if he and his can be filled with God's hid treasure, he is already an undone man. Ps. xvii. 14. Repentance alone can rescue him from an eternal overthrow. When we set an undue value upon our own bodily endowments, as strength, beauty, or agility; or upon our mental faculties, as memory, imagination, reason, wit, or judgment; or on our acquirements, as skill, learning, or eloquence, then we make idols of these things. When Herod received the gross flatteries of the people, and gloried in his eloquence, he was eaten of worms and gave up the ghost. When the daughters of Zion were haughty, and walked with stretched-forth necks and wanton eyes, walking and mincing as they went, they were but preparing themselves for the day of evil, when the Lord should take away the bravery of their tinkling ornaments, and untold calamities should be poured upon them. Isa. iii. 16–26. How many too have an idolatrous regard to their good name and credit among men. They seem as if they would rather be out of the world than out of public favour. They are lovers of themselves and lovers of pleasures more than lovers of God. They are high-minded. 2 Tim. iii. 2–4; Rom. xi. 20. The least thing that goes cross to their ambitious desires, causes them to display the very temper of Haman, the son of Hammedatha, the Agagite, the Jews' enemy. They are ready to inflict vengeance on any who cringe not before their brief authority. Hare: "In short, there are idols for the worldly-minded, and idols for the generous,—idols for the intemperate, and idols for the prudent: there are idols for the affectionate; and again there is an idol for the selfish; young and old have their idols; married and unmarried have their idols; rich and poor have their idols."

*Self-will* is the idol of many. To the will of God they are wholly unsubmissive. Should God take from them half the temporal blessings he has heaped upon them, yea, if he should take but one of a thousand of their mercies from them, you would never find them adopting the language of Job, "The Lord gave, and the Lord hath taken away; blessed be the name of the Lord." Job i. 21. They never say like the suffering Redeemer, "Not my will, but thine be done," O God. Luke xxii. 42. Their will is directly counter to the will of God. They are of course idolaters.

*Self-righteousness* is also idolatry. It dares to put the morality, the prayers, the repentance, the orthodoxy, the zeal, the profession of religion, the ordinances of the gospel, the rites of religion, in the place of the infinite merits of the Son of God. If the self-righteous are right, the Son of God lived and died in vain. How many give to works, all over defiled, the honour, which is due to the spotless righteousness of Christ alone.

Against nothing is true religion more determinately set than against idolatry. When the evangelical prophet foretells the increase of Messiah's government, he says, "The Lord alone shall be exalted in that day." The very next words are, "And the idols he shall utterly abolish." Isa. ii. 17, 18. Again God calls, "Repent, and turn from your idols." Ezek. xiv. 6. When Hosea describes Israel as healed of his backslidings, he makes him say, "What have I to do any more with idols?" Hosea xiv. 8. But how little are the admonitions of Scripture heeded! Even Paul may cry, "What fellowship hath righteousness with unrighteousness? and what communion hath light with darkness? and what concord hath Christ with Belial? or what part hath he that believeth with an infidel? and what agreement hath the temple of God with idols?" 2 Cor. vi. 14–16. Yet how few are thereby moved to holy living! When inspired writers wish to compare an act with some heinous sin, they sometimes liken it to idolatry. "Rebellion is as the sin of witchcraft, and stubbornness is as iniquity and *idolatry*." 1 Sam. xv. 23. And often do they call idolatry by the names of treachery and whoredom. Jer. iii. 6–11. Compare parallel places. If any would see further the enormity of this sin, and the dreadfulness of its punishment, let him examine Eph. v. 5; Rev. ix. 20, 21; xxi. 8, and parallel passages.

The end of some of the idolaters of this world has been exceedingly dreadful. One great British minister, when he came to die, said, "Had I but served my God, as I have my sovereign, he would not have left me thus." Another, no less distinguished, said, "I have always had my mind so occupied with the various affairs of the nation that I have had no time to examine Christianity or any other system of religion." "How can ye believe," said Jesus Christ, "who receive honour one of another, and seek not the honour that cometh from God only?"

Durham thus answers the question, "What idols are the most subtil?"

"1. An idol is then most subtil when it lurketh in the heart, and seateth itself principally in men's mind, aim and inward contentment, and they inwardly ascribe too much to such a thing, and yet it may be in their external practice, there is not much to discover this.

"2. Then are idols most subtil, when they lie in those things to which somewhat of fear, love, delight, &c., is allowable; as in lawful things, which may in some measure be lawfully loved, feared, and sought for.

"3. When they are in negatives, as in omissions, ease, &c., then they are more subtil than when they lie in something men positively seek after, or in the commission of something forbidden.

"4. When they pass under a lawful name, as when pride goeth under the name of honesty, anxiety under the name of lawful care, &c., then they are hardly discovered.

"5. When, sticking to one idol, the man rejecteth

all others, (as he conceiveth) out of respect to God; as may be instanced in the cases of a monastic life, regular obedience, some singular opinion so much stuck to, and laid weight on by many.

"6. When it is in means that have been used, or are allowed by God for attaining such an end; as it is hard to keep bounds in this case, so it is hard to discover the idolatry of the heart in it."

In the idolatry which adopts the heathen mythology, and erects temples to false gods, there is something so sottish and so debasing that it is a marvel men should ever fall into it. But as those who are likely to read this book are probably not worshippers of Jupiter, or Mars, or Budha, and as the denunciations of spiritual idolatry already cited are no less applicable to the grosser forms, the subject is here dismissed, with the simple declaration of our Saviour, "Thou shalt worship the Lord thy God, and him only shalt thou serve." Matt. iv. 10. Compare Deut. vi. 13, 14; x. 20, Josh. xxiv. 14; 1 Sam. vii. 3.

### IS THE CHURCH OF ROME IDOLATROUS?

This is a very solemn and practical question. In all countries nominally Christian, Romanism is urging her claims. Every man must examine and decide for himself.

In discussing the question, let us accept the definition of idolatry given by Cardinal Wiseman in his thirteenth lecture. "It is the giving to man, or to any thing created, that homage, that adoration and that worship, which God hath reserved unto himself." The church of Rome openly, habitually, and systematically gives to creatures honours, veneration, and worship due to God alone; and thus she is guilty of idolatry. This is a grave charge. No good man can make it without sorrow of heart.

I. The church of Rome, in ascribing to the Pope titles and powers peculiar to God, is guilty of idolatry. Some of these he has claimed, and all of them he has accepted from his followers. In a great Lateran Council, one member, says Barrow, called him "Prince of the world;" another, "King of kings, and Monarch of the earth;" another said of him, that "he had all power above all powers of heaven and earth." Bishop Newton says, "The Pope is styled and pleased to be styled 'Our Lord God the Pope, another God upon earth, King of kings and Lord of lords. The same is the dominion of God and the Pope. The power of the Pope is greater than all created power, and extends itself to things celestial, terrestrial and infernal. The Pope doth whatsoever he listeth, even things unlawfully, and is more than God.'" Cardinal Bellarmin says, "If the Pope could or should so far err as to command the practice of vice, and to forbid virtuous actions, the church were bound to believe vices to be good and virtue to be bad." Here, at the very threshold of this discussion, we are shocked by these amazing claims and by the idolatry which concedes them. Is not here that Wicked One, "who opposeth and exalteth himself above all that is called God, or that is worshipped; so that he, as God, sitteth in the temple of God, showing himself that he is God?" 2 Thess. ii. 4. Verily, it looks so much like the fulfilment of the prediction of Paul that while the world stands, we shall not find a more exact likeness. Can these men have well considered the words of that faultless young man, Elihu? (Job xxxii. 21, 22.) "Let me not, I pray you, accept any man's person, neither let me give flattering titles unto man. For I know not to give flattering titles; in so doing my Maker would soon take me away."

II. In his turn, the Pope himself gives to a creature honours peculiar to God. In his first Encyclical letter, Pope Gregory XVI., who died but a few years ago, addressing all Patriarchs, Primates, Archbishops and Bishops, speaking of the Virgin Mary, calls upon the clergy to implore "that she, who has been, through every great calamity, our Patroness and Protectress, may watch over us, writing to you, and lead our mind by her heavenly influence to those counsels which may prove most salutary to Christ's flock." In this matter of guidance, could Gregory have asked more from God himself? From the Bible we learn that *He*, whose eyes never slumber nor sleep, is a present help in trouble; but here the Pope says that Mary is "our Protectress through every great calamity." He adds, "But that all may have a successful and happy issue, let us raise our eyes to the Most Blessed Virgin Mary, who alone destroys heresies, who is our greatest hope, yea, the entire ground of our hope." This is plain. Whoever maintains truth by destroying heresies, and is our *greatest* hope, yea, the *entire* ground of our hope, is to us a God. What pious man ever put higher honour upon Jehovah himself, than by making Him his *greatest hope*, yea, *the entire ground of his hope?*

III. In full accordance with the Pope's declaration, are the books of devotion common in that communion. In them Mary is called upon more frequently than the Father, Son and Holy Ghost. In the "Catholic Manual," published by Fielding Lucas, Baltimore, with the approbation of Archbishop Whitfield, occur the following in the *Confiteor:* "I confess to Almighty God, to blessed Mary, ever Virgin, to blessed Michael, the Archangel, to blessed John the Baptist, to the Holy Apostles Peter and Paul, and to all the saints that I have sinned," &c. How this differs from the practice of holy men of old! Daniel (ix. 4, 5,) said: "O Lord, the great and dreadful God, . . . we have sinned, and have committed iniquity, and have done wickedly, and have rebelled, even by departing from *thy* precepts and from *thy* judgments." Addressing Jehovah, David said (Ps. xxxii. 5,) "I acknowledged my sin unto *thee*, and mine iniquity have I not hid. I said, I will confess my transgressions unto the LORD; and *thou* forgavest the iniquity of my sin." Again he says to God, "Against *thee*, *thee only*, have I sinned, and done this evil in *thy* sight." Ps. li. 4. The publican prayed, "*God*, be merciful to me, a sinner." Romanists say their religion is older than ours, but Daniel and David and the justified Publican lived before either Pope or Papist.

Having finished the *confession* of sin, a Christian would have thought the proper application would have been *first* and *alone* to God. That was the course pursued by the worthies above named, and by Ezra.

But in the Catholic Manual it is different. There we read thus: "Therefore, I beseech the blessed Mary, ever Virgin, the blessed Michael the Archangel, the blessed John the Baptist, the Holy Apostles Peter and Paul, and all the saints to pray to the Lord our God for me." Then follow two short petitions to God, and then this invocation: "O Holy Virgin, Mother of God! my Advocate and Patroness! pray for thy poor servant, and show thyself a mother to me." Our Saviour taught us to pray to our *Father* which is in heaven, but when did the Lord direct us to pray to our *mother* in heaven? Such idolatry is not taught by inspired men. In the Douay Bible (1 John ii. 1,) are these words: "If any man sin, we have an Advocate with the Father, Jesus Christ, the just;" but in the Manual, every one is taught to call Mary "My Advocate," and to seek her intercession. How then is the Romish doctrine older than ours? We agree with John in having but one "Advocate with the Father," and him "the Father heareth always." He is able, he is willing, he is Jesus Christ the righteous.

The next thing in the Manual is in these words: "And thou, O blessed Spirit!" The word Spirit is printed as above. One would have thought the address was now surely to God. But it is not so. "And thou, O blessed Spirit, whom God in his mercy hath appointed to watch over me, intercede for me this day, that I may not stray from the path of virtue." If any ask, What does this mean? he may look back a little and *see* that it is an *invocation* of *your angel guardian*. The next words are these: "Thou also, O happy Spirit, whose name I bear, pray for me," &c. Listen to the Douay Bible. (1 Tim. ii. 5.) "There is one God, and one Mediator of God and men, the man Christ Jesus." This text is as plainly opposed to many mediators as it is to many gods. Yet the Manual teaches that we are to pray to our angel guardian and to the saint whose name we bear to mediate in our behalf. Christ has no higher glory than that which belongs to him as Mediator. To rob him of that or any part of it is as wicked as to rob God of the honour of creating the world. In the Douay Bible (Heb. iv. 15, 16,) we have these words: "We have not an High Priest, who cannot have compassion on our infirmities; but one tempted in all things like as we are, yet without sin. Let us go, therefore, with confidence to the throne of grace; that we may obtain mercy, and find grace in seasonable aid." Thanks be unto God, who has taught us this best, this only way. But does it look like coming "with confidence" to stand off, and cry to Mary, to Michael, to John the Baptist, to Peter and Paul and others, and ask them to intercede for us? Paul told us to "look to Jesus," and to flee for refuge to the hope set before us in the gospel. The Douay Bible (Heb. vii. 25,) says of Jesus, "He is able also to save for ever them that come unto God by himself; always living to make intercession for us." If we are to come to God by Jesus *himself*, we are not to come by his mother, or by any other creature. Blessed be God, that when Jesus was yet with us, he said: "I am the way, the truth, and the life: no man cometh unto the Father, but by ME." "I am the door." "Verily, verily, I say unto you, He that entereth not by the door into the sheep-fold but climbeth up some other way, the same is a thief and a robber." And yet in the Manual we read, "O Holy Mother of God! deliver us from all dangers."

On the 45th page is an address to Mary, in which she is styled "the bright Queen of heaven." The title Queen of heaven is found in Jer. xliv. 17, 25, 26.

But it is in an alarming connection. God there declares his displeasure against the people for "making vows to the Queen of heaven." In the Douay Bible is a note on this passage, saying that the moon is here meant. That is true, but Mary is just as much a creature as the moon. On the next page, she is addressed thus: "O Holy Mother! My Sovereign Queen, receive me under thy blessed patronage, and special protection, and into the bosom of thy mercy, this day and every day, and at the hour of my death. I recommend to thee my soul and body, I commit to thy care all my hopes and comforts, all my afflictions and miseries, my life and my death, that by thy intercession and through thy merits, all my actions may be directed and disposed according to thy will and the will of thy blessed Son." As man, Christ never offered higher worship to God than when in death he said, "Father, into thy hands I commend my spirit." Luke xxiii. 46. Christ in glory never received higher worship from a holy martyr than when dying Stephen said, "Lord Jesus, receive my spirit." Yet in this Manual, all this honour and this worship are offered to Mary.

The same book abounds with like evidences of idolatry. The same is true of the *Ursuline Manual;* and of all the formularies of worship designed for private use among the members of this communion. A very favourite book among Catholics for some time past is entitled, "The Glories of Mary, Mother of God," &c. Its author is St. Alphonsus Liguori. The edition at hand was published by Eugene Cummiskey of Philadelphia, and has the approval of Bishop Kenrick. The translator dedicates the work to Mary, "the

Queen of Angels and of Men," with "all veneration and respect," and says it is "designed to increase the number and fervour of her clients." Here is the table of contents. Chapter I. "How great should be our confidence in Mary *Queen of Mercy.* How great our confidence should be in Mary as our mother. The great love borne us by Mary our mother. Mary is the refuge of repentant sinners. Chapter II. Mary is our life, since she obtains us the pardon of our sins. Mary is our life, because she obtains our perseverance. Mary renders death sweet to her servants. Chapter III. Mary is the hope of all the children of Adam. Mary is the hope of the sinner. Chapter IV. Mary's readiness to assist those who invoke her. The power of Mary to defend those who invoke her in temptations. Chapter V. Necessity of Mary's intercession in order to obtain salvation. Continuation of the same subject. Chapter VI. Mary is a powerful Advocate. Mary is a compassionate Advocate. Mary is mediatrix of peace between God and sinners. Chapter VII. Mary is ever watchful to succour our miseries. Chapter VIII. Mary preserves her servants from hell. Mary succours her servants in purgatory. Mary conducts her servants to heaven. Chapter IX. The greatness of Mary's clemency and goodness. Chapter X. The sweetness of the holy name of Mary in life and in death." The filling up of these chapters in sections is of the same shocking kind with what you would expect from this table of contents.

So also in "the Psalter of the Virgin" we find the last two Psalms of David thus thrown into parody, and applied to Mary instead of Jehovah: "Sing unto our Lady a new song: let her praise be in the congregation of the just," &c. Again, "Praise our Lady in her holiness; praise her in her virtues and miracles; praise her, ye choirs of patriarchs and prophets; praise her, ye army of martyrs; praise her, ye crowds of doctors and confessors; praise her, ye company of virgins and chaste ones; praise her, ye orders of monks and anchorites; let every thing that hath breath praise our lady."

In that form of adoration, which, it is audaciously pretended, was revealed by an angel to St. Bernard, offering worship to many members of her body, we find among others these words: "Adoro et bendico beatissimas pedes tuas," &c. "I adore and bless thy most blessed feet," &c. The effect of this Mariolatry in fostering corruption is manifest in all Papal countries. Even pirates and robbers are often great worshippers of the saints. In "Graham's Three Months' Residence in the Mountains East of Rome," pp. 155, 161, he says: "Every robber had a silver heart, containing a picture of the Madonna and Child, suspended by a red ribbon to his neck, and fastened with another of the same colour to his side. . . . . They talked pretty freely with their prisoners about themselves and their habits of life, which they maintained arose from necessity, rather than choice. They showed them the heart and picture of the Madonna, which each had suspended from his neck, saying, 'We know that we are likely to die a violent death, but in our hour of need we have these,' touching their muskets, 'to struggle for our lives with, and this,' kissing the image of the Virgin, 'to make our death easy.'"

The same was admitted by a very prominent person at Rome in his conversations with Seymour, as reported in his "Mornings among the Jesuits," pp. 104, 105. "The feeling of devotion to the Virgin has a mysterious something in it that will ever linger about the heart of the man who has ever felt it. It is one of those feelings that, once admitted, can never afterward be totally obliterated. There it still clings around the heart; and though there may be coldness to all other religious impressions; though there may be infidelity or even scorn upon all our faith; though there may be the plunging into the wild vortex of every sin, yet still there will not unfrequently be found even among the very worst of our people, a lingering feeling of devotion to the Blessed Virgin. . . Even in the most wild, wicked, and desperate men—even among the bandits in their worst state, there is always retained this devotion to Mary."

The church of Rome authorizes the worship of the cross. Bossuet, (Œuvres 1, 448,) admits that Thomas Aquinas, the great Romish doctor, teaches that the cross is to be worshipped with Latria. The Roman Pontifical expressly says, "Latria is due to the cross." The Missal enjoins on clergy and laity, "on bended knee to adore the cross." In the meantime the whole choir sing, "Thy cross, O Lord, we adore." The Breviary says, "Thy cross, O Lord, we adore." Again, "O venerable Cross, that hast brought salvation to the wretched, by what praise shall I extol thee?" In the service for Good Friday, in the Roman Missal, a hymn is given to be sung to the cross:

"O Crux, ave spes unica,
Auge piis justitiam,
Reisque dona veniam."

Literally, "O Cross, hail thou only hope,
Increase righteousness to the pious,
Give pardon to the guilty."

The church of Rome also requires the worship of the bread and wine in the Mass. The Council of Trent, the last general council of the Romish Church, expressly says, "There is, therefore, no room to doubt that all the faithful in Christ are bound to venerate this most holy sacrament, and to render thereto the worship of Latria, which is due to the true God, according to the custom always observed in the Catholic Church. Neither is it to be less adored because it was instituted by Christ our Lord, as has been stated." There can be no mistake here. The very highest worship [latriæ cultum] which is due to the true God [qui vero Deo debetur] is to be rendered to the sacrament of the Eucharist. Faithfully is this carried out in the elevation and procession of the host. Thus, a wheaten cake and the juice of the grape are worshipped with the very worship offered to God, and a fearful anathema is denounced against those who teach otherwise. The heathen worshipped Saturn, of whom their poets said that he ate his children as soon as they were born; but it was reserved for modern Rome to teach that the priest makes God with flour and water, and that then he and the people adore him and eat him.

These proofs of idolatry in the Church of Rome might easily be multiplied fifty-fold. Where is the difference between Pagan and Papal Rome? Pagan Rome worshipped demons, commonly dead men. Papal Rome worships dead men and women. Papal Rome claims that she invokes holy creatures, whereas

Pagan Rome called upon wicked ones. But *holy* creatures are still *creatures;* and to call upon them is to put them in the place of God, and that is idolatry. Paul sends forth the challenge, "How shall they call on him in whom they have not believed?" This clearly implies that religious service addressed to one that is not the object of religious faith is an absurdity. The invocation of saints, therefore, is either a mockery, or it at once exalts them to the rank of objects of religious belief. Nor is it possible to prove that all whose names are in the Calendar are saints, or even in existence. Let any man prove that there ever lived such a person as St. Veronica, and by the same kind of evidence we can prove the existence of all the fabulous characters in Pagan mythology. But suppose all the saints named in the Calendar were now in heaven; not one of them possesses omnipresence. Not one of them can be in Rome, Vienna, London, Montreal, Mexico, St. Louis, New York, and all over the world at the same time; neither can they be in heaven and on earth at the same moment. Any act, therefore, which attributes to them omnipresence, is idolatry.

Neither can any one of them possibly know all the wants, fears, sorrows, and temptations of all the pious in the church militant. Mary would need to have millions of ears and of understandings. She would require *infinite* intelligence; that is, she must be God in order to know the wants and wishes of all who now address her. To say or do anything that ascribes such knowledge to her is idolatry.

This invocation of saints and angels goes upon the presumption that they pity and love us more tenderly and strongly than the Lord Jesus Christ. A learned priest, holding high position at Rome, distinctly declared to Rev. M. H. Seymour, "that God hears our prayers more quickly when they are offered through the blessed Virgin than when offered through any one else;" and "that even Christ himself was not so willing to hear our prayers, and did not hear them so quickly when offered simply to himself, as when they were offered through the blessed Virgin." Could greater indignity be offered to Christ than is expressed in such sentiments? Himself said: "Greater love hath no man than this, that a man lay down his life for his friends." John xv. 13. Did not Jesus die for us, even while we were yet *enemies?* How then dare any express by word or deed more confidence in the tenderness and love of any creature than of the Lord Jesus Christ? When on earth, he said, "Come unto ME, all ye that labour and are heavy laden, and I will give you rest;" or as it is in the Douay Bible, "Come unto ME, all you that labour and are heavy laden, and I will refresh you." Our Saviour never directed the eyes of penitent sinners to his mother as a source of hope. When on earth, he was told, "Behold, thy mother and thy brethren stand without. But he answered and said unto him that told him, Who is my mother? and who are my brethren? And he stretched forth his hand toward his disciples, and said, Behold my mother and my brethren! For whosoever shall do the will of my Father which is in heaven, the same is my brother, and sister, and mother." Matt. xii. 47–50. Christ could not in more emphatic terms have declared that in his kingdom, a new and spiritual nature, leading to a holy life, infinitely exceeded in value all consanguinity, even with himself. As to the doctrine that Mary is Queen of heaven and has the highest throne of any of Adam's race, it is a mere imagination, and contrary to the Scriptures. Christ expressly said, that to sit on his right hand and on his left hand in his kingdom should be given to them for whom it is prepared of my Father, Matt. xx. 23; Mark x. 40; never intimating that it should be to Mary, or Peter, or any one else known to us. We can, therefore, never prove that Mary is preferred before all the redeemed. But if she were, it would not alter the case, for the most eminent of all the redeemed is but a creature, helpless and dependent, and idolatry consists in giving to anything created, homage and worship belonging to God only. The early preaching of the gospel was hardly a greater blessing than the Reformation. Hare: "The first was a deliverance from idol gods; the second, from the worshipping of idol saints."

When John mistook an angel for the Almighty, and fell at his feet to worship him, the angel said: "See thou do it not; I am thy fellow-servant, and of thy brethren that have the testimony of Jesus: worship God." Rev. xix. 10. Peter Dens says, that "the angel refused this on account of the great holiness of John." The authors of the notes in the Douay Bible say that the angel declined it on account of the dignity of human nature, and of the dignity of John. But the angel assigns no such reason. On the contrary, he assigns a very different one: "I am thy fellow-servant, and the fellow-servant of thy brethren."

To set aside these and like proofs of the idolatry

of Rome her doctors have invented various devices and distinctions. One is that worship is of three kinds, Dulia, Hyperdulia and Latria. These are again distinguished into absolute and respective. Thus we have six grades of religious worship, viz. absolute Dulia and respective Dulia; absolute Hyperdulia and respective Hyperdulia; absolute Latria and respective Latria. These distinctions are both unintelligible and impracticable. The masses of plain people in the Church of Rome neither know them, nor understand them, nor practise them. Moreover not one of them is preserved in the ordinary books of devotion, sent out by the Church of Rome. No warning is given to the devotee that he is to use the Litany to Mary with less exalted feelings of piety than those he exercises when using the Litany of the name of Jesus. Yea, in a prayer sanctioned by the Pope in 1807, his followers are taught to say: "Jesus, Mary and Joseph, assist me in my last agony." So that these refined distinctions are of no practical use, and Dens admits as much. The distinction between civil and religious homage is plain and clear. All men can make it. All men do make it.

If any ask, how do Romanists suppose that saints in glory become acquainted with their prayers, Bellarmin answers thus: "Concerning the manner in which they know what is said to them, there are four opinions among the doctors,—

1. "Some say that they know it from the relation of the angels, who at one time ascend to heaven, and at another time, descend thence to us.

2. "Others say that the souls of the saints, as also

the angels, by a certain wonderful swiftness which is natural to them, are in some measure every where, and themselves hear the prayer of the supplicant.

3. "Others, that the saints see in God all things, from the beginning of their beatitude, which in any way appertain to themselves; and hence even our prayers, which are directed to them.

4. "Others, lastly, that the saints do not see in the word, our prayers from the beginning of their blessedness, but that our prayers are only then revealed to them by God, when we pour them forth."

Surely if Bellarmin, the greatest of their doctors, could give no better account of the matter, it must be dark indeed. The fact is, it is inexplicable, because it is absurd.

Some say that Jacob wrestled with an angel, *i. e.* he prayed to him; and therefore we may pray to saints and angels. The case is given at length in Gen. xxxii. 24–31. There this angel is called a man, that is, he had the appearance of a man. But no sooner did he leave the Patriarch, than it is added, "And Jacob called the name of the place Peniel, [*i. e.* the face of God] for [said he,] "I have seen God face to face, and my life is preserved." This man then was God, and Jacob knew it was God before he left the spot. To this memorable event, the patriarch referred even when dying, thus: "God of my fathers, the God which fed me all my life long unto this day, the *Angel* which redeemed me from all evil, bless the lads." Gen. xlviii. 15, 16. This passage alone determines that the angel was God himself. But we have still further and explicit information on the subject in Hosea xii. 4, 5, 6: "Jacob had power with God, yea, he had power over the angel, and prevailed; he wept and made supplication unto him: he found him at Bethel, and there he spake with us, even the LORD God of hosts; the LORD [or Jehovah] is his memorial; therefore turn thou to thy God." Thus we learn that the man, or the angel, was God, was the LORD God, was the LORD God of hosts, Jehovah.

Listen to God's voice: "Call upon ME in the day of trouble: I will deliver thee, and thou shalt glorify me." Ps. l. 15.

How fully the ancient church testified by her example and teachings against such idolatry can be seen by consulting Church History, and especially the Antiquities of the Christian Church by Joseph Bingham.

V. UNGODLINESS. Perhaps the most comprehensive definition of ungodliness is "Neglect of God." It involves a "disregard of God and his commands, and neglect of his worship; or it is any positive act of disobedience or irreverence." In all cases it supposes some degree of ignorance of the true nature of God and divine things. It implies a want of reverence for God, and of right affections towards him. It supposes men to desire independence of God, to be unsubmissive to his will, to be ungrateful and disobedient. The ungodly may have many notions of the matters revealed in Scripture: but they are not clear nor sound. They are tainted with some degree of superstition or of impiety. They will probably not stand the test of a dying hour. They certainly will not endure the severity of God's judgment. Ungodliness is always deficient in uprightness of conscience. It is not marked by what the Bible calls simplicity and godly sincerity. It is never self-sacrificing or self-renouncing. Whatever it may do for the sake of decency or public opinion, it never mortifies sin. Nor does ungodliness ever enter into the forms of religion with zest and animation. If it serves at all, it is with luke-warmness.

It must be very evident that *ignorance of God* is directly a species of ungodliness, and is in the face of the first commandment. It is never the mother of true devotion, though it may be of superstition. It is everywhere condemned in Scripture. The Lord says: "My people is foolish, they have not known me; they are sottish children, and they have none understanding: they are wise to do evil, but to do good they have no knowledge." Again: "The Lord hath a controversy with the inhabitants of the land, because there is no truth, nor mercy, nor knowledge of God in the land. . . . . My people are destroyed for lack of knowledge." Jer. iv. 22; Hosea iv. 1, 6. All ignorance of God is aggravated by being to a considerable extent wilful.

*Forgetfulness of God* falls into the same class of sins. From the frequency with which it is charged in Scripture, it would appear to be very prevalent, and one of the most obstinate forms of rebellion. Nothing, no alarming judgments, no stupendous displays of mercy, can cure this folly, without the sovereign grace of God. Ps. lxxviii. 11; cvi. 13, 21. From one expression in Scripture, it would seem to be the great sin of the whole heathen world; for there we read of "all the nations that forget God." Ps. ix. 17. To the same class of sins we must refer all false opinions, misapprehensions and unworthy thoughts of

God. We are no more at liberty to liken God to some creature however exalted, than to a creature ever so debased. "We ought not to think that the Godhead is like unto gold, or silver, or stone, graven by art and man's device." Acts xvii. 29. Whenever we think that God is such an one as ourselves, we miserably degrade him. Ps. l. 21.

When we withhold from God any act of service or honour required by himself, we break the first commandment. That is a heavy charge, "Thou hast not called upon me, O Jacob; but thou hast been weary of me, O Israel. Thou hast not brought me the small cattle of thy burnt-offerings; neither hast thou honoured me with thy sacrifices. I have not caused thee to serve with an offering, nor wearied thee with incense. Thou hast bought me no sweet cane with money, neither hast thou filled me with the fat of thy sacrifices: but thou hast made me to serve with thy sins, thou hast wearied me with thine iniquities." Isa. xliii. 22–24.

We greatly sin when we curiously and irreverently *pry into God's secrets*, Deut. xxix. 29, when we put ourselves above God, or make ourselves equal to God in our own estimation or plans, 2 Tim. iii. 2–4; when we hate God, which must always be without a cause, John xv. 25; when we yield to unbelief, Heb. iii. 12; when we give up our hearts to heresy, Titus iii. 10; when we believe God is pleased with our cruelty or with any of our sins, Acts xxvi. 9, when we refuse to set our hopes in God, Ps. lxxviii. 22; when we refuse to believe the promises, and give up our minds to despair, as did Cain and Judas; when we refuse to be amended by God's sore judgments, Jer. v. 3; when we are not brought to repentance by his kind acts of providence, Rom. ii. 4, 5; when we cry Peace and safety, in the midst of our sins, Ps. xix. 13; when we deny God's moral government over the world, Zeph. i. 12; when we tempt God, Matt. iv. 7; when our zeal in religion is ignorant and indiscreet, Gal. iv. 17; Rom. x. 2; John xvi. 2; Luke ix. 54, 55; when we are either dead or lukewarm in the service of God, Rev. iii. 1, 16. In all these cases we violate the first commandment.

Nor do we less sin when we go after wizards and witches, and practise palmistry, spiritualism, and the black art, or use charms and spells. Gal. v. 20; Lev. xx. 6; 1 Sam. xxviii. 7, 11. The sin of such practices is not destroyed by any particular theory that we may hold on this subject. We also violate the first commandment when we yield to any of the suggestions of the devil, Acts v. 3.

Of course, *apostasy* from God is against this commandment. "If any man draw back, my soul hath no pleasure in him." Heb. x. 38. "God will make his sword drunk in the blood of apostates." For a while they may seem to prosper, but it is the prosperity of the bullock preparing for the slaughter. The Bible gives us awful examples of the end of apostates, in the case of king Saul and of Judas Iscariot. The former of these was, in early life, modest, unaspiring, mingling with God's people and even with his eminent ministers, himself a prophet among the prophets. But after he was raised to power, jealousy, malice, ambition, contempt of God and disobedience to the clearest commands began to mark his conduct. Bad became worse, till at length he openly apostatized by refusing to hearken to God, and by consulting the witch of Endor. His doom was as sudden as it was dreadful.

The case of Judas need not be here rehearsed. It is familiar to all.

Nor is uninspired history without its awful lessons on this subject. Early in life Julian embraced the Christian religion. For a time he seemed zealous for its truths. But ere long a change came over him, and in course of time he became one of the bitterest enemies of Christianity, even forbidding Christian youth in the Roman empire to be taught the classics of their mother tongue. Against Christ he was exceedingly enraged. At one time he raised his dagger in the presence of his army and publicly defied the Son of God, whom he called Galilean. The longer he lived, the more envenomed he became. But such wickedness could not be allowed to go unchecked for ever. The day of retribution approached. He received a mortal wound in battle and lay weltering in his own blood. After a while he gathered up a handful of the clotted gore and threw it into the air, exclaiming, *Vicisti Galilæe!* Thou hast conquered, O thou Galilean.

The sixteenth century was a wonderful era in human history. There were great dynasties, managed by great men; great errors, upheld by long established usages; great events, moving all the energies of men; and great heroes, glorying in perils and persecutions for truth and righteousness. The human mind was wrought to the highest pitch of excitement. Hopes aroused some. Fears agitated some. Some were a flame of love. Others showed the most deadly malice. Seldom has virtue risen higher, seldom has wickedness sunk to lower depths.

Several causes united to give the Reformation an unexpected degree of success and stability. One was the faith of its friends. Such a work was never wrought by doubting minds. Allied to this was an intrepidity, that struck terror into enemies, while it mightily emboldened friends. If there were not many martyrdoms, there were yet many who in spirit were martyrs. For more than a thousand years the gospel had not been preached with as much zeal, nor heard with as much zest, as in the first half of the sixteenth century. Catechising among Protestants was generally and earnestly attended to, and gave great success to truth.

Nor were things of a terrible nature wanting in those days. Let one of this class be noticed. Several old writers tell us of one, whose history has often thrilled the hearts of men. Even to this day his name is often met with in print, and sometimes heard in the pulpit. It was a terror while he lived. It is a watchword of alarm, now that he has passed away from earth. Many already anticipate the name of FRANCIS SPIRA.

This great man was a Venitian, wonderfully gifted by nature, and no less remarkable for his acquirements; by profession a lawyer, or advocate, of almost unrivalled power; as a man, just, courteous, friendly, and held in the highest esteem. His career was brilliant till he was past middle life.

When he was over *forty* years of age, he became interested in the great religious controversy then agitating Europe. He examined for himself. He searched into foundation truths. He felt that it was not a little thing; that it was his life. His convictions of the truth were strong, and his zeal in making it known was exemplary. He studied God's word; he told his family and his countrymen the wonderful things of God. He was the source of a new impulse to inquiry. A few such men, in the course of an ordinary life-time, would have reformed all Italy.

This was seen at Rome. Spira was marked for destruction. The Pope's legate applied to the Senate of Venice. The foundations of society were moved. Confiscation, reproach, poverty to his wife and eleven children, a dungeon, torture, and death, all rose up like monsters before his imagination. His purpose faltered, his courage failed, his faith was gone. He went from Citadella, the town of his usual residence, to Venice; there found Casa, the legate, and signed the following paper:

"Having for several years maintained opinions respecting certain articles of faith, contrary to the orthodox and accredited judgment of the Church, and advanced many things against the authority of the Church of Rome, and of the universal Bishop, I acknowledge, in all humility, my fault, mistake, and folly, in seducing others, and in consequence I return in entire obedience to the Sovereign Bishop in the communion of the Church of Rome, without ever desiring to depart from the traditions and decrees of the holy See. I am extremely grieved for all which has passed, and humbly implore pardon for so great an offence."

Twice was he required to sign his recantation, and then to go to his own town, and publicly declare his renunciation of the doctrines he had so lately and zealously defended. But ere this work was fully done, conscience began to awake; a sense of guilt began to take hold of him; shame at his own cowardice unmanned him; but worldly friends urged him on till he had, in the presence of a great assembly, renounced the principles of the Reformation.

The awful deed was now done. But it was the signal for the letting loose of the tormentors. From that moment he regarded himself as an impious apostate, a weak and wicked creature, who had trifled with his own convictions on the most solemn subjects. He always maintained that his sin was against light. He said: "I believed it when I denied it; now I neither believe that nor the doctrine of the Church of Rome. I believe nothing; I have neither faith, nor confidence, nor hope; I am a reprobate, like Cain or Judas, who, rejecting all hope, fell from grace into despair; and my friends do me great wrong in not suffering me to depart to the abode of the unbelieving, as I have justly deserved." Again: "I have denied Christ voluntarily, and against my knowledge; and I feel that he hardens me, and that he will allow me no hope." Again: "I tell you my own conscience condemns me. What need is there for any other judge?"

Those, who had been the instruments of his denying Christ, attempted to comfort him. The priest who had received his recantation came to see him, and made himself known. This awakened new horror. He cried: "Oh the accursed day! Oh the accursed day! Oh that I had never been there! Would to God I had then been dead!" Another Roman

Catholic undertook to satisfy him that he had not denied Christ by abjuring Protestant doctrines. His answer was: "Assuredly, when I renounced those opinions, I believed them to be true; and yet I renounced them." Some Roman Catholics called on him now to believe the doctrines of the Reformation to be false. He cried out: "I cannot, I cannot; God will not permit me to believe them so, nor to take refuge in his mercy."

Others told him of God's mercy to Peter, who had thrice denied his Lord. This gave him no hope. He exclaimed: "It is a fearful thing to fall into the hands of the living God." The sight of the Bible filled him with anguish. He begged that it might be carried out of his sight, and read no more in his hearing. The bitterness of death was in him, and seemed to assimilate every thing to itself.

When he was urged to believe, his answer was, "Oh! I wish I could believe, but it is impossible for me. I HAVE DENIED CHRIST. I can only believe what is contrary to my salvation and my comfort."

When prayer was recommended to him, he said: "I ardently desire to pray to God with my whole heart; but I am unable. I see my condemnation, and know my only remedy is in Christ. Yet I cannot persuade myself to embrace him: such is the punishment of the damned. . . . My crime is not one iota less than that of Judas." One proposed to him that they should together repeat the Lord's prayer. He began, and after each petition, he would express such sentiments as these: "I deplore my misery, for I perceive that I am abandoned by God, and cannot invoke him with all my heart, as I have been accus tomed to do.

In this deplorable state he continued for some time, once attempting self-destruction, and failing; once going to Padua for medical and religious advice, but deriving no benefit from any, until at the age of *forty-eight* years, without comfort, without hope, without confidence, his body being wasted to a skeleton, he left this world, and entered on the realities of eternity. This case teaches many lessons.

1. No man knows what he will do until he is tried.

2. No man has any more religious principle than a fair trial proves him to have.

3. How horrible is sin! "Man knows the beginnings of sin," said Spira, "but who can tell the bounds thereof?"

4. In this, as well as in any other day, men may wickedly and fatally deny Christ. "Whosoever shall deny me before men, him will I deny before my Father, which is in heaven."

5. "If our heart condemn us, God is greater than our heart, and knoweth all things."

6. There is even in this life something worse than the death of the body. Sin is worse. Dishonour is worse. Despair is worse. A guilty conscience is worse.

7. If God chooses to punish, he is at no loss for means. He can let loose on a man his own vile passions, or his memory, or his imagination, or his conscience, and the work is done.

8. There must be a hell. In this world, where

mercy so much prevails, there is often something very much like hell. In the next world, retribution will be perfect, and so there must be a hell.

9. The human mind may be brought, and sometimes is brought, into states of feeling, to be kept out of which evinces infinite goodness on the part of God.

10. God can do good by any means. He made Spira a great means of establishing many, and of converting some. Even Verger, who held a very rich bishopric under the Pope, was so wrought on in his visits to Spira, that he renounced popery, retired to Basle, and died a Protestant.

11. "He that endureth to the end shall be saved." "If any man draw back, my soul hath no pleasure in him."

12. Are you a Christian? Spira used to say, "Do you, who are so assured of your right state, take care that it be such. . . . Look to yourselves. It is no light or easy matter to be a Christian. Look narrowly to your lives. Make a greater account of the gifts of the Spirit of God than I have done. Be constant and immovable in maintaining your profession. Confess it even to death, if you are called to it."

Let us also beware how we give up our convictions of truth and duty as taught by God, and yield to the doctrines and solicitations of men, thus giving them dominion over our faith and lordship over our consciences. Matt. xxiii. 9; 2 Cor. i. 24. The united voice of the world is as nothing on a point of faith or practice, when we have a *Thus saith the Lord* to the contrary.

This commandment also forbids the giving of the praise of any good that has befallen us, or is possessed by us, to ourselves, to fortune or to idols. Deut. viii. 17; Dan. iv. 30; v. 23; 1 Sam. vi. 9.

All impatience under God's dispensations, all discontent and murmuring, all foolish and wicked speeches respecting God, are also sins against this commandment. Ps. lxxiii. 2–17; Jude 16; Phil. ii. 14; 1 Cor. x. 10.

Some never show cheerfulness in bowing to God's will. Others openly fret against it. Many sin by taking no thankful notice of mercies received and remaining. Leighton: "There is more joy in enduring a cross for God, than in the smiles of the world; in a private, despised affliction, without the name of suffering for his cause, or anything in it like martyrdom, but only as coming from his hand, kissing it and bearing it patiently, yea, gladly, for his sake, out of love to him, because it is his will so to try thee. What can come amiss to a soul thus composed?

"I wish that even they who have renounced the vain world, and have the face of their hearts turned Godwards, would learn more this happy life, and enjoy it more; not to hang so much upon sensible comforts, as to delight in obedience, and to wait for those at his pleasure, whether he gives much or little, any or none. Learn to be still finding the sweetness of his commands, which no outward or inward change can disrelish, rejoicing in the actings of that divine love within thee. Continue thy conflicts with sin, and though thou mayest at times be foiled, yet cry to him for help, and getting up, redouble thy hatred of it and attempts against it. Still stir this flame of

God. That will overcome: 'many waters cannot quench it.' It is a renewed pleasure to be offering up thyself every day to God. Oh! the sweetest life in the world is to be crossing thyself to please him; trampling on thy own will to follow his."

Three other sins against this commandment should not pass without notice. One of them consists in resisting and grieving the Holy Spirit. How dreadful this sin is, may be learned from the fact that inspired men speak of it as if it were the sum of all wickedness. Thus said Stephen to his impenitent audience: "Ye stiff-necked, and uncircumcised in heart and ears, ye do always resist the Holy Ghost." Acts vii. 51.

Another form of breaking this commandment is the rejection of Jesus Christ. Without him we can do nothing. John xv. 5. He is the sole and sufficient author of salvation to lost men. To reject him is to reject all the counsels of God for our restoration to the divine favour. The Scriptures employ the most alarming language respecting this sin. Christ himself says, "If ye believe not that I am he, ye shall die in your sins." John viii. 24. "He that despised Moses' law died without mercy under two or three witnesses; of how much sorer punishment, suppose ye, shall he be thought worthy, who hath trodden under foot the Son of God, and hath counted the blood of the covenant, wherewith he was sanctified, an unholy thing, and hath done despite unto the Spirit of grace?" Heb. x. 28, 29.

The last form of breaking this commandment is by insincerity of heart in religious worship. When Christ was on earth, he used more alarming and terrible language to hypocrites than to all others. Their case is indeed sad, and their guilt heinous. Hopkins: "*The hypocrite calls on God to be an accomplice and partaker with him in his crimes;* and so makes God to be the patron of sin, who will be the Judge and condemner of sin."

# CHAPTER XV.

## THE SECOND COMMANDMENT.

THOU SHALT NOT MAKE UNTO THEE ANY GRAVEN IMAGE, OR ANY LIKENESS OF ANYTHING THAT IS IN HEAVEN ABOVE, OR THAT IS IN THE EARTH BENEATH, OR THAT IS IN THE WATERS UNDER THE EARTH: THOU SHALT NOT BOW DOWN THYSELF TO THEM, NOR SERVE THEM: FOR I THE LORD THY GOD AM A JEALOUS GOD, VISITING THE INIQUITY OF THE FATHERS UPON THE CHILDREN UNTO THE THIRD AND FOURTH GENERATION OF THEM THAT HATE ME; AND SHOWING MERCY UNTO THOUSANDS OF THEM THAT LOVE ME, AND KEEP MY COMMANDMENTS.

GOD never gave a command more solemn in its terms, or in the sanction connected with it. Nor are we left in doubt respecting the vast importance of this precept. On this point other parts of God's word are full and urgent. Let us first consider the sanction annexed to it. It is very weighty. The words in which it is delivered seem to have been chosen for the purpose of striking terror into the hearts of the rebellious, and of giving the highest encouragement to the obedient.

I. We have an assertion of God's rightful authority

and sovereignty; *for I the* LORD *thy God*, &c. The phrase rendered *the* LORD *thy God* is precisely the same as found in the preface to the commandments, already considered. It points to the foundation of all religious obligation. It is commonly thought to be a fair mode of estimating the importance of a principle by the frequency with which it is stated in Scripture. Applying this rule to the present case, there is no more important truth than this, *I am the* LORD *thy God.* "He is thy Lord, and worship thou him." "O come, let us worship and bow down: let us kneel before the LORD our maker. For he is our God." Ps. xlv. 11; xcv. 6, 7. From the fact that the Scriptures frequently compare idolatry to whoredom, some suppose that the phrase *thy God*, has special reference, not only to a covenant relation in general, but to a covenant relation well represented by that of marriage; and so Isaiah says: "Thy Maker is thine husband; the LORD of hosts is his name; and thy Redeemer, the Holy One of Israel; The God of the whole earth shall he be called." Is. liv. 5. See also Rev. xv. 3, 4. There can be no true religion except as the doctrine of God's sovereign and rightful authority over us is received.

II. As the human mind is exceedingly prone to practical atheism, and to idolatry also, God takes pains to inform us respecting his nature. He says, I am *a jealous God.* The word here rendered *God* is not *Elohim*, but *El.* This latter word rendered God, when used as an adjective, signifies *strong* or *mighty;* and when used as an abstract term, it signifies *might* or *power.* As a name of God, standing alone, it is chiefly found in the poetic parts of Scripture. It occurs about two hundred and forty times in the Hebrew Bible, and in a majority of cases refers to the true God. Whether we render it here *God* or *strong*, the sense is the same, for the LORD is mighty, nor can any number of persons or nations resist his omnipotence. Leighton: "*El.*—Able to right myself upon the mightiest and proudest offender. *Do we provoke the Lord to jealousy?* says the apostle. *Are we stronger than he?* 1 Cor. x. 22; thus joining these two together, as they are here, His *strength* and his *jealousy.*" He is able to punish any insult that is offered him by any of his creatures. He is strong and *jealous,* too. The same thing is repeatedly declared in Scripture. "Thou shalt worship no other God; for the LORD, whose name is Jealous, is a jealous God. Ex. xxxiv. 14. Compare Deut. iv. 24; v. 9; vi. 15. The word rendered *jealous* could not be better translated. Elsewhere the corresponding noun is used to express the strongest passion of man towards man: Num. v. 14, 15, 18, 25, 29, 30. It is several times rendered *zeal;* 2 Kings xix. 31; Ps. lxix. 9; Isa. ix. 7; xxxvii. 32; lix. 17. A like word is used, Numbers xxv. 13, where it is said, that Phinehas was *zealous* for his God. So here the meaning is, that God has a *zeal* for his own honour and glory. The special reference here is doubtless to the intense emotions of men respecting their domestic peace. Hopkins: "Jealousy is an affection or passion of the mind, by which we are stirred up and provoked against whatsoever hinders the enjoyment of that which we love and desire. The cause and origin of it is love; the effect of it is revenge." In its very nature it is apprehensive of rivalship. A sovereign is jealous of his authority. Freemen are jealous of their rights. The term always expresses exceedingly strong disapprobation and indignation against the withholding of that which is our due, particularly in the marriage relation. Jealousy is never satisfied except with perfect fidelity. No compliments, no services however beautiful in themselves, and no rewards, can quiet its imperious demands. "Neither their silver nor their gold shall be able to deliver them in the day of the Lord's wrath; but the whole land shall be devoured by the fire of his jealousy, for he shall make even a speedy riddance of all them that dwell in the land." Zeph. i. 18. No virtuous husband will rest satisfied with less than the love and fidelity of his wife. Nor will a holy God be content with less than the heart, the homage, and the holy living of his people. So he has said: "I have heard the voice of the words of this people, which they have spoken unto thee: they have well said all that they have spoken. Oh, that there were such an heart in them, that they would fear me, and keep all my commandments always, that it might be well with them and their children for ever." Deut. v. 28, 29.

Nor will jealousy ever rest satisfied till its doubts are removed. It is exceedingly eager in its pursuit of what it supposes to be evidence calculated to put an end to all uncertainty. God indeed is never in doubt about the state of our minds; for he searches the heart. "God is light; and in him is no darkness at all." 1 John i. 5. His searching will therefore tear away every disguise, and bring out the whole truth.

Men are never more determined to risk every thing

than in securing and guarding the sanctity of their own marriage. Nor does their indignation ever rise higher than against any crime, which destroys their domestic peace. "Jealousy is cruel as the grave; the coals thereof are coals of fire, which hath a most vehement flame." Jealousy is indeed "the rage of a man; therefore he will not spare in the day of vengeance." Cant. viii. 6; Prov. vi. 34. So the Almighty threatens: "The LORD will not spare him, but the anger of the LORD and his jealousy shall smoke against that man, and all the curses that are written in this book shall lie upon him, and the LORD shall blot out his name from under heaven." Deut. xxix. 20.

III. God declares that, as Governor of the world, he is not indifferent to the sins of men; but that he *visits iniquity.* The word *visits* is used in Scripture both in a good and in a bad sense. It is found in a good sense in Gen. xxi. 1, l. 24; Ex. xiii. 19; Ps. lxxx. 14; Luke i. 68, 78, vii. 16; Acts xv. 14. It is found in a bad sense in the following passages. Ps. lix. 5; Jer. v. 9, 29; Jer. ix. 9; Isa. xxiii. 17. Leighton says God will visit "as judges and magistrates use to visit those places that are under their jurisdiction, to make inquiry after abuses committed in time of their absence, and to punish them." 1 Sam. vii. 16." To *visit iniquity*, to *visit transgression* and to *visit sins* are phrases which always threaten punishment. The meaning, therefore, is, that God will terribly and condignly punish infractions of this commandment.

IV. The LORD declares that his jealousy is such that he *visits the iniquity of the fathers upon the chil-*

*dren unto the third and fourth generation of them that hate him.* This declaration is repeated in so many words in Ex. xxxiv. 7; Num. xiv. 18; Deut. v. 9. Nor is there any doubt respecting the genuineness of the text, or the fairness of the translation. The following passages of Scripture are supposed to be to a considerable extent parallel or explanatory. "I remember that which Amalek did to Israel, how he laid wait for him in the way, when he came up from Egypt. Now go and smite Amalek, and utterly destroy all that they have, and spare them not." 1 Sam. xv. 2, 3. This command was given to Saul, nearly four hundred years after the Israelites had entered Canaan. So that not a single man who had opposed Israel in the march to Canaan was then living; but only the descendants of such. Again: "Because Ahab humbled himself before God, the Lord brought not the evil upon his house in his days, but in his son's days." 1 Kings xxi. 29. In a time of great public calamity, when the heathen had come into God's inheritance and had defiled the holy temple, Asaph prayed, "O remember not against us former iniquities." Ps. lxxix. 8. When Belshazzar was suddenly cut down, a part of the song sung by the children of Israel was in these awful words: "The seed of evildoers shall never be renowned. Prepare slaughter for his children, for the iniquity of their father; that they do not rise, nor possess the land." Isa. xiv. 20, 21. Again: "Thou shewest loving-kindness unto thousands, and recompensest the iniquity of the fathers into the bosom of their children after them." Jer. xxxii. 18. Again: "That upon you may come all the righteous blood shed upon the earth, from the blood of righteous Abel unto the blood of Zacharias son of Barachias, whom ye slew between the temple and the altar." Matt. xxiii. 35. Thus it appears that whatever God intended to teach us by such language, he designed deeply to impress it on our minds, because he repeats it very often.

The following additional remarks on the commination contained in the second commandment are here offered.

I. Candour requires the admission that it is an exceedingly awful threatening, and well suited to make men stop and think, and fear before the Lord. All threatenings to visit iniquity are alarming, because they are declarations of the inflexible justice of God. But when God declares that our moral conduct shall have a bearing on our posterity for generations, surely none but the desperately hardened can be insensible.

II. Candour no less requires the admission that this threatening is not of easy explication. The difficulty arises principally on three accounts. 1. It seems to be counter to the sense of justice and equity felt by men generally. But we should not forget that man is not a competent judge of the best rules for conducting a moral government; and that, therefore, any objection arising from his views of things ought to be stated with great modesty. He ought to be willing patiently to wait and carefully consider the whole case. Many things seem harsh or unfair, until the principles, on which they are founded, are well understood. 2. Another source of difficulty arises from the fact that in organizing the Jewish commonwealth under the theocracy, and in providing for the administration of penal justice, God expressly ordained that "the fathers shall not be put to death for the children, neither shall the children be put to death for the fathers: every man shall be put to death for his own sin." Deut. xxiv. 16. This statute was observed in Israel in their generations; 2 Kings xiv. 5, 6; 2 Chron. xxv. 3, 4. So that in the threatening connected with the second commandment, there is involved no principle which ought to make our laws harsh to the descendants of wrong-doers. God himself thus teaches. Some nations still retain the principle of attainting blood for certain crimes. Happily, the Constitution of the United States prohibits the passage of any law of attainder. 3. A still greater difficulty arises from the declarations of God made elsewhere. In Jeremiah (xxxi. 29, 30,) God says, "In those days they shall say no more, The fathers have eaten a sour grape, and the children's teeth are set on edge. But every one shall die for his own iniquity: every man that eateth the sour grape, his teeth shall be set on edge." "Those days" here mentioned are shown by the context to refer especially to gospel times, when the Mosaic dispensation should be fully ended. See verses 31–34. We have a like declaration, but much more extended, in the prophecy of Ezekiel, (xviii. 2–28.)

Whatever may be the import of the threatening in the second commandment, or of these declarations by the prophets, we are certain that they would entirely harmonize if we correctly understood them. The right course, therefore, for us to pursue, is to receive them all, as they are indeed, the word of God, and reverently study to find out what they teach. It is not right to array one of these passages or classes of texts of Scripture against the other. No man is at liberty to receive one or more of them more fully or cordially than the others.

III. The evil threatened in the second commandment is said to extend to *the third and fourth generation.* This is the fundamental passage on the subject; and yet in Jeremiah xxxii. 18, there is no such limitation, but the prophet declares that God "recompenses the iniquity of the fathers into the bosom of the children after them." And in some other passages already cited, it appears that the curse extended beyond the fourth generation. So also in the punishment of the ten tribes, the evil consequences were felt far beyond four generations. The third and fourth generation are particularly mentioned, "partly, because a parent may live so long, and see the dreadful effects of his sin in his children's children; partly, because so far the memory of a father may extend, and be matter of imitation to his children; and partly, to show the difference between his exercise of justice and mercy, as appears by comparing the next verse."

IV. Some have supposed that we find an explanation of the whole principle here involved in the ruin of our race by the sin of Adam. But this cannot be admitted. Adam was a public person, the federal head and representative of his posterity. Had he stood his probation without sinning, they all would have been for ever confirmed in holiness and in the favour of God. But he sinned and cut off from all possibility of standing accepted on the ground of the covenant of works every one who descended from him by ordinary generation. No man is now so the representative of his posterity as that they will be lost for his sin alone; or that they will be saved on the ground of his piety.

V. Some have thought that the threatening here contained has exclusive reference to idolaters. No doubt idolatry is exceedingly offensive to God. So much is God incensed at it that he directed the inhabitants of idolatrous cities in Palestine to be exterminated. Deut. xiii. 12–17. And it is true that the most terrible denunciations of Heaven's wrath, made in Scripture, or executed in providence, are against idolatry and kindred sins. Maimonides confines the curse in the second commandment to idolaters, because, he says, they are *haters of God;* and it cannot be denied that wherever God specifies the particular class of sinners, against whose posterity he threatens evil for the sins of their ancestry, idolaters, persecucutors, bloody men, or other atrocious offenders are the subjects of consideration. There seems to be something exceedingly dreadful in the operation of idolatry on communities. It strikes so deep into the very essence of moral character, that to root it out from among a people, where it has once obtained acceptance, seems to be all but impossible. Jer. ii. 11. Even after it is driven from street and temple, it lurks in families and chambers; and images are often carried concealed under the vestments. Thus it is apt to be perpetuated from generation to generation. While we may admit as much as the foregoing, it is not true that the curse is *confined* to idolaters. All the unregenerate *hate God.* Rom. viii. 7. Atheists, infidels, all wilful violaters of any of the commandments, and all rejecters of the gospel of Jesus Christ are the *enemies* of God by wicked works. The special reason of speaking of idolaters as those that hate God is not merely to express that simple truth, but to cut off all pretext and pretence of love to him on the part of those who essentially corrupt his worship.

VI. It cannot be denied that temporal calamities have been sent and are still sent on children in consequence of the wickedness of their ancestry. We see this principle carried out in all countries, whatever may be the form of government. The children of the thief, of the drunkard, and of the flagrant wrong-doer, do always commence life under great disadvantages. The grace of God, leading to uprightness, may enable them to overcome all these. But in some cases vice transmits diseases or entails poverty, from the effects of which, no virtuous living on the part of the children relieves them. Moreover, the Scriptures record instances of temporal suffering in children, even where the damning guilt of the parents' sin has been forgiven: "And David said unto Nathan, I have sinned against the LORD. And Nathan said unto David, The LORD also hath put away thy sin; thou shalt not die. Howbeit, because by this deed thou hast given great occasion to the enemies of the LORD to blaspheme, the child also that is born unto thee shall surely die." 2 Sam. xii. 13, 14. The evil *here* threatened is exclusively temporal. So David understood it; for after his child was dead, he expressed strong confidence not only that his child was immortal and happy in heaven, but that he should soon join him. See verse 23. Pool thinks that all the evil threatened in the second commandment relates to temporal punishments. But this cannot be proven any more than that all the mercy promised in the next verse relates to temporal prosperity.

VII. While for the glory of his justice, the honour of his kingdom, and the good of his chosen, the LORD may afflict even the godly children of idolaters and of other great offenders with temporal calamities, for the sins of their ancestors, yet none of the pains of eternal death shall fall on the humble, penitent believer, either for his own sins, the sins of his immediate progenitors, or for the first sin of his representative Adam, just as the Most High grants eternal mercies to none of the children of those who love him, if they forsake the God of their fathers, and walk on in sin. So he clearly declares, "When the son hath done that which is lawful and right, and hath kept all my statutes and hath done them, he shall surely live;" and, "When a righteous man turneth away from his righteousness and committeth iniquity and dieth in them; for his iniquity that he hath done shall he die." Ezek. xviii. 19, 26. Thus, individual responsibility is fully retained; and a door of mercy is opened wide to all who, forsaking the evil practices of their ancestors, renouncing the works of the devil, and fleeing for refuge to the hope set before them in the gospel, accept the grace that is in Christ Jesus. Thus Hezekiah, though the son of wicked Ahaz, who had greatly defiled the house of God, was a truly pious man, walked with God, had great temporal prosperity, and died in faith.

VIII. Where children walk in the footsteps of their vicious ancestors and thus justify all their wickedness, as the descendants of idolaters and of other heinous violaters of God's law are very apt to do, there is no difficulty in perceiving at once the perfect justice of the evil here threatened. Ps. xlix. 13. That indeed is visiting the iniquity of the fathers upon the children in the most terrible form. Spiritual judgments are the most terrific of all judgments. To be given over on any account, particularly in imitation of the wickedness of our forefathers, to work iniquity with greediness, is the heaviest of Heaven's curses.

IX. It would probably not a little quiet some of our rebellious thoughts respecting the evil here threatened, if we would duly remember the following things. 1. Sin is a horrible evil. It deserves God's wrath and curse both in this life and that which is to come. God has never punished it excessively. He never will punish it more than it deserves. 2. We are all "by nature the children of wrath." None of us are in ourselves innocent. As we come into the world, we are under the just curse of the covenant of works. 3. It is of God's mere grace that kindness is shown to any of our race. No man deserves mercy at the hand of God, either for himself or his posterity.

X. Let us for a moment suppose that there was no such principle as social liability incorporated into the government of the world; that the husband could not be made to pay the fines imposed upon his wife; that wives and children were subjected to no inconveniences on account of the criminal conduct of husbands and fathers; would we thus be led reasonably to expect an improved state of morality? Lord Bacon says, "He who marries gives hostages to society." That is, he gives additional pledges of his good behaviour as a citizen. So also the father has motives for good behaviour, which can never be felt by the childless. The love of our offspring is not only natural, but exceedingly strong. Even infidels, who have lived and died reckless of their own spiritual interests, have been known to exhort their dying children to believe in Christ; so mightily did parental love, at least for the time, over-ride their skepticism and enmity. But suppose when a man was tempted to do wrong, he could truly say, My evil conduct shall injuriously affect no one but myself, would not one of the strongest inducements to resist temptation, in many cases, be quite taken away? Even a heathen said, "It is nothing strange and absurd for the posterity of lewd and wicked men to suffer what belongs to them."

XI. Hopkins: "*God doth not always observe this method of revenging the offences of fathers upon their children in temporal punishments.* Neither doth this threatening in the commandment oblige him to do it, but only shows what their sins deserve, and what he might justly do, if he pleased to use his power and prerogative. . . . If children themselves be pious and holy, this may be for their comfort, that whatever afflictions they lie under, shall be for their benefit and advantage; and they are not punishments to them, but only fatherly corrections and chastisements: for the very things which they suffer may be intended by God as a punishment to their ancestors, but a fatherly correction to themselves; and what to the one is threatened as a curse, to the other may prove a blessing and an advantage, as it gives them occasion of exercising more grace and so of receiving the greater glory."

XII. It may be well here to present the views of some of the best commentators on this threatening.

Diodati: "As concerning eternal judgment upon the soul, every one dieth for his own iniquity. Jer. xxxi. 30. But for the father's sins, the children are often punished in body, in goods, and other things, which they hold, and derive from their fathers. Num. xiv. 33; 2 Sam. xii. 11, xxi. 5, 14. And besides, God oftentimes curseth the generation of the wicked, withdrawing his grace and Spirit from it, whereby imitating their parents' wickedness, they are punished in the same manner." 1 Sam. xv. 2; Matt. xxiii. 32, 35.

Boston: "Not that God properly punishes one for another's sin; but that from the parents' sin, he often takes occasion to punish children for their own sins, and such their parents' sins ofttimes are by imitation, or some way approving of them."

Ridgley has three remarks on the threatening contained in the second commandment: 1. "That though God does not punish children with eternal destruction for the sins of their immediate parents, yet these oftentimes bring temporal judgments on families. 2. These judgments fall heavier on those children that make their parents' sins their own, by approving them and committing the same. . . . . 3. Whatever temporal judgments may be inflicted on children for their parents' sins, shall be sanctified and redound to their spiritual advantage, as well as end in their everlasting happiness, if they do not follow their bad example."

Scott: "If Israel, or any Israelites, revolted to

idolatry, they would be deemed *haters of God;* as the wife would be supposed to hate her husband, when she preferred every worthless stranger to him: and the national covenant, with its peculiar blessings, being forfeited, the sins of the parents would involve their offspring in the punishment, even to the third and fourth generation."

Stowell gives much the same explanation. He says, "God's dealing with the seed of Abraham must be examined on the principles of that national covenant into which he entered with that people."

XIII. There is nothing in this threatening, which goes counter to the exceeding great and precious principle laid down by the apostle. (1 Cor. vii. 14.) "The unbelieving husband is sanctified by the wife, and the unbelieving wife is sanctified by the husband; else were your children unclean, but now are they holy." So that the wickedness of one parent can never make null and void the covenant of God with the other believing parent. In this case, as in many others, though sin abounds, grace does much more abound. God, who would not have destroyed Sodom had there been ten righteous people in it; God, who spares the world for the sake of his elect that are in it, will never put beyond the reach of his grace, or the pale of his covenant, the child, either of whose parents is found faithful with God, except for the personal sins of such child.

XIV. It is an exceedingly great relief to a tender heart to find this declaration of God's justice immediately followed by a promise unspeakably more large and glorious, viz.: "*shewing mercy unto thousands of them that love me and keep my command-*

*ments*." So that even here at the foot of Sinai, "mercy rejoiceth against judgment," triumphing over it. James ii. 13. Compare Ezek. xxxiii. 11. The chief difficulty respecting this promise is in bringing our hearts to understand and embrace the exceeding riches of the grace here offered. The *thousands* here spoken of are not thousands of *persons* merely, but *thousands of generations*. The context teaches as much, and this is the interpretation approved by a great body of the soundest expositors, among them John Calvin. The promise will stand for ever good: "I will be a God unto thee, and to thy seed after thee." Gen. xvii. 7. And Solomon says, "The children of a just man are blessed after him." Prov. xx. 7. "This," says Calvin, "is not only the effect of a religious education, which is of no small importance, but it is also in consequence of the blessing promised in the covenant, that the grace of God shall perpetually remain in the families of the pious." So that if any of the effects of divine wrath are felt to the *third* and *fourth* generation of gross offenders, mercy is shown to *thousands of generations* of the truly pious. If God is glorious in holiness, and terrible in justice; he is matchless in loving-kindness, and unparalleled in tender mercy. And that we may labour under no misapprehension as to the infallible proof of love to God, it is stated in the same connection that it is evinced by *keeping his commandments*. Jesus himself repeated the same truth: "He that hath my commandments, and keepeth them, he it is that loveth me." John xiv. 21.

Under the influence of the due consideration of these great truths, 1. *I am Jehovah*, 2. *I am thy*

*God*, and 3. *I am a jealous God;* and 4, of the alarming threatening of *visiting iniquity*, and 5, of the very glorious promise of *shewing mercy*, let us consider

WHAT THE SECOND COMMANDMENT REQUIRES.

The first commandment clearly points out the one, glorious, exclusive object of religious worship. The second commandment chiefly relates to the manner in which such worship is to be offered to him. The word, *worship*, either means civil respect, or religious reverence. It is in the latter sense that it is here employed. It has already been shown that neither the word of God nor the practice of men grades the veneration offered in religious worship, as the church of Rome vainly pretends to do. The worship of God consists, says Buck, "in paying a due respect, veneration, and homage to the Deity under a sense of religious obligation to him."

Fisher says, "Religious worship is that homage and respect we owe to a gracious God, as a God of infinite perfections, by which we profess subjection to, and confidence in him, as our God in Christ, for the supply of all our wants; and ascribe the praise and glory that is due to him, as our chief good, and only happiness."

Hopkins: "The true and spiritual worship of God *in general* is an action of a pious soul, wrought and excited in us by the Holy Ghost; whereby, with godly love and fear, we serve God acceptably according to his will revealed in his word; by faith embracing his promises, and in obedience performing his commands; to his glory, the edification of others, and our own eternal salvation."

One of these definitions may be more full than another; but they are all right as far as they go.

While the second commandment, no less than all the other precepts of the decalogue, should be regarded as designed to regulate our tempers, it no doubt has special reference to the external worship of God. The things forbidden in it relate to outward acts. It is true the most gross form of violating God's worship is mentioned, just as the most flagrant form of sinning against our neighbour's life, and peace, and property are mentioned in the sixth, seventh and eighth commandments.

I. Let us then consider *God's worship.* Whenever worship is acceptable to God, it must have the following properties:

1. It must be sincere and ingenuous. Hypocrisy is odious to all right-minded men; to God it is detestable. Without this heartiness in God's service, it is impossible to "worship the LORD in the beauty of holiness." 1 Chron. xvi. 29. An attempt to serve him without sincerity calls in question the Divine Omniscience, and is a gross insult to his infinite purity and majesty. Of course true worship will be cheerful, free from moroseness, and from sanctimonious grimace. It never teaches men to disfigure their faces. It abhors whining cant. In all approaches to God, let the oil of gladness run through our souls.

2. It must be marked by solemnity and reverence, excluding levity, vanity, and profaneness of mind in the worshipper. Nothing can be more offensive to God than rushing thoughtlessly into his presence. "Keep thy foot when thou goest to the house of God, and be more ready to hear than to give the sacrifice

of fools: for they consider not that they do evil. Be not rash with thy mouth, and let not thine heart be hasty to utter any thing before God; for God is in heaven, and thou upon earth: therefore let thy words be few." Eccles. v. 1, 2. "God is greatly to be feared in the assembly of the saints, and to be had in reverence of all them that are about him." Ps. lxxxix. 7.

3. All worship offered to God must be humble. It is with the lowly that he takes up his abode; while the proud he sends empty away. The great difference between the Pharisee and Publican in the temple was, that the former was bloated with self-conceit, while the latter was bowed down in deep self-abasement. "God resisteth the proud, but giveth grace unto the humble."

4. God's worship must be intelligent. If it may be truly said to us as to the Samaritans, "Ye worship ye know not what," our service is utterly worthless. Charnock: "Worship is the fruit of knowledge. . . . There is no worship acceptable to God without the knowledge of Christ. . . . . Without this knowledge of God, we should never worship him in a *right manner*. . . . Whatever the principle of the worship is, it must have knowledge for the foundation. Without a knowledge of God we cannot affect him; without a strong knowledge, we cannot love him ardently. . . . When we understand not his justice, we shall presume upon him; when we are ignorant of his glorious majesty, we shall be rude with him; unless we understand his holiness, we shall leap out of sin to duty; and the risings of our lusts will be as nimble as the desires of our souls. If we are ignorant of his excellency, we shall want humility before him;

if we have not a deep sense of his omniscience, we shall be careless in his presence."

Ignorance of the true God will clearly lead to atheism or to the worship of false gods; while a true saving knowledge of him will surely preserve us from so great sins. Gal. iv. 8. Dan. iii. 18.

5. Our worship of God must be spiritual. Its seat must be in the soul. So taught Christ himself: "The hour cometh, and now is, when the true worshippers shall worship the Father in spirit and in truth; for the Father seeketh such to worship him. God is a spirit; and they that worship him must worship in spirit and in truth." John iv. 23, 24.

6. Our worship must be according to divine directions. Every sovereign, as every court, has a right to regulate the manner in which petitioners shall approach. Nothing more effectually destroys all acceptableness in worship than that our fear towards God be taught by the precept of men. Isa. xxix. 13. Compare Matt. xv. 9. Acceptable worship is therefore pure and simple, and free from superstition, pomp, and idle ceremony. All will-worship and all displays of magnificence invented by man are an offence to God. True worship, like real "beauty, when unadorned is adorned the most." We may not, therefore devise any false worship, Num. xv. 37–40; nor recommend it to others, Deut. xiii. 6, 7, 8; nor enjoin it upon others, Hosea v. 11; nor use it ourselves, 1 Kings xi. 33; nor in any wise countenance it. Rev. ii. 14.

7. All acceptable worship must be offered in true faith. "Without faith it is impossible to please him; for he that cometh to God must believe that he is, and

that he is a rewarder of them that diligently seek him.' Heb. xi. 6. Mason: "There wants nothing but a be lieving prayer to turn every promise into a performance." Unless we have this faith, the most appropriate public worship will soon become a burden, and we shall cry out, "What a weariness is it!" Mal. i. 13. Then we may indeed draw nigh to God with our mouth and honour him with our lips, but our hearts will be far from him. Matt. xv. 8.

8. All acceptable worship must be offered to God by and through Jesus Christ, the only Mediator. "Hitherto have ye asked nothing in my name; ask, and ye shall receive, that your joy may be full." John xvi. 24. "If ye shall ask anything in my name, I will do it." John xiv. 14. The Saviour takes our imperfect services, puts them into his golden censer, sprinkles them with his own most precious blood and presents them before God for a sweet-smelling savour.

Worship is either internal or external. Internal worship consists in right thoughts and intentions, right views and desires, humility of soul united with warm and tender affections towards God. This is the fountain of all religious service, pleasing to the Most High. It is of great price in the sight of him who knoweth our thoughts afar off. When some one spoke to Leighton of his very valuable library, he said, "One devout thought is worth it all." But there is no contrariety between internal and external worship. The former naturally leads to the latter. In external worship, we use words and actions expressive of inward emotions. That worship exercising both soul and body is proper, can be made manifest in many ways. 1. We have the examples of good men recorded in Scripture and of the Saviour himself. 2. External worship is specially ordained in many parts of Scripture. Time would fail us to cite all the texts pertinent. 3. Just so sure as we feel aright towards God, our pious affections will seek suitable modes of outward expression. Matt. xii. 35; Luke vi. 45; Rom. x. 10. 4. Our bodies are no less redeemed than our souls. If the soul shall be glorified, so shall the body; if the soul shall be lost, so shall the body. The law is explicit: "Glorify God in your body and in your spirit, which are God's." 1 Cor. vi. 20. Compare Matt. xvi. 24. 5. Suitable outward worship greatly aids the spirit of devotion and cultivates pious affections. Many Scriptures say as much. In some things in external worship, God has left us free to do that which seems to us most becoming and convenient. But he has prescribed the entire matter, and motive, and spirit with which he will be worshipped.

Worship is again distinguished into that which is taught us both by the light of nature and by revelation; and that which is taught us by revelation alone. There is nothing in nature to suggest that the offering of bloody sacrifices would be acceptable to God. That was learned by revelation alone. The same is true of the sacraments instituted by Christ. On the other hand, prayer and thanksgiving seem to be taught by the light of nature. At least all nations have practised them. But enough of distinctions.

The Westminster Assembly thus sums up the requirements of this precept: "The duties required in the second commandment are, the receiving, observing, and keeping pure and entire, all such religious worship and ordinances as God hath instituted in his word; particularly prayer and thanksgiving in the name of Christ; the reading, preaching, and hearing of the word; the administration and receiving of the sacraments; church government and discipline; the ministry and maintenance thereof; religious fasting; swearing by the name of God; and vowing unto him; as also the disapproving, detesting, opposing all false worship; and, according to each one's place and calling, removing it, and all monuments of idolatry."

This general view of what is required in this commandment must for the present suffice. As the commandment itself is in the negative form, it will be most convenient to consider the various topics in detail, when we shall speak of WHAT THE SECOND COMMANDMENT FORBIDS.

### I. HOW THE CHURCH OF ROME BREAKS THIS COMMANDMENT BY IDOLATRY.

The church of Rome has long found this a very troublesome commandment. Her devices for evading its force are many. The Douay Bible reads thus: "Thou shalt not make to thyself a graven thing, nor the likeness of any thing that is in heaven above, or in the earth beneath, nor of those things that are in the waters under the earth. Thou shalt not adore them, nor serve them." Ex. xx. 4, 5. Again: "Thou shalt not make to thyself a graven thing, nor the likeness of any things, that are in heaven above, or that are in the earth beneath, or that abide in the waters under the earth. Thou shalt not adore them, and thou shalt not serve them." Deut. v. 8, 9. Again: "You shall not make to yourselves any idol or graven thing, neither shall you erect pillars, nor set up a remarkable stone in your land, to adore it." Lev. xxvi. 1. The word (*Pesel*), which in the second commandment we render *graven image*, is the same word which we render *carved image*, and in the plural *carved images* in 2 Chron. xxxiii. 7, 19, 22. There is no difference between *graven images* and *carved images*. This word (*Pesel*) is derived from a verb that signifies to grave, hew, or carve. In the singular it occurs twenty-nine times, and invariably means a *graven* or *carved image*. In the plural it occurs twenty-three times, and always means *graven* or *carved images*, unless Judges iii. 19, 26 form an exception. There the common version renders the word *quarries* (margin *graven images*). Possibly the word does here designate the beds of rock, whence stones were *hewn*. But both the Vulgate and the Douay Bible in each of these verses have *idols;* "where were the idols," &c., "the place of the idols;" so that in the only places where the word may possibly mean something else than graven images, Rome decides that it means *idols*. But in the second commandment, the church of Rome for *images* reads *things*. If we should yield that *things* should be preferred to *images*, with the candid scholar it would really not aid the cause of idolatry. But so clearly does the word mean not *thing* but *image* that the church of Rome herself has to admit it in Deut. iv. 16. "Lest perhaps being deceived you might make you a *graven similitude*, or image of male or female." So at last Rome yields even this point. Again, in 2 Chron. xxxiii. 7, 19, in the Douay Bible we have *statue* and *statues*, not *things*. Here it is fairly admitted that the word does not mean *thing*, but statue or *image*. In 2 Chron. xxxiv. 3, 4, the Douay Bible twice renders it *idols*. The Vulgate has *simulacra*. Indeed the word uniformly points to some figure or representation containing a similitude of some thing that is supposed once to have had life.

The Hebrew word [Temunah] rendered *likeness* occurs ten times. In the common version it is once rendered *image*, Job iv. 16; four times *similitude*, Num. xii. 8; Deut. iv. 12, 15, 16; and five times *likeness*, Ex. xx. 4; Deut. iv. 23, 25, v. 8; Ps. xvii. 15. Patrick says: "The difference between *Pesel*, which we translate *graven image*, and *Temunah*, which we translate *likeness*, seems to be, that the former was a protuberant image, or a statue made of wood, stone, &c., and the other only a *picture* drawn in colours upon a wall or board." &c.

Besides *graven* or *carved images*, God forbade the making or worshipping of *molten images* [Mas-seh-chah]. The word occurs twenty-seven times in the Hebrew Bible, and with the exception of Isa. xxx. 1, it is uniformly rendered *molten*, *molten image* or in the plural *molten images*. In Deut. ix. 12, the Douay Bible has "molten idol;" and in 3 Kings xiv. 9, "molten gods;" and in 2 Chron. xxviii. 2, "statues." So that every kind of representation of the object of worship by casting melted metals, by carving, and by painting, is here forbidden.

The cherubim which stood over the ark, are never called *pesel* or *peselim*, because they were not worshipped. For the same reason the brazen serpent is never called *pesel*. The *graven images* were worshipped as the representation or habitation of some deity. They presented to the eye of the worshipper something claiming religious veneration. So that any representation of the true God or of a false god would have been a *pesel*. It was an image used in religious worship.

The church of Rome also renders by the word *adore* the word [shah-gah] which we translate *bow down* in this commandment. The reason of this difference is, that Rome teaches that there is due to certain objects much religious homage and veneration which yet do not amount to *adoration*. The word does indeed mean *worship*, but worship by *bowing down*. So clear is this that the Douay Bible renders the same verb *make obeisance*, Gen. xliii. 28; *falling flat*, Num. xxii. 31; *bowed*, Gen. xxxiii. 6; *bow down*, Gen. xxiii. 7, 12; Gen. xxvii. 29; also in Gen. xxxiii. 3; and twice in xxxiii. 7; also in xxxvii. 7, xlii. 6, xliii. 26, xlviii. 12, xlix. 8; and *worship*, Gen. xxii. 5; see also Ex. xviii. 7, &c. So true is it, that whenever her doctors have no sectarian ends to accomplish, even they admit that *bow down* or *worship* is the right rendering, and not *adore*, in their sense of that word. In fact, the Douay Bible (Gen. xxiii. 7) reads thus: "Abraham rose up, and bowed down to the people of the land." To this is this note affixed: "*Bowed down to the people*, *adoravit*, literally *adored*. But this word here, as well as in many other places in the Latin Scriptures is used to signify only an inferior honour and reverence paid to men, expressed by a bowing down of the body." This concedes the whole point in dispute.

The church of Rome is so much annoyed by this second commandment, that she wholly omits all the words of it in vast numbers of her formularies. Nor is this wonderful. For she authorizes and practises the use of graven images, or carved images, and of molten images, and of pictures in her worship.

This worship of images has long been maintained with great earnestness by "the woman that sitteth on the seven hills." Sir Edward Coke (Inst. 3, p. 49), informs us that when Popery reigned in England a law was passed that "any persons, who affirm images ought not to be worshipped, be holden in strong prison, until they take an oath and swear to worship images." And the last general council of that corrupt communion, the Council of Trent, says, "Let them [*i. e.* all bishops, and others who have the care and charge of teaching] teach that the images of Christ, of the Virgin, Mother of God, and of other saints, are to be had and retained, especially in churches, and due honour and veneration paid to them." None will deny that in all countries, where worship is conducted by ministers of the church of Rome images do abound, and that the devotees do *bow down* before them, and *kiss them*, as Trent directs. All this is directly in the teeth of the second commandment.

That the church of Rome authorizes a like use of *pictures* is evident from her uniform usage, and from the decrees of the same council of Trent: "Let the Bishops teach further, that by the records of the mysteries of our redemption, expressed in pictures or other similitudes, men are instructed and confirmed in those articles of faith which are especially to be remembered and cherished; and that great advantages are derived from all sacred images, not only because the people are thus reminded of the benefits and gifts which are bestowed upon them by Christ, but also because the divine miracles performed by the saints, and their salutary examples, are thus placed before the eyes of the faithful, that they may give thanks to God for them, order their lives and manners in imitation of the saints, and be excited to adore and love God, and cultivate piety. Whoever shall teach or think in opposition to these decrees, let him be accursed."

That in practice the Romish church does carry out this decree, none will deny. That she goes still further, and represents the Father, Son and Holy Ghost in pictures, is also matter of notoriety. In one of the public buildings of the Jesuit College at Georgetown, D. C. was, and perhaps still is, a picture representing the Trinity. A draft of the picture and certificates of its existence have been before the public for more than twenty years. They are now in the author's possession, and have been seen by many.

That all this is according to the teaching of the doctrines of the Romish church, none will deny. Peter Dens says, "ARE IMAGES OF GOD OR OF THE MOST HOLY TRINITY PROPER? Yes: although this is not so certain as concerning the images of Christ and the saints; as this was determined at a later period.

"But it is to be observed that the Divinity cannot be depicted, but those forms are depicted under which God hath sometimes appeared, or to which divine attributes are paid in some similitude: thus GOD THE FATHER is represented under the form of an old man; because, Dan. vii. 9, we read that he appeared thus:

*And the Ancient of days sat;* and the Holy Ghost under the form of a dove; because he appeared thus: Matt. iii. 16. *He saw the Spirit of God descending like a dove;* or under the form of cloven tongues, such as he appeared on the day of Pentecost, Acts ii. 3. *And there appeared unto them cloven tongues as it were of fire.*"

That all this is directly contrary to the express teaching of God's word may be learned by a reference to its earliest books. Thus says Moses: "The LORD spake unto you out of the midst of the fire: ye heard the voice of the words, but saw no similitude; only ye heard a voice. Take ye therefore good heed unto yourselves; for ye saw no manner of similitude on the day that the LORD spake unto you in Horeb out of the midst of the fire: lest ye corrupt yourselves, and make you a graven image, the similitude of any figure, the likeness of male or female, the likeness of any beast that is on the earth, the likeness of any winged fowl that flieth in the air, the likeness of anything that creepeth on the ground, the likeness of any fish that is in the waters beneath the earth. Take heed unto yourselves, lest ye forget the covenant of the LORD your God, which he made with you, and make you a graven image, or the likeness of any thing, which the LORD thy God hath forbidden thee. For the LORD thy God is a consuming fire, even a jealous God." Deut. iv. 12, 15–18, 23, 24.

It is doubtless on this ground that Isaiah utters the fearful challenge: "To whom then will ye liken God? or what likeness will ye compare unto him?" Isa. xl. 18. Verily men are fearfully blind when they can "change the glory of the uncorruptible God into an image made like to corruptible man, and to birds, and four-footed beasts, and creeping things." Rom. i. 23.

The same Council of Trent says: "They are to be wholly condemned, as the church has long before condemned them, and now repeats the sentence, who affirm that veneration and honour are not due to the relics of the saints, or that it is a useless thing that the faithful should honour these and other sacred monuments, and that the memorials of the saints are in vain frequented, to obtain their help and assistance." Some plea, if possible, must be set up for this species of idolatry. In his "Defence of Catholic Principles," Gallitzin says: "The Israelites venerated the brazen serpent, a type or figure of Christ." Num. xxi. 9. p. 129. This indeed is as good authority as can be brought for this purpose. How God regarded this veneration shown to the serpent appears from the record of Scripture itself. Good king Hezekiah, who "did that which was right in the sight of the Lord," and who was a great reformer in the church of God, "destroyed the high places, and broke the statues in pieces, and cut down the groves, and broke the brazen serpent, which Moses had made: for till that time the children of Israel burnt incense to it: and he called its name Nohestan." This is the record given in the Douay Bible, 4 Kings xviii. 4. At the bottom is a note saying, that it was called Nohestan, *their brass* or *a little brass* in contempt, because they had made an idol of it. See Common Version, 2 Kings xviii. 4. But Gallitzin says, that in all this worship of images, pictures, and relics, there "is nothing but what every Christian must approve as conformable to the word of God and to reason. St. John the Baptist venerated the very latchets of our Saviour's shoes." Mark i. 7. The entire record of this matter in the Douay Bible is in these words: John said, "There cometh after me one mightier than I, the latchet of whose shoes I am not worthy to stoop down and loose." Truly these are slender foundations on which to rear the immense fabric of Popish idolatry. John expresses no veneration for Christ's shoes, but simply declares that he himself was not worthy to perform the humblest office of kindness to the Saviour. As if to cut off all occasion for this species of idolatry, our blessed Saviour left no keepsakes among his disciples. It was his executioners that divided his raiment and cast lots upon his vesture. On the foregoing topics, see Bingham, vol. ii., pp. 511–518, 523–525; vol. iv., pp. 140, &c.; vol. vii. 458–462.

### II. IDOLATRY ABSURD AND CRIMINAL.

Idolatry, in all its forms, is a sin so gross, and expressive of so much folly and stupidity, that it is marvellous that men should ever commit it. To inspired writers it is a theme of just and severe ridicule, not the less pungent because a simple statement of its grossness is all that is required to show its absurdity. The Psalmist says, "Their idols are silver and gold, the work of men's hands. They have mouths, but they speak not; eyes have they, but they see not; they have ears, but they hear not; noses have they, but they smell not: they have hands, but they handle not: feet have they, but they walk not: neither do they speak through their throat." Well does he add, "They that make them are like unto them: so is every one that trusteth in them." Ps. cxv. 4–8. In like manner Isaiah ridicules at length the whole process of making and worshipping idols: "They that make a graven image are all of them vanity; and their delectable things shall not profit: and they are their own witnesses; they see not, nor know; that they may be ashamed. Who hath formed a god, or molten a graven image that is profitable for nothing? Behold, all his fellows shall be ashamed; and the workmen, they are of men: let them all be gathered together, let them stand up; yet they shall fear, and they shall be ashamed together. The smith with the tongs both worketh in the coals, and fashioneth it with hammers, and worketh it with the strength of his arms: yea, he is hungry, and his strength faileth; he drinketh no water, and is faint. The carpenter stretcheth out his rule; he marketh it out with a line; he fitteth it with planes, and he marketh it out with the compass, and maketh it after the figure of a man, according to the beauty of a man; that it may remain in the house. He heweth him down cedars, and taketh the cypress and the oak, which he strengtheneth for himself among the trees of the forest: he planteth an ash, and the rain doth nourish it. Then shall it be for a man to burn; for he will take thereof and warm himself; yea, he kindleth it, and baketh bread; yea, he maketh a god, and worshippeth it; he maketh it a graven image, and falleth down thereto. He burneth part thereof in the fire; with part thereof he eateth flesh; he roasteth roast, and is satisfied: yea, he warmeth himself, and saith, Aha, I am warm, I have seen the fire: and the residue thereof he maketh a god, even his graven image: he falleth down unto it, and worshippeth it, and prayeth unto it, and saith, Deliver me; for thou art my god. They have not known nor understood: for he hath shut their eyes, that they cannot see; and their hearts that they cannot understand. And none considereth in his heart, neither is there knowledge nor understanding to say, I have burned part of it in the fire; yea, also I have baked bread upon the coals thereof; I have roasted flesh, and eaten it: and shall I make the residue thereof an abomination? shall I fall down to the stock of a tree? He feedeth on ashes: a deceived heart hath turned him aside, that he cannot deliver his soul, nor say, Is there not a lie in my right hand?" Isa. xliv. 9–20. In like manner Elijah *mocked* the priests of Baal, and said: "Cry aloud, for he is a god: either he is talking, or he is pursuing, or he is in a journey, or peradventure he sleepeth, and must be awaked. And they cried aloud, and cut themselves after their manner with knives and lancets, till the blood gushed out upon them." 1 Kings xviii. 27, 28. In all this ridicule there is no caricature, no exaggeration. It is all fair, because it is simple truth.

Yet absurd as are the usages of open idolatry, there is no light in science, literature, philosophy, civilization, or the arts, that can show its silliness so glowingly as to banish it from among men. As Athens rose in eloquence and philosophy, so did she rise in her devotion to false gods, until in the days of Paul, besides hosts of idols famous in Greece, she had her altar erected to the *Unknown God*, and was, as the Scriptures testify, wholly given to idolatry, Acts xvii. 16, or as it is in the margin, she was "full of idols."

The very word in Hebrew, which we render *idol*, means a *vanity*, *nothing*, *naught*. In Jeremiah (xiv. 14,) the same word is rendered "a thing of nought." The man of Uz says to his friends, "Ye are all physicians *of no value*," literally, *idol* or *vain* physicians. Job xiii. 4. The "idol shepherd" of Zechariah (xi. 17,) is a worthless shepherd, whose care of the flock amounts to nothing. It may be to this signification of the word, as well as to the futility of all idol worship, that Paul alludes when he says: "What say I then? that the idol is any thing, or that which is offered in sacrifice to idols is any thing?" Again: "We know that an idol is nothing in the world." 1 Cor. viii. 4, x. 19. Men never do a more vain and empty thing than when they make or serve an idol. It is as foolish and as unproductive of good, as when one beats the air.

Idols themselves and the worship of them are in Scripture often styled an *abomination*. Ex. viii. 26; Deut. vii. 26; 1 Kings xi. 7, xiv. 24; 2 Chron. xv. 8; Isa. xliv. 19; Ezek. xviii. 12. Some also explain Daniel xi. 31, as referring to the images carried by the Romans, and to the pictures on the Roman standard, which were an *abomination* to the Jews, who after the captivity fell no more into the worship of either images or pictures, but all such things were an *abomination* to them. In 1 Maccabees, i. 54, we have the very phrase "abomination of desolation" applied to the image of Jupiter Olympus, which Antiochus had caused to be set up on the altar of God.

That idolatry is the abhorrence of God and of good men, is evident from the New Testament. Peter (1st Epistle, iv. 3,) speaks of "abominable idolatries."

So carefully did God guard his ancient people against idolatry, that he would not permit them to bring home with them as trophies the idols of the nations whom they conquered in war. He required all such images to be at once burnt with fire. Nay more, he would not permit them to strip the idol of its rich ornaments, before they destroyed it, "lest they should be snared therein." The reason he assigns is, that "it is an abomination to the LORD thy God." Deut. vii. 25.

How often and earnestly God condemns all idolatry may be seen in many Scriptures. The following are mere samples of what he often says: "Ye shall make you no idols nor graven image, neither rear you up a standing image, neither shall ye set up any image of stone in your land, to bow down unto it: for I am the LORD your God." Lev. xxvi. 1. Compare Deut. iv. 15, xii. 2, 3, xxxii. 16–20; Josh. xxiv. 20, 23. By David God clearly declares a fact, which ought never to be forgotten, as it can never be safely denied, viz.: that idolatry is productive of untold miseries, even in this life: "Their sorrows shall be multiplied that hasten after another God." Ps. xvi. 4. See also Jer. ix. 14, 15, xliv. 2–9; Ezek. xx. 18–26; Acts xvii. 29; 1 Cor. x. 14, xii. 2; 2 Cor. vi. 16; 1 John v. 21; Rev. ix. 20. If any doubt the horrible wretchedness of ancient heathenism, let him read the writings of the early fathers of the church, who had been converted from Gentilism. They often write like men, who had escaped from horrors, of which those who had been born in Christian lands, can hardly form a conception. And if any suppose that modern heathenism is a whit better, let him hear the testimony of many, who have been eye-witnesses of its cruelties.

The whole process of consecrating a heathen idol has in no important particular probably varied for thousands of years. The present mode of dedicating an idol is described by the prophet Daniel, five hundred and eighty years before Christ. Dan. iii. 5–7.

The following passages of Scripture condemning idolatry can be added to those already cited. They are all from the New Testament. 1 Cor. vi. 9; Gal. v. 20; Eph. v. 5; 1 Thess. i. 9; Rev. xxi. 8, xxii. 15.

## III. THE WORDS OF PROHIBITION EXPLAINED.

Let us revert for a little time to the words of the second commandment. One would think their import unmistakable. They positively forbid the making of images or likenesses for any religious use. The Douay Bible itself has a full pause or period at the end of the fourth verse of the twentieth chapter of Exodus. If it had not, the prohibition is clear against *making* images and against *bowing down* to images, and against *serving* them. The prohibition to *make* is repeated in Lev. xxvi. 1, and Deut. v. 8. That the second commandment does not forbid the cultivation of the fine arts, is generally agreed. But *making* any images or likenesses for religious service is forbidden. The terms of prohibition are very comprehensive. The image or likeness is not to be of any thing *in heaven above.* According to the Jews there were three heavens. 1. The aerial or atmospheric. No image or likeness of any flying bird or fowl may therefore be made for religious service, even though it be a dove. 2. The Jews spoke of the starry heavens. As we are forbidden to worship the sun, moon, and stars, so are we forbidden to make images of them for worship. 3. The Jews spoke of the third heaven, or heaven of heavens, the abode of God, the residence of saints and angels. No image or likeness of any inhabitant of this celestial city is to be made. Then the commandment forbids the making of any image or likeness of any thing that is *in the earth beneath.* These are men, beasts, fowls that walk the earth and do not fly, trees, plants, timber, crosses, bodies of men, living or dead, &c. Then we are forbidden to make an image or likeness of any thing that is in the water *under the earth,* such as of fishes of almost countless varieties and monsters of the deep. Of none of these may we *make* any representation for religious service. We are not only forbidden to make them, but to *bow down* to them. We may not bow the head, or the knee, or the whole body to them, nor uncover the head to them, nor kiss the hand to them, nor kiss them. Josh. xxiii. 16; Judges ii. 17; 1 Kings xix. 18; Job xxxi. 26, 27; Hos. xiii. 2. Nor may we show them the least token of respect, nor make to them any manner of obeisance.

Nor may we *serve* them, either as God's people serve him, or as the heathen serve their false gods by praising them, praying to them, building houses, or altars for their worship, carrying them in processions, or in any manner whatever commending them.

The reasons, why this precept is so often repeated and so much insisted on, are that God has a great zeal for the purity of his worship; that man is very gross and corrupt in his conceptions of God; that he has a peculiar dislike to spiritual worship: that all history shows his special liability to fall into idolatry; that the least corruption of worship, however well intended, is sure in the end to mislead many; and that men who fall into errors in worship, especially into any form of idolatry, are full of all bitterness and horrible malice in promoting at all costs their abominable practices. Matt. xv. 9; Isa. xlii. 8; Rom. i. 23, 28; Ex. xxxii. 1–8; Jer. ii. 11; 1 Kings xviii. 28; Ps. cvi. 36–38. The world furnishes not a single instance of an idolatrous people, who were not a bitterly persecuting people. Very strikingly does the author of the Apocryphal book of *Wisdom of Solomon* speak of idolatry: "The devising of idols was the beginning of spiritual fornication, and the invention of them, the corruption of life. For neither were they from the beginning, neither shall they be for ever. For by the vain-glory of men, they entered into the world, and therefore shall they come shortly to an end. For a father afflicted with untimely mourning, when he hath made an image of his child soon taken away, now honoured him as a god which was then a dead man, and delivered to those that were under him ceremonies and sacrifices. Thus in process of time an ungodly custom grown strong was kept as a law, and graven images were worshipped by the commandments of kings." Chap xiv. 12–16. See much more in the same chapter.

### IV. EXAMPLES OF WORSHIP CORRUPTED.

The Scriptures record four cases of introducing human inventions into the worship of Jehovah. Every one of them proved a snare to men's souls, and was an offence to the Most High.

1. The first was the making of the golden calf at the foot of Mount Sinai. The whole account is given in the thirty-second chapter of Exodus. That this was a professed attempt to honour the God of heaven seems evident from the record itself, as well as from the circumstances of the case. Indeed, Aaron said, "To-morrow is a feast to the LORD;" the original word is *Jehovah.* Israel could hardly have sunk so low as now to admit that the idols of Egypt, or rather, that a calf not made till they reached Horeb had delivered them. But they attempted to worship Jehovah under this sacred sign of the Egyptians. And yet, no sooner had they the calf, than down went all their conceptions of a spiritual God, and they cried, "These be thy gods, O Israel, which brought thee up out of the land of Egypt." They wanted some visible object to "go before them;" and in this they committed great sin. God himself says, "They have corrupted themselves." v. 7. And Moses says, "Oh this people have sinned a great sin," and Paul says, that they were *idolaters.* 1 Cor. x. 7. Compare Ex. xxxii. 6. And Stephen, in his last address says, "They made a calf in those days, and offered sacrifice unto the idol, and rejoiced in the works of their own hands." Acts vii. 41.

Kurtz: "The stringency and exclusiveness of the Mosaic monotheism, and the earnestness with which it held fast to the notion of the absolute spirituality of God, required that the worship of Jehovah by images and symbols should be held up as equally reprehensible with actual idolatry, that both should be punished as rebellion against Jehovah; in fact, that both should be represented under exactly the same point of view. It is easy enough to distinguish them in theory; but in practice the limits drawn by theory are quickly disregarded and overstepped. Aaron was a theorist of this kind: he said, (Ex. xxxii. 5,) 'To-morrow is the feast of Jehovah;' but the people had 'asked for a god to go before them.' (Ex. xxxii. 1.) Hence they had rejected *the* God who had gone before them in the pillar of cloud and fire, and demanded to be led in a different way; they wanted a God to go before them in a more tangible form, and not enveloped in the pillar of cloud. They probably had no intention of rejecting and denying their God, Jehovah, for they said: 'This is the God who brought us up out of the land of Egypt,' (Ex. xxxii. 8,) but they merely retained the name of Jehovah, and substituted a different and totally heterogeneous idea. The Jehovah worshipped by the people in the form of the golden calf was as much an idol as Apis, Moloch, and Dagon; and the people acted in violation of the command in Ex. xx. 3, quite as much as of that in Ex. xx. 4." The only grammatical difficulty in admitting Kurtz's explanation relates to the demonstrative pronoun *these* in the eighth verse. It is plural; but the translators of our English Bible in Ex. xxxviii. 21, render it in the singular *this*, and Gesenius says that some suppose it is used in the sense of a singular in 2 Chron. iii. 3; Ez. i. 9; Ezek. xlvi. 24; though he says these passages are uncertain. There is not much doubt that it sometimes has a singular sense. In 1 Chron. xxiv. 5, it is rendered *one sort* with *another*.

2. The next case in point of time of an attempt to worship Jehovah by symbolical representations was that of Micah and his mother, recorded in the seven-

teenth and eighteenth chapters of Judges. His mother blessed Micah in the name of *Jehovah*, (xvii. 2.) She said, "I had wholly dedicated the silver unto the LORD (Hebrew, *Jehovah*) from my hand for my son, to make a graven image and a molten image." When Micah had done so, a Levite came to Mount Ephraim, to the house of Micah, and Micah said to him, "Dwell with me, and be unto me a father and a priest." When he had secured the services of this man, he said, "Now know I that the LORD (Jehovah) will do me good, seeing I have a Levite to my priest." (xvii. 13.) When the Danites came and found this priest, he said to them, "Before the LORD (Jehovah) is your way wherein ye go." (xviii. 6.) And yet, by confession of all, this entire worship was gross idolatry.

3. The next case is that of Jeroboam, who made and set up the calves to be worshipped by the people. There is hardly a doubt that he intended these images as representations of the true God. His object is generally thought not to have been to withdraw Israel from the worship of Jehovah, but to prevent the kingdom from returning to the house of David. So he distinctly avows. He wanted a worship which would as well satisfy the ten tribes as the splendid service in Jerusalem. One of the calves he put in Bethel, and the other in Dan. He wanted some sensible signs that would fill their imaginations with the belief that Jehovah was present there as well as at Jerusalem. That he did not design the introduction of the worship of new gods, seems to be evident from a declaration in 1 Kings xvi. 31, where God says of Ahab that "it came to pass, as if it had been a light thing for him to walk in the sins of Jeroboam, the

son of Nebat. . . . and went and served Baal and worshipped him." And yet God says to Jeroboam, "Thou hast done evil above all that were before thee: for thou hast gone and made thee other gods, and molten images, to provoke me to anger, and hast cast me behind thy back." For this sin, Jehovah threatened the extinction of all the males of Jeroboam's family; and in due time he did "take away the remnant of the house of Jeroboam, as a man taketh away dung, till it be all gone." 1 Kings xiv. 10. The destruction of this race became a by-word in Israel. 1 Kings xvi. 3. And long after the death of Jeroboam, this sin of his is mentioned to his disgrace; for thus he "made Israel to sin." Kurtz, having spoken of the idolatry respecting Aaron's calf, says: "In the same way may Jeroboam have set up the bulls at Dan and Bethel as images of *Jehovah*, but in practice the people were not able to make so nice a distinction as he. Now, such dangerous distinctions as these, the law would at once cut up by the root, if it placed the false worship of Jehovah in precisely the same category as the worship of idols, and this it has done. For it is a false idea to suppose that Ex. xx. 4, refers to symbolical images of *God* alone, and not to *idolatrous* images also." However Jeroboam refined, the people came right out and said, "Behold thy gods, O Israel, which brought thee up out of the land of Egypt." 1 Kings xii. 28; or, Behold thy God, O Israel, &c.

4. The fourth kind of human invention leading to idolatry, was the use of groves and high places in the worship of Jehovah. God claimed the right of fixing the place as well as the manner of his worship. Deut.

xii. 5. He solemnly declared against these imitations of heathen worship, while the people were yet at the foot of Sinai. Lev. xxvi. 30. Yet so firmly rooted was the devotion of Eastern nations to this mode of worship that it required a long time and the judgments of Heaven, and the zeal of great reforming kings wholly to abolish it. See 2 Chron. xxxiii. 17; 2 Kings xxiii. 13, 14, and many other places. Solomon himself fell into this sin. 1 Kings iii. 3. The Assyrians were by sore judgments brought so far to confess Jehovah that they worshipped him in the same manner. 2 Kings xvii. 24–33. See, also, 2 Chron. xiv. 4. When great reformers were raised up, they found it necessary to cut down the groves and utterly to demolish the apparatus of worship in high places. So dangerous is it to tamper with the worship of God instituted by himself. Men always err when they revise the wisdom of Omniscience, particularly so in matters of worship.

### V. VAIN PLEAS FOR BREAKING THE SECOND COMMANDMENT.

The plea of modern idolaters that they do not worship the image, but God by the image, that the material effigy is nothing but a sign used to help devotion; and that it cannot be unlawful to make an image of God somewhat resembling the figure of a man, because God made man in his own image, were anticipated by the heathen long ago, in vindication of their idolatry. If God has said that the use of the cross in baptism is a part of the ordinance, then we are bound to use it. If he has said no such thing, we are not only at liberty to reject it, but we are bound to do so, as often as men or churches attempt to *make it obligatory* upon our consciences. The same is true of immersion and of trine-immersion, and of sprinkling, and pouring. So in respect of kneeling at the Lord's supper. If any choose in a spirit of devotion to Christ then to kneel, they are at liberty to do so. But if men refuse us the elements unless we will perform this gesture before them, we may not yield to their invention. The same is true respecting days of Fasting or of Thanksgiving, resting solely upon human authority. Each man must be his own judge whether the providence of God calls him or not to such a service. The same is true of festival-days in the church of God. All the religious liberty that is now upon earth is the fruit of resistance to attempts on the part of churches and civil authorities to bind men's consciences where God has left them free. Human ingenuity is great, but it is expressly forbidden to bring its inventions into God's worship: "Ye shall not do after all the things that we do here this day, every man whatsoever is right in his own eyes." Deut. xii. 8. Compare Deut. xii. 29–32. We do then grossly violate this commandment when we make any representation of the Most High, or of any of his perfections either by image or painting; when we make an image of any creature or thing for religious use; when we worship the true God in the use of images, or by adopting any of the practices of idolaters; when we believe the Most High is peculiarly present in any one place, house, statue, painting or relic; when any reverence due to God alone is given to any creature, as when the inhabitants of Lystra brought oxen and garlands to sacrifice to Paul and

Barnabas. Acts xiv. 11–15. It was idolatry in Cornelius to worship Peter, and would have been highly criminal had he persisted in it, when warned not to do it. Acts x. 25, 26. It would have been idolatry in John had he worshipped the angel, when told that he was a creature. Rev. xxii. 8, 9. It cannot be innocent, therefore, for European Christians to make images of Hindoo and Chinese gods, and transport them as articles of merchandize, to be dedicated and worshipped in Eastern countries; nor for any one to represent the Omniscience of God by a huge eye, sometimes denominated the All-seeing Eye. We are no more at liberty to worship the true God in a false way than we are to worship false gods.

VI. WE OFFEND AGAINST THIS PRECEPT IN DOCTRINE.

We do this when we entertain carnal views and gross apprehensions of God, Acts xvii. 29; Ps. l. 21; when we give heed to the doctrine of devils, 1 Tim. iv. 1; when we are carried about with strange doctrines, Heb. xiii. 9; when we are unwilling to hear sound doctrine, 2 Tim. iv. 3; or do not relish that which is according to godliness, 1 Tim. vi. 3; when we are not nourished in the words of good doctrine, 1 Tim. iv. 6; when we do not obey the form of doctrine delivered to us in the Scriptures, Rom. vi. 17; when we are carried about with every wind of doctrine, Eph. iv. 14; when we do not honestly inquire after the truth, Acts xvii. 5; when we are not willing to practise what we do know, John vii. 17; when we are not on our guard against self-righteous teachings and against loose and Antinomian opinions. Matt. xvi. 6, Rev. ii. 14, 15. There is not a truth of Scripture that is not "profitable for doctrine, for reproof, for correction, for instruction in righteousness." 2 Tim. iii. 16. We are no more at liberty to entertain loose opinions, however popular or plausible, than we are to indulge in loose practices, because they are common or agreeable. We have no more right to modify or alter the principles of church government, as learned from the revealed will of God, than we have to change the objects of religious worship. The Bible tells what elements shall be used both in baptism and the Lord's supper. It has declared one day in seven to be holy time; and all attempts to introduce into the church more holy days, or more elements in the sacraments, are as truly offensive to God as idol worship itself. The same is true of all attempts to make *canonical*, books that are apocryphal. All this is taught by God's word. Deut. iv. 3, Rev. xxii. 18, 19. It is sad indeed, because it is sinful, when we introduce will-worship into God's service. Col. ii. 18–23. If penances, pilgrimages, postures in worship, days and times are laid before us as matters to be conscientiously observed, it is mere superstition to yield to such demands.

## VII. THE SECOND COMMANDMENT IS OFTEN BROKEN IN PRAYER.

There is no form of religion upon earth which does not include prayer. It is noticed in the Scriptures more than five hundred times. No duty is more clearly enjoined. Were it possible to find a man giving all the other evidences of piety and yet leading a prayerless life, that one fact would sufficiently show the vanity of his professions. We are never in circumstances of joy or sorrow, sickness or health, where, if opportunity offered, the truly devout would not love to pray. No official station, no excellence of gifts, no experience in grace can put us beyond the need of prayer, till we enter the heavenly Jerusalem. Jesus Christ has left us two parables to encourage importunity in prayer. Nothing more effectually destroys the life of prayer than secret sin. "If I regard iniquity in my heart, the Lord will not hear me." Ps. lxvi. 18.

Prayer is either secret or public. Secret prayer should, as far as possible, be secluded from the eyes of men. A church, street-corner, or a market is no fit place to offer our personal devotions. In the sermon on the mount, our Lord puts this matter beyond all doubt: "And when thou prayest, thou shalt not be as the hypocrites are: for they love to pray standing in the synagogues, and in the corners of the streets, that they may be seen of men. Verily I say unto you, They have their reward. But thou, when thou prayest, enter into thy closet, and when thou hast shut thy door, pray to thy Father which is in secret; and thy Father, which seeth in secret, shall reward thee openly." Matt. vi. 5, 6.

Public prayer may be in the hearing of two or three friends, in a family, in a large company, or in the great congregation. Let us notice some particulars.

1. There are some things which in no wise affect the efficacy of prayer. One of these is the posture. Standing, kneeling, and prostration are all sanctioned in Scripture. Let no man judge his brother in this matter. Church history informs us that in early

times, the whole congregation stood with hands uplifted towards heaven. Another non-essential is the use or disuse of written or printed forms. There is not much room for doubt that extemporaneous prayer, if the heart is rightly affected, is the most edifying. But in either method, wickedness, pride, and unbelief may reign, or love, faith, and confidence in God may prevail. Nor does the prevalence of prayer depend on the language employed. In public prayer, the words used should commonly be plain and simple. A scriptural phraseology is usually the best. But God looks beyond the words to the heart. His ears are never charmed with any sounds, however melodious, if the heart is wanting. Neither is he ever offended at our language, because it is broken, or rude, if it engage the pious affections. Nor does fluency, or the want of it cause God either to hear or to reject our petitions. He cares not for eloquence. He knows the meaning of a sigh—the language of a groan—the pleading of a tear. Nor does the length of a prayer determine its character. The thief on the cross used a prayer of less than ten words and obtained all he asked. David prayed all night for the life of his child, and in the morning it died. The publican's prayer consisted of one short sentence, and was heard; the Pharisee's was long, and wordy, and worthless. Scriptural example seems to favour brevity. We are not heard for our much speaking.

2. But there are some things which greatly hinder our prayers. When we do not really desire what we ask for, God is offended at our cries. Augustine says, that in the days of his unregeneracy, he "prayed for chastity and continence, but not yet." All such

prayer is a mockery of God. And how many, too, are heedless respecting the answer to their petitions! Men leave their prayer, as the ostrich does her egg in the sand, to care for itself. It is well, when in our pious fervour, we cry out, "O Lord, how long?" When we ask God to gratify our wicked desires, or accomplish our evil purposes, we may know that he will be offended with us. If our reason for desiring personal usefulness is that we may be conspicuous, it is a mercy in God to deny us our request. Men may pray for zeal, or gifts in God's cause, that they may be set on high. Our prayers are always wrong, when we do not, in our measure, exercise towards men the sentiments which we ask God to show, without measure, towards us. If any ask for mercy, let him be careful to show it. If any pray for comforts, let him do what he can to make all happy around him. If he desires God not to mark iniquity in him, let him beware lest severity of judgment form a part of his own character. "With what measure ye mete, it shall be measured to you again." Matt. vii. 2. If we pray with a right spirit, we will gladly use the right means, and be willing that God should employ the right measures to secure us an answer. If one ask for an abundant harvest, let him be careful to cultivate his crops, and let him not find fault with God for sending soaking rains. If one prays that he may be made a "workman, that needeth not to be ashamed," let him not refuse the course of study, discipline, and prayer, requisite to make him such. Some fail to secure an answer in peace, because they are impatient. "Blessed are all they that wait for him." Isa. xxx. 18. "They shall not be ashamed that wait for me."

Isa. xlix. 23. "I waited patiently for the LORD; and he inclined unto me, and heard my cry." Ps. xl. 1. Impatience is the offspring of turbulence, rebellion, and unbelief. Impatience is apt to lead to the forsaking of prayer. Nor can we expect cold, heartless prayers to prevail. "Elijah's prayer brought fire down from heaven, because, being fervent, it carried fire up to heaven."

3. We all ought to pray more. As every faculty of body and mind, so every grace of the soul is improved by exercise. Prayer exercises all our graces. If we do not love to pray, we have no genuine piety. None of God's children are born dumb. They can all, at least, cry. Our religious comfort materially depends upon our having much of the spirit of prayer. Our usefulness is also thereby greatly affected. Moreover the Scriptures settle the question that prayer has powerful efficacy. The Bible, and all church history abound in records of its prevalence. Christ himself prayed much. "In the days of his flesh, when he had offered up prayers and supplications with strong crying and tears unto him that was able to save him from death, and was heard in that he feared." Heb. v. 7.

4. We do, therefore, greatly sin against God's ordinance of prayer when we lightly esteem it, in secret, in the family, or in the public assembly, Matt. vi. 6; Jer. x. 25; Acts ii. 42; Mal. iii. 14; when we do not seek the Spirit's aid in prayer, Rom. viii. 26; when we make light of those who are much exercised in this duty, 1 Sam. i. 14; when we are not constantly in possession of the spirit of prayer, 1 Thes. v. 17; when our hearts are reluctant to this duty, Job xv. 4; when we

do not shake off our sluggishness, and stir up ourselves to this duty, Isa. lxiv. 7; when we are impatient of God's delays in answering our prayers, Ps. xl. 1; when we do not prepare our hearts to this exercise, 1 Sam. vii. 3; when our prayers are full of words and not of desires, Eccles. x. 14; when our thoughts are like the fool's eyes, wandering everywhere, Prov. xvii. 24; when we do not earnestly desire to know what we ought to pray for, Rom. viii. 26; when we are satisfied with the gift without the grace of prayer, Matt. xv. 8; when we offer up our prayers without any lively faith, Heb. xi. 6; when we do not unite watching with prayer, Matt. xxvi. 41; Mark xiii. 33; when we are not burdened with a due sense of the sins which we confess before God; when we limit God's power to grant us things lawful, Ps. lxxviii. 41; 2 Kings vii. 2; when our prayers are chiefly for ourselves and do not embrace all sorts and conditions of men, even those who are malignant towards us, 1 Tim. ii. 1–4; when we desire our petitions rather for our own advantage than for the glory of God, 1 Cor. vi. 20; James iv. 3; when we are satisfied with the act of devotion without the presence and blessing of God; when we use vain repetitions; though all repetitions are not vain, for Augustine spent a whole night in offering up this one short prayer: *Noverim te, Domine, noverim me;* Grant that I may know thee, O Lord, and that I may know myself. We also sin when our prayers are self-righteous; when, another leading our devotions, we do not heartily say, Amen, to all proper petitions, 1 Cor. xiv. 16; when we are not duly thankful for gracious answers; when we are not duly humble for the defects in our prayers, and when we do not flee continually to the blood of Christ for cleansing from the sins of our holy things.

## VIII. WE BREAK THIS COMMANDMENT IN THE MANNER OF PRAISING GOD.

Praise is offered to God for what he is, and for what he does. In the latter case it is commonly called thanksgiving. Both Scripture and providence frequently summon us to this duty. If it is a mark of bad manners not to thank men for acts of kindness; surely it is a mark of a bad heart not to thank the Lord for his boundless goodness. Like prayer, praise is mentioned several hundred times in the Scriptures. It seems to be taught by natural religion. Even the heathen praise their gods. Judg. xvi. 23, 24; Dan. v. 4. Let us notice several particulars.

1. Our great error respecting this duty is, that we do not engage in it with sufficient frequency or fervency. If we were more thankful for the mercies we receive, we should doubtless receive more mercies to be thankful for. As God's nature is unchangeable and his compassions infinite, it is impossible for us to praise him too much. It is much to be lamented that the children of sorrow should ever feel themselves exempt from the obligations of this duty. The most afflicted of mere men in the depth of his sorrows, cried out, "Blessed be the name of the LORD." Job i. 21. It should greatly commend this duty to us, that it is very delightful and refreshing to a contrite heart; and that if through grace, we shall ever reach the kingdom of God, praise will be our employment for ever. No soul, that has been washed in atoning blood, shall, in passing Jordan, lose its harp. No!

on the other side of "the river that has no bridge," the hand that had on earth touched its strings but feebly and awkwardly, shall strike them with a vigour and accuracy that shall entrance itself, and shall be well-pleasing to God. Paul says love is greater than faith or hope, not because it is more necessary here, but because it shall last for ever. By parity of reasoning, praise is greater than prayer or fasting. Ps. civ. 33, cxlvi. 2. The chief revenue God gathers from our lost world, is from the praises of his loving, penitent people. Can it be doubted that many of the dismal fears and terrible misgivings of God's children would vanish, if they did properly abound in this duty? "Whoso offereth praise glorifieth me: and to him that ordereth his conversation aright, will I show the salvation of God." "Is any merry? Let him sing psalms." Ps. l. 23; James v. 13.

2. Some seem to have the impression that under the old dispensation, abundant praise was more required than under the new. But that is surely a mistake. "Be careful for nothing: but in every thing by prayer and supplication, with *thanksgiving*, let your requests be made known unto God." Phil. iv. 6. "Be filled with the Spirit: speaking to yourselves in psalms, and hymns, and spiritual songs, singing and making melody in your heart to the Lord; giving thanks always for all things unto God and the Father, in the name of our Lord Jesus Christ." Eph. v. 18–20. If Old Testament saints had much cause for abounding in praise and thanksgiving, as none but the wicked will deny; surely New Testament saints have much greater cause for doing the same. "For if the ministration of condemnation

be glory, much more doth the ministration of righteousness exceed in glory. . . . . If that which was done away was glorious, much more that which remaineth is glorious." 2 Cor. iii. 9, 11. And if we are thus surrounded by the "glory that excelleth," we ought to say so in praises, and thanksgivings, and thundering hallelujahs.

3. We sin against the ordinance of praise and thanksgiving when we reject it altogether, either from public or private worship, Ps. l. 23; when we do not abound in it, Ps. lii. 9; when we engage in it in a frivolous spirit, Ps. iv. 4; when neither our understandings nor our hearts are truly engaged in the work, 1 Cor. xiv. 15; when we waver in this duty; when we look upon it as a task, Mal. i. 13; when we go from this duty and are no more thoughtful or watchful than we were before, Haggai i. 5–7; when we are willing the work of praise should be performed in an unedifying manner, 2 Chron. xxix. 11; when we enter into this service with malignant hearts, Luke vi. 37; when without sufficient cause, we excuse ourselves from uniting our voices with God's people in this service, Ps. xvi. 9, xxx. 12, lvii. 8; when in our praises we have not a due reference to the mediation of Jesus Christ, Heb. xiii. 15; when we hinder or discourage others from engaging in this duty; and when this part of divine worship is performed in any way contrary to the requirements of God in all acts of worship previously stated.

## IX. WE BREAK THE SECOND COMMANDMENT WHEN WE DO NOT RIGHTLY USE GOD'S WORD.

Revealed truth is to be read, preached, heard, and

meditated upon. This was true even under a darker dispensation. That none is exempt from the study of God's word is manifest from the Scriptures. John v. 39; Acts xv. 21; 2 Tim. iv. 2. The Lord gave it for a perpetual statute respecting the man who should be king over his people: "He shall write him a copy of this law in a book, out of that which is before the priests, the Levites: and it shall be with him, and he shall read therein all the days of his life: that he may learn to fear the LORD his God, to keep all the words of this law and these statutes to do them: that his heart be not lifted up above his brethren, and that he turn not aside from the commandment, to the right hand, or to the left: to the end that he may prolong his days in his kingdom, he, and his children, in the midst of Israel." Deut. xvii. 18–20. No cares of state, no engagedness in any office, can exempt its incumbent from the obligation of making himself acquainted with the word of life; and this with devout reverence and all the attributes of religious worship. In the council at Jerusalem, James declared, "Moses of old time hath in every city them that preach him, being read in the synagogues every Sabbath day." Acts xv. 21. And Jesus Christ has instituted a permanent gospel ministry, the great object of whose appointment is to proclaim salvation, and cause the people to understand the word of the Lord. Rom. x. 15; Eph. iv. 11, 12; Neh. viii. 7, 8, 13. So important is this ministry that God has ordained that it shall be supported at the charge of the people, 1 Cor. ix. 14; 1 Tim. v. 18; and that all who are inducted into the sacred office shall be first proven to be fit and capable men. 1 Tim. iii. 6. All to whom the truth is preached are required to receive with meekness the engrafted word, which is able to save their souls, and to be doers of the word, and not hearers only, deceiving themselves. James i. 21, 22. We are bound carefully to guard the word of God against all corruption in doctrine or practice.

We do not give good heed to the second commandment when we read or hear God's word in a prayerless temper, 2 Thess. iii. 1; when we do not labour to attend upon the word without distraction, 1 Cor. vii. 35; when we are not thankful for the privilege of hearing God's word, Ps. ciii. 2; Heb. xiii. 15; when we do not, as new-born babes, desire the pure word of God, 1 Peter ii. 2; when we read or hear with our minds full of prejudice, 1 Kings xxii. 8; when we are actuated by no regard to God, but are merely following a custom, being satisfied with a decent appearance, Ezek. xxxiii. 31; when we do not earnestly lay hold of divine truth, Heb. ii. 1; when we do not believe the truth read or heard, Heb. iv. 2; when we soon forget the truth, or fail to practise it, James i. 22–25; when we do not tremble at God's word, Isa. lxvi. 2; when from mere stupidity of mind, we sleep when we should be all attention; Rom. xi. 8; when we are offended at the truth, Acts vii. 54; when we have itching ears, 2 Tim. iv. 3; when we are satisfied with the gifts of the preacher, though there be no growth of grace in our own hearts; when we go to the house of God rather to see and be seen, to notice and be noticed, than to hear what God the Lord will say; when we are more pleased with enticing words of man's wisdom than with the words and wisdom of the Holy Ghost, 1 Cor. ii. 1–5; when we do not set our hearts as a fair mark for the arrows of truth; when we dislike clear, discriminating, searching sermons; when we are more anxious after the curious than the profitable; when we do not embrace the promises of God; when we believe that we have little more to do with God's word than to hear it and criticise the preacher; when we irreverently treat any sacred truth; when we have little or no love to the truth as it is in Jesus; when slight excuses hinder us from hearing God's word; and when we put a low estimate upon the gospel ministry.

### X. WE MAY BREAK THE SECOND COMMANDMENT IN REGARD TO THE SACRAMENTS.

Christ has instituted two sacraments in his house. Some corrupt communions have added four or five more without the slightest authority from Heaven. The sacraments of the Christian church are baptism and the Lord's Supper. Respecting these, we offend against God when we despise or neglect them; when we do not regard them both as signs and seals of the righteousness which is by faith; when we do not observe them under the binding force of Christ's authority; when we observe them merely in conformity to custom, general usage, or the persuasion of others; when we expect salvation by the sacraments themselves; when we exalt them to the place assigned to the Saviour himself; when we observe them in a superstitious frame of mind; when we are more eager after the sign in the sacraments, than after the things signified thereby; when we put a higher estimate on sacramental observances than on faith, justice, mercy or the love of God; when we add to the Scriptural mode of their administration; when we do not duly prepare our hearts by prayer and self-examination, 1 Cor. xi. 28; when we rush thoughtlessly to the celebration of either of them, or needlessly delay their observance; when we go from their celebration and become careless or carnal in our affections; when we do not endeavour to have an abiding sense of the solemnity of sacramental acts; when we do not duly lament our imperfections and the low esteem in which the sacraments are held; when we do not earnestly desire our own edification and the glory of God in these ordinances; when we indulge in censorious and uncharitable tempers toward fellow-professors, refusing Christian communion with those whose profession and practice require the judgment of charity in their favour; when we wish the sacraments, which are holy things, to be given unto the dogs; or, when our observance of the sacred rites is marked by any of the deficiencies more particularly noticed in acts of worship discussed in previous pages.

XI. ANOTHER DUTY RESPECTING WHICH WE HAVE FULL INSTRUCTIONS AND MANY WARNINGS IN GOD'S WORD IS THAT OF FASTING.

This may be either of persons, as in the case of the great prophet of the captivity, Dan. ix. 3; or of families, as with Queen Esther and her maidens, Esth. iv. 16; or of churches, Acts xiii. 2, 3; or of cities, as of Nineveh, Jonah iii. 5; or of nations, Judg. xx. 26. Christ instituted no stated fast, or fasts to be observed by individuals, families, churches or communities. But he declared for the reasonableness of fasting under the gospel. He said, "Can the children of the bride-chamber mourn as long as the bridegroom is with them? but the days will come when the bridegroom shall be taken from them, and then shall they fast." Matt. ix. 15. We have also apostolic example for fasting; and in every age, "Christians of the finer mould have had their private fasts."

It is worthy of notice that fasting is a branch of worship in every system of religion now upon earth. From this some have inferred, perhaps not illogically, that it is a duty of natural religion.

The Jews had but one annual fast, prescribed by the LORD. Lev. xxiii. 27–32. From this they could not plead exemption. The Pharisee, mentioned in the 18th chapter of Luke, regarded himself as pre-eminently pious, because he added one hundred and three days of fasting over and above all that was required by that dispensation. Note these particulars.

1. In fasting, abstinence from food is to be either total or partial so long as the fast lasts. Daniel says, "I ate no pleasant bread, neither came flesh nor wine in my mouth, neither did I anoint myself at all." Dan. x. 3. This was his mode of observing a fast which lasted three whole weeks. Where the fast is of short duration, the abstinence from food is total. Some say that all the fasting required under the gospel is, that we abstain from sin. But this we should do every day and all our lives. A Christian may indeed observe a day of penitence and humiliation without fasting. But if he would observe a fast, let him abstain from all food or from pleasant food. It is but mocking God to eat, as some do, very heartily just before a fast and very greedily just afterwards. Epicures themselves sometimes do as much as that, in

order to increase their relish for food. The fast of Moses, of Elijah, and of our Saviour, each lasting forty days (Ex. xxxiv. 28, 1 Kings xix. 8, Matt. iv. 2) are no patterns to us. They ate no food, but were miraculously sustained.

2. Others sin in the matter of fasting, because although they themselves abstain from labour, they relieve not those who are in their service. God charges it upon the Jews, that on their fast-days, they "exacted all their labours." They did not "undo the heavy burdens," they did not "let the oppressed go free," they did not "break every yoke." Isa. lviii. 3, 6. Some are as severe and uncharitable on a fast-day as any other. At such a time, the wealthier should deal their bread to the hungry, and bring the poor that are cast out to their houses; when they see the naked they should cover them, and they should not hide themselves from their own flesh. Isa. lviii. 7. If we can do no more, we can at least give the value of the food we would that day have eaten to such as really need it.

3. A real fast calls for humiliation and repentance before God. Sorrow for sin should be deep and personal, Zech. xii. 9–14. The miserable substitute offered for this consists in bowing the head as a bulrush, Isa. lviii. 5; in disfiguring the face, Matt. vi. 16; and putting on sanctimonious grimaces. Such arts are hateful to all right-minded men. How God abhors them, the Scriptures fully declare.

4. To all right fasting, prayer should be added. So teach the Scriptures in many places.

5. Some spoil their fasting by making it a cloak of maliciousness, 1 Pet. ii. 16. To such God says, "Behold ye fast for strife and debate, and to smite

with the fist of wickedness." Isa. lviii. 4. If our fasting make us ill-natured, fretful, irritable or stubborn, surely it has done us no good. True fasting does not convert men into wild beasts. It does not make them resemble a bear robbed of her whelps. It does not foster anger, jealousy, discontent or suspicion; but it makes men kind, gentle, and charitable in their thoughts, words, and deeds.

6. We always abuse a fast when we pervert it to self-righteousness as did the Pharisees; when we fast for human admiration, Matt. vi. 16; when we have no solemn reference to God's authority and honour, Zech. vii. 5, 6; when we fast for a pretence, Mark xii. 40; when on a fast day, we find our own pleasure, Isa. lviii. 3; when we become weary of it, Amos viii. 5; when we do not earnestly address ourselves to this solemn duty; and when in general we observe it in violation of any Scripture principle respecting God's worship.

Although the subjects of oaths, vows, and lots, are naturally suggested in this connection, they may perhaps as well be considered when we come to the third commandment.

## XII. LET US BRIEFLY CONSIDER CHURCH GOVERNMENT AND DISCIPLINE.

These are expressly instituted by Christ himself, Matt. xvi. 19; Matt. xviii. 15–20. Nor are we at liberty to invest particular persons with power over their brethren in the ministry of the gospel. Matt. xx. 25–28. God has appointed all the officers who shall bear rule in his house, both ordinary and extraordinary. 1 Cor. xii. 28; Eph. iv. 11. The use of discipline and the general principles by which it is to be administered are alike determined by the word of God. Matt. xviii. 15–17; 1 Cor. v. 4, 5; 1 Tim. v. 20. While it is sinful, therefore, to oppose church discipline in any of its proper ends, we are not at liberty, on the other hand, to make men lords of our faith. God's genuine servants disclaim all dominion in his house in this matter. 1 Cor. iii. 5; 2 Cor. i. 24; 1 Pet. v. 3. Nor are we at liberty to yield, even for an hour, to those who would usurp such lordship over us. Gal. ii. 5.

### XIII. HOW THE CHURCH OF ROME BREAKS THIS COMMANDMENT BY SUPERSTITION.

Johnson defines superstition to be "Unnecessary fear or scruples in religion; observance of unnecessary or uncommanded rites or practices; religion without morality." Brown defines it to be "Excessive exactness or rigour in religious opinions or practice: extreme and unnecessary scruples in the observance of religious rites not commanded, or of points of minor importance; excess or extravagance in religion; the doing of things not required by God, or abstaining from things not forbidden; or the belief of what is absurd, or belief without evidence." Perhaps a still more exact definition is "The observance of unnecessary and uncommanded rites in religion; reverence for objects not fit for worship; scruples about matters lawful or indifferent; and extravagant devotions."

Superstition is almost always connected with a strange credulity on some points, and a singular incredulity on others. It is often solemn respecting what is unimportant or even ludicrous, and is yet irreverent and frivolous on at least some solemn subjects and occasions. It is exceedingly dangerous. Robert Hall: "Enthusiasm is an evil much less tc be dreaded than *superstition.* Superstition is the disease of nations; enthusiasm that of individuals; the former grows inveterate by time, the latter is cured by it." John Owen: "As superstition is an undue fear of the divine nature, will, and operations, built on false notions and apprehensions of them, it may befal the minds of men in all religions, true and false. It is an internal vice of the mind." All superstition is based upon ignorance more or less gross. Minds not capable of close and just discrimination are peculiarly liable to it. A carnal state of the heart works up the imagination, and the fleshly mind seizes with great vigour upon its own conceptions. When one has not been made wise by God's word, and the affections become highly excited, plausible pretences are sufficient to mislead. Once enlisted in the cause of superstition, self-love causes persistence in it. Having some persuasion that holiness is essential, and the natural heart rising in opposition to the requirements of God's law, the excited mind perversely seeks out some method whereby to delude itself into the persuasion that it is holy. The growth of superstition is by a very gradual process. Its whole history is written in three words, *little by little.* The only sure defence against it is the true knowledge and genuine love of God, accompanied by a firm determination to do what he commands, to worship as he directs, and to follow human devisings in nothing. "This is the fountain and principle of all error, that men think that those modes of worship which please them, must needs please God; and what displeaseth them, must also displease him."

Surely these principles are clear; God alone has a right to state how he will be worshipped; his word is the only means by which we can know his will; his word clearly forbids all attempts to alter his worship, Ex. xxiii. 13; Deut. iv. 2; Gal. iv. 10, 11; and the great business of God's church is to defend his truth, and service from all corruption, Phil. i. 7, 17; Jude 3; Rev. iii. 10. Let the church do her duty.

Having previously noticed the breaking of the second commandment by the church of Rome through her idolatry, let us now see how she breaks it by her superstition. There is superstition in all idolatry; but there is not necessarily idolatry in all superstition.

1. The Romish church is guilty of superstition in conducting her worship in an unknown tongue. In Italy, in Spain, in France, in England, in China, among the Indians of North America, indeed wherever her priests are found, they offer public devotions in Latin, which is now nowhere a living language. Even in Rome, it is no better understood by the common people than it is in America. It is mere mummery to pretend to worship God by the use of words which convey no idea whatever to the mind of the assembly. If I render to God a service which I do not understand, how can it be a *reasonable* service? If it be not intelligent, how does it differ from the unmeaning chattering of swallows, or a cawing of rooks? The Bible has settled this question. Paul insists upon it that the edification of the church requires that the language used in her worship should be understood.

The quotation is from the Douay Bible: "He that speaketh in a tongue, edifieth himself; but he that prophesieth, edifieth the church. And I would have you all to speak with tongues, but rather to prophesy. For greater is he that prophesieth, than he that speaketh with tongues; unless, perhaps, he interpret, that the church may receive edification. But now, brethren, if I come to you, speaking with tongues, what shall I profit you, unless I speak to you either in revelation, or in knowledge, or in prophecy, or in doctrine? Even things without life that give sound, whether pipe or harp, except they give a distinction of sounds, how shall it be known what is piped or harped? For if the trumpet give an uncertain sound, who shall prepare himself to battle? So likewise you, unless you utter by the tongue plain speech, how shall it be known what is spoken? For you shall be speaking into the air. There are, for example, so many kinds of tongues in this world: and none is without a voice. If then I know not the power of the voice, I shall be to him, to whom I speak, a barbarian, and he that speaketh, a barbarian to me. So you also, forasmuch as you are zealous of spirits, seek to abound unto the edifying of the church. And, therefore, let him that speaketh a tongue, pray that he may interpret. For if I pray in a tongue, my spirit prayeth, but my understanding is without fruit. What is it then? I will pray in the spirit; I will pray also in the understanding: I will sing with the spirit; I will sing also with the understanding. Else if thou shalt bless in the spirit, how shall he that holdeth the place of the unlearned say Amen to thy blessing? because he knoweth not what thou sayest.

For thou indeed givest thanks well: but the other is not edified. I thank my God, I speak with all your tongues. But in the church I had rather speak five words with my understanding, that I may instruct others also; than ten thousand words in a tongue. Brethren, do not become children in sense; but in malice be children; and in sense be perfect." 1 Cor. xiv. 2–20. The church of Rome feels this passage to be very condemnatory of her conduct; so there must needs be a *note* affixed declaring herself free from violating it. The note is indeed wonderful. It is on the word, *Amen*, found in the sixteenth verse, and is in these words: "*Amen.* The unlearned not knowing that ye are then blessing will not be qualified to join with you by saying Amen to your blessing. The use or abuse of strange tongues, of which the Apostle here speaks, does not regard the public liturgy of the church, (in which strange tongues were never used) but certain conferences of the faithful, v. 26, &c., in which, meeting together, they discovered to one another their various and miraculous gifts of the Spirit, common in those primitive times; amongst which the apostle prefers that of prophesying, before that of speaking strange tongues, because it was more to the public edification. Where also note, that the Latin used in our Liturgy, is so far from being a strange or unknown tongue, that it is perhaps the best known tongue in the world." Whew!!!

But do Romanists assign no reason for this practice that converts public worship into gross superstition? The answer is, they do not, except such as sets aside the word of God. A private member of that communion being asked, Why the Liturgy was kept in a dead language? replied, "The devil does not understand Latin." Whether this is a general opinion need not now be determined. But Reynolds Scott, a writer of great learning, says, "Our witching writers saie that divells speake onelie the language of that countrie where they are resiant, [resident,] as French, or English," &c.

But must the people be kept from worshipping God understandingly, for fear the devil will know what is going on? And is it so certain, after all, that Satan is excluded from assemblies where the Latin is used?

Some learned Papists tell us of the "numberless, barbarous, half-formed, and daily changing languages of modern Europe;" and ask, would it have been respectful, or secure, or prudent, or practicable, to have their Liturgy in these languages? The answer is, Why not? The prophets, and Christ and the apostles, used the vernacular of the people to whom they spoke in their day. No part of the Bible was originally written in the Latin. Romanists have translated both Testaments into English. If God's word may lawfully be in our language, why may not the Roman Missal also? But the whole question is settled by God himself. In the passage already cited from Paul, it is shown that a religious service, conducted either in speaking, singing, or praying, in a language not understood by the congregation, is to be avoided, and that God's servants must earnestly desire gifts whereby they may edify the people.

2. The use of relics in the church of Rome clearly proves the power and extent of superstition in that communion. Till of late, relics made but little noise in the United States. But no doubt we shall hear

very soon and commonly of wonders performed by means of some old rag, or tooth, or bone, said once to have belonged to some one now esteemed a saint. In Rome itself, "they show the heads of St. Peter and St. Paul, encased in silver busts, set with jewels; a lock of the Virgin Mary's hair, a phial of her tears, a piece of her green petticoat, a robe of Jesus Christ sprinkled with his blood, some drops of his blood in a bottle, some of the water which flowed out of the wound in his side, some of the sponge, a large piece of the cross, all the nails used in the crucifixion, a piece of the stone of the sepulchre on which the angel sat, the identical porphyry pillar on which the cock perched when he crowed after Peter denied Christ, the rods of Moses and Aaron, and two pieces of the real ark of the covenant." Volumes might be filled with simiiar statements. In the Mass House at Dobborane, in Mechlenburg, Nugent says, they show the following relics: "1. Flax for spinning, which belonged to the Virgin Mary. 2. Hay, which the wise men had for their camels and left behind them at Bethlehem. 3. A piece of the garment of Lazarus. 4. A piece of linen worn by the Virgin Mary. 5. A piece of the head of Tobit's fish. 6. A part of Judas' bowels that fell out. 7. The scissors with which Delilah cut off Samson's hair. 8. A piece of the apron which the butcher wore when he killed the fatted calf for the feast of the prodigal son. 9. One of the five stones which David put in his sling when he went out to meet Goliath. 10. The branch of the tree on which Absalom hung by the hair. 11. A part of Peter's fishing net. 12. The heads of the apostles Thomas, Peter, and Paul."

3. In like manner one might refer to the super stitious use of charms, by which the Romish church leads those in her communion to expect to avoid or expel certain natural evils, asserting her authority over noxious insects by means of holy water and certain other superstitious acts and doings.

4. The Romish church makes also high, though false pretences to the power of working miracles. The Catholic Herald, of Feb. 1, 1844, intimated an expectation that some miracles might ere long be wrought at the graves of two deceased Roman bishops in this country. How perfectly idle all these claims are, it is not necessary here to discuss. Not one of them is accompanied by such evidences as to satisfy a reasonable spirit of inquiry.

5. Nor are the tortures self-inflicted by members of the Romish church less superstitious. But enough of these disgusting themes.

# CHAPTER XVI.

## THE THIRD COMMANDMENT.

THOU SHALT NOT TAKE THE NAME OF THE LORD THY GOD IN VAIN; FOR THE LORD WILL NOT HOLD HIM GUILTLESS THAT TAKETH HIS NAME IN VAIN.

THE verb *take*, found in this commandment, occurs very often in the Bible. It is also rendered *take up*, *take away*, *bear*, *bring*, *bring forth*, *stir*, *lift up*, *fetch*, *set up*. Here, and in many other places, it has the sense of *use* or *employ*.

The *name of God* is a phrase of frequent occurrence in the Bible. Few words are employed in more varied senses than the word *name;* and yet there is seldom difficulty in ascertaining its precise signification. The name of God stands 1, for his proper name, as *Jehovah*, *God*, *the Most High*, *the Almighty*, *I am what I am*, &c., Deut. iv. 35; vi. 4; Num. xxiv. 16; Rev. i. 8; 2, for his titles, as *Creator*, *Shepherd*, *Saviour*, *Redeemer*, &c., Eccles. xii. 1; Ps. xxiii. 1; Isa. xliii. 11; Ps. xix. 14; 3, for his attributes or perfections, Ex. xxxiii. 19; xxxiv. 6, 7; 1 Tim. vi. 1; 4, for his word, Ps. cxxxviii. 2; Acts ix. 15; 5, for his grace and mercy shown to sinners through Christ,

John xvii. 6, 26; 6, for his help and assistance, 1 Sam. xvii. 45; Ps. xliv. 6; 7, for his honour, Ps. lxxvi. 1, and in many places; 8, for the display of his perfections in the works of creation, Ps. viii. 1, 9; 9, for the illustration of his attributes in providence, Ps. xx. 1, 7; 10, for his worship and service, 1 Kings v. 5; Ex. xx. 24; 11, for God himself, Ps. xxxiv. 3; lxi. 5; Prov. xviii. 10. The name of the Lord therefore is either Jehovah himself, or any thing whereby he is known. Hopkins: "It is not an unusual figure to put the name for the thing or person that is expressed by it." Any thing relating to the true God, his being, his nature, his will, his works, his worship, any thing relating to the service rendered him, or to the doctrine concerning him, pertains to his *name*.

The phrase *the* LORD *thy God* has been explained in the preface to the ten commandments.

The word rendered *in vain* is a noun. It occurs nearly fifty times in the Hebrew Bible. The Lexicons define it, *evil*, *iniquity*, *wickedness*, *falsehood*, *emptiness*, *vanity*, *nothingness*. Twice in this commandment it is rendered *in vain;* twice also in Deut. v. 11, and once in Ps. cxxvii. 1, and cxxxix. 20. Its most comprehensive meaning is *vanity*. It is often so rendered, Job vii. 3, xv. 31, xxxi. 5, xxxv. 13; Ps. xii. 2, xli. 6; Isa. v. 18, xxx. 28. It is frequently rendered *vain*, and several times *false* or *lying;* Ex. xxiii. 1; Deut. v. 20; Ps. xxxi. 6; Jonah ii. 8. Some render the prohibition of this commandment thus: *Thou shalt not utter the name of Jehovah unto a falsehood.* The original fully bears this translation. Perhaps it is better than that of the common [illegible]n. As in other commandments, God may here design to condemn the most atrocious form of a given species of sin. But if we follow the common rendering, which is good, we at once give to the commandment a wider scope. If we may not use God's name in a light and frivolous manner, surely we may not use it in vindication of our wicked falsehoods. A great design of true religion is to bring men to habitual and controlling reverence for the divine majesty. "Neither shall ye profane my holy name; but I will be hallowed among the children of Israel: I am the Lord which hallow you." Levit. xxii. 32. "If thou wilt not observe to do all the words of this law that are written in this book, that thou mayest fear this glorious and fearful name, THE LORD THY GOD; then the LORD will make thy plagues wonderful." Deut. xxviii. 58, 59. "God is greatly to be feared in the assembly of the saints, and to be had in reverence of all them that are about him." Ps. lxxxix. 7. "Holy and reverend is his name." Ps. cxi. 9. When our Lord gave us an outline of ordinary prayer, the first petition was, "Hallowed be thy name." Indeed all religious service, which does not hallow the name of God, or which is without godly fear, is miserable trifling. The inhabitants of heaven are much purer and more elevated than we. Yet when they sing the song of Moses, the servant of God, and the song of the Lamb, they say, "Great and marvellous are thy works, Lord God Almighty; just and true are thy ways, thou King of saints. Who shall not fear thee, O Lord, and glorify thy name? for thou only art holy." Rev. xv. 3, 4.

To take God's name in vain, therefore, is to use it in any frivolous, false, inconsiderate, irreverent, or otherwise wicked manner. Hare: "This may be done in two ways; either by calling God to witness a lie,—for lies and falsehoods of all kinds are in many places of Scripture called vanity; or else it may be done by using that holy Name on small and irreverent occasions; for light and empty things are also called vanity."

The scope of this commandment is to secure the holy and reverent use of all that whereby God makes himself known to his people; and so to guard his sacred name against all that is calculated to make it contemptible.

These things enter into the very essence of obedience to the requirements of this precept.

1. That we propose the glory of God, the good of our fellow-men, or the defence of ourselves, in all cases when we take the name of God upon our lips. Josh. vii. 19; Heb. vi. 16; Ex. xxii. 11.

2. Of course the manner of so taking his name is to be grave, solemn, intelligent, aforethought, and with godly fear.

3. We should not use the name of God, where there is no fitness or necessity; even in prayer it should not be employed to fill up our vacancies of thought. Nor should we use it in swearing, or in casting lots, where the matter can be otherwise properly adjusted.

4. We are not at liberty to use God's name in any way to promote superstition, false doctrine, perjury, blasphemy, profanity, cursing, or any such thing. We must therefore see to it, that what we propose to promote by the use of God's name is something which he approves.

Just reflection must satisfy any good man that the non-observance of this commandment would utterly subvert all true religion. The very moment mankind cease to believe that God is holy, that moment their worship becomes polluted. When God's creatures come into his presence with thoughtless familiarity, forgetting that he is in heaven, and they upon earth, they will surely lightly esteem the Rock of their salvation. The world furnishes no case of a despiser of the third commandment, who is not guilty of gross breaches of one or more of the other precepts of the moral law. There is not a country having written statutes but has ordained heavy penalties against one or more of the sins clearly condemned in this commandment.

In answer to the question, *what is required in the third commandment*, the Westminster Assembly answers, "The third commandment requires, that the name of God, his titles, attributes, ordinances, the word, sacraments, prayer, oaths, vows, lots, his works, and whatsoever else there is whereby he makes himself known, be holily and reverently used in thought, meditation, word, and writing; by an holy profession, and answerable conversation, to the glory of God, and the good of ourselves and others." Further note.

That this commandment extends to the state of men's hearts, is clear, from the fact that God commends those who rightly *think upon* his name and *meditate* on his works. Mal. iii. 16; Ps. viii. 1–9. That it includes our speech, is clear from Ps. cv. 2, 5; Mal. iii. 16; Col. iii. 17. That we are as much bound to honour God by our pen as by our tongue, is evident from the nature of the case, and from Ps. cii.

18. This precept binds us to a holy profession of the true religion. We are required to be always ready to give an answer to every man that asketh us a reason of the hope that is in us, with meekness and fear. 1 Pet. iii. 15. All men are bound to adopt the good resolution of the church in the days of Micah: "We will walk in the name of the LORD our God for ever and ever." Micah iv. 5. Nor should this profession be light or inconsistent. Our whole deportment must be as it becometh the gospel of Christ. Phil. i. 27; Rom. x. 10; 1 Pet. ii. 12; Luke i. 6; Rev. xiv. 1.

It is not necessary here to repeat remarks previously made on the right use of God's word, the sacraments, prayer, praise, fasting, and the government and discipline of the church, as those subjects came up in considering the first and second commandments. But as those matters belong also to the requirements of this precept, let them be regarded with new and increased solemnity; and let all the principles here elucidated, be applied to them.

The general spirit of this command requires us to keep at the greatest possible distance from mingling in our doctrines, affections, or thoughts, the name of the true God with any corruption whatever. The Lord forbade the Israelites to make any mention of the name of other gods or to let it be heard out of their mouth. Ex. xxiii. 13. The meaning of the prohibition evidently was, that they should keep their minds as pure as possible from the contamination of familiarity with heathenism. For the same reason, no doubt, God required the Israelites utterly to destroy all the places where the heathen had served their gods, upon the high mountains, and upon the hills, and under every green tree; and to overthrow their altars and break their pillars and burn their groves with fire, and hew down the graven images of their gods, and destroy the names of them, Deut. xii. 2, 3. In the days of Joshua, Israel was again forbidden to make mention of the name of these false gods, Josh. xxiii. 7. And when God promises a revived and healthful state of religion to his church, he says, "I will take away the names of Baalim out of her mouth, and they shall no more be remembered by their name." Hos. ii. 17. And still more explicitly, God says by the mouth of Paul, "It is a shame even to speak of those things which are done of them in secret." Eph. v. 12.

The reverent use of God's name requires all the attributes of acceptable worship, as stated at length in the foregoing pages; that is, we must have faith and love, and fear and godly sincerity, and singleness of heart, &c., &c.

It is clearly implied in this commandment that we do not keep it by observing a profound silence respecting the Almighty. Though we are not to take the name of God *in vain*, we are still to *take it*. More than once in Scripture, are pious men described as those who make mention of the Lord. Isa. xxvi. 13, xlviii. 1, lxii. 6. There may be sinful silence respecting God as well as a profane use of his name.

Besides acts of worship already discussed, it is proper here to call special attention to some things immediately suggested by this commandment.

### I. SOLEMN OATHS.

Swearing is an appeal to God as a witness to the truth of what we say. It is always accompanied with an expressed or implied imprecation of his curse, or renunciation of his favour, if we perform not our oath. It is therefore a very solemn act of worship. The form of the oath is different in different ages and countries. All forms are an appeal to God. Some are more decent or appropriate than others; but our laws properly leave every one to select that which in his own judgment is most becoming. The binding obligation of an oath is in no wise diminished by the form of its administration. Abraham's servant swore to his master by putting his own hand under his master's thigh. Gen. xxiv. 2. Another form mentioned in Scripture is that of lifting up the hand towards heaven. Rev. x. 5. But the word of God binds us to no particular form. Whatever be the mode of administration, let us not forget that the essence of an oath consists in a solemn appeal to God as the Searcher of hearts and the Judge of quick and dead. It either expresses or implies a declaration that we are willing God should subject us to his dreadful curse, if we swear falsely. The proper use of an oath is the termination of strife concerning matters which cannot otherwise be adjusted. Heb. vi. 16. Oaths are authorized by the example of God, who swears by himself as he can swear by none greater. Gen. xxii. 16. Isa. xlv. 23. Jer. xlix. 13. Amos vi. 8. Oaths are sinful when they are not necessary or called for by proper authority. It deserves the consideration of all, who have the control of the administration of public justice, whether the great number and frequency of oaths do not seriously impair their sanctity in the public mind, and thus wound justice, morals and religion. The lax observance of oaths is a very painful subject. Still, the slight regard paid to them argues nothing against their lawfulness. Every well-instructed Christian ought to be willing to worship God in this as well as in other appointed ways. Our Saviour himself allowed an oath to be administered to him by the High Priest. Matt. xxvi. 63, 64. Paul uses forms of expression which have the nature of an oath: "I call God for a record upon my soul," 2 Cor. i. 23; "God is my record," Phil. i. 8; "I say the truth in Christ, I lie not," Rom. ix. 1. We have at least one example of a holy angel swearing: "The angel which I saw stand upon the sea and upon the earth, lifted up his hand to heaven, and swore by him that liveth for ever and ever, who created heaven, and the things that therein are, and the earth," &c. Rev. x. 5, 6. It is promised in the Old Testament that in the latter days this mode of worshipping God shall prevail. "To me every tongue shall swear," says God. Isa. xlv. 23. "He that sweareth shall swear by the God of truth." Isa. lxv. 16. "Thou shalt swear, The Lord liveth in truth." Jer. iv. 2. Those Scriptures therefore which forbid swearing evidently refer to passionate, unnecessary, common or profane swearing.

Swearing is either lawful or unlawful. Unlawful swearing will be considered hereafter. Lawful swearing is always a solemn act. It is an acknowledgment of the omniscience, truth, and justice of the Most High. Commonly it is required by the laws of the land. Yet there may be cases where one may receive from another the confirmation of a promise by an oath.

This subject is much spoken of in the Scriptures. The general law respecting swearing is that it be done by an appeal to the true God, and in truth, in judgment, and in righteousness. Jer. iv. 2. To appeal to any but the true God is an insult to the Heavenly Majesty. If the act is performed with any devoutness of feeling, it is idolatry; if with levity of mind, it is profaneness. God's word carefully enjoins that our appeal should be to Jehovah. Isa. lxv. 16; Jer. xii. 16; Zeph. i. 5. Then we must swear *in truth.* The ordinary form of a public oath requires "the truth, the whole truth, and nothing but the truth." We may not ask God to witness to a lie, or to a thing that we do not know to be true. The lips and the conscience must agree. Let all reservations and equivocations be put far from us. Ps. xv. 2, 4. We must also swear in *judgment;* that is, we must understand the nature of an oath; we must have God's fear before us when we swear; and we must know that concerning which we testify. According to Scripture, every *good* man feareth an oath. Eccles. ix. 2. Then we must swear in *righteousness.* The cause in which we testify must be so far just. We may not give evidence to establish iniquity. In swearing we are not at liberty to show partiality to friends, or enmity to foes; but are to speak what truth requires.

No doubt it greatly tends to the honour of God and to the execution of public justice, when the officers of the law administer oaths with due solemnity. We ought to be careful that the matter of every oath is *something possible.* Abraham's servant showed a proper conscientiousness on this subject. Gen. xxiv. 5. Of course the matter of every oath must be *something lawful.* A man can never lawfully or firmly bind himself to do an act of iniquity.

### II. VOWS.

Vows belong to every dispensation of true religion. Gen. xxviii. 20; Isa. xix. 21; Acts xviii. 18. The word *vow* is used in three senses in our language. Sometimes, it is equivalent to worship or devotion, or a public profession of religion. Isa. xliv. 5; Jer. l. 4, 5. Again, it signifies a promise to serve God in a way to which his word obliges us, even before we make the promise. But in the strict sense, a vow is a solemn promise made to God, that we will do something which we were not bound to do till we made the voluntary engagement. Like promises or oaths, vows are either lawful or unlawful according to circumstances. A vow to do a wicked thing is of course wicked. We ought to repent of it and of our sin in making it. God is more honoured in its breach than in its observance. It is a great mercy when God hinders men from fulfilling such vows. This, however, does not diminish the wickedness of making them. A man made a vow that he would never comb his hair till he could wreak his vengeance on an adversary. He never had the opportunity of gratifying his malice, and he never combed his head. But such promises are not properly vows. They are rather curses. Acts xxiii. 12.

Vows are commonly distinguished into conditional and unconditional. Unconditional vows are solemn resolutions that we will do or abstain from doing certain things; as that we will practise certain acts of self-denial, or forego certain lawful indulgences, in order thereby to give to our character more firmness, or the more effectually to keep ourselves from habits of effeminacy. Conditional vows are such as according to their original form are not binding unless God shall perform or cause to be performed some condition annexed. One says to God, "If thou wilt do this or that, I will do thus and so." Thus "Jacob vowed a vow, saying, If God will be with me, and will keep me in this way that I go, and will give me bread to eat, and raiment to put on, so that I come again to my father's house in peace; then shall the LORD be my God, and this stone which I have set for a pillar shall be God's house: and of all that thou shalt give me, I will surely give the tenth unto thee." Gen. xxviii. 20–22. God performed the condition, which the patriarch annexed, and Jacob kept his vow:—a pleasing instance of paternal love on the part of God; and consistent, steadfast piety on the part of his servant. From their very nature, conditional vows are voluntary. They are not required of us by any positive precept of God's word, but, like many things else, are left to the conscience, discretion, thankfulness, zeal, and general piety of each individual. They have a reference to the receipt of future good, in view of which one chooses to bring himself under the sanctions of a solemn promise to prove his gratitude, if the favour shall be granted. When we vow before a good is received, we express our judgment of its value, and the obligations under which the receipt of it will bring us. This helps us to resist the base ingratitude to which we are so prone after mercies have been received. All vows should be kept most conscientiously. "When thou shalt vow a vow unto the LORD thy God, thou shalt not slack to pay it: for the LORD thy God will surely require it of thee: and it would be sin in thee." Deut. xxiii. 21. "When thou vowest a vow unto God, defer not to pay it; for he hath no pleasure in fools: pay that which thou hast vowed. Better is it that thou shouldest not vow, than that thou shouldest vow and not pay. Suffer not thy mouth to cause thy flesh to sin; neither say thou before the angel, that it was an error: wherefore should God be angry at thy voice, and destroy the work of thy hands." Eccles. v. 4–6. "It is a snare to a man after vows to make inquiry." Prov. xx. 25. Vows may be rash, and the fulfilment of them may cost us a great deal; but if they are not wicked we ought to keep them, however hard they may bear upon our pride, or sloth, or covetousness.

### III. THE LOT.

The lot is an appeal to God, to determine a matter which the parties themselves are unable to adjust. It is a confession of the universal providence and particular government of God. "The lot is cast into the lap; but the whole disposing thereof is of the Lord." Prov. xvi. 33. A recognition of this important truth is essential to the lawfulness of the lot in any case. This acknowledgment should be made in a religious and becoming manner; and the lot must be employed only in some grave and important matter, concerning which God's will cannot otherwise be known, or a satisfactory decision cannot otherwise be had. The general design of the lot is very much the same as that of the oath, viz.: the adjustment of difficulties, and the settlement of disputes.

Thus Solomon says: "The lot causeth contentions to cease, and parteth between the mighty." Prov. xviii. 18. Lots are never to be used for divination. We have examples of the use of the lot both in the Old and New Testaments. The whole land of Canaan was thus divided as an inheritance among the descendants of Jacob. Num. xxvi. 55, and xxxiii. 54. The apostles thus chose a successor to Judas, who fell from his office by transgression. Acts i. 26. The lot seems to be taught by the light of nature. Jonah i. 7.

The abuses to which the lot is liable are very great. Vast schemes of lotteries under various pretexts have been introduced into society, and have greatly corrupted the morals of the people. Hardly a more appalling history could be written than that of persons who have become devoted to endeavours at accumulation in this form. When they have been successful, in many cases, reason has tottered and fallen from her throne; or sudden wealth has begotten extravagance and dissipation. But in a larger number of cases, the want of success has driven to crime and then to despair those who have risked much or all in this hazardous scheme.

Gambling by means of lotteries dates as far back as an early period of Roman history. The Republic of Genoa, among the moderns, first resorted to the lottery. It was employed as a state measure for supplying the treasury. Thence it was brought into other countries, especially France and England. The first public lottery known in English history dates as far back as 1567. The institution was soon felt to be injurious and mischievous. Parliament undertook to control it. Through the influence of the mother country, lotteries were introduced into the colonies of North America. After the establishment of the independence of the United States, the system grew by degrees, till it threatened the most alarming consequences. All classes of citizens finally became roused by the extensive ruin wrought by the system. It perpetuated poverty among the humbler classes; it produced much insolvency, many frauds, embezzlements, larcenies and robberies. Its effects on those who drew large prizes were hardly less injurious than on those who drew nothing. It led both classes to intemperance and suicide. In one of the large cities of the North, some years since, the feelings of the community were most painfully and indignantly excited by the case of Mr. A. He had been for ten years the "chief clerk in one of the first importing houses in the city; and to the hour of his death he enjoyed the unbounded confidence of his employers.

"His character for integrity and purity was unsullied. Modest and amiable in his manners, temperate and domestic in his habits, he was endeared to all who knew him as one without a vice.

"When the distressing tidings were first spread abroad, that he had been found dead, not the most distant suspicion was entertained that he had ended—that he *could* have ended his quiet existence by his own act. The rumour which momentarily prevailed, that he had been robbed and *murdered*, was received, it is true, with horror, but with implicit confidence;

nor was it until the fatal evidence of his rashness was found in his own hurried hand-writing, that they who had known, and loved, and trusted him so long, were made to feel that he had cruelly deceived them; and that in the distraction of remorse he had attempted to atone for one crime by committing another—the darkest crime of all. . . . In the short space between seven and eight months, he embezzled the sum of $18,000, every cent of which was lost on lottery tickets."

This unfortunate man became so tortured in mind that he resolved on self-destruction. In his desk, after his death, a paper was found, probably written very shortly before the fearful deed which ushered him into the presence of his Judge. "It is a simple picture of human woe. In its untutored language, we see to what a depth of wretchedness, one false step reduced a man upon whose whole life before, not a blot had rested."

(*Copy.*)

"I have for the last *seven months* gone fast down the broad road to destruction.

"There was a time, and that too but a few months since, that I was happy, because I was free from debt and care.

"The time I note my downfall, or deviation from the path of rectitude, was about the middle of June last, when I took a share in a company of lottery tickets, whereby I was successful in obtaining a share of one half the capital prize; since which I have gone for myself, and that too, not on a very small scale, as you can judge from the amount now due J. R. & Co., every dollar of which has been spent in that way.

"I have lived or dragged out a miserable existence for two or three months past. Sleepless nights and a guilty conscience have led me on to the fatal act.

"Only the hope of making Messrs. J. R. & Co. good for the defalcation has postponed it till the present time; a smaller amount, I did hope, would be the result, for the worse luck I had the more I bought.

"Since I have reflected on my rashness, I cannot look back, and see how it is possible I could have conducted in this way. When the situation I occupied, and the confidence reposed in me, and the long time I have been engaged, and the reward for my poor services by ——, that all should be lost in one moment—but the loss is too much for me to bear.

"Oh! that seven or eight months past of my existence could be blotted out—but no, I must go—and ere this paper is read my spirit is gone to my Maker, to give an account of my misdeeds here, and receive the dreadful sentence for self-destruction and abuse of confidence.

"Relatives and friends I have, from whom I do not wish to part under such circumstances, but neces sity ——

"Oh, wretch! *Lotteries* have been my ruin. I cannot add more."

Let all who have influence in controlling public affairs, either on a large or small scale, see to it that so corrupting an institution gain no footing in the community.

Those amusements called games of *chance*, if they are indeed such, are liable to the same objection. If there is any thing put at stake, God has already in the regular way of his providence made known his will concerning the property that is thus staked. Rev. Eliphalet Nott, D. D., President of Union College, has testified to the world that even a young gambler has been so hardened as to play at cards on the coffin of his dead brother. And the Gospels tell us that the Roman soldiers went to gambling at the foot of the cross of the Redeemer.

## IV. DOXOLOGIES.

It is not without cause that some have expressed surprise that doxologies were so little used in social and public worship, in the pulpit and in the choir. True, we often have them sung at the close of public worship, but they ought to be *said* as well as *sung*. In printed works, and in familiar letters, they ought to occur more frequently. So the Bible would teach. In the Old Testament doxologies abound. A literary friend lately collected a list of doxologies from the Old Testament. Those who saw it were constrained to admit that too little attention was paid to this branch of worship.

It seems to be forgotten by some that we have a rich variety of doxologies in the New Testament also. So that they belong no less to Christian than to Jewish worship.

The outburst of holy joy in the mother of our Lord was of the nature of a doxology. That of Zacharias was so in form; Luke i. 46–55, and 68–79. So also Simeon's song over the infant Jesus was a doxology; Luke ii. 28–32. In like manner, "praising and blessing God" was a good part of the work of the disciples between Christ's resurrection and the day of Pentecost. So in the triumphant entry of Christ into Jerusalem, the people uttered the loud shout, "Hosanna! Blessed is the King of Israel, that cometh in the name of the Lord."

But it is in the Epistles and in Revelation that we have the fullest and most formal doxologies. Thus, in Romans xvi. 25–27, we find the following, than which we could hardly conceive any thing more fit to bring in at the close of a missionary sermon, or a discourse on the excellence of the gospel: "Now to him that is of power to establish you according to my gospel, and the preaching of Jesus Christ, according to the revelation of the mystery, which was kept secret since the world began, but now is made manifest, and by the Scriptures of the prophets, according to the commandment of the everlasting God, made known to all nations for the obedience of faith: to God only wise, be glory through Jesus Christ for ever. Amen." As no one now living can fitly say "*my gospel*" a change may there be made, and we may say "*the blessed gospel*," or "*the glorious gospel.*"

Another very precious doxology is found in Ephesians i. 3–6, "Blessed be the God and Father of our Lord Jesus Christ, who hath blessed us with all spiritual blessings in heavenly places in Christ: according as he hath chosen us in him before the foundation of the world, that we should be holy and without blame before him in love; having predestinated us unto the adoption of children by Jesus Christ to himself, according to the good pleasure of his will, to the praise of the glory of his grace." Observe—1. This doxology was written by Paul, a prisoner. No chains, or bars, or stripes, could repress his adoring praises. 2. We may have all "spiritual blessings," when we have few or no temporal blessings. 3. When the scriptural doctrine of election and predestination offends people, it is either because they misunderstand it, or because their hearts are not right. It filled Paul with praise, and it is honourable to God. It is conducive to *holiness*.

The same Epistle to the Ephesians (iii. 20, 21) contains another precious doxology: "Now unto him that is able to do exceeding abundantly above all that we ask or think, according to the power that worketh in us, unto him be glory in the church by Jesus Christ, throughout all ages, world without end. Amen." On this notice—1. That God's *ability* fairly implies his *willingness*. 2. That no difficulties to us are hinderances to God. 3. That no words, no thoughts of ours, ever rise to the dignity of the blessedness reserved for saints. 4. That the whole plan of salvation shall eternally and more and more redound to God's honour.

The doxology in 1 Tim. i. 17, is very sublime: "Now unto the King eternal, immortal, invisible, the only wise God, be honour and glory for ever and ever. Amen." I marvel not that the chanting of this in some of our churches produces so marked an effect on the audience. In each of his Epistles the apostle of the Circumcision has a short doxology: "To him [the God of all grace] be glory and dominion for ever and ever. Amen." 1 Pet. v. 11. "To him [our Lord and Saviour Jesus Christ] be glory both now and for ever. Amen." 2 Pet. iii. 18.

The doxology in Jude 24, 25, is very full and very

consolatory: "Now unto him that is able to keep you from falling, and to present you faultless before the presence of his glory with exceeding joy, to the only wise God our Saviour, be glory and majesty, dominion and power, both now and ever. Amen." Could brighter or more glorious prospects be presented? Could *glory to God* be more fitly sung than in view of such prospects?

But the Apocalypse excels all the books of the New Testament in the ardour, variety and copiousness of its doxologies. See Rev. i. 5, 6, iv. 11, v. 12, 13, and vii. 12. "Unto him that loved us, and washed us from our sins in his own blood, and hath made us kings and priests unto God and his Father; to him be glory and dominion for ever and ever. Amen." "Thou art worthy, O Lord, to receive glory and honour and power: for thou hast created all things, and for thy pleasure they are and were created." "Worthy is the Lamb that was slain to receive power, and riches, and wisdom, and strength, and honour, and glory, and blessing." "Blessing, and honour, and glory, and power, be unto him that sitteth upon the throne, and unto the Lamb for ever and ever." "Amen: Blessing, and glory, and wisdom, and thanksgiving, and honour, and power, and might, be unto our God for ever and ever. Amen." These doxologies clearly show—1. That the worship of heaven is, *in substance*, the same as the worship of earth; and 2. That the honours paid to the Father in heaven and on earth are properly paid to the Son. So that if men have no heart to love and praise the Son, they do not love the Father; and if they have no heart for spiritual worship here, neither would they have if taken to heaven.

Other forms of doxology are found in the New Testament. Let them be sought out, and studied. If we shall be saved, doxology will be our work eternally. Will not the ministers of Christ more abound in doxology, at least in the conclusion of public worship?

### V. BENEDICTIONS.

Another act of worship is blessing the people. A benediction is the ministerial and authoritative pronunciation of a blessing upon the people in the name of the Lord, and is therefore not merely or chiefly the expression of the private wishes of the minister.

The ordinary blessing of the Jewish dispensation, used by the priests to each worshipper, who had brought his offering, and to the congregation of Israel was: "The LORD bless thee, and keep thee: The Lord make his face to shine upon thee: The LORD lift up his countenance upon thee, and give thee peace." This form is very full and very precious. The original of the word LORD is *Jehovah*—a name applied to the Father, Son and Holy Ghost. From its being repeated thrice, as the word *Holy* is in Isaiah vi. 3, some have thought there was an allusion to the doctrine of the Trinity. Perhaps there may be. The Father, Son and Holy Spirit are the one, self-existent, independent, eternal and unchangeable *Jehovah* revealed in Scripture. This form is used as a salutatory in opening the worship of some of our churches.

The forms of benediction in the New Testament are numerous, various and very precious. Of the twenty-one epistles, five do not *close* with a benediction. These are the epistle of James, of 2d Peter, the 1st and 2d epistles of John and the epistle of Jude.

James nowhere has any form of blessing. In the *opening* of his second epistle, Peter has this form: "Grace and peace be multiplied unto you through the knowledge of God, and of Jesus our Lord." So, near the beginning of his second epistle, John says: "Grace be with you, mercy and peace from God the Father, and from the Lord Jesus Christ, the Son of the Father, in truth and love." So also Jude, at the beginning, says: "Mercy unto you, and peace and love be multiplied." So that there are but two epistles in the Bible entirely without some form of benediction. These are James and 1st John. The shortest benediction in the Bible is that of 3d John: "Peace be with thee." In Colossians we have: "Grace be with you. Amen." In Titus we have: "Grace be with you all. Amen." In Peter we have: "Peace be with you all that are in Christ Jesus. Amen." In 1st Timothy we have: "The grace of our Lord Jesus Christ be with thee. Amen." In Philemon we read: "The grace of our Lord Jesus Christ be with your spirit. Amen." In 2d Timothy it is: "The Lord Jesus Christ be with thy spirit. Grace be with you. Amen." In Romans, Philippians, and 2d Thessalonians, it is: "The grace of our Lord Jesus Christ be with you all. Amen." In 1st Corinthians it is: "The grace of our Lord Jesus Christ be with you." In 1st Thessalonians it is the same, with the addition of the *amen*. In Galatians the apostle says, "Brethren, the grace of our Lord Jesus Christ be with your spirit. Amen." In Ephesians he says: "Grace be with all them that love our Lord Jesus Christ in sincerity. Amen." In Hebrews we have two forms of blessing in the last chapter. The last is the same as that in Titus. The other is exceedingly rich, and might be appropriately used with much greater frequency than it is: "Now the God of peace, that brought again from the dead our Lord Jesus, that great Shepherd of the sheep, through the blood of the everlasting covenant, make you perfect in every good work to do his will, working in you that which is well pleasing in his sight, through Jesus Christ; to whom be glory for ever and ever. Amen." In 2d Corinthians we have what has often been called by way of pre-eminence, *the* apostolic benediction, though it is no more entitled to that designation than others. Yet it is rich and full: "The grace of our Lord Jesus Christ, and the love of God, and the communion of the Holy Ghost be with you all. Amen." But the fullest form of benediction is that given by John in Rev. i. 4, 5. "Grace be unto you, and peace, from him which is, and which was, and which is to come; and from the seven Spirits which are before his throne, and from Jesus Christ, who is the faithful Witness, and the First begotten from the dead, and the prince of the kings of the earth."

Besides these *seventeen* forms of blessing, we have in the beginning of *ten* of Paul's epistles this form of blessing: "Grace to you and peace from God our Father, and the Lord Jesus Christ;" and in each of his three pastoral epistles this form: "Grace, mercy and peace from God our Father and Jesus Christ our Lord."

Thus we have nineteen forms of benediction given us in the New Testament. Ought they not all to be used? Why should ministers confine themselves to one, that in 2 Corinthians, xiii. 14? It is precious indeed, but no more so than several others. Some of the others have also peculiar appropriateness to special occasions. The last thing said in the Bible is a benediction. "The grace of our Lord Jesus Christ be with you all. Amen."

The Hebrew form of blessing was: "Mercy to you;" the Greek, "Grace to you;" and the Roman, "Peace to you." Paul uses them all, and tells us whence they come, even "from God the Father and from our Lord Jesus Christ."

Interpreters are in doubt whether the phrase, "through the blood of the everlasting covenant," in Heb. xiii. 20, qualifies one of the preceding clauses or that next succeeding, or whether it has special reference to the word *great*, meaning that the Shepherd of the sheep is *great* through the blood of the everlasting covenant. Why may it not refer to all these?

By "the seven spirits" in Rev. i. 4, is meant the Holy Spirit, *seven* being the number of perfection, and the Holy Ghost being the absolute perfection of spiritual existence.

Generally the benedictions are plain. Let them all be studied and used at appropriate times. A part of God's worship in every dispensation has been blessing the people in his name.

### VI. CARE AND THE FEAR OF GOD IN THE USE OF SPEEECH, AND IN MAKING IMPRESSIONS ON OUR FELLOW MEN.

He who has so little reverence for the Most High as carelessly to utter whatever comes into his mind, whether it be true or false, will not be long in becoming a gross violater of this commandment. The subject is now merely hinted at. So also whatever use is made of God's name should be sincere. We should never employ it to deceive our fellow-men, to make an impression that we are pious and so trustworthy, and thus lead men to confide in us.

This commandment clearly forbids the following sins.

### I. BLASPHEMY.

In Scripture language, to blaspheme is to reproach or revile either God or man. 1 Kings xxi. 10. But for a long time, blasphemy in the English language designates an offence against God. Dr. George Campbell says, "*Blasphemy* invariably implies an expression of contempt or detestation, and a desire of producing the same passions in others." Linwood says, "Blasphemy is an injury offered to God, by denying that which is due and belonging to him, or attributing to him what is not agreeable to his nature." Blackstone defines it as a crime "against the Almighty, by denying his being or providence; or by contumelious reproaches of our Saviour Christ. Whither also may be referred all profane scoffing at the holy Scripture, or exposing it to contempt and ridicule." In the Apocalypse, John describes the great beast as "having a mouth, speaking great things and blasphemies." "And he opened his mouth in blasphemy against God, to blaspheme his name, and his tabernacle, and them that dwell in heaven." Rev. xiii. 6. According to modern usage, intelligence, scorn and malignity against God are essential to the commission of this crime. In some of the states of North America, legal blasphemy is punishable at common law. See the 8th vol. of Johnson's Reports, the case of *The People* vs. *Ruggles*. In the Jewish commonwealth it was punishable with death. Lev. xxiv. 16. Of the offence as against municipal law, nothing is here said. But of it as a breach of the third commandment, a few things are offered. Boston says, "Blasphemy is a wronging of the majesty of God by speeches tending to his reproach." Durham says, "There are three sorts of blasphemy. 1. When anything unbecoming God is in word attributed to him; as that he is unjust, unholy, unmerciful, &c., such as that complaint, (Ezek. xviii. 25,) *The way of the Lord is not equal.* 2. When what is due to him is denied him; as when he is said not to be Eternal, Omniscient, Almighty, Sovereign, &c., as when Pharaoh said, *Who is the Lord that I should obey his voice? &c.*, Ex. v. 2, or as when railing Rabshakeh in his master's name said, *Who is the Lord that is able to deliver you out of my hand?* Isa. xxxvi. 20. 3. When what is due to God is attributed to a creature, or arrogated by a creature: thus the Jews, supposing Christ to be a creature charged him with blasphemy, (Luke vii. 49; John x. 33,) because he forgave sins and called himself God."

In strict propriety of modern parlance, blasphemy always includes insolence. But in the Bible use of the term, it is much more comprehensive. So that we blaspheme, not only when we speak against God directly, but when we revile his word, his way, his children, his ordinances, or his works. 1 Tim. vi. 1; Titus ii. 5; 2 Pet. ii. 2; 1 Cor. iv. 13; Mark iii. 29, 30.

The judgment of the Christian world is that blasphemy is the greatest possible violation of the third commandment. Durham: "The great breach of this command is blasphemy, though perjury be more direct." Boston: "Blasphemy is the most atrocious of all sins." It is clearly our duty to express our abhorrence of it. The Jews rent their garments at the hearing of blasphemy. Our mode of testifying against it must depend upon our circumstances; but it should always be decided. At such a time even silence is sinful, much more then is smiling or laughing at it. It is truly appalling to reflect how even good men sometimes, by an untender walking, excite the blasphemies of their fellow-men. 2 Sam. xii. 14, Rom. ii. 24. Nor is it possible for some truly converted men to forget how in the days of their own unregeneracy they led others to commit this crime. Even inferiors in station may lead their superiors into this sin, 1 Tim. vi. 1.

A great source of blasphemy is ignorance, 1 Tim. i. 13. No doubt it is committed also from want of watchfulness over our hearts and lips. The great source of blasphemy is the corrupt heart of man, as the Saviour himself explicitly taught, Matt. xv. 19.

The Scriptures speak of blasphemy against the Father, Son and Holy Ghost. Lev. xxiv. 16, Matt. xii. 31, 32, Mark iii. 28, 29, Luke xii. 10. Of all blasphemies that against the Holy Ghost alone, is unpardonable. It hath never forgiveness, neither in this world nor in that which is to come, Mark iii. 29. It is the sin unto death, 1 John v. 16. Of course it is a sin that is never committed by one of God's chosen people. There is an impression very common among the best theologians that it is not often committed. But that it has been committed, we have the most alarming evidence in the New Testament. Some have said that this sin could not be committed in our day. But why not? It is a sin against light. And are not men much instructed in our time? Is not the truth preached with great clearness and power at least by some? and does not the Holy Ghost bear witness in many hearts by strong convictions and clear impressions of religious truth? and do not men assail the great fundamental truths of religion now as in the days of our Saviour? Does not their opposition assume the form of deadly malice against the gospel itself? Have they not both seen and hated both Christ and his Father? John xv. 24. Yea, do they not show despite not only to the Saviour, but to the Spirit of grace? Heb. x. 29. It is commonly agreed that if Peter had denied his Lord with the malice with which Saul of Tarsus persecuted the church, he would have committed this sin. Or if Saul of Tarsus, with the threatenings and slaughter which he breathed out, had enjoyed the light and advantages of Peter in his intercourse with Christ, he would have committed this sin.

It is pretty clear that in all cases where there is a sincere desire to turn from sin and cleave to God, the unpardonable sin has not been committed. But let men beware how they embrace damnable heresies; how they deliberately set themselves against God; how by words, or writing, or painting, or acting, they represent any thing sacred in an odious or ridiculous light; or how they stand silently by and connive at the blasphemies of others, Jer. xxxvi. 24, 25; or how they excuse, defend, or plead for, any form of ungodliness; or how in any wise they walk untenderly. Especially let them be very guarded against all scornful words and acts towards the Most High; against all mocking and derision of sacred things; against all jibes and jests at the things of God; against all thoughtless use of God's name, or irreverent speaking, as using the names of God in mere exclamation, or as by-words. All these things lead directly to blasphemy against the persons of the Godhead, and particularly against the Holy Ghost.

### II. PERJURY.

Cicero says that an oath is *a religious affirmation*. Of course perjury is an ungodly use of a solemn institution, the object of which is the ascertaining of the truth. Perhaps the most correct definition of legal perjury is that it consists in making a false oath, when lawfully administered, in some judicial proceeding, by a person who swears wilfully, absolutely and falsely, in a matter material to the issue. Blackstone: "The law takes no notice of any perjury, but such as is committed in some court of justice, having power to administer an oath; or before some magistrate or proper officer invested with a similar authority, in some proceedings relative to a civil suit, or a criminal prosecution." But we are interpreting the law of God and not the municipal regulations of men. In the sight of Heaven, all false swearing is perjury. Boston: "Perjury is falsehood confirmed with an oath." In God's esteem a man commits perjury, when upon oath he affirms as truth that which he knows to be false, or that which he does not know to be true, 1 Kings xxi. 10; or, when one engages upon oath to do something which is impossible, or which he is afterwards careless to perform.

The word *perjure* is of Latin origin. The word

*forswear* is of Anglo-Saxon origin. In ordinary language they have the same signification; though some have pretended to refined distinctions between them. Hopkins: "Perjury is the chief and most notorious abusing of God's name. And indeed what greater sin can there be, than to bring God to be a witness to our lie? to make him, who is truth itself, attest that which is falsehood or deceit?"

"SUBORNATION OF PERJURY is the offence of procuring another to take such a false oath, as constitutes perjury in the principal." All nations have punished perjury and subornation with severity. By ancient English law the punishment was death; afterwards expatriation or cutting out the tongue; then forfeiture of all property. Although the punishment of this crime has been somewhat varied, yet in England and America, the criminal party is for ever disqualified from bearing testimony, and so is subjected to perpetual infamy. The judicial regulation of the Jewish commonwealth on this subject was excellent, Deut. xix. 16–19. For a long time it was, and perhaps still is the law of France. It provided that perjury in the case of prosecution for capital offences was itself a capital crime. And surely he who takes a false oath to screen a murderer from death, or to punish an innocent man with death, deserves to die. This crime is as ancient as perhaps any other. Paul mentions *perjured persons*, 1 Tim. i. 10; but long before his time God ordained by his prophet Moses severe laws against swearing falsely, Lev. xix. 12, Deut. xix. 18, 19. Indeed the Scriptures array themselves with great rigour against perjury. "Love no false oath," Zech. viii. 17. "I will be a swift witness against false swearers," Mal. iii. 5. See also Zech. v. 4, Hos. x. 4.

OATHS OF OFFICE. Perjury may be committed not only by deponents in judicial proceedings, but by merchants in the custom-house, and by the servants of the public, who bind themselves by an oath faithfully to perform the duties of their office. Every partial judge is a perjured monster. Every magistrate, who violates the laws, which he is sworn to execute, is guilty of perjury. Every legislator, who has sworn to maintain the Constitution under which he is acting, and then is led away by selfish or sectional considerations, is perjured. And the executive officer, who for fear or favour, for bribe or reward, fails to do all he has sworn to do, is also a perjured wretch. The commonness of these sins does in no degree whatever abate their enormity.

A CASE OF CONSCIENCE. May we press a man to swear when we have good reason to think he will swear falsely? This is a very serious question. In one sense indeed, every man shall bear his own burden. But on the other hand, we are warned not to be partakers of other men's sins. The correct answer seems to be, that if the matter is of no great weight, Christian tenderness on our part should not press him to the oath, if we seriously fear that in testifying he will commit perjury. This reason derives strength, if the matter in contest involves our own private interests only. In such a case, we may lawfully yield our rights. But if the matter at stake is of great importance to the public, or to private parties, then we may require the oath; for it is the appointed instrument of public justice. We cannot certainly know but that God will so fill the mind of the witness with a sense of his fear, as that the truth may come out. In no case has a judge a right to release a competent witness, duly brought forward, by either party.

### III. PROFANENESS.

The general definition of profaneness is irreverence for sacred names, or things, or institutions, or persons. A more specific definition is, that profaneness is the act of violating any thing sacred. The grossest form of profaning the name of God is by common swearing, in which oaths and curses are usually united; for very few men swear profanely without cursing also. Blackstone speaks of this as one sin, and calls it, "the offence of profane and common *swearing* and *cursing.*" This sin consists, (besides the cursing,) in making an appeal to God in a light, passionate, or wicked manner, for no important purpose, and when not required to do so by any competent authority. Perhaps there is no branch of morals concerning which it is more difficult to preserve a healthy state of the public conscience. The difficulty is found, 1. In the natural lawlessness of the heart. It does not like to be under restraint to God. 2. The habits of men are extensively corrupted in this matter. 3. Some moralists have written loosely on the subject. 4. Men in high places often set a very bad example. These causes have always been at work. They were felt in the days of our Saviour. Strict as the Pharisees were, in some things, they held that common swearing was no sin, even if it were by the name of God, provided what we swore was true; that no oath was binding where the name of

God was not expressly used; and that we might swear as much as we pleased without offence, if we swore by heaven, by Jerusalem, &c. Thus they subverted the entire system of morality of speech built on the third commandment. The rebuke of our Saviour to them was terrible. "Woe unto you, ye blind guides! which say, Whosoever shall swear by the temple it is nothing; but whosoever shall swear by the gold of the temple, he is a debtor! Ye fools and blind! for whether is greater, the gold, or the temple that sanctifieth the gold? And, Whosoever shall swear by the altar it is nothing; but whosoever sweareth by the gift that is upon it, he is guilty. Ye fools and blind! For whether is greater the gift, or the altar that sanctifieth the gift? Whoso therefore, shall swear by the altar, sweareth by it, and by all things thereon. And whoso shall swear by the temple, sweareth by it, and by him that dwelleth therein. And he that shall swear by heaven, sweareth by the throne of God, and by him that sitteth thereon." Matt. xxiii. 16–22. The Old Testament no less distinctly condemns swearing by any thing but God. "How shall I pardon thee for this? thy children have forsaken me, and sworn by them that are no gods." Jer. v. 7. To the same effect our Lord speaks in Matt. v. 33–37, where he notices the fact that the Pharisees condemned perjury, requiring the fulfilment of oaths to the Lord, but admitting common swearing. "Ye have heard that it hath been said by them of old time, Thou shalt not forswear thyself, but shalt perform unto the Lord thine oaths: But I say unto you, Swear not at all: neither by heaven; for it is God's throne: nor by the earth; for it is his footstool: neither by Jerusalem;

for it is the city of the great King: neither shalt thou swear by thy head; because thou canst not make one hair white or black. But let your communication be, Yea, yea; Nay, nay: for whatsoever is more than these cometh of evil."

The sin of swearing by any thing but God is positively forbidden of old. "Thou shalt fear the LORD thy God, and serve him, and shalt swear by his name." Deut. vi. 13; Deut. x. 20. Swearing is an act of worship. When it is right to swear, such worship should be offered to none but him who searches the heart, and knows whether we swear truly; and who has almightiness, and justice, and sovereignty, and so can punish if we swear falsely. Swearing by any creature is therefore so far an act of idolatry, and yet, because it is a creature of God, we do in the esteem of Heaven take an oath, when we swear by it; and so, if we swear not truly, even by a creature, we do commit perjury in the sight of God. God's creatures were given us for other and lawful uses, and not to supplant our Maker.

The reasons against profane swearing are many, and entitled to the most solemn consideration.

1. Profane swearing never does any good. It makes no one wiser, better or happier. It inspires no respect for him who uses it. It casts no light on any subject. It gives force to no argument. It strengthens no assertions. It gives no edge to wit. It does not promote cheerfulness, justice, truth or any good thing. It is a wholly useless practice. More than this,

2. It always does harm. It must give pain to all right-minded people, who hear it. It is so much the

language of passion that it either grieves or irritates. It often makes enemies, and weakens a good cause.

3. It is, therefore, a wanton sin, committed for the love of sinning, and not for any good to be secured in time or eternity. It is a gratuitous expression of contempt towards God and all that is sacred.

4. It is confessedly a vulgar practice. Even Chesterfield says that swearing is inconsistent with the character of a gentleman. In a world like this, virtue and happiness greatly depend on good manners. Every one is bound to be truly gentle and polite. He owes it to his neighbours, not to offend against good breeding. Have you ever seen a man, who justified profane language as a branch of good manners?

5. Profane swearing is forbidden by the laws of every well regulated government. The wisdom of lawgivers, sitting in council on the affairs of nations, has uniformly condemned profane oaths. We are bound by all the principles of patriotism to maintain, both by speech and example, all good rules and laws made for the country in which we live.

6. Swearing leads to other evil practices. He who uses profane words, easily falls into the use of angry and bitter language. Cursing commonly goes with swearing. It is also generally conceded that swearing leads to obscene conversation. So utterly subversive of all good was profane swearing considered by the heathen, that the ancient Scythians punished it with the loss of the estate, the Persians with slavery, the Greeks with cutting off the ears, the Romans with hurling from a high rock.

7. Profane swearing is a shocking sin. South: "All profanation and invasion of things sacred is an

offence against the eternal laws of nature." It is never found alone. It dreadfully hardens the heart against God, and inclines men to reject both his mercies and his authority. It indisposes them to pray, to repent, to forsake any sin. While indulged it makes prayer a mockery. To swear one hour and pray the next is so inconsistent that very few men do both. Yet the poor, profane swearer is as feeble and dependent as his pious neighbour, and constantly needs the divine blessing to make existence desirable. How dreadful then must be that sin, which cuts off the soul from access to God! How seldom are the profane inclined to repentance! Dwight: "Profaneness is the mere flood-gate of iniquity, and the stream once let out, flows, with a current daily becoming more and more rapid and powerful. It is the very nurse of sin; the foster-parent of ingratitude, rebellion and impiety. This witness is true." Thousands have testified as much. Boston, who had long noticed the effects of evil habits on mankind, says, "Profane swearers do seldom reform. Many are very extravagant otherwise in youth, who afterwards take up themselves; but ofttimes swearing grows gray-headed with men." How much like a madman the swearer is in closing even the door of repentance and mercy against himself!

8. The corrupting influence of profane swearing on society is terrible. The prophet Jeremiah says, "Because of swearing the land mourneth." Jer. xxiii. 7. How our land mourns by reason of this sin, almost all classes are made to feel. Among all profane swearers, you shall not find a teacher of Sabbath Schools, or one who reproves sin in his family, or

who seeks the salvation of his fellow-men, or is otherwise a safe guide to those around him. You may search nations and empires throughout, and you shall not find a Howard among all the armies of profane swearers. This crime diminishes reverence for God, relaxes the force of solemn oaths, and prepares men for perjury and general irreligion. If the people of this nation continue thus to insult the Most High, we may look for even more dire calamities than are now, (1864) in the midst of civil war, poured upon us out of the vials of God's wrath. "The mischiefs of evil examples," says one, "are always great; in the present case they are dreadful. The tongue is obviously the prime instrument of human corruption; of diffusing and perpetuating sin; of preventing the eternal life of our fellow men; of extending perdition over the earth; and of populating the world of misery. . . . Among all the evil examples, which I have heard mentioned, I do not remember that a dumb man was ever named as one. No person, within my recollection, ever attributed his own sins to the example of such a man. Men corrupt each other pre-eminently by their speech. No individual, perhaps, ever began to swear profanely by himself: and few, very few, ever commenced the practice but from imitation. Let every profane person, therefore, solemnly remember how much guilt will be charged to him in the great day of accounts."

9. God has put this sin in a catalogue of the worst offences. "The Lord hath a controversy with the inhabitants of the land, because there is no truth, nor mercy, nor knowledge of God in the land. By swearing, and lying, and killing, and stealing, and com-

mitting adultery, they break out, and blood toucheth blood. Therefore shall the land mourn," &c. Hos. iv. 1–3.

10. Dreadful judgments often overtake persons and communities, on account of this sin. This has often been declared by inspired and uninspired men. Jer. vii. 9–16; Zech. v. 4. But should no curse fall on the profane in this life, there is an eternity of retribution before us all. We must reap that which we sow. We must give an account to Him, who says of all profane swearers, that he will not hold them guiltless. What everlasting sorrows await all who go to the next world with their souls defiled with wicked oaths!

And now, dear reader, are not these reasons good? Ought they not to decide the case? You are a poor feeble worm, living on God's daily bounty. You need his favour. At any moment you may be called out of time into eternity. How dare you provoke his wrath by treating his name with contempt? If even one profane oath has escaped your lips, humble yourself before God, heartily repent of your iniquity, and plead for forgiveness through the blood and righteousness of the Lord Jesus Christ. To the penitent who forsake sin, there is mercy. Ask for it now. Give your heart to Christ. How dreadful it will be to spend an eternity with all the foul-mouthed who shall day and night curse and blaspheme the God of heaven, and with all the vile from among men sink down in endless, hopeless sorrow!

The following little scrap, written by a pious man, has been used so often to impress upon the minds of men a sense of the sin of profane swearing, and even to persuade them to turn to God and live, that it is here inserted without alteration. It is entitled, "THE SWEARER'S PRAYER, OR HIS OATH EXPLAINED."

"What, a swearer pray! Yes, swearer, whether thou thinkest so or not, each of thine oaths is a prayer —an appeal to the holy and Almighty God, whose name thou darest so impiously to take into thy lips.

"And what is it, thinkest thou, swearer, that thou dost call for, when the awful imprecations, *damn* and *damnation*, roll so frequently from thy profane tongue? Tremble, swearer, while I tell thee! Thy prayer containeth two parts: thou prayest, First, that thou mayest be deprived of eternal happiness! Secondly, that thou mayest be plunged into eternal misery!

"When, therefore, thou callest for damnation, dost thou not, in effect, say as follows? 'O God! thou hast power to punish me in hell for ever, therefore, let not one of my sins be forgiven! Let every oath I have sworn—every lie that I have told—every Sabbath that I have broken—and all the sins that I have committed, either in thought, word or deed, rise up in judgment against me, and eternally condemn me! Let me never partake of thy salvation! May my soul and body be deprived of all happiness, both in this world and that which is to come! Let me never see thy face with comfort—never enjoy thy favour and friendship; and let me never enter into the kingdom of heaven!'

"This is the first part of thy prayer. Let us hear the second.

"'O God let me not only be shut out of heaven, but also shut up in hell! May all the members of my body be tortured with inconceivable agony, and all the powers of my soul tormented with horror and despair, inexpressible and eternal! Let my dwelling be in the blackness of darkness, and my companions accursed men and accursed devils! Pour down thy hottest anger; execute all thy wrath and curse upon me; arm and send forth all thy terrors against me; and let thy fierce, thy fiery, thy fearful indignation rest upon me! Be mine eternal enemy, and plague, and punish, and torment me, in hell, for ever, and ever, and ever!'

"Swearer, *this is thy prayer!* Oh dreadful imprecation! Oh horrible, horrible, most horrible! Blaspheming man, dost thou like thy petition? Look at it. Art thou sincere in thy prayer, or art thou *mocking* thy Maker? Dost thou wish for damnation? Art thou desirous of eternal torment? If so, swear on,—swear hard. The more oaths the more misery; and perhaps, the sooner thou mayest be in hell. Art thou *shocked* at this language? Does it harrow up thy soul? Does the very blood run cold in thy veins? Art thou convinced of the evil of profane swearing? How many times hast thou blasphemed the God of heaven? How many times hast thou asked God to damn thee in the course of a year, a month, a day? Nay, how many times in a single hour hast thou called for damnation? Art thou not yet in hell? Wonder, O heavens and be astonished, O earth, at the goodness and long-suffering of that God whose great name swearing persons so often and so awfully profane! Swearer, be thankful, O be exceedingly thankful, that God has not answered thy prayer, thy *tremendous* prayer—that his mercy and patience have withholden the request of thy polluted lips. Never let him hear another oath from thy unhallowed tongue lest it should be thy last expression upon earth, and thy swearing prayer should be answered in hell. O, let thine oaths be turned into supplications. Repent and turn to Jesus, who died for swearers as well as his murderers: and then, O then, though thou mayest have sworn as many oaths as there are 'stars in the heavens, and sands upon the seashore, innumerable,' then thou shalt find, to thy eternal joy, that there is love enough in his heart and merit sufficient in his blood, to pardon thy sins, and to save thy soul for ever. Swearer, canst thou ever again blaspheme such a God and Saviour as this? Does not thy conscience cry, *God forbid?* Even so, Amen."

It is a vain endeavour on the part of some to avoid the guilt of profane swearing by mincing their oaths, as is the practice of many whose consciences still trouble them so much as to hinder them from the more outbreaking forms of this sin. Minced oaths are either oaths, or they are nonsense. If oaths, they are of course profane. If they are nonsense, they are not "good nonsense," and are clearly forbidden by Matt. xii. 36. They are certainly offensive to good manners and to God's people, 1 Cor. xv. 33, Matt. xviii. 6, 7.

The following hints may be useful in restraining men from all profane swearing. 1. Hare: "I do not know that when a man is called to account for this his sin at the bar of God's judgment seat, that he will much mend the matter by pleading that he had been guilty of it so often, at last it became a second nature to him, and he got to swear ever and anon without so much as intending it. For God perhaps may ask him in return, How camest thou by that nature?"

2. Commit to memory the third commandment. Its language is clear and solemn. Very few men are able to remember its words and to swear profanely at the same time.

3. Cultivate the fear of God in the heart. Let a sense of the awful majesty of the Most High fall upon you.

4. Beware of needless social intercourse with men who are habitually profane.

5. Control your passions amid needless and violent excitements.

6. Whenever you go out into the world, try to carry with you the spirit of prayer.

7. If at any time you fall into this sin, deeply humble yourself on that account and repent in deep sorrow.

SWEARING REPROVED. The following narrative is known to many to be substantially correct. It has found its way into the public prints. In the city of ——, Dr. —— left his residence to ride on horseback towards the lower part of the main street. He had not proceeded far when he met a well-mounted man, who was much excited with liquor. He hailed the doctor in an earnest and rather bluff manner. The latter stopped and looked him steadily in the face. Soon the excited man asked, "Have you seen a young man passing this way with a wagon?" The doctor replied in the negative. From the lips of the inquirer soon escaped a number of profane and foolish oaths respecting the strange disappearance of the team and driver.

The doctor sat still on his horse, greatly moved with compassion, and tenderly but steadily fixed his large eyes on the face of his neighbour. Presently the excited man asked for some trifling favour. The doctor promptly gave it, saying, "I take great pleasure in doing anything to oblige you, although you have greatly hurt my feelings." The other replied, "How can that be? I did not intend to do so." The doctor replied, "You have spoken very disrespectfully of my best friend." The reply was, "What do you mean? I have said nothing against any one." The doctor answered, "The best Friend I have in the universe is God. Both to you and me He has done more kindness than all others besides. You have used his name here in my presence in a very profane way, and yet you ask, 'What have I said to hurt your feelings?' Can I hear my God and Saviour spoken of contemptuously, and not be hurt?" "Sir," said the man, "I ask your pardon." The doctor replied, "My pardon is nothing. I am a worm of the dust. Like you, I must soon stand before the judgment-seat of Christ, and give up my last and solemn account. Ask pardon of God." By this time the countenance of the man betrayed shame and remorse, and he said, "Sir, allow me to ask your name." The doctor said, "Oh, that is a matter of no importance. I shall soon meet you at the bar of God. I hope for salvation through the grace of our Lord Jesus Christ. Do you?" Thus saying, he bade good-bye to the excited man, and rode away. Neither party in this strange interview knew the name of the other.

About nine or ten months after this, the doctor was delivering an address on temperance, and when the meeting was over, a man well-dressed and having an appearance of respectability, came to him and said, "I suppose you do not know me." "I do not," was the reply. "Do you not remember," said he, "that last summer you met a man at the corner of F. and F. streets, and reproved him for swearing?" "I do," said the doctor. "I am that man," he replied. "I went home distressed, and wondering who you were. I described your appearance to my son. He told me you were a minister of the gospel, and gave me your name. Since that day I have drunk no liquor; I have stopped swearing; and that is not all"—tears starting in his eyes—"the best of all is, I hope God has converted my soul."

The affecting character of this meeting can be better conceived than described. Subsequent inquiry showed that the reformation was entire, and that the former swearer was now a praying man, and the former drunkard was leading a consistent Christian life. From this narrative it appears,

1. There may be exceptions to the rule laid down by that wise and good man, Rev. Dr. Ebenezer Porter: "I will not talk to a man intoxicated with strong drink." Such conversation is sometimes dangerous, seldom improving, but not always without advantage. Let us be civil to even drunken men. Who knows but that we may do them good?

2. "Love, and say what you please." A stern or objurgatory manner commonly makes men worse; but true tenderness commonly disarms enmity.

3. "In the morning sow thy seed, and in the evening withhold not thy hand; for thou knowest not whether shall prosper, either this or that, or whether they both shall be alike good." Let us be always at work, both in season and out of season.

4. Let us overcome the fear of man. It brings a snare. It makes us cowardly. It excites the contempt of the wicked. "Be of good courage." When the council saw the boldness of Peter and John they marvelled, and they took knowledge of them that they had been with Jesus.

5. We must not treat all wicked men alike. Of some we must "have compassion, making a difference." They must have none but gentle, persuasive words and tones. Others we must "save with fear, pulling them out of the fire." To such we must often present the terrors of the Lord, and in his awful name point them to the wrath to come.

6. How rich is divine grace! how abundant is divine mercy! It saves even profane swearers and drunkards. It can do all things. Oh that men would accept the salvation so freely and so sincerely offered to them by the Lord!

## IV. ASSEVERATIONS.

An asseveration may be either with or without an oath. The primary signification of the term pointed to an oath. But now we are said to asseverate when with repetition or solemnity we aver positively: a declaration without repetition is a simple assertion. An asseveration expresses vehemence, and is designed to give emphasis to one's declarations. Asseverations are right or wrong according to the occasion and manner of using them. When lawful, they do not materially differ from persistent declarations. Thus Rhoda, the damsel, *constantly affirmed* that Peter was at the gate. Acts xii. 15. We may make our asseverations very strong, even as Elisha did to Elijah, when he said, "As the Lord liveth, and as thy soul liveth." 2 Kings ii. 2, 4, 6. This is not really an oath; and yet it is an appeal to God and an assertion hardly less solemn than an oath. But asseverations are sinful when they are made without thoughtfulness or without any proper call for them. Ray: "Another abuse of the tongue, I might add; vehement asseveration upon slight and trivial occasions." We ought especially to guard against making any asseveration rashly or needlessly, as it tends to weaken our regard for sacred things.

### V. ATTESTATIONS.

Attestations are nothing more than giving evidence without oath. But ordinarily they have in them a tone of positiveness and peremptoriness, not belonging to ordinary testimony, and they may partake and often do partake of an appeal to God. If the occasion is sufficiently solemn and important, and the attestation reverent, it is not sinful. It is frequently accompanied with such phrases as *truly*, *indeed*, *I solemnly declare*, &c. But when made in rashness, or on frivolous occasions, or with irreverence of manner or of heart towards God or sacred things, it is contrary to the spirit of this commandment.

### VI. OBTESTATIONS.

Obtestations are exceedingly earnest entreaties or supplications, made to our fellow-men, respecting something which we desire. When lawful, they are solemnly made. Paul used such: "I beseech you, brethren, by the mercies of God, that ye present your bodies a living sacrifice, &c." Rom. xii. 1. Again,

"I, Paul, beseech you by the meekness of Christ." 2 Cor. x. 1. These too are contrary to the spirit of the third commandment, when made without just cause; much more when employed to persuade men to that which is sinful.

### VII. IMPRECATIONS.

Imprecations are prayers, by which we seek evil to ourselves or others. They are conditional or unconditional. If unconditional, they are mere curses. The general spirit of the gospel and of its precepts is counter to them. "Bless, and curse not." "The wrath of man worketh not the righteousness of God." "Vengeance is mine; I will repay, saith the Lord." When directed towards others, if they partake of the spirit of railing, this adds to their sinfulness. Jude 9. There may be solemn occasions when we may conditionally imprecate evil upon ourselves, as did the royal Psalmist. Ps. vii. 3–5. All imprecations, however, are sinful, when our appeal is to Satan; when they are made to establish a falsehood; to express malignant passions against others, and when there is no solemn occasion for them.

### VIII. SUPERSTITIOUS OBSERVANCES.

These are so numerous, and vary so much with the country, and even the neighbourhood where they prevail, that a detail of them would fill a volume. Sailors are superstitious about having a minister of religion on board their vessels; and about sailing on Friday. Some farmers are superstitious about almost every thing they do. Some will hardly sow flax, except on Good Friday. Some persons are alarmed if they spill salt on the table; if they sneeze when putting on their shoes; or if they have a burning sensation in the left ear. All these and like things are senseless, are calculated to make life miserable, and to reduce us to slavery to perpetual apprehensions.

### IX. GENERAL IRREVERENCE.

Our Saviour and his apostles very carefully guard us against all needless introduction of the name of God into common conversation. "Let your communication be Yea, yea; Nay, nay: for whatsoever is more than these cometh of evil." Matt. v. 37. "But above all things, my brethren, swear not, neither by heaven, neither by the earth, neither by any other oath: but let your yea be yea; and your nay, nay; lest ye fall into condemnation." James v. 12. It may greatly encourage us to pay a strict regard to these injunctions, to know that those who keep at the greatest distance from all irreverence and needless appeals to God, other things being equal, probably suffer least in their reputation for veracity. And in general, we should avoid every thing that seems to us inconsistent with profound and awful reverence for the Divine Majesty.

The Westminster Assembly say: "The sins forbidden in the third commandment are, the not using of God's name as is required; and the abuse of it in an ignorant, vain, irreverent, profane, superstitious, or wicked mentioning, or otherwise using his titles, attributes, ordinances, or works, by blasphemy, perjury; all sinful cursings, oaths, vows, and lots; violating of our oaths and vows, if lawful; and fulfilling them, if of things unlawful; murmuring and quarrelling at, curious prying into, and misapplying of God's decrees and providences; misinterpreting, misapplying, or any way perverting the word, or any part of it, to profane jests, curious or unprofitable questions, vain janglings, or the maintaining of false doctrines; abusing it, the creatures, or any thing contained under the name of God, to charms, or sinful lusts and practices; the maligning, scorning, reviling, or any ways opposing of God's truth, grace, and ways, making profession of religion in hypocrisy, or for sinister ends; being ashamed of it, or a shame to it, by uncomfortable, unwise, unfruitful, and offensive walking, or backsliding from it."

## THE THREATENING ANNEXED TO THIS COMMANDMENT.

This is expressed in terms well-suited to fill the mind with awe: for "the LORD will not hold him guiltless that taketh his name in vain." The threatening is delivered in a figure of speech, common to all languages, wherein much more is implied than is expressed. When the apostle Peter, exhorting the early Christians to holiness, says, "The time past of our life may suffice us to have wrought the will of the Gentiles," he means to say, that we have spent far too much time in that wicked course of life. This threatening clearly implies, 1. That we shall have a solemn and awful reckoning with God—a reckoning in which his creatures shall have all their conduct investigated with the scrutiny of omniscience, shall all be found innocent or guilty, and shall all be condemned or acquitted. 2. In that awful account, we shall answer to God for all irreverence of thought, or feeling, or speech, or action. 3. God will by no means clear the guilty, and in particular, by no means clear those who shall then be found guilty of breaking this commandment. 4. No mercy shall be shown to men whose souls shall then be found defiled with the guilt of this sin. Yea, THE LORD WILL NOT HOLD HIM GUILTLESS THAT TAKETH HIS NAME IN VAIN. Such a one may perhaps hold himself guiltless; he may esteem himself a fine fellow; he may think that he graces his profanity with the air of a gentleman; he may imagine that he is quite above all responsibility even to God. Moreover his fellows may hold him guiltless; may make light of his sin; may call him brave and elegant. But Jehovah, the lawgiver of heaven and earth, will not acquit him. To God he is responsible, and in God's sight he is criminal. If the profane man, at the last day, stands alone, still God will reckon with him. If hand has joined in hand, and he is surrounded by a crew of the ungodly, their numbers shall not protect him. Pr. xi. 21. If he is poor, and steals, and takes the name of his God in vain, Prov. xxx. 9, still his poverty shall not screen him. If he is rich and gifted and honourable in men's esteem, and violates this command, his pomp shall be brought down to the grave, yea, he shall be brought down to hell, to the sides of the pit. Isa. xiv. 11, 14. In all cases the violation of this commandment has many aggravations. It is committed immediately against God. It is in the teeth of the expressed letter of the law. It is outbreaking. It is suited to lead others astray. It admits of no reparation. It is against the law of nature. It is against all the religious instruction we have ever received. It is against the laws of common politeness. If open, it is against every man's convictions of right.

It is exceedingly impudent. It is heaven-daring. It is an expression of deep malignity against God. Ps. cxxxix. 20.

While indeed the profane person, who shall repent, shall obtain forgiveness, profaneness is a sin which greatly disinclines men to turn to God. To the penitent, the offence is not unpardonable. But how hard it is to bring a man to cry for mercy, when for a long time he has been insulting the Father of all mercies and the God of all grace.

# CHAPTER XVII.

## THE FOURTH COMMANDMENT.

REMEMBER THE SABBATH-DAY TO KEEP IT HOLY. SIX DAYS SHALT THOU LABOUR, AND DO ALL THY WORK; BUT THE SEVENTH DAY IS THE SABBATH OF THE LORD THY GOD: IN IT THOU SHALT NOT DO ANY WORK, THOU, NOR THY SON, NOR THY DAUGHTER, THY MAN-SERVANT, NOR THY MAID-SERVANT, NOR THY CATTLE, NOR THY STRANGER THAT IS WITHIN THY GATES: FOR IN SIX DAYS THE LORD MADE HEAVEN AND EARTH, THE SEA AND ALL THAT IN THEM IS, AND RESTED THE SEVENTH DAY: WHEREFORE THE LORD BLESSED THE SABBATH-DAY, AND HALLOWED IT.

NO man can seriously read and consider this precept without seeing that it is of vast importance. It is a law claiming to regulate a *seventh* portion of human life. If a man lives twenty-one years, this law claims the entire control of three of them; if he lives fifty years, it disposes of more than *seven* of them. It is therefore important. But it also devotes this portion of time to *religious* purposes; and these are the highest ends of life. All other time is secular. This is holy. That *may* be occupied with things which perish in the using. This *must* be given to things which take hold on eternity. Many questions may be raised concerning this law; but one question is at the foundation of all the rest: "Is this law still in force?" If it is not binding now, it never will be; and if it is binding now, it will bind while the world stands. The inquiry is of great practical interest. Public manners are vastly affected by the esteem in which the Sabbath is held. It is, therefore, right to look well to the foundations.

### DOES THE LAW OF THE SABBATH BIND US?

It is evident that laws may cease to be of force; that is, they may cease to be laws. When this occurs, it must be in one of the following ways.

*The condition of a people* may be so changed as to render obedience to the law impracticable. In human governments such cases often arise, and the law, unless administered by tyrants, becomes a dead letter. No good government will inflict the penalty on the transgressor to whom obedience is impossible, even though the law remains on the statute-book. But the law of the Sabbath can as well be kept now as at any former period of the world. Indeed, when given from Mount Sinai, it was given to a people on a long journey, to whom were wanting many conveniences which we enjoy for its careful observance. If this law was in its nature ever practicable, it is so now.

Some laws *expire by limitation.* Such are many of the laws of every country. Such were many of the laws given by Moses. They were in force until Christ, who was their end, came; and then they bound no longer. Thus the whole ceremonial law ceased to bind after the death of Christ, to which it was limited.

But no limit was fixed to the observance of the fourth commandment, either when first given or afterwards.

A competent authority may *repeal* a law, and thus its obliging power may cease. Every free government affords numerous instances of the repeal of laws once useful, but no longer so. In a regular government, the repeal must be passed by the power which enacts the law. The great Lawgiver of the world is God. He ordained the law of the Sabbath, and he has never repealed it. Is any evidence of such repeal found in Scripture? If so, where is the book, the chapter, the verse containing it? All admit that the law was in force until Christ. Christ did not repeal it, for he says so, Matt. v. 17; nor did the apostles anywhere declare that it was repealed.

If this law, therefore, had ceased to bind, it must be in some way utterly unknown to us. It is still practicable; it has not expired by limitation; it has not been repealed.

THIS LAW IS PART OF A CODE WHICH IS IN FORCE.

It may also be said that this law is *in the middle of a code*, all the rest of which is acknowledged to be binding; and why not this? Were the other precepts of this code spoken by God from Sinai amidst blackness and darkness, and tempest and terrors? So was this. Were the others written by the finger of God, on tables of stone? So was this. Were the others deposited in the ark of the testimony, in the holy of holies, under the wings of the cherubim? So was this. No ceremonial or repealable law, given to the Jews, had these marks of honour put upon it. Did Christ say, "I came not to destroy, but to fulfil the law?" He said it as much of this as of any other precept. Did Christ's most devoted followers keep the other commandments? So did they keep this. Luke xxiii. 56.

## THIS LAW ENACTED WITH GREAT CARE.

On the face of this law are found some things which prove that God, who gave it, regarded it as of great importance.

In the wording of it, a more full explanation of its true intent is given than in any other commandment. It is enacted both positively and negatively: positively, "Remember the Sabbath-day to keep it holy;" negatively, "In it thou shalt do no manner of work." No other precept of the decalogue is given in both these forms, although every fair rule of interpreting them requires, that when they enjoin a duty, we should regard them as forbidding the contrary sin: and when they forbid a sin, we should regard them as enjoining the contrary duty. Yet in this command, but in no other, both forms are used.

This shows that God has a great zeal for the observance of the Sabbath, and that he is determined we shall not misunderstand his will concerning it. It also intimates the peculiar proneness in our nature to forget the sacredness of this day; and so God puts us on our guard in the most solemn manner; and has taken "an especial care to fence us in on all sides to the observance of this precept."

This command is also introduced as no other is. The very first word of it is a solemn memento—"Remember." This word is not found elsewhere in the decalogue.

Moreover, this command not only addresses men in the singular, "Thou shalt," &c., but it goes further, and tells who is thereby intended, namely, not only the head of the family, but also the son, the daughter, the man-servant and the maid-servant, the cattle and the stranger. No such particularity is found in any other precept of either table of the law.

### THREE REASONS CONTAINED IN THE COMMANDMENT FOR OBSERVING IT.

1. God reasons with us *on the equity of his demands.* He says, he gives us six days out of seven, as if he had said, "I am no hard master; I do not act unreasonably. I give you ample time to do your necessary work. I give you *six* days; therefore, if you have any conscience, give me the *seventh.*" For, says he, "It is mine—it is the Sabbath of the Lord your God." Surely, you will not deny to your God a right so equitable, a demand so fair.

2. It is also stated by God in the command itself, that he *set us the example on the completion of the creation.* And shall we not follow *such* an example? Calvin: "It is no small stimulus to any action, for a man to know that he is imitating his Creator." If we ought to be holy because God is holy, if we ought to forgive *our* enemies because God forgives *his* enemies, we ought also to keep the Sabbath-day because God kept it. Teaching by example is the highest kind of instruction. "Be ye followers of God, as dear children." Eph. v. 1.

3. *The* LORD *blessed the Sabbath-day, and hallowed it.* There is an important sense in which God has blessed each day of the week, but he has blessed this

peculiarly, so that Ignatius calls it "THE PRINCE AND SOVEREIGN OF DAYS." Strike out of the history of pious men the instructions, the warnings, the devotions, the refreshments, which they have received on this day, and what a blank would there be! Hare: "The same difference which there is between common down and a cultivated garden, the same is there also between worldly days, worldly books, worldly names, worldly people, and God's day, God's book, God's name, and God's people. The former are common, and may be treated as such: the latter are not common; because God has taken them to himself, and brought them within the limits of his sanctuary, and thrown the safeguard of his holiness around them." It was on our Christian Sabbath, that the conversation between Christ and the disciples on the way to Emmaus took place. And from that day to this have the hearts of pious men been made to burn within them as in the sanctuary they have attended to the wonderful discoveries of his grace and truth. It is also said that God *hallowed* it; that is, he set it apart from a common use to his own solemn worship. Some think that the phrases *blessed* and *hallowed* are explanatory of each other. Perhaps to an extent they are. But there is no tautology here.

### THE SABBATH GIVEN IN EDEN.

Nor did the Sabbath originate with Moses, or with any sinner. It was an ordinance in Eden. So that the first whole day that man ever spent on earth, was in the observance of this holy day. "The Sabbath is but one day younger than man: was ordained for him in the state of his uprightness and innocence, that his faculties being then holy and excellent, he might employ them, especially on that day, in the singular and most spiritual worship of God his Creator." When, for his sins, man was driven out of Paradise, God permitted him to carry with him two institutions, established for his good before his fall. Which of these institutions is the greatest mercy to our world, or which is the dearest to the heart of a good man, I will not undertake to say. One of them is *marriage*, the other *the Sabbath-day*. If he is the enemy of virtue who would abolish the former, he cannot be the friend of God or man who would set aside the latter. By restoring marriage, as far as possible, to its original purity in Eden, that is, by confining it to the pairs and rendering it indissoluble, the Christian religion has incalculably advanced civilization, peace, and all the domestic virtues. By restoring the Sabbath, as near as possible, to its purity in Eden, that is, by the holy observance of all of it, man makes his nearest approach to primitive innocence and to future glory. There is no example of any community, large or small, ancient or modern, continuing virtuous or happy for a considerable time, if they slighted either marriage or the Sabbath-day.

That the Sabbath was instituted in Eden, is expressly stated in Gen. ii. 2, 3. The same is repeated in the decalogue. Some have indeed said that there was no Sabbath observed by the patriarchs from Adam until the giving of the law on Mount Sinai. But this is surely a mistake. In Ex. xvi., the Sabbath is spoken of as an ancient institution well-understood. In the 5th verse, all Israel is required to prepare for its observance by gathering twice as much manna on the day preceding the Sabbath, as on any other day in the week. Again, in the 23d verse, it is said, "This is that which the LORD hath said, To-morrow is the rest of the holy Sabbath unto the LORD." And in verses 28, 29, is a sharp rebuke for not strictly observing the day. "The LORD said unto Moses, How long refuse ye to keep my commandments and my laws? See, for that the LORD hath given you the Sabbath, therefore he giveth you on the sixth day, the bread of two days: abide ye every man in his place, let no man go out of his place on the seventh day." Then, in the 30th verse, it is added, "So the people rested on the seventh day." And when God does actually give the law from Sinai, he does not declare that he is giving a new institution, but says, "Remember the Sabbath-day," as though it were an institution that they had known in all their generations. Some say that the patriarchs had no Sabbath, because it is nowhere stated that they kept such a day. But this cannot prove that there was no Sabbath from Adam to Moses, any more than the fact that no mention of the Sabbath is made during the time of the judges, of Samuel, or of Saul, proves that Israel wholly neglected the fourth commandment, from Joshua to David. "Arguments based on the silence of history are generally inconclusive." Moreover the patriarchs counted by weeks, and this shows that the ordinance of Eden was in force. Gen. viii. 10, 12; Gen. xxix. 27, 28.

The foregoing remarkable peculiarities of this precept justly entitle it to as high and sacred regard as can be claimed for any command given from Mount

Sinai. If we admit that this is not of binding force, we cannot show the obligation of any of the rest, unless we can show that they are in some way written in the constitution of man, and that this is not. But it would be easy to show, by innumerable testimonies, that life is not only rendered miserable, but also much shortened by not observing the day of rest. The world over, those men do the most work, and do it with the most comfort, who rest from labour one day in seven. Nor is there one exception to this remark. It applies as much to mental as to bodily labour.

### THE LAW OFTEN ENACTED.

The law of the Sabbath is frequently noticed in other parts of the Bible besides the moral law; it is frequently and solemnly declared to be binding, and its spiritual nature is often explained. Indeed, the law of the Sabbath is several times solemnly reënacted. It is mentioned with the highest reverence in the second chapter of Genesis, as a day "blessed and sanctified" by God. It is especially mentioned as binding during the journey through the wilderness, in the sixteenth chapter of Exodus, four chapters before that containing the moral law. It is repeated in the thirty-first chapter of the same book. It is also made by God the pattern for the solemn feasts of his ancient church. Leviticus xxiii. In short, it is often noticed by Moses, by David, by Isaiah, Jeremiah, and Ezekiel. The 92d Psalm is by its author denominated "A Psalm or Song for the Sabbath-day." One of these passages could not have pointed more plainly to a *spiritual* service on the Sabbath, if it had been given by Christ or Paul. It is in Isaiah lviii.

13, 14: "If thou turn away thy foot from the Sabbath," that is, from trampling on it, "from doing thy pleasure on my holy day; and call the Sabbath a delight, the holy of the LORD, honourable; and shalt honour him, not doing thine own ways, nor finding thine own pleasure, nor speaking thine own words; then shalt thou delight thyself in the Lord; and I will cause thee to ride upon the high places of the earth, and feed thee with the heritage of Jacob: for the mouth of the Lord hath spoken it."

In the New Testament, also, frequent mention is made of a day of rest and solemn worship. It is not necessary now to examine more than one of these passages. It is in the fourth chapter of Hebrews, where the rest of the Sabbath in Eden is made the figure of the rest of the Jews in Canaan, then of the rest of God's people under the gospel dispensation, and lastly, of the everlasting rest of all good men in heaven. Surely, so clear and evangelical a writer as Paul, in an epistle, one great object of which was to show that the ceremonial law had passed away, would not have made the Sabbath on earth a type of the bliss of heaven even to Christians, if he had thought they were at liberty to regard it otherwise than as a holy, religious day. From the Scriptures the following things are clearly made out.

In both the Old and New Testaments God claims the day as his. Exod. xx. 10; Isa. lviii. 13; Rev. i. 10.

Pious men have always acknowledged this claim. Neh. ix. 14; Luke xxiii. 56. Was there ever a community on earth who feared God and did not reverence his Sabbaths? When that company of heathen and mutineers who settled Pitcairn's Island, repented and gave evidence of piety, although there was but one Bible and one man from a Christian country among them, yet the Sabbath was strictly observed.

There walked of late in this world a man of conceptions as sublime as they were philosophical, of views as benevolent as they were accurate. Recently, "he was not, for God took him." Before he left us, Chalmers said,

"We never, in the whole course of our recollections, met with a Christian who bore upon his character *every other evidence* of the Spirit's operation, who did not *remember the Sabbath-day and keep it holy.* We appeal to the memory of all the worthies who are lying in their graves, that, eminent as they were in every other grace and accomplishment of the new creature, the religiousness of their Sabbath-day shone with equal lustre amid the fine assemblage of virtues which adorned them. * * * *

"Rest assured, that the Christian, having the law of God written in his heart, and denying the Sabbath a place in his affections, is an anomaly that is nowhere to be found. Every Sabbath image, with every Sabbath circumstance, is dear to him. He loves the quietness of that hallowed morn. He loves the church-bell sound that summons him to the house of prayer. He loves to join the chorus of devotion, and to sit and listen to that voice of persuasion, which is lifted in the hearing of an assembled multitude. He loves the retirement of this day from the din of worldly business and the inroads of worldly men. He loves the leisure it brings along with it; and sweet to his soul is the exercise of that hallowed hour, when there is no eye to witness him but the eye of Heaven, and when, in solemn audience with the Father who seeth him in secret, he can, on the wings of celestial contemplation, leave all the cares and all the secularities of the world behind him."

So it has ever been. He, who loves God's word and worship, he, who delights in prayer and praise, loves the day devoted to the study of Scripture, and the service of Jehovah. Among the thousands of religious biographies now before the world, is there one which shows that any heart loved the other precepts of the decalogue and disregarded this?

It is generally agreed that Christ came to enlarge, not to curtail the privileges of his people, and especially of the poor and afflicted, many of whom are not the masters of their own time. But if he abolished the Sabbath, he cut off the pious poor from one of their dearest privileges, one no less necessary to relieve their heavy hearts than to refresh their toil-worn bodies.

The Scriptures contain many precious promises to those who reverently keep this day, and take pleasure in its appropriate duties. Isa. lvi. 1–7, and lviii. 14; Jer. xvii. 21–26. To such God will give, in his house and within his walls, a place and a name better than of sons and of daughters. He will give them an everlasting name, that shall not be cut off. He will make them joyful in his house of prayer, and will accept all their sacrifices; and blessings like those which came upon Jacob shall fall upon them.

The Scriptures denounce many terrible curses against those who profane this holy day. Jer. xvii.

27; Ezek. xx. 21. These curses are none the less dreadful because expressed in general terms.

God has often visited, and does still visit sore calamities on many violators of his holy day. From the days of the man who perished for his sin in the camp of Israel, Num. xv. 36, to this day, God has made awful examples of Sabbath-breakers. The man has been blind who has not seen them. Almost all felons in prison and under the gallows are known to have provoked God by a series of open violations of the law of the Sabbath. Of six ladies who spent their Sabbaths at cards, five died either objects of pity or without a moment's warning. Not one in fifty of known criminals in the land even outwardly keeps the Sabbath. Men forsake God, and he forsakes them. They despise him, and he takes away the restraints of his providence, and they are lightly esteemed, yea, become vile in the eyes of even wicked men.

In both the Old and New Testaments God declares that the Sabbath is a benevolent institution. He says, he "has *given* us the Sabbath." Exod. xvi. 29. It is not a vexatious or injurious restriction upon us, but a gift, a mercy. "I gave them my Sabbaths, that they might know that I am the LORD that sanctify them," Ezek. xx. 12; that they might have proper time to acquire the most important of all knowledge, the knowledge of God and salvation. Christ himself taught the same, when he said, "The Sabbath was made *for* man." Mark ii. 27. It was made to do him good, and not evil. Nor was it made for the Jew alone. It was made for MAN, for the whole race.

Both the Old and New Testaments record the observance of this day by godly men as an act approved by God, and appointed in Scripture. Even after the death of our Lord, the holy women, who wished to anoint his sacred body, would not do it until the Sabbath was over, but "rested the Sabbath-day according to the commandment." Luke xxiii. 56.

### PROPHECY REQUIRES A CHRISTIAN SABBATH.

The Old Testament requires that under the gospel, in times of its universal prevalence, "from one sabbath to another, all flesh shall come to worship before the Lord." Isa. lxvi. 23, and Ezek. xlvi. 1. This is an argument of great importance. The holy observance of the Sabbath is made by the prophets one of the tests by which the evangelical character of any people, after the coming of Christ, shall be judged. The prophets declare that the offering of prayer and praise, and solemn oaths, in the name of the true God, shall be marks of a true gospel church. Psalm lxxii. 15; Isa. lvi. 7; lxv. 16. Suppose a church should be found, whose members in solemn oaths swore by some other than the true God, and never prayed to the Lord, nor daily praised his name, could any man fail to see that it was without the marks of a true church? And if no Sabbath was observed in the church of God, it would prove that Messiah's reign had not yet commenced. Christianity would not be what prophecy required that it should be. The test is a fair one. Just in proportion as churches decline in the practice and power of godliness, become unsound in doctrine, licentious in life, and lax in discipline, wedded to human inventions, and heedless of the law of God in other respects, in the same proportion do they lightly esteem the Sabbath of the Lord. *No Sabbath, no Church*, is the rule laid down in Scripture. It is a correct rule. Without that holy day, all true religion would soon vanish from the earth.

### A SABBATH AFTER CHRIST'S RESURRECTION.

When our Lord was upon earth, he foretold the destruction of Jerusalem, stating that the enemies of the holy city should cast a trench about it, and that the Roman eagle, the abomination that maketh desolate, should be seen from its walls. He directed his disciples how they should, with the utmost haste, flee from the city, and said, "But pray ye that your flight be not in the winter, neither on the sabbath-day." Matt. xxiv. 20. Now, Jerusalem was not destroyed for more than thirty years after Christ's ascension, and this prophecy was delivered for the direction of Christ's disciples, when the siege, leading to its destruction, should take place. They were to pray that their flight "be not in the winter," on account of the difficulty of fleeing at that season, "neither on the sabbath-day." Whatever may have been the reason why the Sabbath-day was undesirable for flight, whether because it was not deemed lawful to travel far on that day—a Sabbath-day's journey being less than three miles—or because their tender consciences might cause them to hesitate, and not embrace the favoured hour of escape, yet the fact is clear, that Christ foretold that at the destruction of Jerusalem, long after his ascension to glory, long after tens of thousands had been converted to the faith of Jesus, his people should have a day of rest, called by himself, "the Sabbath-day." Human perverseness may annul the force of any reasoning, but candour and piety will be satisfied with fair argument. All admit that all laws and ordinances given by Moses, and not binding to the end of the world, ceased to be of force from the ascension of Christ. But the flight of the Christians from the holy city was more than thirty years after that event, and yet Christ speaks of a "Sabbath-day" that should at that date, in the mother church at Jerusalem, bind the consciences, not of Jews wedded to the law of Moses, but of Christians, converted, baptized, and formed into churches taught by apostles themselves.

### THE EARLY CHRISTIANS HAD A SABBATH.

If we look into the early history of the Christians, we see that they did observe a day of sacred rest; the first day of each week. On that day of the first week after the crucifixion, Jesus rose and was worshipped: on that day of the second week after his death, he assembled his disciples, and said, "Peace be unto you," and confirmed their faith. The first day of the eighth week after his death, was the day of Pentecost, a glorious Christian Sabbath. In several passages of Scripture, we find a record of the meeting of the disciples and churches of Christ on that day, to worship God, to preach the gospel, to administer baptism and the Lord's supper, and to collect alms, so that when Paul wrote his first epistle to the Corinthians, he directs that collections for charitable purposes be made weekly upon that set day. The work he directs them to perform is a work of piety, of proper love to their poor brethren, who were suffering through the violence of persecution—a work proper to a holy day; for it always was "lawful to do well on the Sabbath-days." Matt. xii. 12. "Pure religion and undefiled before God, even the Father, is, to visit the fatherless and widows in their affliction." Paul says that he had given the same command to other churches—the churches of Galatia, 1 Cor. xvi. 1—so that the observance was general. Paul gave these directions by the Holy Ghost. Galatia was quite remote from Corinth, several countries and a sea lying between them; so that the religious observance of the first day of the week was very general, and by no means confined to any one nation or class of Christians.

When we come to the last book of Scripture, we find John, Rev. i. 10, saying, "I was in the Spirit on the Lord's day." We read in the New Testament once of the "Lord's supper," and once of the "Lord's day." Does any one doubt that these expressions designate a feast and a day well known to the early Christians, and distinguished from all other days and feasts by their religious character?

Such are some of the arguments, by which it is shown that the Sabbath should be observed by us. Are they not fair, solid, and conclusive? Are we not bound by the law of the Sabbath?

The most common method of attempting to destroy or lessen the force of these arguments, is by asserting, that if we are bound to observe any day, it is the seventh, and not the first, as the seventh was the day observed from the creation till the death of Christ. It is sufficient to reply,

1. That the term Sabbath signifies rest; and that

rest by divine appointment may, without at all changing its nature, be transferred from one day to another. Some other Jewish festivals were called sabbaths, but never is one of them called "*the Sabbath*," "*the rest*."

2. There is nothing in the fourth commandment, fixing this weekly rest to the seventh day of the week. The law in the decalogue does not point out any day of the week, but only a day succeeding six days of labour. It is said, "God blessed the *Sabbath*-day and hallowed it."

3. The resurrection of Christ was a very glorious event, to which the highest importance is properly attached, and which is well worthy of a weekly and joyful commemoration. His resurrection was life from the dead to all his people, and to all their hopes. If the completion of creation was worthy of a weekly celebration, much more is the same true of the completion of redemption. For Christians to celebrate the seventh day, would be to keep a feast on the gloomiest day of the week—the day on which their Lord lay in the sepulchre of Joseph.

4. Apostolic example is as safe and correct a guide as apostolic precept, and no serious and candid reader of the New Testament can doubt that the apostles and early Christians did observe the first day of the week as the rest appointed by God. This fact, therefore, clearly determines our duty. Many duties are taught us by the example of inspired men. An appeal to such example is fair, and the example itself is binding.

In Acts xx. 7 we read, "Upon the first day of the week, when the disciples came together to break bread,

Paul preached unto them." So from the early part of the first century to the present time, the whole Christian world has observed the first day of the week as the sacred rest approved by Christ.

5. It is believed by many sound writers, that prophecy foretold that the day of Christ's resurrection should be kept as the Sabbath under the gospel. This prophecy is in the 118th Psalm: "The stone which the builders refused is become the headstone of the corner." They refused him when they demanded his death. He became the headstone by his resurrection; for by that "he was declared to be the Son of God with power," Rom. i. 4. The very next words in the Psalm are, "This is the day which the LORD hath made; we will be glad and rejoice in it."

Some have suggested that the weekly day of rest under the gospel, which is an eminently spiritual dispensation, is not to be a rest from labour or business, but only from sin. To such it is sufficient to reply, that every day of life ought to be a day of abstinence from all sin: and when it shall be shown that we are at liberty to indulge in sin six days out of seven, and then avoid it for one day only, it will be time enough to make a more serious and extended answer.

But some persons of more seriousness ask, "Does not the apostle Paul, Rom. xiv. 5, 6, declare the observance of days a matter of indifference?" He does; but the context clearly shows that he speaks not of the weekly Sabbath, nor of any institution of the decalogue, but of matters besides the moral law. The same remark is substantially applicable to what he says in Gal. iv. 10, and in Col. ii. 16.

Every law is to be known by its position and connection in a code. This is an invariable rule in interpreting every body of laws, and ought to be applied to the laws of God and the teaching of the apostles. When the whole connection of one of their arguments shows that they are simply endeavouring to wean their converts from Jewish ceremonies, it is most unfair to extend their general remarks to institutions as old as the creation, and observed before the fall of man, and by all the pious after the fall, up to the giving of the ceremonial law, and then not reënacted as a part of the ceremonial law, but put in the middle of the moral law. "The handwriting of ordinances which was *against* us," is indeed "blotted out;" but that can never prove that the Sabbath, which is *for* us, is blotted out also.

### WHAT SHALL WE DO WITHOUT THE SABBATH?

If no time be set apart by a competent authority for public worship, there will be no public worship. When Paul rebuked some of the early Christians, for "forsaking the assembling of themselves together," Heb. x. 25, it would have been ample justification for them to have replied, "No such thing is required, and no time is set for it." But we hear of no such plea. It never was made. There was as much agreement among the early Christians in observing the Lord's day as in observing the Lord's supper. It would be mere will-worship to observe the Lord's day, if it had not been appointed to be so observed by God himself. Is it credible that God should have left the whole church so ignorant of his will, that all believers for eighteen hundred years should have been mistaken as to their duty in so important a matter as this? The apostle James says, "He that keepeth the whole law, and yet offendeth in one point, is guilty of all." That he here means the moral law is evident, for he cites two of the precepts of it in the next verse: "Do not commit adultery," "Do not kill." James ii. 10, 11. Now, if you do not kill, or swear profanely, yet if you violate the fourth commandment, you are "become a transgressor of the law." Let those who indulge in Antinomian laxity concerning the law of the Sabbath, solemnly consider the course of reasoning adopted by James, and be warned in time.

### WHEN DOES THE SABBATH BEGIN?

There is some diversity in the Christian world respecting the time, at which the Sabbath begins. Some date it from sunset on Saturday till sunset on Sabbath. When asked for their authority, they refer to a phrase which occurs several times in the first chapter of Genesis: "And the evening and the morning were the first day." This has not been considered sufficient proof by the great mass of the Christian world. Nor ought it to be, as all the world knows that no day of creation began in the evening; but all of them began in the morning. That saying of Moses therefore only declares that the day was made up of two parts, the after part, and the fore part. Indeed the evidence in the New Testament seems to be clearly against this view. "Our Sabbath begins where the Jewish Sabbath ended; but the Jewish Sabbath did not end towards the evening, but towards the morning. Matt. xxviii. 1. 'In the end of the Sabbath, as it began to dawn towards the first day of the week,' &c. In the New Testament, the evening following, and not going before this first day of the week, is called the evening of the first day. John xx. 19. 'The same day, at evening, being the first day of the week,' &c. Our Sabbath is held in memory of Christ's resurrection, and it is certain that Christ rose early in the morning of the first day of the week."

### IS THIS PRECEPT MORAL?

The correct answer is in the affirmative.

1. All admit that the other precepts of this law are moral; and this is in the very midst of the law. It would be very remarkable indeed if three preceding and six succeeding precepts were moral and this ceremonial. None but practical atheists will deny that God is to be worshipped; that if he is to be worshipped, some time must be appropriated for that service; and that where this worship is to be public, it is convenient that the time be fixed and known.

2. Nor is any reason given in the commandment for its own observance except such as is moral. The equity of the case, God's example and the blessing and hallowing of the day, are all moral considerations of the highest character.

3. The law of the Sabbath was binding in Paradise, and has been binding ever since. As long as man is on earth, he needs the Sabbath, and the evidence of this necessity is found in both his moral and physical constitution. Blackstone: "The keeping one day in seven holy, as a time of relaxation and refreshment, as well as for public worship, is of admirable service

to a state, considered merely as a civil institution. It humanizes, by the help of conversation and society, the manners of the lower classes; which would otherwise degenerate into a sordid ferocity, and savage selfishness of spirit: it enables the industrious workman to pursue his occupation in the ensuing week with health and cheerfulness: it imprints on the minds of the people that sense of their duty to God, so necessary to make them good citizens; but which yet would be worn out and defaced by an unremitted continuance of labour, without any stated times of recalling them to the worship of their Maker." The example of the ancient nations would prove the same thing. Even the heathen who knew nothing of the Sinaitic covenant regarded every seventh day as holy. Hesiod, Homer, and Callimachus, speak of the seventh day as "holy." Theophilus of Antioch speaks of the seventh day as "The day which all mankind celebrate." Porphyry says, "The Phenicians consecrated one day in seven as holy." Linus says, "A seventh day is observed among saints, or holy people." Eusebius says, "Almost all the philosophers and poets acknowledge the seventh day as holy." Clemens Alexandrinus says, "The Greeks as well as the Hebrews observe the seventh day as holy." Josephus says, "No city of Greeks, or barbarians can be found, which does not acknowledge a seventh day's rest from labour." Philo says, "The seventh day is a festival to every nation." These and other testimonies may be seen in Dwight's Theology, and in many other writings. They go to show that the law of the Sabbath, like the law of marriage, was known at the origin of the human family, and was not derived from the Jews; and that there was an adaptation in it to the felt wants of our nature. Ussher: "The heathens had their knowledge of God and the Sabbath by tradition from the first fathers, which lived before the dispersion." It would be easy to fill pages with the testimonies of eminent physiologists as to the value of the Sabbath as a day of rest to the physical constitution of man, and of beasts of burden and of labour. Duncan says, "Neither men nor animals are capable of sustaining for any length of time the continual waste of uninterrupted toil. The rest of the Sabbath, while it does not diminish the productive amount of their labour, adds incalculably to their comfort and happiness." Another physiologist says, "Of a single Sabbath spent in labour, without any great inconvenience or suffering, we can readily enough conceive; but we can have little idea of the degree in which uninterrupted, unrelaxing toil, going on from week to week, and from year to year, would be injurious and destructive to the health, and comfort, and life of multitudes of our fellow-creatures." In the French Revolution it was not proposed to abolish all days of rest. Every *tenth* day was reserved for that purpose. And yet such was the waste of human life and the decay of human vigour during the time that this arrangement was carried out, that even irreligious men themselves acknowledged its dwarfing and injurious effects.

4. If it is necessary to maintain the worship appointed by God, it is necessary that we observe the fourth commandment. And if this law is not moral, why should we explain it and urge the practice of it

upon all God's people, as has been done from the beginning of the world?

5. It is a remarkable fact that when this law is clearly stated and ably defended, the human conscience gives as strong a response to its morality as to any other precept of the decalogue. Man feels and knows that God has a right to a reasonable portion of time for his own worship. So clear is this assent of the conscience that it is among the last things that wicked men find themselves able to do, to get rid of awful compunctions for trenching on sacred time.

6. Both in temporal and spiritual matters, especially in the latter, God has connected blessings with the observance, and curses with the breach of this commandment; and that in a very remarkable manner. All over the world men have confessed as much. Many a criminal, about to suffer capital punishment, has confessed that as long as he obeyed his conscience respecting the Lord's day, he was sensibly held in check as to other commandments. But that when he cast off the cords of the Almighty concerning sacred time, he was then prepared for almost any deed of darkness. It was a remarkable saying of Judge Hale, that of all persons convicted of capital crimes, while he was upon the bench, he found few who did not confess that they began their career of wickedness by neglect of the Sabbath.

The good also have borne a like testimony to the blessing of God on their right observance of this precept, and to the displeasure of the Almighty manifested against their infractions of its righteous requirements. One of the most remarkable men, that his own or any other age has ever produced, was Sir Matthew Hale, chief-justice of England. He says,

"I will acquaint you with a truth, that above forty years' experience, and strict observation of myself, hath assuredly taught me. I have been, near fifty years, a man as much conversant in business, and that of moment and importance, as most men; and I assure you I was never under any inclination to fanaticism, enthusiasm, or superstition.

"In all this time I have most industriously observed in myself, and in my concerns, these three things:

"1. Whenever I have undertaken any secular business on the Lord's day, which was not absolutely necessary, that business never prospered and succeeded well with me.

"2. Nay, if I had set myself that day but to *forecast* or *design* any temporal business, to be done or performed afterwards, though such forecasts were just and honest in themselves, and had as fair a prospect as could be expected, yet I have always been disappointed in the effecting of it, or in the success of it. So that it almost grew proverbial with me, when any importuned me to any secular business on that day, to answer them, that if they expected to succeed amiss, then they might desire my undertaking it upon that day. And this was so certain an observation with me, that I feared to think of any secular business on that day; because the resolution then taken would be disappointed, or unsuccessful.

"3. That always the more closely I applied myself to the duties of the Lord's day, the more happy and successful were my business and employments of the week following. So that I could, from the loose or strict observance of that day, take a just prospect and true calculation of my temporal success in the ensuing week. Though my hands and mind have been so full of secular business, both before and since I was a judge, yet *I never wanted time in my six days to ripen and fit myself for the business and employments I had to do; though I borrowed not one minute from the Lord's day to prepare for it, by study or otherwise.* But on the other hand, if I had at any time borrowed from this day any time for my secular employments, I found that it did further me less than if I had left it alone; and therefore, when some years' experience, upon a most attentive and vigilant observation, had given me this instruction, I grew peremptorily resolved, never in this kind to make a breach on the Lord's day, which I have strictly observed for above thirty years.

"This relation is most certainly and experimentally true, and hath been declared by me to hundreds of persons, as I now declare it unto you."

All this is but the fulfilment of what is often declared in Holy Scripture, that it shall be well with the righteous, and ill with the wicked; that in the keeping God's commands there is great reward; and that none hath hardened himself against God and prospered. Compare Isa. lvi. 2–7, and lviii. 14.

Nor is it necessary to explain these phenomena by a supposition of any miraculous interposition. He, who exhausts the vigour of his nature by overwork, must expect ere long, sensibly to feel the penalty.

If by a moral law, therefore, is meant a law providing for the necessities of our nature under all circumstances, and enforcing its observance by penal consequences certainly felt by persons and communities which disregard it, it is clear that the fourth commandment is moral.

In further considering this commandment, it will be most convenient first to inquire,

### WHAT IT FORBIDS.

1. It forbids all labour not required by necessity or mercy. The divine example, recorded in Gen. ii. 2, 3, teaches as much. "And God rested on the seventh day from all his work which he had made." So also, in the very words of the fourth commandment we are required to do "*all our work*" in six days, and are forbidden to do "*any work*" on the Sabbath. In Exodus xxiii. 12, God says, "Six days shalt thou do thy work, and on the seventh day thou shalt rest." And in Ex. xxxi. 15, "Six days may work be done; but in the seventh is the Sabbath of rest, holy unto the Lord." So in Lev. xxiii. 3, "Six days shall work be done; but the seventh day is the Sabbath of rest, a holy convocation: ye shall do no work therein; it is the Sabbath of the LORD in all your dwellings." And in Jer. xvii. 21, 22, "Bear no burden on the Sabbath-day, nor bring it in by the gates of Jerusalem; neither carry forth a burden out of your houses on the Sabbath-day, neither do ye any work, but hallow ye the Sabbath-day." They disobeyed this command, and God was greatly displeased. Yet he mercifully renewed the same proposal, and promised them great and marvellous blessings if they would

obey, and threatened the direst calamities if they would persist in profaning the Sabbath. Jer. xvii. 23–27. These several commands are in plain words, are clearly expressed, are given by divine authority, in the most solemn language, and are subject to no exceptions but those of necessity and mercy, as God has himself laid down the law in Matt. xii. 1–13; Mark iii. 1–6; Luke vi. 6–11; Luke xiii. 10–17; Luke xiv. 1–6; and John v. 10–17. Although carnal men will abuse the doctrine of necessity and mercy to defend their violations of the Sabbath-day, yet "the law is good if a man use it lawfully."

Works of necessity are of two kinds—permanent, and occasional. Permanent works of necessity chiefly consist in preparing for the house of God, going to it, and returning from it. Occasional works of necessity arise from unusual events; as the burning of a house, the inundation of a flood, or the destruction of a tempest. In either case the necesity should be real, and not feigned; and should be such as previous care could not have avoided.

Works of mercy are also permanent, or occasional. Permanent works of mercy, are such as the use of necessary and sufficient food and drink for ourselves, and the giving of them to our families, and to guests, and to brute animals. Occasional works of mercy, are such as the providence of God unexpectedly brings before us; as dressing a wound, nursing the sick, and visiting the poor and afflicted, for the purpose of administering relief and comfort.

We ought to be very careful that we do not neglect works of necessity and of mercy, which might be done by us during the secular days of the week, in order that we may make a mere convenience of the Lord's day for doing things which ought to have been done before, although it would be wrong longer to omit them. How very sternly our Saviour rebuked those who would hinder others from doing good on the Sabbath-day may be seen from his address to such a caviller, beginning, "Thou hypocrite." See the whole address in Luke xiii. 15–17. See also Matt. xii. 10–12. Also Mark iii. 4.

2. Nor should the Lord's day be made a day of indulgence in sumptuous feasting. This sin seems to be pointed at in Ex. xvi. 23; in Ex. xxxv. 2, 3; and in Num. xv. 32–36. It is true, God has never commanded that the Sabbath be a fast-day; nor would it be proper so to observe it. But let us not run to the other extreme. This is important, because sumptuous feasting produces drowsiness in religious exercises; because, as far as possible, servants should be relieved from labour, and have an opportunity of going to the house of God; and because, in such feasts, we are too apt to seek the presence of others, who could better keep the Sabbath at home.

3. God, who has promised that "while the earth remaineth, seed-time and harvest, and cold and heat, and summer and winter, and day and night, shall not cease," has expressly said, in Ex. xxxiv. 21, "Six days shalt thou work, but on the seventh day thou shalt rest: in earing time and in harvest thou shalt rest." Very diverse from this law is the practice of many. But if man and beast ever need refreshment from rest, is it not during seed-time and the excessive heat and labours of harvest? It is also a solemn question, and may be pertinently pressed, Who hath

hardened himself against God, in violating this law, and prospered? But even if apparent success has attended any man in profaning the Sabbath in seed-time or harvest, let him remember, that "the prosperity of fools shall destroy them."

4. It was a resolution of pious men, in the days of Nehemiah, that "if the people of the land bring ware or any victuals on the Sabbath-day to sell, they would not buy it of them on the Sabbath, or on the holy day." Neh. x. 31. The thirteenth chapter of Nehemiah, from the fifteenth to the twenty-second verse, records the efforts of that resolute and pious man to enforce this solemn purpose. He did not regard it as a merely civil regulation, but says to the nobles of Judah, "What evil thing is this that ye do? Ye bring more wrath upon Israel by profaning the Sabbath." From these passages it is very evident, that the law of God forbids the opening of markets and shops, and the driving of bargains, on the Lord's day.

5. The Scriptures, with equal explicitness, forbid travel upon the Sabbath-day. The exception is to what is known in the Scriptures as a Sabbath-day's journey. Acts i. 12. From very early times, it seems to have been regarded as proper to visit God's prophets at any time that men's distress required, even though it were upon the Sabbath-day. 2 Kings iv. 23. After the erection of synagogues in Palestine, the distance from a man's house to the nearest synagogue was his ordinary Sabbath-day's jonrney. With this exception, travelling was forbidden on the Sabbath. "Thy stranger that is within thy gates" is put down by name in the fourth commandment,

and is as much required to keep the Sabbath holy as any other person. So in Ex. xxiii. 12, "the stranger" is required to "rest," and the reason is given, that he "may be refreshed." Many and ingenious, but wicked are the pleas urged by men for disregarding the fourth commandment when on a journey; but they are "refuges of lies," which will be swept away the moment man appears in the presence of God. This is a great sin in our nation. Its influence is vastly mischievous. The traveller is seen by many, and sins openly. He requires the services of those who conduct the public conveyances; or if travelling privately, he at least demands the services of keepers of public or private houses. The whole moral law, including the fourth commandment, was given from Sinai to a whole nation on a journey.

6. The fourth commandment, like all the precepts of the decalogue, is spiritual, "and is a discerner of the thoughts and intents of the heart." It forbids us not only to do and to speak what we please on that day, but it binds our thoughts and hearts, and requires us to "delight" in its holy services. By the prophet Isaiah, lviii. 13, 14, God says, "If thou turn away thy foot from the Sabbath, from doing thy pleasure on my holy day; and call the Sabbath a delight, the holy of the LORD, honourable; and shalt honour him, not doing thine own ways, nor finding thine own pleasure, nor speaking thine own words: then shalt thou delight thyself in the LORD; and I will cause thee to ride on the high places of the earth, and feed thee with the heritage of Jacob thy father: for the mouth of the LORD hath spoken it."

Dwight: "We may as easily and grossly profane

the Sabbath, so far as ourselves only are concerned, by *thoughts* which are unsuited to its nature, as we can by any actions whatever. If our minds are intent on our business or our pleasures; if our affections wander after them; if we are cold or lukewarm with respect to our religious duties; if we are negligent of a serious and cordial attention to them; if we regard with impatience the interruption occasioned to our secular concerns; if we wish the institution had not been appointed, or that the time in which it is to be kept were lessened, then plainly we do not esteem 'the Sabbath a delight,' nor abstain from *finding our own pleasure.* Every oblation from such a mind will be vain, and all its incense an abomination. The Sabbaths and the calling of assemblies among persons who act thus, will be such as God cannot away with; and their solemn *meeting* will be *iniquity.*

"The heart gives birth to all the movements of *the tongue.* We profane the Sabbath whenever we employ the time in worldly conversation. Such conversation is, in the text, denoted by the phrase 'speaking thine own words.' There is no way in which the Sabbath is more easily, more insensibly, more frequently, and more fatally violated, than this. Temptations to it are always at hand. The transgression always seems a small one; usually a doubtful one at the worst; and often no transgression at all.

"Multitudes of persons, beginning with religious subjects, slide imperceptibly towards those which are considered moral in such a degree as scarcely to differ from religious ones; thence to secular themes bordering on these; and thence to mere matters of business or amusement. Such persons, before they are aware, find themselves conversing about the affairs of the neighbourhood, the strangers who were at church, the new dresses, fashions, business, diversions, news, and politics. To these they are led by mere *worldly conversation* concerning the prayers, the psalmody, or the sermon, as having been well or ill-devised, written, spoken, or performed; by a history, merely secular, of the sickness and deaths in the neighbourhood or elsewhere, or of the dangerous or fatal accidents which have lately happened; the weather, the seasons, the crops, the prospects, the affairs of the family, and by innumerable other things of a similar nature.

"The next step is, ordinarily, an habitual employment of this holy day in open, cool, and self-satisfied conversations about business, schemes of worldly pursuits, bargains, gains, and losses. It is not to be understood that *Christians* go all these lengths. It is greatly to be feared, however, that they often go much farther than they can justify, and thus fail of their duty, and of the improvement, the usefulness, the hope, the joy, and the peace which they would otherwise attain.

"The profanation of the Sabbath by *actions* is seen and conceded by all decent men who acknowledge it as a day consecrated by God to himself. The common and favourite modes of profaning the Sabbath in this way, are spending our time in dress, in ministering to a luxurious appetite, in walking or riding for amusement, in writing letters of friendship, in secular visits, and in reading books which are not of a decidedly religious character.

"The end of this progress is the devotion of this sacred day to downright business, such as writing letters of business, posting accounts, visiting post-offices, making bargains, transmitting money to correspondents, going or sending to markets, making journeys, at first with, and afterwards without pretences of necessity, and ultimately labouring openly in the ordinary employments of life. This is what is called in Scripture *doing our own ways*."

Some have contended that the law of the Sabbath was considerably relaxed under the gospel. There is no such relaxation anywhere recorded. There is no evidence of its having been made. The reason why many have supposed that this commandment was less rigorous than formerly, may be found in their misunderstanding of Old Testament prohibitions respecting its violations. A right interpretation of the Old Testament would show that in no case did God prohibit the preparation of food necessary for the nourishment of men's bodies, nor that his ancient people were forbidden to do any work of necessity or mercy upon the Sabbath-day. They were not indeed allowed to gather the manna, to grind it in mills, to beat it in mortars, or bake it in pans upon that day; because all that work could be previously done. Our Lord himself lived under the ancient law of the Sabbath; and yet he did not hesitate to take a meal in the house of another man upon the Lord's day. Luke xiv. 1. At the same time he vindicated kindness to brute animals; much more, therefore, is real kindness to human beings pleasing to God. Stowell: "A very common error prevails respecting the strictness with which the Sabbath was observed under the Mosaic dispensation. We have no reason to suppose that its *requirements* were more rigid than they are now;

though, being incorporated in the political laws, they were enforced by *immediate* and severe penalties."

### WHAT IT REQUIRES.

There has perhaps been more difference of opinion respecting the requirements of this than of any other commandment. The human heart earnestly pleads for lawlessness. Men are much accustomed to yield to public opinion around them. The fear of being esteemed singular is a snare to thousands. He, who is not prepared to stand in a minority of one with a majority of millions against him, will not keep a good conscience respecting the Lord's day. It is clear that this commandment not only requires something, but that it requires it in a very urgent manner. This is expressed by the word *Remember*, the most solemn form of memento used in Scripture. By the same word Moses calls upon the Israelites never to forget their redemption from Egypt. Ex. xiii. 3. It is the strongest form of calling attention to a matter. Deut. xxiv. 9; Josh. i. 13. It is found in many parts of Scripture, as the word expressive of our wishes respecting the divine providence over us, as when men ask God to *remember* them, where the prayer evidently is that God may have them in his thoughts and so in his holy keeping. Then we have another word, Remember the Sabbath-day to *keep* it holy. This word expresses great vigilance, as of a guard over his prisoner; as of a tiller of ground over his garden; as of a shepherd over his flock. We must see to it that we do not let this commandment *slip*. In some of its forms the same word is often rendered *beware* and *take heed*. We are to *remember* the Sabbath-day before it arrives and prepare for it. We are to *remember* and keep it when it shall arrive. We are to *remember* it when it is gone, and humble ourselves for the imperfect manner in which we have kept it. In looking into books of Moral Theology, written by authors in the church of Rome, nothing strikes one more painfully than that this one day set apart by God to be observed to the end of time, is put on a level with other days appointed by mere human authority. Thus, the old sin is committed of "setting their threshold by my thresholds, and their post by my posts," and their days by the Lord's days. Ezek. xliii. 8.

This command is as careful to render the observance of the Lord's day practicable, as it is to enjoin its observance at all. It says, "Six days shalt thou labour and do all thy work." Some have raised the point, whether this last clause is a command or a permission. It is not necessary to enter into that question. No human power can make it unlawful for men to pursue their industrial avocations during the six secular days. The New Testament plainly discourages the attempt to fill up the calendar with holidays. Gal. iv. 9–11; Col. ii. 16–23. Even days of fasting or thanksgiving are not holy days; but they are a part of secular time voluntarily devoted to God's service. And if we are to perform these things at all, we must take some time for them. Yet none but God can sanctify a day so as to make it holy. The attempt to do this was one of the sins of Jeroboam. 1 Kings xii. 33. If the clause, *Six days shalt thou labour*, is merely permissive, it is still enough for us. For who dare take away the liberty which God has here given us? Let us then consider particularly what it is for us to keep the Sabbath holy. It should be begun, and, as far as circumstances permit, occupied with the duties of devotion. These are either private or public, personal or social.

### I. THE PRIVATE DUTIES OF RELIGION.

These are chiefly: 1. Devout reading of the Scriptures. 2. Prayer. 3. Praise. 4. Meditation. 5. Self-examination. Into each of these we should enter heartily. We should pour out our souls before him. We should give our minds free scope. We should rejoice in the opportunity to admire his glory and to think upon his name. If we have no heart for the secret duties appropriate to the Sabbath, it is probable we shall find it a burden on our minds, and its public duties a task. Coleman says that in early ages, "the several members of a Christian family were accustomed to rise very early in the morning, and address their thoughts to God by silent ejaculations, by calling to mind familiar passages of Scripture, and by secret prayer." Basil the Great says, "One must arise before the twilight of the morning, to greet with prayer the coming day. . . Let the sun at his rising find us with the word of God in hand. . . . Let the day begin with prayer. . . Let the child be accustomed early in the morning to offer prayer and praise to God." This is said indeed of every day. It is peculiarly appropriate to the Lord's day.

### II. THE SOCIAL DUTIES APPROPRIATE TO THIS DAY.

Besides prayer, praise, and the study of God's

word, in which two or more may join, these consist very much in an interchange of pious sentiments and in edifying discourse. See Luke xxiv. 13, 15. If we are bound to have our speech seasoned with salt, that we may minister grace to the hearers at all times, much more at times by God himself set apart for our edification.

### III. FAMILY RELIGION.

The prophet Jeremiah puts prayerless families and the heathen in the same category. If God's wrath falls on the latter, it will certainly descend on the former. The language the prophet uses is truly startling: "Pour out thy fury upon the heathen that know thee not, and upon the families that call not on thy name." Jer. x. 25. Such families are truly heathenish in their dispositions and practices.

Perhaps there never was a godly pastor, who did not feel that the cultivation of family religion was very important to the success of his ministry and to the progress of true piety; and who did not regret the neglect of it as a sad injury to the cause of God. But what is the cultivation of family religion? It consists, 1. In a devout reading, hearing, and studying of the Scriptures. The word of God is able to make us wise unto salvation, and Timothy knew it from a child. We should acquaint ourselves and all our household with the sacred volume, because it is the word of God, because it is as fit to be read and spoken of in the family as anywhere else, and because we are specially commanded to teach all its truths to our children in the most familiar manner. 2 Tim. iii. 15; Deut. iv. 9; vi. 7; Ps. lxxviii. 4. 2. A portion should be spent in praising God for his mercies. Where it can be done to edification, families should sing God's praises. If it is impossible to sing them, it is well even to read some sacred hymn. 3. To these should be added prayer, including adoration, thanksgiving, confession, and supplication. 4. Religious conversation guided and conducted by the head of the family, consisting of familiar explanations. This commandment also requires Scripture and catechetical instruction. In these endeavours to maintain domestic piety, all the family as far as possible should unite. Some may be too young. Others may be sick; but none should be absent except for good cause. Servants should be kindly invited to unite with the rest of the family, and comfortable seats should be provided for all. What a blessed sight is that, when the pious head of a family, "with solemn air," says, "Let us worship God," and then devoutly reads the Bible, and sings the praises of the Most High.

> "Then kneeling down to heaven's eternal King,
> The *saint*, the *father*, and the *husband* prays;
> Hope springs exulting on triumphant wing,
> That *thus* they all shall meet in future days;
> There ever bask in uncreated rays,
> No more to sigh or shed the bitter tear,
> Together hymning their Creator's praise,
> In such society, yet still more dear,
> While circling time moves round in an eternal sphere."

Great care should be taken that this family religion should be attended to at the most fitting time; and not at hours so early as to make it necessary for the members of a household to neglect their private devotions in the morning, nor so late in the evening as to render it certain that children and others will be drowsy, and of course, unedified. That this whole matter may be truly useful, family worship, and attention to family religion should be 1. Stated and regular. No light or trivial cause should be allowed to postpone or hinder it. 2. It should be decorous, orderly, quiet, and serious. If it fails in this respect, it can scarcely edify any one. All trifling behaviour should be carefully avoided. 3. It should be cheerful, and not austere and morose. God, who loves a cheerful giver, no less loves a cheerful worshipper. Every thing said and done should be suited to secure attention, and to awaken an interest in the service. 4. Therefore, tediousness should be avoided. A wise man regardeth both time and judgment. Where exhaustion begins, edification ceases. It would often prevent weariness, if there was more variety in conducting Sabbath-day instruction and worship. Prayers, expositions, and remarks should be short and comprehensive. 5. But we should avoid both the appearance and reality of being hasty, and of attending to this matter as though we were desirous of finishing it as speedily as possible. 6. Family instruction and worship should take proper notice of family mercies and afflictions. Such are continually occurring. But we should be very careful not to wound the feelings of even the youngest or most ignorant. It is seldom well to lecture one member of a family for personal faults in the presence of others. 7. In this matter, widows, who are the heads of families, should remember that they are held responsible for the order and religious education of their households, even as if the family had never had another head. 8. It is sometimes asked, what should pious wives and mothers do, when the husband and father are absent? The correct answer is, Take his place and see to it that God is honoured in the house. 9. But what shall wives and mothers do, when husbands and fathers, even when at home and well, decline to give proper religious instruction, and to conduct family worship? In answer, it may be stated that it is not the duty of the wife to assume the husband's place, and therefore she may not in his presence, with an air of authority over him, convene the family and give instruction. But though she is not the head of her husband, yet with him and under him she is the head of the rest of the family, and she ought to assemble her children and servants in some suitable apartment, and there teach them, and unite with them in suitable acts of devotion. This course has often been followed by the happiest consequences. 10. As the great object of all religious instruction and worship is to please God, and secure his blessing; so let great care be taken, that whatever is done, be sincere, humble, and fervent. A heartless form is idle; yea, it is worse. Be zealous, not cold.

The following considerations show the propriety and obligation of family religion:

I. The very heathen, who profess and practise any form of religion, do, without exception, maintain some form of domestic religion. Though they call not on the name of Jehovah, yet they call upon their gods, and teach their children to do the same. This certainly argues a strong presumption that family religion is a dictate of nature. It is only in countries nominally Christian that we find men failing to cultivate some form of devotion at home. The presumption, therefore, would be fearful against any system, which should be found fit only for temples or churches, because it would fail to meet the serious convictions and wants of men.

II. The condition of every family calls for such instruction and devotion. We are very ignorant. Every appliance is necessary to diffuse light into our darkened understandings. Every family has wants, which should lead it to unite in prayer. Every family has mercies, which demand a united song. Every family has trials, where each should shed with the rest the tear of sympathy. Afflicted souls can find no better way to staunch their bleeding wounds than thus to unite in solemn acts of worship. Sometimes a household is threatened with some dire calamity. Then, what is more proper than united petitions to Him, who is Lord of all, to avert the dreaded evil?

III. The maintenance of domestic religion has a happy effect on the peace and order of families. If one is absent, or sick, or peculiarly afflicted, how it awakens and strengthens proper affection in the rest, to speak of that one, to utter words of kindness to him, and to pray for his return or deliverance! How many little heart-burnings and jealousies are thus extinguished! How sweet is the sight, when old and young quietly and lovingly meet, and put away all else, that they may speak, and hear, and think, and pray, and praise before the Father of their spirits! There can hardly be an unamiable, disobliging family, whose habit is to make common confession of sin, common acknowledgments of mercies, and common supplications for needed blessings, attended with the correct understanding of God's mind and will. They may lack much that the world calls courtliness. But of that politeness which consists in "real kindness, kindly expressed," such a family can hardly be destitute. There is real love there. Every act of joint devotion strengthens it. Temptation may assail it. It may even be temporarily interrupted; but it will seldom or never be destroyed. Such bonds as these are the ligaments of the whole social system. A good writer says, "That is the best system of economy, which as far as possible causes every family in an empire to be the most prosperous." Any thing, therefore, which serves to promote the peace, order, thrift, and happiness of families, must be a great blessing to all their members. The best "normal school" in the world is a well-regulated family. There, the first lessons of government, law, literature, science, and religion are taught to purpose. A nation made up of such families can never be despicable. It is an alarming fact that during the nineteenth century, infidelity has directed its most formidable enginery against the family institution and against family religion.

IV. The primitive church, and indeed every thriving evangelical church has set us an example in this matter, which it cannot be safe to despise. Church history informs us that after their private devotions, the members of the family in primitive times met for united prayer, the reading of the Scriptures, the recital of doctrinal and practical sentiments and mutual edification generally. This indeed, to some extent, was done every day. Each day was also closed by similar devotions. But the Lord's day abounded in them.

V. This maintenance of family religion is eminently useful. It has nearly every advantage attending every possible method of teaching. It gives a little at a time and repeats it often. It is varied in its modes. It cuts up ignorance by the roots. Prideaux says, "The excessive ignorance I have met with in some, who offered themselves for holy orders, is to be attributed in a great measure to the neglect of family devotion. For, while religion remained in families, and God was daily worshipped, children were early bred up by their parents and instructed in the knowledge of him. And the principles of Christianity thus instilled into them, continued to grow up with them into further knowledge, as themselves grew to be further capable of it. Thus young men carried some knowledge of religion with them to the universities."

VI. Family instruction and worship are of great importance in promoting pure and undefiled religion in the world. When Richard Baxter settled in Kidderminster, there were but few devout families. Consequently, iniquity abounded. But as the spirit of religion revived, so did family worship, until at last, in some whole streets, not one family was found, where God was not honoured by even daily worship. The Rev. Thomas Scott, the Commentator, was very successful in leading his children and servants to Christ. He thus describes his general course with his family: "The grand secret of my success appears to have been this, that I always sought for my children as well as for myself, IN THE FIRST PLACE, *the kingdom of God and his righteousness.*" He says, "he had not attempted a great deal in the way of talking directly to his children, and drawing them forth to talk upon religious subjects; but much indirectly, by explaining the Scriptures, and by conversation in the family, especially by the improvement of passing events, of occurrences relating to their own conduct, and that of others, as the occasions of religious remark, teaching them to take a religious and Christian view of whatever took place."

VII. Besides the solemn passage already cited from Jeremiah, other Scriptures show that pious men did not neglect family religion. Of Abraham, God said, "I know him, that he will command his children, and his household after him, and they shall keep the way of the LORD, to do justice and judgment." Gen. xviii. 19. Joshua said, "As for me and my house, we will serve the Lord." Josh. xxiv. 15. David says, "I will behave myself wisely in a perfect way. When wilt thou come unto me? I will walk within my house with a perfect heart." Ps. ci. 2. Solomon says, "The curse of the Lord is in the house of the wicked: but he blesseth the habitation of the just." Prov. iii. 33. See also Acts x. 2, and all those passages of Scripture which speak of *praying always, praying always with all prayer and supplication, praying every where, praying without ceasing*, &c.

LET FAMILY RELIGION BE MAINTAINED IN ALL ITS PURITY AND POWER, COST WHAT IT MAY; BUT THIS HAS NEVER BEEN DONE WHERE FAMILIES HAVE SLIGHTED THE HOLY SABBATH. Stowell: "It may be seriously questioned whether any one duty is so lamentably neglected among all classes of professing Christians, as *the domestic observance of the Sabbath.*"

### IV. THE PUBLIC WORSHIP OF GOD.

"How amiable are thy tabernacles, O Lord of hosts! A day in thy courts is better than a thousand. I had rather be a door-keeper in the house of my God than to dwell in the tents of wickedness." Such are some of the exclamations of the Psalmist respecting the public worship of God. How well they express the sentiments of God's true people has been testified in every age. It is, therefore, a great mercy that God has not only given us permission but made it obligatory upon us to frequent his sanctuary. No man has ever been the loser by complying with the scriptural ordinances of public worship. Lev. xxv. 20–22. It is an act of atrocious wrong to deny to God the service or the time which he claims as his due. "It is a snare to the man who devoureth that which is holy." Prov. xx. 25. "Will a man rob God? Yet ye have robbed me. But ye say, Wherein have we robbed thee? In tithes and offerings. Ye are cursed with a curse: for ye have robbed me, even this whole nation." Mal. iii. 8, 9. Prophecy requires that in the most glorious times of the gospel solemn worship shall be maintained from one Sabbath to another. Isa. lxvi. 23. Our Saviour's example teaches the same thing. Luke iv. 16. The people of Macedonia, to whom the gospel brought countless blessings, were stated and devout worshippers. Acts xvi. 13–15. The apostles all lived in perilous times. It often cost a man his life to be known as a worshipper of the true God and of Jesus Christ our Lord. Yet Paul, writing to the Hebrews, says, "Let us consider one another to provoke unto love and to good works: not forsaking the assembling of ourselves together, as the manner of some is; but exhorting one another: and so much the more as ye see the day approaching." Heb. x. 24, 25. Indeed, there never was a prosperous church that did not continue steadfastly in the apostles' doctrine and fellowship, and in breaking of bread and in prayers. Acts ii. 42. They who separate themselves from the assembly of God's people are commonly sensual, having not the Spirit. Jude 19.

It therefore seems clear from Scripture and from the nature of the case, that one of the duties we owe on the Sabbath-day, is "a diligent and conscientious attendance upon all the ordinances of God and the duties of his worship, appointed to be performed on this day."

Which duty of public worship could we safely neglect? Shall it be *prayer?* Public prayer is a great nourisher of secret devotion. To united prayer, special promises are made. "If two of you shall agree on earth as touching any thing that they shall ask, it shall be done for them of my Father which is in heaven. For where two or three are gathered together in my name, there am I in the midst of them," Matt. xviii. 19, 20. Shall we give up the public *preaching* and *hearing* of God's word? How can we? True, the preaching of the cross is to them that perish foolishness; but to all that believe, it is the power of God, 1 Cor. i. 18. Yea, it pleased God by the foolishness of preaching to save them that believe, 1 Cor. i. 21. Where was there ever a pious minister, filled with the spirit of his office, yet perhaps sorely tried and cruelly persecuted, who did not yet say with Paul and his co-adjutors, "Now thanks be unto God, which always causeth us to triumph in Christ, and maketh manifest the savour of his knowledge by us in every place?" 2 Cor. ii. 14. True, if the Son of man were to come, he would probably find but little faith on the earth. But of whatever there is, it may be truly said, "Faith cometh by hearing, and hearing by the word of God," Rom. x. 17.

Shall we give up the public *praises* of Jehovah? In this degenerate world he is forgotten, despised, reviled, blasphemed. If he has any friends, shall they keep silence? Shall they not rather show forth his praise all the day long? If our Sabbath is a type of heaven, and much of the work of heaven is praise, shall we not get our organs in tune and in training for uniting in the hosannas and hallelujahs of the upper sanctuary? It is chiefly after a day thus fitly spent in the private, family and public worship of God, that good men are able to say with Philip Henry, "If this is not heaven upon earth, surely it is the road to a heaven above." Similar remarks may be made respecting the due celebration of the *sacraments* of God's house. It is one of the evidences of the low state of piety in the Christian world that so many professors and churches are satisfied with annual, semi-annual, or quarterly communions. Perhaps there never was a revived state of piety in which there was not a desire awakened for increased frequency in the celebration of The Supper.

### TO WHOM IS THIS COMMAND ADDRESSED?

The answer is, To all who have authority; to the

magistrate, who holds the gates of the city; to the parents, who hold the gate of the house; to the principal of the literary institution, who holds the gate of the seminary; to the military chieftain, who holds the gates of the camp; to each man who holds the gates of his own heart; in short, to all and in particular to those, whose word controls the actions of others. "In it *thou* shalt not do any work, *thou*, nor *thy son*, nor *thy daughter*, *thy man-servant*, nor *thy maid-servant*, nor *thy cattle*, nor *thy stranger* that is within thy gates."

### GENERAL REMARKS.

I. Some make conscience of rising earlier than usual; while others sleep later on the Lord's day than is their custom. What is our duty in this matter? It is certain that edification either in public or private devotion ceases when languor prevails. Drowsiness is very apt to overtake a labouring population, when they repair to the house of God, and are quietly seated. It is a shame to see our churches filled with sleepers. From Psa. xcii. 2, some have urged that we should rise earlier than usual on Sabbath morning. Surely the Lord's day was not made for the indulgence of indolence. The right course to be pursued seems to be this: let all persons retire rather earlier than usual to rest on Saturday night. Let them get sufficient sleep, and then awake at the ordinary hour and enter on the service of God. To those who indulge their drowsiness in the house of God, we might make a parody on the words of the Apostle: "What! have ye not beds to sleep in, or despise ye the church of God? What shall I say to you? Shall I praise you in this? I praise you not."

II. In this no less than in all the other precepts, love is the fulfilling of the law. He, who has no heart or relish for the appropriate exercises of this day, can never remember the Sabbath-day so as to keep it holy. All the characteristics of worship described in considering the second commandment, must enter into the services of the Lord's day.

III. Many able writers and more pious persons have remarked on the dreadful plagues, which God has often made to attend on the violation of holy time. Boston's last remark on the Fourth Commandment is this, "Many begin with the sin of profaning the Lord's day, and it brings them at length to an ill hour, both in this world and that which is to come." Calvin: "The Lord is hardly so strict in his requisitions of obedience to any other precept. (Num. xiii. 22; Ezek. xx. 12, xxii. 8, xxiii. 38.) When he means to intimate, in the prophets, that religion is totally subverted, he complains that his Sabbaths are polluted, violated, neglected and profaned, Jer. xvii. 21, 22, 27; Isa. lvi. 2." Durham says, "No breach of any command hath more aggravations; for 1. It is against reason and equity. . . . 2. It is high ingratitude. . 3. It is against love. . . 4. It is cruelty against ourselves." . He adds, "that no sin doth more evidence universal untenderness and that it occasioneth and breedeth other sins." Indeed many writers do not hesitate to say that breaches of this commandment are generally to be regarded as more aggravated than breaches of the subsequent commandments; inasmuch as violations of them are primarily directed against man, and violations of this are directed against God himself. Stowell: "No terms are strong enough to express the impiety of that man, whatever be his creed or his connexions, who wilfully absents himself from the public solemnities of the Sabbath."

IV. What shall those do who have not decent apparel for visiting the house of God? Shall they wholly stay away from public worship, or shall they be urged to attend in their rags? The correct answer seems to be this. Let the rich help the poor. Let them in a delicate way provide for them suitable apparel. But if this cannot be done, let the poor man reason thus: "Shall I stay away from a place of worship because my clothes are old, and worn, and patched? But do I go there to be looked at by others, to mind what others think and say? My business is with God; and if I bring with me a broken and contrite heart, no matter what my dress, God will not despise my sacrifice. Ps. li. 17."

V. Let us endeavour to cultivate more love for the sanctuary. It is a great reproach to the Christian religion that so many of its professors are for slight reasons detained from the house of God. Rather let us say with one, "*Thither* let me go, with willing feet, on the morning and evening of every Sabbath; *thither* a sense of guilt should urge me; *thither* the hope of mercy should draw me; *there* God the Father waits to be gracious; *there* God the Son exhibits his atoning blood, and God the Holy Ghost his sanctifying grace. With so much sin to confess, with so many mercies to acknowledge, with such darkness in my mind, and such hardness in my heart, how can I absent myself from the Lord's house on the Lord's day! *There* a crucified Saviour holds forth wisdom to the ignorant, strength to the weak, comfort to the broken-hearted, pardon to the penitent, and salvation to the lost."

VI. Let us in a right spirit and in Christian fidelity reprove the profanation of the Lord's day. Even Sabbath-breakers often have consciences, capable of being roused, when faithfully warned.

VII. We should frequently remember that holy time will soon be gone for ever. Well may each one say, "Who can tell whether more Sabbaths are reserved for me in this world? Perhaps the next may be my last, and I may never again hear the glad tidings of salvation through Jesus Christ. And shall I then dare to stay away from public worship, with death and judgment at hand, with heaven or hell before me? Shall I let some trifling excuse, which I should be ashamed to make to any earthly friend, deprive me of the only remaining opportunity of meeting God in his own house? Oh what would many a soul give, one hour *after* death, for the Sabbaths and sermons that are now so slighted?" Two things will probably have a keener edge in wounding the lost soul than all others. One will be the recollection of Christ rejected; the other will be, the remembrance of TIME, especially HOLY TIME misspent.

VIII. The Sabbath is, and in Scripture is made to be a type of the glorious rest of the people of God in heaven. If men do not relish the type, it is proof positive that they are not prepared for the antitype. Let us all diligently ask for grace to prepare us for the 'employments, the society and worship of that SABBATH WHICH REMAINS FOR THE PEOPLE OF GOD.'

Thus we have considered the first commandment,

which requires us to worship the true God and him alone; the second commandment which prescribes how that worship shall be offered; the third commandment, calling for reverence in the heart and in the manner of worship; and the fourth commandment, which designates the time to be appropriated to God's service. Thus we conclude the first table of the law.

# CHAPTER XVIII.

## THE SECOND TABLE OF THE LAW.

THE sum of the last six commandments is by our Lord given in these few words: "Thou shalt love thy neighbour as thyself." Matt. xxii. 39. He says of the second table of the law that "it is like unto the first." It is *like* unto it in these things: that it proceeds from the same divine authority; that in order to the fulfilling of it, we must have genuine love; that it is very comprehensive, involving many duties; that it requires our utmost care and vigilance to avoid transgression; that if we have a right spirit towards God, we shall not practise wickedness towards man; that the scope and aim of both are purity; that he who requires holiness in the church no less requires it "in the market, in the shop, at home, abroad; not only in prayer but at the plough." The law would have been an imperfect rule for the government of human beings, existing in society, if it had not as clearly taught us our duty to man as our duty to God. Domat: "Man's first law is the spirit of his religion. . . . This implies a second law which obliges men to unity among themselves, and to the love of one another." It was particularly necessary that we should have the second table, in order to avoid that fatal mistake made by many, that if we are strict in our conduct towards God, we may be lax in our demeanour towards men.

At the very beginning of a revelation of true religion, God would have us to understand that genuine piety will surely manifest itself towards those around us. And in all the Scriptures God "hath showed thee, O man, what is good; and what doth the Lord require of thee, but to do justly, and to love mercy, and to walk humbly with thy God?" Micah vi. 8. If men "keep the way of the Lord," they will be sure to do justice and judgment. Gen. xviii. 19. No possible devotion to prescribed forms of religious worship is ever pleasing to the Almighty, or can save a people from ruin, unless they learn "to seek judgment, relieve the oppressed, judge the fatherless, plead for the widow." Isa. i. 17. Indeed, when God would save a backslidden church from utter extinction, he says, "These are the things that ye shall do; Speak ye every man the truth to his neighbour; execute the judgment of truth and peace in your gates: and let none of you imagine evil in your hearts against his neighbour; and love no false oath: for all these are things that I hate, saith the LORD." Zech. viii. 16. In like manner does God instruct us by the pen of Paul. Rom. xiii. 8–10.

The second table contains six precepts, beginning with the fifth commandment, which points out the duties of our stations in society; the sixth commandment is a bulwark around human life; the seventh is God's protection to chastity and domestic peace; the eighth warns all evil doers against infractions of rights of property; the ninth is God's law respecting the good name of man; and the tenth is the keystone to this arch of morals, covering every thing that involves the temporal good of our fellowmen.

We have an excellent help in the study of the second table. It is given us by our Lord himself. It is simple, easily remembered and easily applied to all the diversified cases that arise in intercourse between men: "Therefore all things whatsoever ye would that men should do unto you, do ye even so to them: for this is the law and the prophets." Matt. vii. 12. Another evangelist gives it in still fewer words. "As ye would that men should do to you, do ye also to them likewise." Luke vi. 31. There is no possible situation in which men can be placed in their dealings with each other, where, if the heart be honest, this rule will not furnish a sufficient guide to our conduct. True indeed, no man will rightly use even this plain maxim, unless he has learned the meaning of Paul, when he says, "Look not every man on his own things, but every man also on the things of others." Phil. ii. 4.

The second table of the law is well sustained by many parts of Scripture, in showing that the will of God is that man's earthly existence should be social and not secluded. The Author of our existence brings us into this world in a state of entire dependence on our fellow-creatures, and this dependence lasts longer in the case of man than of any other creature. Like dependence often recurs in old age. Nor can the perfection of man's nature in any sense be attained in absolute solitude. Hare: "Were we all so many hermits, made to live each by himself, having no ties or dealings with other men, the first table of the law would perhaps have been sufficient; as in that case, man would have owed no duties, except to God only. God, however, did not form men to live alone, but to live in society."

# CHAPTER XIX.

## THE FIFTH COMMANDMENT.

HONOUR THY FATHER AND THY MOTHER: THAT THY DAYS MAY BE LONG UPON THE LAND WHICH THE LORD THY GOD GIVETH THEE.

IN Deut. v. 16, this commandment is given thus: "Honour thy father and thy mother, as the LORD thy God hath commanded thee; that thy days may be prolonged, and that it may go well with thee, in the land which the LORD thy God giveth thee." The substance of this command is also given in the opposite form in the chapter next succeeding that which contains the moral law. "He that curseth his father or his mother shall surely be put to death." Ex. xxi. 17. Again: "Every one that curseth his father or his mother shall surely be put to death: he hath cursed his father or his mother; his blood shall be upon him." Levit. xx. 9. Jesus Christ unites these two forms of the commandment, when he explains it and rescues it from the glosses of the scribes and Pharisees. Matt. xv. 4–6. The apostle thus refers to this commandment: "Honour thy father and mother; which is the first commandment with promise; that it may be well with thee, and thou mayest live long on the earth." Eph. vi. 2, 3. When he says this "is the *first* commandment," the meaning probably is, it is the first commandment of the second table, or that it is the first commandment that has a particular promise annexed to it; for there is a general promise of a very comprehensive nature annexed to the second commandment.

The general design of this precept is to regulate our conduct in the several vocations of life. The foundation of all the social relations is that of husband and wife. But this subject will naturally come up, when we consider the seventh commandment, and is for the present passed over.

The next relation is that of parent and child. The word *father* is used in the Scriptures to express the relation between God and his creatures. He is the Father of spirits. We are his offspring. Heb. xii. 9; Acts xvii. 28, 29. In him we live, and move, and have our being. God is our Father in a sense higher than is any other being. And as in the first table, God fitly provides for due honour to himself, it is by an easy transition that he provides for due honour to our parents. Stowell: "In the care and interest, the tenderness and authority of the parent, we behold a faint image of the superintendence, compassion, and government of God." Some have misconstrued the teachings of our Saviour, when he taught us to "call no man father." The whole passage reads thus: "Be not ye called Rabbi: for one is your Master, even Christ; and all ye are brethren. And call no man your father upon the earth; for one is your Father, which is in heaven. Neither be ye called masters: for one is your Master, even Christ. But he that is greatest among you, shall be your servant.

And whosoever shall exalt himself, shall be abased; and he that shall humble himself shall be exalted." Matt. xxiii. 8–12. From this it is evident that what our Saviour forbade was assuming dominion over the faith of others, or allowing others to assume dominion over our faith.

The word *father* may be taken in several senses: 1. As the teacher or inventor of any art. Jabal was the father of such as dwell in tents; and Jubal the father of all such as handle the harp or organ. Gen. iv. 20, 21. 2. Sometimes it is a mere term of civil respect, as when Naaman's servants said, "My father," &c. 2 Kings v. 13. 3. Again, it designates persons who are our superiors in age, or experience. "The elders intreat as fathers, and the elder women as mothers." 1 Tim. v. 1, 2. 4. Again, it is the title of a wise and influential counsellor. Joseph says, "God hath made me a father to Pharaoh." Gen. xlv. 8. 5. It describes the relation between converts and those honoured of God as the means of their salvation. Paul says, "Though ye have ten thousand instructors in Christ, yet have ye not many fathers: for in Christ Jesus I have begotten you through the gospel." 1 Cor. iv. 15. 6. A respectful term for a religious teacher. Thus Elisha addressed Elijah, "My father, my father, the chariots of Israel and the horsemen thereof." 2 Kings ii. 12. 7. A respectful title given in many nations to the chief magistrate. There was a line of kings in Philistia, called Abimelech, which word signifies, *The King, my Father.* For many centuries the king of France was styled *Sire*, &c.; and 8, the fathers of our flesh, Heb. xii. 9; the instruments of our earthly existence.

In the fifth commandment, the father being the head of the wife is named first. But that no slight was thereby intended to be put upon the female parent is evident from other Scriptures. "Ye shall fear every man his mother and his father, and keep my Sabbaths: I am the LORD your God." Lev. xix. 3. No child, however great or good, ever repaid a mother's love, a mother's care, and a mother's sorrow, manifested during all the trials of child-bearing, and child-rearing, and child-caring. Hare: "For a mother's heart is not like the heart of an animal, which, when its young have ceased to suck, drops them out of its memory. The human heart is of more lasting stuff. . . The mother, the good mother at least, will go on caring for her children, long, long after they have become men and women. Let them be men and women to others: to her they will always be children."

Let us then consider,

### I. THE DUTIES OF PARENTS TO CHILDREN.

1. One duty of parents to children is suitably to provide for them when young and helpless. Nature teaches this duty. God's word enjoins it. Matt. vii. 9, 10; 2 Cor. xii. 14; 1 Tim. v. 8.

2. Another duty is to protect them. They are feeble. They are liable to wrong and injury. Reason suggests that the strong defend the weak.

3. Another duty generally confessed is to secure to them an education suitable to their talents and circumstances; that they may not enter upon the offices of life wholly unprepared for their stations, and thus find themselves most awkwardly situated. The secu-

lar education of children is in many ways important. This includes good manners, 1 Pet. iii. 8, industry, Prov. xxxi. 27, and humility of deportment, Prov. xiv. 3.

4. But their religious and moral training is of so great value as that ruin, temporal and eternal, is likely to follow the neglect of it. In a religious education the first thing to be done is to teach children. In teaching, the *matter* and *manner* both claim attention. He, who takes heed *what* but not *how* he teaches, or *how* but not *what* he teaches, does at the most but half his duty. Teach truth, and not its semblance, fiction. Teach truth, and not its opposite, error. Teach the truths God has taught you. Teach the whole word of God. The law is holy, just, and good. The promises are many, sweet, and faithful. The doctrines are true, sublime, and purifying. The threatenings are wise, righteous, and terrible. The examples are striking, various, and instructive. The encouragements are great, necessary, and seasonable. The invitations are kind, sincere, and persuasive. Omit nothing, abate nothing, add nothing. God's word is perfect. He, who made the Bible, made the mind of your child, and knew perfectly what would be best for it.

Teach things in the proportion in which God has taught them. If God is just and holy, he is also good and merciful. If he forgives iniquity, transgression, and sin, he will also by no means clear the guilty. If his wrath is dreadful, his love is infinite. If he is a Saviour, he is also a Judge. If he is a Sovereign, he is also a Father. If he pardons, it is not because sin is not infinitely hateful to him.

Give clear ideas of the covenant of works, and the

covenant of grace. Show how they differ. Never confound works and grace. Let Mount Sinai and Mount Calvary be set over against each other. Sinai without Calvary will fill the mind with terrors. Calvary without Sinai will breed contempt of mercy. The angels, who never sinned, are accepted for their works. "Do and live," is a law that suits them well. But eternal justice will smite to death the sinner who seeks acceptance by his own merits. He is a thief and a robber. "By the deeds of the law shall no flesh be justified."

Give to the person, teaching, miracles, sufferings, death, resurrection, offices, and glory of Christ the place assigned them in Scripture. He is our wisdom, righteousness, sanctification, redemption, light, life, prophet, priest, king, shepherd, surety, sacrifice, advocate. We are complete in him. He is all, and in all. He is Alpha and Omega, the first and the last.

Draw from the Bible the duties you inculcate, and the motives you urge. If you would repress self-will, stubbornness, immodesty, impatience, idleness, pride, deceit, selfishness, bigotry, cruelty, profaneness, or any vice, show that God forbids it. Always take sides with God against the sins and vices of even your own child. Explain the nature and urge the necessity of submission, patience, industry, humility, sobriety, moderation, truth, candour, honesty, justice, kindness, charity, faith, hope, repentance, fidelity, benevolence, respect for superiors, and reverence for God's name, word, Sabbath, worship, and ordinances. Take not the duty from the Bible, and the motives from Chesterfield, Rochefaucault, Seneca, or Plato.

Present scriptural motives to an upright and virtuous life.

Think not to be wise above what is written: but try to be wise, and to make your children wise up to what is written. "All Scripture is given by inspiration of God, and is profitable." Mix it not up with dreams and fancies, and loose opinions. "What is the chaff to the wheat?"

In teaching, great diligence is essential. So says God: "These words, which I command thee this day, shall be in thine heart; and thou shalt teach them diligently unto thy children, and shalt talk of them when thou sittest in thine house, and when thou walkest by the way, and when thou liest down, and when thou risest up. And thou shalt bind them for a sign upon thine hand, and they shall be as frontlets between thine eyes. And thou shalt write them upon the posts of thy house, and on thy gates." Deut. vi. 6–9. "Be instant in season, out of season." The holy Sabbath, sickness or death in your family or neighbourhood, a narrow escape from some great evil, a time of drought or of plenty, any event that excites notice, even the common incidents of life, furnish fit occasions for dropping the precious seeds of truth in the heart. Occasional remarks are no less impressive than stated instructions. They are often more pithy, and more easily remembered.

Take not too much for granted. Children are feeble and heedless. A little at a time, and often repeated, is the great secret of successful teaching. "Line upon line, line upon line, precept upon precept, precept upon precept," is the scriptural method.

Though you may have taught a lesson twenty times, it is not certain that it has been perfectly learned.

Avail yourself of the love of narrative, so common in children. God has revealed much of his will in this way. The stories and parables of Scripture are not only admirable for their plainness and simplicity, but they enforce truth with unsurpassed power. Almost every principle of religion and morals is thus illustrated and enforced in the word of God.

A good teacher must be gentle and patient. It is hardly worse not to speak divine truth at all, than not to speak it in love. Teach the same lesson a hundredth time. Upbraid not a child for its dulness. Be like Jesus, who said: "Learn of me, for I am meek and lowly." Terror produces agitation, and thus precludes the power of learning. Nor can any thing be more undesirable than to have religious instruction associated in the mind of a child with moroseness and harshness. The human heart is sufficiently opposed to the truth of God without our strengthening it by roughness or severity.

Do not be easily discouraged. Persevere. He has seen but little of mankind, who has not witnessed the sad failures of the precocious, and the final success of the slow. "Long patience" is even more essential to the teacher than to the husbandman. Let both parents heartily unite in this work. King Lemuel has given us the prophecy that his mother taught him. Prov. xxxi.

Enter with spirit and zeal on the work of instruction. Put off all languor and sloth. "Whatsoever thy hand findeth to do, do it with thy might." A lifeless formalism is as truly mischievous at the fireside as in the pulpit.

To your own efforts add those of well-selected pious teachers, both during the week and on the Sabbath. Every school, even every Sabbath-school, is not well taught. Exercise your best judgment in the choice of teachers.

Know what books your children read. The world is deluged with books, which abound in error. Guard the minds of your children against a fondness for novel-reading. It has ruined thousands.

Hopkins: "The instruction of children must not be nice and critical, but familiar and obvious; teaching them such fundamental truths and principles of Christian doctrine, as are of absolute necessity to be known, and in such a manner as may be most suitable to their capacity and discretion.

5. Another duty of parents to their children is that of governing them. The elements of good family government are strength, justice, discrimination, uniformity, and love. Act not the tyrant, yet be master or mistress of your own house. In your superior years, place, experience, and vigour, God has given you all that is necessary for making your government strong. Let it be a government, and not mere counsel. But let its provisions and administration be just. A child can *feel* injustice as soon and as keenly as a man. Impose no impossible tasks. Take into account all the weaknesses of childhood. In governing your children make a difference, not from partiality, but from a proper estimate of their various capacities, years, dispositions, and temptations. The varieties of character even in the same family are

often surprising. Yet be uniform. Be not lax to day and rigid to-morrow. Have settled principles, and let your children know them. Yet beware of making too many laws. They will not only ensnare your children, but destroy your government. Children may be governed too much. Do not expect perfection. In all you do, be guided by enlightened and pure affection. Never chide, nor correct in passion. If you cannot rule your own spirit, you may break the spirit of your child, but you cannot establish a wholesome government over him.

That we are bound to use authority is manifest from many parts of Scripture. Of Abraham, God says: "I know him that he will command his children and his household after him, and they shall keep the way of the Lord, to do justice and judgment." Behold the dreadful end of the sons of Eli, and be warned. He was a good man, hated sin even in his own children, and reproved it, saying: "It is no good thing I hear of you, my sons." But he used not authority, as their father and as the high-priest, to *require* reformation. Follow not so dangerous an example.

With reproof God has united the rod. When it is necessary, use it. It commonly is necessary in cases of wilful and deliberate disobedience. "Foolishness is bound up in the heart of a child, but the rod of correction shall drive it far from him." Hopkins: "This severity is to be used betimes, before age and spirit have hardened them against the fear or smart of correction. The wise man hath told us, 'He that spareth the rod hateth his son: but he that loveth him chasteneth him betimes,' Prov. xiii. 24; see also

Prov. xxiii. 13, 14." Never use the rod to gratify a feeling of anger, nor without being sure that it is deserved. I have somewhere read the following story, which well illustrates the matter. Two stages, belonging to opposite lines, left the same place at the same hour every day for London. Both drivers had orders to make the distance in the shortest time possible. One driver mounted the box, with whip in hand, was excited, spoke angrily to his horses, and alternately relaxed and jerked the reins, at the same time using his whip freely. In a few miles his horses gave signs of distress, and before he reached London some of his team were usually broken down. The other driver coolly took his seat, spoke gently to his horses, held a steady rein all the time, and seldom even cracked his whip. He was often hindmost for a few miles, but while the horses of the other team were in a foam, hardly a hair of his horses was moist. The last few miles, his team not being jaded, he took the lead, and seldom even distressed a horse. The reason of the difference was, not that one driver had a better team than the other; but one was a better driver than the other. One held a steady rein, and never used the whip unless it was necessary. The other constantly used the whip, fretted his team, and wasted both their spirit and strength.

Who has not seen this precise difference in the government of families? The first driver would have done as well, perhaps better, without a whip. And many a family would not have been in a worse state, if a rod had never been in it. Family government is always a failure when it does not secure prompt obedience and sincere affection from the child to the parent

Parents should be agreed in the government of their children. If they do not support each other's authority, it must fall. A divided house cannot stand. Nor should they permit grand-parents, aunts, or any person whatever to weaken their authority.

Hare: "I am aware, this strict and ready obedience, which does every thing it is bid, as soon as it is bid, without asking why or wherefore,—this unquestioning obedience, I am aware, is rather out of date. But God's words are still true, and God's commandments are still good and reasonable, whatever the world, which is at enmity with God, may think or say. . . . There is the same difference between a father and son, a mother and daughter, as between a person who knows a road and one who does not." "Hear, ye children, the instruction of a father; for I give you good doctrine;" "Hear, O my son, and receive my sayings, for I have taught thee in the way of wisdom; I have led thee in right paths. When thou runnest, thou shalt not stumble," Prov. iv. 1, 10, 11, 12. How different would have been the history of Rehoboam, had he duly obeyed this counsel of his father Solomon. There is a race of people said still to be found on the earth in thrift and honour, who are mentioned in history more than 2500 years ago, upon whom a blessing was then pronounced by the Almighty in these words: "Because ye have obeyed the commandment of Jonadab, your father, and kept all his precepts, and done according to all that he hath commanded you; therefore thus saith the Lord of hosts, Jonadab, the son of Rechab, shall not want a man to stand before me for ever," Jer. xxxv. 18, 19. "Train up a child in the way he should go." Hare: "Train him up in obedience to his parents, while a child, in order that he may be less unwilling to obey his heavenly Father when he becomes a man. 'It is good for a man that he bear the yoke in his youth,' (Lam. iii. 27.) But what yoke? First, The yoke of obedience; Secondly, The yoke of self-denial; Thirdly, The yoke of the cross, which is the sign and token of humility."

But beware of so conducting the government of children as to dishearten them. "Ye fathers, provoke not your children to wrath, lest they be discouraged," Eph. vi. 4; Col. iii. 21. David set a noble example of encouragement to his son, 1 Chron. xxviii. 20. Let the parent allure as well as command.

6. Parents should so walk before their children as that they may safely follow in their footsteps. Set a good example in all things. "Tinder is not more apt to take fire, nor wax the impression of the seal, than the young are to follow example." If your child may in his heart say: "Physician, heal thyself," your influence for good in that matter is at an end, at least until you reform. He, who delivers good precepts, sows good seed. He, who adds good example, ploughs in that seed. Children are the most imitative creatures in the world. The different species of ape excite the laughter of fools by their powers of mimicry, but children excite the admiration of wise men by their powers of imitation. Quintilian rightly says that nurses should not have a bad accent. The reason is that children will soon acquire it. And Dr. Watts well says, "It is far less difficult to learn than to unlearn." In his Ode to the Romans, Horace says: "Brave men are made by brave men." Nor

is there any other way of making men brave. Precept, eloquence, and poetry cannot do it. Cowards breed cowards. The same is true of all the virtues and vices.

The power of good examples above bare precepts is threefold; *first*, they most clearly show what the duty is; *then*, they prove that it is practicable; and *lastly*, they awaken a more lively desire to perform it, by arousing the imitative principle of our nature. I have known two men, by precept and authority, without example, to try to restrain their sons from intemperance and profanity. They both failed. I have known many a parent, whose precepts were few, and whose use of the rod was sparing, to raise a family to virtue and honour chiefly by a blameless example. It is as true of parents as of preachers, that a bad example will destroy the good that might be expected from sound instruction. "Do as I say and not as I do," is a sentence that converts the best teaching into poison, and dreadfully hardens the heart. Precepts give the theory, but example instils principle. Words impart notions, but example carries conviction. One plain man, of blameless life and good sense, will more enforce the obligations of true piety than a hundred orators of godless lives. A heathen once gave as a reason for his guarded behaviour in the presence of the young, "I reverence a child." If you deceive your child, break your promises to him, or practise any sin before him, you cannot fail to teach him to do the same.

7. But as he that soweth is nothing, and he that watereth is nothing, even though he be a tender and judicious parent, we should always look to God in

humble prayer for his blessing. "Pray always with all prayer and supplication in the Spirit, watching thereunto with all perseverance." "Pray without ceasing." Pray in the house of God, in your family, in your closet, in your daily walks. Ask others to pray for you and your children. This should not be a mere formal, but an earnest request. You need special wisdom and grace to preserve you from error, and sin, and folly. The heart of your child is corrupt, and all your culture will be lost without God's blessing. You cannot change the heart, renew the will, or wash away the sins of your child. God alone can impart to him a love of the truth, or give him repentance. You may use your best endeavours, but all will be in vain without God's Spirit. Sails are necessary, but a thousand yards of canvas will not carry forward a vessel, unless the wind blows.

Be fervent in your supplications. Monica, the mother of Augustine, said she "had greater travail and pain that her son might be born again, than that he might be born." God answered her prayers, and that too, at a time when he seemed to be utterly lost. John Newton tells of a mother of eleven pious children, who being asked how she came to be so much blessed, said, "I never took one of them into my arms to give it nourishment, that I did not pray that I might never nurse a child for the devil." It is as true now as in any former age of the world, that "the effectual fervent prayer of a righteous man availeth much." Never despair of the salvation of a child. While there is life, there is hope. Wrestle with God like Jacob, and you shall prevail like Israel. Never by unbelief deliver over a child to sin, and to the wrath of God. Pray on. Hope on.

For the encouragement of all who are charged with the religious education of the young, let these promises of the covenant of peace be well considered: "I will be a God to thee and to thy seed after thee." "The promise is to you and to your children." "Suffer little children to come unto me, and forbid them not, for of such is the kingdom of God." "Train up a child in the way he should go, and when he is old he will not depart from it." More precious promises could not be made. Believe them. Plead them before God. Richard Baxter has said, that if pious education, family worship, parental instruction, and a holy example were properly regarded by parents, even the *preaching* of the gospel would not be the most common means of conversion. The best encouragement to effort is found in the hope of success. In this case that hope is well-founded. God's word and providence both prove it. The great mass of the pious now on earth is made up of those who from childhood have been taught the ways of God. Many foolish things have no doubt been said concerning the religious impressions of children. Yet there have been many well-authenticated cases of early piety. Our children cannot too soon begin to live to the glory of God. He who is old enough to sin against God, is old enough to love God. Whether your children shall be early or late converted, yet if they shall obtain salvation at all, they will be kings and priests unto God for ever and ever. Does a sweeter hope ever visit the parental mind than that of standing before God in the last day, and saying: "Behold, I and the children, whom the Lord hath given me?" "A whole family in heaven" will for ever be matter of greater wonder and louder praise, than can be found in all the works disclosed by microscopes and telescopes in the boundless dominions of God.

But if you neglect the religious education of your children, dreadful will be the consequences. "A child left to himself bringeth his mother to shame." Parental love is often blind and foolish.

"A parent's heart may prove a snare;
The child she loves so well,
Her hand may lead with gentlest care,
Down the smooth road to hell."

Trust not your heart. Trust God's word. Give not place to evil tempers and ways in yourself or your child. It is not many years since a young lady thus addressed her parents: "You have been the unhappy instruments of my being. You fostered me in pride, and led me in the paths of sin. You never once warned me of my danger, and now it is too late. In a few hours you will have to cover me with earth, but remember, while you are casting earth upon my body, my soul will be in hell, and yourselves the miserable cause." If you would escape the scourges of a guilty conscience, the reproaches of a lost child, and the rebukes of an angry God, do your duty to your children. Only when the heart of the fathers is turned to their children, and the heart of the children to their fathers, may we hope that God will not come and smite the earth with a curse. As a town without walls, as a house without a roof, as a garden without a hedge, and as sheep without a shepherd, so is a family, whose thoughts and affairs are not moulded by the fear and love of God.

### II. THE DUTIES OF CHILDREN TO PARENTS.

These are many, weighty and of great importance. They are summed up in the word HONOUR. This word is well chosen. It contains the sum of the duty here required. The same word is found in Prov. iii. 9. "Honour the Lord with thy substance, &c." It is often rendered *glorify*. Isa. xxiv. 15. "Glorify ye the LORD, &c." God himself uses the word in 1 Sam. ii. 30. "Them that *honour* me, will I *honour*." Dwight: "The word *honour* is chosen with supreme felicity; as being sufficiently comprehensive, and sufficiently definite, to express with as much exactness as can easily be compassed, all the several branches of duty which parents can equitably demand of their children." Pool: "The word *honour* doth not only note the reverence, love, and obedience we owe them, but also support and maintenance, as appears from Matt. xv. 4–6, and from a like signification of that word, 1 Tim. v. 3, 17."

1. One duty of children to parents is sincere, strong, unwavering love. To be "without natural affection" makes either parent or child a monster of depravity. Rom. i. 31. What a beautiful instance of filial love we have in Joseph, even when he was well-advanced in years. His venerable parent was coming to him; indeed had arrived in Goshen. "And Joseph made ready his chariot and went up to meet Israel his father, to Goshen, and presented himself unto him; and he fell on his neck, and wept on his neck a good while."

Gen. xlvi. 29. Love is no less the fulfilling of the fifth commandment than of any other.

2. Another duty of children to parents is to give them filial fear. Heb. xii. 9. This is not inconsistent with love. Because the child is affectionate, he is devoted. Because he is filled with awe, he is free from unbecoming familiarity. There is no substitute for this kind of filial regard. Mal. i. 6; Prov. xxxi. 28. This kind of reverence Solomon manifested to his mother. 1 Kings ii. 19. It was a good resolution of Jonathan Edwards of Northampton, "Never to allow the least measure of any fretting or uneasiness at my father or mother. *Resolved*, To suffer no effects of it, so much as in the least alteration of speech, or motion of my eye, and to be especially careful of it with respect to any of our family." This is quite in accordance with holy Scripture. "He that curseth his father or his mother shall surely be put to death;" "He that curseth his father or his mother, his lamp shall be put out in obscure darkness;" "The eye that mocketh at his father, and despiseth to obey his mother, the ravens of the valley shall pick it out, and the young eagles shall eat it." Ex. xxi. 17, Prov. xx. 20, xxx. 17. With what great delight does a rightly ordered mind review the account of the reverence with which Joseph treated Jacob, when he went to see that venerable man. Joseph was then actually the wisest and most powerful man on earth; and yet when he approached his father, "he bowed himself with his face to the earth." Gen. xlviii. 12. Where parents are wrong and show vile tempers, the speech of their children towards them should be mild and gentle, even in using the language of re-

monstrance. Thus said Jonathan to Saul: "Let not the king sin against his servant, against David; for he did put his life in his hand, and slew the Philistine." 1 Sam. xix. 4, 5. This reverence to parents should be sincere, uniform, profound. It should not indeed be servile, nor tormenting; but it should be full of sweet submission and of obliging dispositions. However worthless or wicked a parent may be, this duty still binds. One natural effect of reverence is docility. If parents are bound to give instruction, children are bound to receive it. "My son, hear the instruction of thy father, and forsake not the law of thy mother."

3. Out of love and fear naturally grows obedience, which should be prompt, cheerful and universal, unless the parent requires the child to do something wicked. "My son, keep thy father's commandment, and forsake not the law of thy mother: bind them continually upon thine heart, and tie them about thy neck." Prov. vi. 20, 22. See also, Prov. xiii. 1, and xxiii. 22. "Children, obey your parents in the Lord, for this is right." Eph. vi. 1. "Children, obey your parents, in all things: for this is well-pleasing unto the Lord." Col. iii. 20. No expectation of future eminence, no consciousness of present superiority in attainments can exempt us from this obligation. Two examples of Scripture delightfully settle this question. One is that of David, who after displaying amazing prowess, was yet entirely submissive to the authority of Jesse. 1 Sam. xvi. 11. The other is that of the Blessed Master himself, of whom we have this short but comprehensive record; that "he went down with his father and mother, and came to Nazareth, and was subject

unto them." Luke ii. 51. Let all children who are tempted to disobedience, or even to the slightest disrespect to either parent, remember the case of Canaan. Gen. ix. 25. It is true that the kind of obedience due to parents differs according to the age of the child. At first, it is implicit, and rests entirely upon the authority of the parent. Young children must obey without reserve or examination. As children advance in years, it is reasonable that they should understand the grounds of many things required of them. In due time, by the law of their nature and of Scripture, ordinarily God sets them also in families, when it is agreeable to the divine will that a man should leave his father and mother and cleave to his wife. Gen. ii. 24; Matt. xix. 5; Mark x. 7. Yet there can never come a time when the child may cease to honour the parent, in every way expressing love and esteem, and especially by yielding to all his reasonable commands. There have been cases and may be again, where parents require of their children to lie, to steal, to commit trespass and even to murder. In all such cases, children may not obey, because it is directly counter to the supreme will of God.

4. Another duty of children is to contribute as circumstances demand, and as their parents require, to their temporal support and comfort. The law on this subject is explicit. "If any widow have children or nephews, let them learn first to show piety at home and to requite their parents: for that is good and acceptable before God." 1 Tim. v. 4. See also Ruth iv. 15. Indeed that alarming statement in 1 Tim. v. 8, is brought out to enforce the duty of lineal and collateral descendants to provide for their helpless or

dependent relatives. In nothing did those corrupt creatures, the Scribes and Pharisees, more grossly misinterpret God's will than in regard to the fifth commandment. Our Saviour said to them, "Why do ye transgress the commandment of God by your tradition? for God commanded, saying, Honour thy father and mother: and, he that curseth father or mother, let him die the death. But ye say, Whosoever shall say to his father or his mother, It is a gift, by whatsoever thou mightest be profited by me; and honour not his father or his mother, he shall be free. Thus have ye made the commandment of God of no effect by your tradition." Matt. xv. 3–6. The tradition of these false teachers seems to have been in almost all respects wrong. They appear to have held that a sacrifice offered in the temple was of such great value as to relieve children from the duty of showing piety at home; and that if we would say of any thing, it was devoted to religious uses, that cut off all claim of parents to assistance. But all this was mere hypocrisy. Joseph set a good example in this respect. Gen. xlvii. 12. Our Lord himself in the agony of crucifixion did not fail to show filial piety to his aged mother, now probably a widow. John xix. 27.

It is also especially obligatory upon children well to consider and closely to follow the right counsel and worthy example of their parents. It is mentioned to the everlasting honour of Jehoshaphat that "he walked in the first ways of his father David, and sought not unto Baalim; but sought to the LORD God of his father, and walked in his commandments, and not after the doings of Israel." 2 Chron. xvii. 3, 4.

Let us now consider,

### III. THE PROMISE ANNEXED.

Although the promise annexed to this commandment has reference more or less to the right performance of all relative duties, yet it has special application to dutiful children. It is in these words: "that thy days may be long upon the land which the LORD thy God giveth thee." In Deut. v. 16, it is, "that thy days may be prolonged, and that it may go well with thee in the land which the LORD thy God giveth thee." It is either to this latter form of the promise, or to the Septuagint translation of Ex. xx. 12, or to both of them, that Paul alludes in citing this promise in Eph. vi. 3. The literal rendering of the Hebrew is, *that they may prolong thy days*, or *cause thy days to be prolonged.* If we follow this rendering, then the meaning is either that the commandments when rightly observed will prolong the days of dutiful children; or that their father and mother whom they honour will by their prayers, and protection, and example, be the means of lengthening their lives. So Diodati: "That they (the parents) may be instruments, and a means of it, by their blessing, and that this good may befal thee from God for their sakes." Pool: "*That thy days may be long*, Hebrew, *that they*, i. e., thy parents *may prolong thy days*, or the days of thy life, to wit, instrumentally, by their prayers made to God for thee, and by their blessing in my name conferred upon thee; though the active verb is commonly taken impersonally, as Job vii. 3; Prov. ix. 11; Luke xii. 10; and so it may be here, *they prolong* for *be prolonged.*"

What then is the meaning of this promise?

Ridgley says, "there are three things which tend to make a long life happy. 1. Experience of growth in grace, in proportion to our advance in age, according to that promise, 'They shall bring forth fruit in old age; they shall be fat and flourishing.' Ps. xcii. 14. 2. When we retain our natural abilities, and that strength and vigour of mind, which we have formerly had. This some are deprived of, through the infirmities of age; whereby they may be said to outlive themselves. It was a peculiar blessing, which God granted to Moses; concerning whom it is said, that he was an hundred and twenty years old when he died; and yet his eye was not dim, nor his natural force abated. Deut. xxxiv. 7. 3. Old age is a blessing, when our usefulness to others, in our day and generation, is continued. Thus Joshua died an old man; but it was a peculiar blessing that he was useful to the end. Josh. xxiv. 25, 29." Henry: "Those who, in conscience towards God, keep this and the rest of God's commandments, may be sure that it shall be well with them, and that they shall live as long on earth as Infinite Wisdom sees good for them, and that what they may seem to be cut short of on earth shall be abundantly made up in eternal life, the heavenly Canaan which God will give them." Doddridge: "These words express the peculiar care of the divine providence for the continuance and comfort of the lives of those who should observe this precept, the benefit of which those children might generally expect, who were dutiful to their parents." Scott: "The annexed promise of long life to obedient children, might have a peculiar reference to the covenant of Israel; yet careful observers of mankind have noted its remarkable fulfilment in other nations. Subordination in the family and community tends to personal and public felicity; and the dislike, which the human heart bears to *submission*, renders it proper to enforce it by motives of every kind." Calvin: "The meaning is, Honour thy father and thy mother, that through the space of a long life, thou mayest enjoy the possession of the land, which will be to thee a testimony of my favour." "The hoary-head is a crown of glory if it be found in the way of righteousness." Prov. xvi. 31. Compare Lev. xix. 32; 1 John ii. 13.

It is evident from the interpretation of this promise given in providence that it is of a general, and not of a universal nature. The land of Canaan was a type of the heavenly blessing. "God has linked our duty and our interest together, so as there is no separating of them." The author wishes here to record his testimony. During a life neither short nor uneventful he has mingled much with mankind. In that time he has seen many children forego their own gratification and apparent interest for the sake of parents, not always amiable, sometimes intemperate. Yet he has in no case seen such children losers in the end. A blessing has followed them.

The relation of master and servant is recognized in the most ancient writings. In some form it will probably last to the end of the world. Let us consider,

## IV. THE DUTIES OF MASTERS.

It is clear that heads of families ought to be exceedingly careful in the selection of their servants.

It was a good resolution of David, "I will walk within my house with a perfect heart: I will not know a wicked person. Whoso privily slandereth his neighbour, him will I cut off: him that hath an high look and a proud heart will not I suffer. Mine eyes shall be upon the faithful of the land, that they may dwell with me: he that walketh in a perfect way, he shall serve me. He that worketh deceit shall not dwell within my house: he that telleth lies shall not tarry in my sight." Ps. ci. On many accounts we should be careful in the selection of servants. 1. The thing is right. 2. Our own peace, quiet, and comfort greatly depend upon the conduct of those who serve us. 3. We owe it to our children not to bring them into habitual association with those who would corrupt them. 4. We owe it to our other servants, not to subject them to the annoyance and bad influence of those who are vicious. 5. It is a great blessing to have good servants, even as "the Lord blessed the Egyptian's house for Joseph's sake; and the blessing of the Lord was upon all that he had in the house, and in the field." Gen. xxxix. 5. One evil-disposed person can keep an establishment in an uproar, and make it difficult for even the right-minded to maintain a proper course of behaviour.

2. Another duty of masters is government. This should be uniform, firm, and gentle, never rash, inconstant nor tyrannical. It is a great error in some masters that they totally lack dignity. If they have a good servant, they rest not until they are on such terms of familiarity as breed contempt. The commands of masters should be reasonable. They should require no impossible service. Masters may never

command that which is sinful. In that case no discretion is left to servants, but to obey God. Acts iv. 19, v. 29. Nor should commands be vexatious. The tone and language of command should be clear and firm, not accompanied with bluster or threatening. So says Paul: "Ye masters, do the same things to your servants, forbearing threatening: knowing that your Master also is in heaven; neither is there respect of persons with him." Eph. vi. 9. And yet masters should command and not merely request. It subverts the entire order of society when servants bear rule. "For three things the earth is disquieted, and for four which it cannot bear: for a servant when he reigneth; and a fool when he is filled with meat; for an odious woman when she is married; and an handmaid that is heir to her mistress." Prov. xxx. 21–23. "Delight is not seemly for a fool; much less for a servant to have rule over princes." Prov. xix. 10.

The authority of masters is to be enforced first, by moral considerations drawn from Scripture; secondly, by the wholesome laws of the land; and thirdly, by the power which in many cases he has over his servants, which often extends as far as his power over his own children. "There is a servant who will not be corrected by words, for although he understand he will not answer." Prov. xxix. 19. But great care should be taken that the government of masters should not be harsh or severe. So said God, "Thou shalt not rule over him with rigour, but shalt fear thy God." Lev. xxv. 43.

3. Another duty of masters is making suitable provision for their servants. "Masters, give unto your servants that which is just and equal; knowing that

ye also have a Master in heaven." Col. iv. 1. Where the servant is a hireling, his reward should be given him promptly. "The wages of him that is hired shall not abide all night with thee until the morning." Lev. xix. 13. Compare Deut. xxiv. 14, 15, James v. 4. The compensation allowed should be fair and reasonable. Mal. iii. 5. There ought to be constant care on the part of masters to secure the comfort and consult the best interests of those who serve them. They should lack for no necessary thing. It was a great shame in that Amalekite to leave his servant when he fell sick. He seems to have wholly neglected his wants, for he gave him neither bread nor water, nor figs, nor raisins. 1 Sam. xxx. 11–13.

4. Masters should also be slow to take up an ill report against their servants. Prov. xxix. 12; xxx. 10.

5. Masters should also be kind and liberal even beyond what they promised, or beyond what is customary, when they have old and faithful servants. Prov. xiv. 35.

6. According to their relations, masters are bound to make the best provision they can for the religious improvement, comfort and instruction of their servants. Gen. xviii. 19.

Difficult as is the relation of master, yet good men may sustain it. 1 Tim. vi. 2. Abraham, the father of the faithful, Job, and persons mentioned in the New Testament seem to have performed their duties in this relation as conscientiously as in any other. Matt. viii. 5–8; Luke vii. 2–9.

How great a matter it will be to all masters, if in the day of sore trial and still more of eternal judgment, they shall be able as Job to quote their innocence respecting their dealings with their servants. Job xxxi. 13–15.

### V. THE DUTIES OF SERVANTS.

The New Testament very clearly states the duties of servants. Thus says Paul: "Servants, be obedient to them that are your masters, according to the flesh, with fear and trembling, in singleness of your heart, as unto Christ; not with eye-service, as men pleasers, but as the servants of Christ, doing the will of God from the heart; with good will doing service as to the Lord, and not unto men; knowing that whatsoever good thing any man doeth, the same shall he receive of the Lord, whether he be bond or free." Eph. vi. 5–9. So again: "Servants, obey in all things your masters, according to the flesh; not with eye-service, as men-pleasers, but in singleness of heart, fearing God; and whatsoever ye do, do it heartily, as to the Lord, and not unto men; knowing that of the Lord ye shall receive the reward of the inheritance: for ye serve the Lord Christ. But he that doeth wrong, shall receive for the wrong which he hath done; and there is no respect of persons." Col. iii. 22–25. Again: "Let as many servants as are under the yoke count their own masters worthy of all honour, that the name of God and his doctrine be not blasphemed. And they that have believing masters, let them not despise them because they are brethren; but rather do them service, because they are faithful and beloved, partakers of the benefit. These things teach and exhort. If any man teach otherwise, and consent not to wholesome words, even the words of our Lord Jesus Christ, and to the doctrine which is according to godliness, he is proud, knowing nothing, but doting about questions and strife of words, whereof cometh envy, strife, railings, evil surmisings, perverse disputings of men of corrupt minds, and destitute of the truth, supposing that gain is godliness: from such withdraw thyself." 1 Tim. vi. 1–5. Again: "Exhort servants to be obedient unto their own masters, and to please them well in all things; not answering again; not purloining, but showing all good fidelity; that they may adorn the doctrine of God our Saviour in all things." Titus ii. 9, 10. With Paul fully concurs Peter: "Servants, be subject to your masters with all fear; not only to the good and gentle, but also to the froward. For this is thank-worthy, if a man for conscience toward God endure grief, suffering wrongfully. For what glory is it, if, when ye be buffeted for your faults, ye shall take it patiently? But if, when ye do well, and suffer for it, ye take it patiently, this is acceptable with God. For even hereunto were ye called." 1 Pet. ii. 18–21.

These scriptures are clear in condemning two things in servants. One is *answering again*, *i. e.* gainsaying, contradicting, or speaking against their master's persons, or commands, or plans. To this sin they are very liable from their position in life. The other is *purloining*, *i. e.*, robbing, snatching, taking, embezzling, or going away. See Robinson's Lexicon.

These and other texts also require of servants these clear duties: 1, that they *honour* their masters, yea, that they count them worthy of *all honour;* 2, that they *reverence* them, serving them with *fear and trembling*. See also Mal. i. 6; 1 Pet. ii. 18; 3, that they carefully study to please them well in all things; 4, that they shew *all good fidelity*, *i. e.* study to promote their master's interests; and 5, that they yield a prompt, cheerful, diligent, and universal obedience to all their lawful commands, (see also Matt. xxv. 26,) and this with *singleness of heart*, *i. e.* with simplicity, kindness, benevolence, liberality, and with *good will*, *i. e.*, a willing mind, a good disposition, and *religiously*, *as unto the Lord;* 6, that they carefully at all times speak the truth to their masters. See an awful warning to lying servants in 2 Kings v. 20–27. Compare Ps. ci. 7.

The motives urged for doing these duties are weighty and solemn. 1. The opposite doctrine and conduct are full of the worst mischiefs. 1 Tim. vi. 3–5. 2. If servants neglect these duties, they will bring great reproach upon religion. 1 Tim. vi. 1, 3. In faithfully doing and suffering God's will, servants are really serving the Lord Christ. Col. iii. 24. 4. God is not unmindful of their labour and patience. They shall receive of the Lord a full recompense; they shall of him receive the reward of the inheritance. Eph. vi. 8; Col. iii. 24.

Of all the duties which Christians owe to mankind, none are more clearly inculcated and none more deeply involve human happiness and the honour of religion than those which regard *civil government.* Error here will lead to much misery, and will tend to destroy much of the influence for good, which might otherwise be exerted. The matter assumes the graver importance, because there is much confusion in the public mind respecting it. Some religious teachers are truly erratic in their doctrines on this subject.

God's word makes it entirely clear that government is a divine ordinance. Rom. xiii. 1–7; Titus iii. 1; 1 Pet. ii. 13–15.

A few preliminary remarks are offered.

1. There is nothing said in Scripture commanding, much less instituting any particular form of government, monarchical, aristocratical, democratical, or mixed, despotic, or free, constitutional or arbitrary. The kingdom which Christ has set up is not of this world, and was not designed to interfere with civil institutions, adapted to promote the good of mankind.

2. There is no intimation in Scripture that indifference to the affairs of one's country, and exclusion from ordinary intercourse with society are themselves virtues, or in any wise promotive of virtue. Patriotism and public spirit in the true sense of those terms have been illustrious in good men of all ages. He who loves not his own country, which he has seen, loves not other lands, which he has not seen. We cannot think too little of the patriotism, which swells, and swaggers, is noisy and boastful, nor too highly of that meek, pure, humble, benevolent temper, which cheerfully makes sacrifices of private interests for the public good.

3. Christianity proposes to take all men as it finds them, kings and subjects, rulers and ruled, husbands and wives, parents and children, high and low, rich and poor, and by divine grace to make them better fitted for their several spheres. By edict or otherwise, it proscribes no lawful or useful occupation. It never intimates that the member of the body politic loses his status in civil society by a Christian profession.

Christianity does neither elevate its devotees above their proper social position, nor depress them below it. Christianity does not alter man's civil condition.

4. So great a blessing is civil government that probably the most imperfect form on earth, if regularly administered, is not so undesirable as anarchy. The latter carries in its train such a multitude of evils and those of so hideous a character that all good men shudder at the contemplation of them. Yet wicked rulers can do much harm. "As a roaring lion, and a ranging bear; so is a wicked ruler over the poor people." Prov. xxviii. 15. "When the righteous are in authority, the people rejoice: but when the wicked beareth rule, the people mourn." Prov. xxix. 2. The language of Scripture in describing the benefits of good government is striking and beautiful. See 2 Sam. xxiii. 3, 4. 1 Kings iv. 25, x. 8, 9, 27; Let us then consider,

### VI. THE DUTIES OF MAGISTRATES.

In scriptural and theological language a magistrate is any officer of civil government. The distinction of the functions of government into the legislative, the judiciary, and the executive is not preserved in the Scriptures. They oppose no objection to such distinction, neither do they require it. Nor do they express any preference for an elective over an hereditary magistracy. Paul lived and suffered under Nero, and yet he obeyed in word and deed. But it is clear that free governments, which depend much on the popular will, ought to be promptly and cheerfully obeyed, not that they have so much terror perhaps as others, but they confer greater blessings and privileges. In them, laws are a nullity, if public opinion is against them. If a revolution is to follow every act of mal-administration, society would soon be dissolved. Magistrates may err, sometimes through mistake, sometimes through prejudice, sometimes through bad counsel, and sometimes through bad passions; but a wise man will bear with these errors as long as he can.

It is the more important that this matter be more clearly stated and frequently presented, because the present age is remarkable for contempt of authority, and for a tendency to loosen all the bands which hold bad men in restraint and secure quiet to the virtuous.

1. One great duty of a magistrate is to understand that branch of government committed to him. "Woe to thee, O land, when thy king is a child." Eccles. x. 16. "The prince that wanteth understanding is also a great oppressor." Prov. xxviii. 16. A strong mind and correct information respecting the duties of the office to be filled are essential to the magistrate. While it is not right that any class of citizens should be excluded from office, in general it is true that the ministers of religion ought not to rule the state. In ordinary cases, such of them as are conscientious, feel that they have more important work on hand, and are willing to say, "Let the dead bury their dead."

2. But some public men who have good understandings and are well-informed, are sordid, selfish, and have contracted views, and thus are unfit for their posts. A magistrate should be a man of magnanimity, leading him to avoid the thousand little arts and meannesses resorted to by many to retain

office and promote their private interests. A magistrate should feel a common interest with those around him. He should not be a miser, a sharper, a buffoon, a jester, a glutton, or a drunkard. "It is not for kings, O Lemuel, it is not for kings to drink wine; nor for princes strong drink: lest they drink, and forget the law, and pervert the judgment of any of the afflicted." Prov. xxxi. 4, 5. A magistrate should be eyes to the blind, and feet to the lame, and strength to the feeble. He ought to have a tender regard for widows and orphans, the stranger, the poor, the abused, the oppressed. In Scripture magistrates are called shepherds; and if of a sordid character, they will love the fleece, but be careless of the flock.

3. Magistrates must also be men of great firmness and fortitude. A timid man, who can be overawed by the clamour of the public, or led away by the violence of the mob, is not fit to hold the reins of any government. Such pusillanimity and instability of character, as were exhibited by Pilate on the trial of our Saviour, wholly disqualify any man for office. The history of criminal jurisprudence in most countries gives like illustrations of unworthiness. The fear of man brings a snare to rulers no less than to others. True courage and calm intrepidity are desirable qualities in any man. Without them a public functionary is a public curse.

4. A good ruler must be a man of integrity and fidelity; alike beyond the power of bribery and the power of flattery. He must have no favourites in the orders of society. Towards rich and poor, high and low, he must be impartial. When public men fan the flame of hatred between classes, or oppress

the poor, or favour the rich, their power becomes a curse. Some have maintained the doctrine that piety was in all cases necessary to fit a ruler for his office. But is this so? Clearly there is many a truly pious man, who from ignorance and narrowness of mind, and timidity of character, is wholly unfit to fill any civil office. Nor do the Scriptures require that Christians promote the appointment of none but professed servants of God to high trusts. Besides, where ungodly men hold the reins of government, God's people are bound to obey them in all their lawful commands, and have a right to claim the protection of their authority. It is true that where piety is genuine, it is an ornament to any character; and in a public officer it is a guaranty for the conscientious discharge of the duties of his station. Robert Walpole must have dealt with mere worldlings, or he never would have said, "Every man has his price." It is a decision of some of our laws and courts that men who deny the doctrine of future rewards and punishments, or embrace other dangerous opinions, subversive of religion and morality, are not competent witnesses in a court of law. On such what binding force can an oath of office have?

5. A good magistrate must set a good example. In vain will he enforce the laws against good morals, if he tramples them under his own feet. What a blessing was good king Josiah in this respect, as well as in averting, at least for a time, the awful judgments of God is declared in Scripture, 2 Kings xxiii. 25; xxii. 19, 20. Indeed among rulers or ruled he is the best patriot who most faithfully serves God, and he is the worst traitor, who by sin most provokes

the majesty of Heaven. Compare Prov. xi. 11; xiv. 34; Isa. i. 4–7.

A general summary of the duties of rulers is the enactment and execution of good laws, 2 Chron. xix. 5–7; Zech. viii. 16; the maintenance of authority with wisdom, justice, and clemency, 2 Chron. i. 10; the punishment of evil doers, and the encouragement of them that do well; the protection of the people and providing for their common safety, seeking their prosperity and not oppressing them. 1 Tim. ii. 2; Prov. xxviii. 16.

## VII. THE DUTIES WHICH PEOPLE OWE TO THEIR RULERS.

It is evident that the particular form of the government under which men live will somewhat modify their duties to their rulers. In a free commonwealth more liberty is granted and the people are citizens, with their rights guaranteed. In a despotic form of government they are subjects of a prince whose will is the supreme law of the land. But the form of government can never absolve any one from the solemn duties he owes his rulers.

1. As a general principle, we are to recognize the actual incumbent of any office as having been appointed thereto by Providence. "Promotion cometh neither from the east, nor from the west, nor from the south. But God is the judge: he putteth down one, and setteth up another." Ps. lxxv. 6, 7. When our Saviour was on earth, it was much debated whether the Roman power in Judea was lawful. The question was submitted to him. He made no decision of the matter further than this; that it was lawful to pay tribute, and so submit to the civil

magistrate in the exercise of actual authority. "Infidelity, or difference in religion, doth not make void a magistrate's just and legal authority, nor free the people from their due obedience to him.' Nor do the illegal or wicked acts of a ruler in some things, exempt us from obedience to him in those things which he may lawfully require. Papists have sometimes maintained the right of the Bishop of Rome to depose temporal princes. But the church has no sword except that of spiritual authority for spiritual ends. 2 Cor. x. 14. The case they sometimes urge from 2 Chron. xxvi. 16–18, does not help their cause. In that case Uzziah sinned by intruding himself into the sacred office, and Azariah and the other priests did not attempt to depose him from his kingly office. They only warned him against persisting in sin. It was God that excluded him from the functions of his civil office by smiting him with leprosy. Nor is the case mentioned in 2 Kings xi. 15, any more in their favour. For Athaliah was a woman and was not permitted to rule. Joash was also the lawful successor to the throne, and before the death of Athaliah had been proclaimed, anointed, and owned by the people as their king. 2 Kings xi. 12, 14.

2. It is the duty of all men to treat all the officers of the government from the highest to the lowest with respect, and to give to each the honour that is his due, never using reviling or railing language to them or concerning them. All this is clear from God's word. See Ex. xxii. 28; 1 Sam. xxvi. 19; Eccles. x. 20; Acts xxiii. 5; Rom. xiii. 7; 1 Pet. ii. 17; Jude 8, 9. Nothing can release us from this duty. Beyond his place and out of his place, an officer is to be

treated as other men, according to his merits. But in his official duty he must be honoured. Until Daniel was sent to denounce the judgments of God, and pass sentence of death on the guilty Belshazzar, he ever treated the court of Babylon with profound respect.

3. We ought earnestly and fervently to pray for all that have authority over us, whatever their rank or character may be. This is a most reasonable duty, and it is expressly commanded, 1 Tim. ii. 1, 2. Such prayers ought to be offered in the closet, in the family, and in the great congregation. Nothing will justify formality or heartlessness in presenting such supplications. Our approval or disapproval of the leading measures of a government, neither increases nor diminishes this obligation. The command is clear and peremptory. It is not possible that Paul approved of the cruelties and enormities of Nero, yet he prayed for him, and charged others to do the same. A due attention to this course would save us from an immense amount of misery. Nor should we forget that rulers, especially those very high in office, have a vast amount of worldly cares, which do bring their souls into extreme peril. Benevolence therefore urges us to this duty. Do you pray for public men? They are in one sense your servants. Ought you not to ask for them grace to be faithful and wise? They are in another sense your rulers. Is it not a duty frequently enjoined by God that men should pray for their rulers? Does not nature teach as much? Would not a warmly pious heart compel you to do it? One hearty prayer will do more good than a thousand angry remarks, and when you shall

have offered such a prayer, you will be a better man for having done it.

4. We ought to pay all the taxes of every kind legally demanded of us by the government. We ought to do this honestly, promptly, cheerfully. So Christ taught us by his own example. Matt. xvii. 27. So he taught us with his own blessed lips. Matt. xxii. 20, 21; Mark xii. 16, 17; Luke xx. 24–26. So Paul teaches us, Rom. xiii. 6, 7. Other passages are parallel. The Scriptures mention two kinds of taxes which are to be paid. One is *custom*, or a tax on property. The other is *tribute* or a poll tax. It is as truly wicked to defraud the government of its pecuniary dues, as it is to rob the poor.

5. We ought also to give a prompt, cheerful and conscientious obedience to all the lawful commands of our government. This is made very clear from God's word. See Rom. xiii. 1–5; Titus iii. 1; 1 Pet. ii. 13–17. These proofs derive great force from the fact that certainly one and perhaps all of them were written when a monster of wickedness ruled the Roman empire. The Scriptures are careful to note that our obedience is to be rendered, not for our attachment to a person or a party, but "for conscience' sake," that is, from religious principle. If the government should go beyond its duty and require us to do something wicked, then, indeed, we must obey God rather than man. Thus Daniel and the three young Hebrews refused to obey the commands of the mightiest monarch on earth, because his decrees were wicked. He had no right to forbid the prophet to worship the God of heaven, nor to require the three young men to fall down before his idol. In disobey-

ing his wicked behests, these four men obtained a good report. On the other hand, the Israelites obeyed the wicked commands of Jeroboam, and the curse of God came upon them for their temerity. Where rulers go out of their office and meddle with things not belonging to them, they are not our rulers in that behalf, and so we are not bound to follow their dictation. The obedience we owe to the laws is due to them as laws, and not as the caprices of men out of office, or beside their office.

6. All the acts and measures of a government are entitled to a just and candid construction. We are never at liberty to deal unfairly with any man, or set of men, much less with those who are borne down with the weight of public responsibilities. It is human to err. It is the glory of a man to pass over both serious mistakes and real wrongs as long as God's providence subjects him to them; and so long as they are bearable. Blind submission and fond admiration are not required of us. But is it not true that in some circles, at least, our public men receive great injustice? Is there not a greater readiness to take up an evil report against the private character of public than of private men? Is it certain that many do not greatly disregard the divine rule, "Thou shalt not speak evil of the ruler of thy people?" In 1827, an editor in Germany, forming his opinions from the journals of this country, said: "In the United States there are two candidates for the next presidency, neither of whom can be worthy of the least confidence. Indeed, they must be two of the worst men in the world." When we remember that this was said of two pure patriots, whose reputation is

now no small part of our country's honour, how must every good man blush!

Indeed, these atrocious attacks on private character, have, in some cases, deterred good men from consenting to be candidates for important offices. Not long since, a worthy and fit man was solicited to accept a nomination for the office of Governor of his State. His reply was in substance that he had maintained through life such a reputation as his children might not be ashamed of; but should he lend his name for such a place, he should expect some infamous story to be fabricated, and by some believed. He therefore respectfully, but positively refused. Should such refusals become common, our statesmen will soon be as bad as some in their uncharitableness are now ready to declare them all to be.

It may, indeed, be said that the characters of public men are public property. Grant it, and yet it may solemnly be asked, Has any man a right to injure the public property? Can any act of wantonness be more wicked than to spread a false report concerning a public man? And it is not true that the private character of any man so belongs to the public, that it may be innocently assailed without mercy. The official conduct of every representative and functionary is proper matter of just criticism, and thorough but fair investigation. But if all the indiscretions of childhood and youth are to be sought out and dragged before the public, or if old and vile slanders are to be dug up and sent forth afresh, where is love? where is justice? where are the bonds of society? where are Christian morals?

It is true that men are often elected to carry out

certain views which they honestly entertained and avowed before their election. If their views should change, all they have to do is to resign. Less than this would be highly dishonourable. It is true that when men differ from us on any subject, we are prone to think their arguments weak; but is it thereupon right to say that they are not honestly held? And warm discussions, whether on the whole operating for good or evil, are inseparable from freedom of opinion. Call them, if you choose, the evidences of feebleness in the human understanding. But they are essential to the maintenance of our great interests.

It is also true that men, who do not actively and long engage in public affairs, seldom understand the bearings of many measures. A principle is often involved in a vote, which, if once adopted, carries millions of money, and finally the liberties of the people with it. To reject a bill reasonable in most of its provisions, because it incorporates such a principle, may be a solemn duty.

Let us at least hear before we condemn. "He that answereth a matter before he heareth it, it is folly and shame unto him." A large number of public measures, which, at the time of their adoption caused the greatest outcries in any country, are now generally confessed to have been wise and necessary.

Let all good men remember these things.

1. Our rulers have souls to be saved or lost like other men. And their souls are in great danger from the ever-pressing and exciting nature of their duties. Public men are often separated from their families, from the best opportunities of secret devotion, and from the most impressive preaching of the gospel.

Other and peculiar temptations beset them. But they can be saved. Among them are fine specimens of evangelical piety and Christian consistency. It was, while a member of Congress, that Mr. (afterwards Rev. Dr.) Milnor became a follower of the prophet of Galilee.

2. Public men have passions and consciences like other men. They often think of a future state, and a judgment to come. They often wish that some one would deal honestly and kindly with their souls. They wonder that they so often get letters from pious men, full of news, business, and politics, but seldom containing a word about God, eternity, the soul, or salvation. Who writes letters to politicians, exhorting them to work out their salvation with fear and trembling? Yet such letters would be highly prized by many, if written in a tone of modesty, kindness, and earnestness.

3. What a powerful influence the testimony of public men exerts in behalf of religion, when it is publicly and honestly given. No sentiment of any minister of the gospel of the same weight has probably been read or felt by so many persons as the following paragraph from one of our leading politicians, uttered on occasion of the death of a friend: "Political eminence and professional fame fade and die with all things earthly. Nothing of character is really permanent, but virtue and personal worth. They remain. Whatever of excellence is wrought into the soul itself, belongs to both worlds. Real goodness does not attach itself merely to this life, it points to another world. Political or professional fame cannot last for ever, but a conscience void of offence before

God and man, is an inheritance for eternity. *Religion*, therefore, is a necessary, an indispensable element in any great human character. There is no living without it. Religion is the tie that connects man with his Creator, and holds him to his throne. If that tie be all sundered, all broken, he floats away, a worthless atom in the universe, its proper attractions all gone, its destiny thwarted, and its whole future, nothing but darkness, desolation and death. A man with no sense of religious duty is he whom the Scriptures describe—in so terse but terrific a manner—as 'living without God in the world.' Such a man is out of his proper being, out of the circle of all his duties, out of the circle of all his happiness, and away, far, far away from the purposes of his creation."

7. When our good rulers die, it is our duty publicly to manifest our sorrow in some becoming manner. Thus "the children of Israel wept for Moses in the plains of Moab, thirty days," Deut. xxxiv. 8. Thus also "all Judah and Jerusalem mourned for Josiah. And Jeremiah lamented for Josiah; all the singing men and the singing women spake of Josiah in their lamentations to this day." 2 Chron. xxxv. 24, 25. It is true indeed we can show no such respect as this to the memory of those monsters of wickedness, who sometimes bear rule over men. "When the wicked perish there is shouting," Prov. xi. 10. God inspired Isaiah to compose the sublimest poem found in any language, to be sung on the occasion of the death of that great oppressor, the king of Babylon, Isa. xiv. 4–23.

The duties of both magistrates and people are enforced by the most solemn sanctions. If the ruled have their duties, so have the rulers. If the line of conduct is pointed out to the governed, it is also pointed out to governors. If the one, by misconduct, exposes himself to reprehension, so by misrule does the other. If the oath of fidelity and allegiance in the one cannot be broken without treason; the oath of office in the other cannot be unheeded without perjury. If the thief and the robber, and the murderer and the assassin shall not escape condemnation, shall tyrants and licentious rulers, who delight in blood, and gather around them unprincipled miscreants, be innocent? If history points to the miserable end of wicked Shimei, who cursed the Lord's anointed, it no less warns us by the terrible punishments which came upon Saul, once the Lord's anointed, but for his iniquities delivered over to wrath.

In like manner, we might show in detail the relative duties of teachers and pupils, of church-officers and church-members, of commanders and soldiers, of old and young, of rich and poor, and indeed of all the relations of life. Lest we be tedious, these are passed over, not because they are unimportant, but because the chief duties arising out of them have been hinted at in considering other relations, or may easily be learned by reference to Scripture. Men are divided into three classes, superiors, inferiors, and equals. 1. In general the duties of superiors are to "love, pray for, and bless their inferiors; to instruct, counsel, and admonish them; countenancing, commending, and rewarding such as do well, and discountenancing, reproving, and chastising such as do ill, protecting and providing for them things necessary for soul and body; and by grave, wise, holy, and exemplary carriage, to procure glory to God, honour to themselves, and so preserve that authority which God hath put upon them." 2. The duties of inferiors are "due reverence in heart, word and behaviour; prayer and thanksgiving for them; imitation of their virtues and graces; willing obedience to their lawful commands and counsels; due submission to their corrections; fidelity to them; the defence and maintenance of their persons and authority; bearing with their infirmities, and covering them in love." 3. Because the law of God is perfect and comprehends all possible cases, no doubt the relations of equals are included in this precept. For, if superiors and inferiors owe duties to others, surely equals are not exempt from obligations to their fellows. The Westminster Assembly thus well sums up the duties of equals. "The duties of equals are, to regard the dignity and worth of each other, in giving honour to go one before another; and to rejoice in each other's gifts and advancement as their own." The same respectable authority says, "The sins of equals are, besides the neglect of the duties required, the undervaluing of the worth, envying the gifts, grieving at the advancement or prosperity one of another; and usurping pre-eminence one over another."

## CHAPTER XX.

### THE SIXTH COMMANDMENT.

THOU SHALT NOT KILL.

THIS commandment, as well as others, was greatly perverted by the traditions and glosses of the Scribes and Pharisees. So when our Saviour came, the design of a part of his teaching was to rescue it from perversion: "Ye have heard that it was said by them of old time, Thou shalt not kill; and whosoever shall kill shall be in danger of the judgment; but I say unto you, That whosoever is angry with his brother without a cause shall be in danger of the judgment; and whosoever shall say to his brother, *Raca*, shall be in danger of the council; but whosoever shall say, *Thou fool*, shall be in danger of hell-fire," Matt. v. 21, 22. The general scope of this teaching of our Lord is to show that not only actual murder is thus forbidden, but also all that leads to it.

A few preliminary remarks seem to be called for.

1. The command reads, "*Thou shalt not kill;*" and upon the face of it, we seem to be prohibited from taking the life of any creature. But other Scriptures inform us, that it is lawful for us to eat the flesh of beasts, birds, and fishes. Thus God says to Noah, "Every moving thing that liveth shall be meat for you; even

as the green herb have I given thee all things," Gen. ix. 3. This grant is the more remarkable as it was not made until more than 2300 years after the creation. The New Testament fully sustains this grant to Noah. Our Lord himself partook of animal food, Luke xxiv. 42. And Paul says, "I know and am persuaded by the Lord Jesus that there is nothing unclean of itself," Rom. xiv. 14. And again, "Whatsoever is sold in the shambles, that eat, asking no questions for conscience' sake," 1 Cor. x. 25. And again, "Every creature of God is good, and nothing to be refused, if it be received with thanksgiving," 1 Tim. iv. 4. So that it is clear that we are not forbidden to take the life of animals for food.

Nor is it wrong to take the life of animals which are dangerous or ravenous. By miracle David slew a bear and a lion; and Paul shook off the serpent into the fire. The law of self-preservation fully justifies our destruction of noxious animals.

But lest this liberty be misunderstood, it is proper to state that all cruelty to the brute creation is clearly forbidden. Durham: "God once made a dumb ass to rebuke the madness of a prophet," Num. xxii. 28. "A righteous man regardeth the life of his beast." The emperor Domitian began his career of crime and cruelty by torturing flies with a bodkin. Benedict Arnold, when a lad, delighted in tormenting calves, colts, and lambs, thus preparing for his end of infamy.

2. There are three reasons why we are bound to be careful of human life. The first is, that mankind are our brethren and our flesh. Gen. xxxvii. 27; Isa. lviii. 7; Acts xvii. 26, 28. Nature ought to move,

and if we were not sadly depraved, would mightily move us in this direction. The second is, that God made man in his own image. Gen. ix. 6. Although by the fall, man has lost the moral image of God, yet he still has his natural image, consisting in his intellectual nature, which though marred is not destroyed. A third reason is, a clear and explicit command of God, hedging about human life with great care, as in this commandment, and often elsewhere; so that God requires that every beast that shall shed the blood of man shall itself be slain. Gen. ix. 5; Ex. xxi. 28.

3. Important as is the preservation of our own lives and the lives of our fellow-men, yet we are not at liberty to use unlawful means for that purpose. We may not lie, or steal, or swear falsely, or deny God's truth, even to save life, our own or that of others. Gen. xii. 12, 13; Rom. iii. 8; 1 Tim. i. 19, 20. Honour, truth, and conscience are worth more than life. It was the devil (and not God) who said: "Skin for skin, yea, all that a man hath will he give for his life." Job ii. 4.

4. There is nothing in this command forbidding us to take the life of men, who are seeking our lives, if we have no other way of escaping their malicious plots. This was clearly settled just after giving the moral law from Sinai. "If a thief be found breaking up, and be smitten that he die, there shall no blood be shed for him." Ex. xxii. 2. Our Lord, himself, may allude to this law as of force in his day. Matt. xxiv. 43. The reason of the law is, that there is always a strong presumption that a house-breaker will commit murder, if necessary to effect his nefarious designs. Nearly the whole Christian world has united in de-

claring the right of self-defence against murderous assaults.

5. Nor is there anything in this command prohibiting war, when necessary for the defence of a nation, or for the recovery of unquestioned rights. Gen. xiv. 13–16; Ex. xvii. 8–12; Judges v. 23; 1 Sam. xxx. 3–20, &c. John the Baptist called upon soldiers to "do no violence, and accuse no man falsely, but be content with your wages," Luke iii. 14; but he never hinted to them that their calling was unlawful. Our Lord also greatly commended the faith of the centurion, but never called on him to renounce his profession. Luke vii. 8, 9. While all this is so, the world ought not to forget what Dwight says: "Aggressive war is nothing but a complication of robbery and murder;" and what Robert Hall says: "War is nothing but a temporary repeal of all the principles of virtue." We are also warned in Scripture that war is full of terrors and horrors.

The prophet Isaiah thus describes war:

"Howl ye, for the day of the Lord is at hand; it shall come as a destruction from the Almighty. Therefore shall all hands be faint, and every man's heart shall melt; and they shall be afraid; pangs and sorrows shall take hold of them; they shall be in pain as a woman that travaileth; they shall be amazed one at another; their faces shall be as flames. Behold, the day of the Lord cometh, cruel both with wrath and fierce anger, to lay the land desolate: and he shall destroy the sinners thereof out of it. For the stars of heaven and the constellations thereof shall not give their light; the sun shall be darkened in his going forth, and the moon shall not cause her light to shine. Every one that is found shall be thrust through. Their children also shall be dashed to pieces before their eyes; their houses shall be spoiled, and their wives ravished. Their bows also shall dash the young men to pieces, and they shall have no pity on the fruit of the womb; their eye shall not spare children. For every battle of the warrior is with confused noise, and garments rolled in blood." Compare Jer. iv. 19–31.

6. Although this commandment is against the murder of men's bodies, and against all that may lead thereto, it could be by fair and easy inference shown that the murder of their souls is even more dreadful; and we may therefore expect God to inflict the direst judgments on those on whom the blood of souls is found. Ezek. xxxiii. 8.

We are now prepared to consider several classes of sins against this commandment.

## I. WRONG FEELINGS.

"A tart temper never mellows with age, and a sharp tongue is the only edged-tool that grows keener with constant use."—*Irving.*

1. One of the tempers very unfriendly to our own life and the lives of others is discontent. When indulged, there is no telling to what length it will go. It is very deceitful, and comes to us under the most plausible pretences. "A change of situation is but a change of one class of trials, temptations, and duties for another." "Hell and destruction are never full, so the eyes of man are never satisfied." Prov. xxvii. 20. Discontent is well-nigh universal. Through divine grace it does not *reign* in the righte-

ous, but it annoys them. How much unseemliness it produces. "As a bird that wandereth from her nest, so is a man that wandereth from his place." Prov. xxvii 8. When discontent becomes strong and violent, it exhibits itself in ill-nature towards man and in hard thoughts and wicked speeches respecting God. It makes our fellow-creatures around us unhappy. It converts us into "murmurers and complainers." Jude 16. It is entirely counter to the Lord's prayer, "Thy will be done." It produces pining, and often ends in the destruction of human life. It would be well if mankind had clear apprehensions of the sinfulness of discontent. When it assumes a violent form and becomes impatient, it makes us quarrel with providence, and foolishly declare life undesirable. The prophet sent to warn Nineveh was in such a frame. "Now, O Lord, take, I beseech thee, my life from me; for it is better for me to die than to live. . . . I do well to be angry even unto death." Jonah iv. 3, 9. How much more befitting was the language of Job in his deep afflictions: "All the days of my appointed time will I wait, till my change come." Job xiv. 14. Luther, seeing a bird light on a twig by his window, to roost for the night, wrote: "Ah, dear little bird! he has chosen his shelter, and is quietly rocking himself to sleep without a care for to-morrow's lodging, calmly holding by his little twig, and leaving God to think for him." Irrational creatures act as if they had more faith in God than men who profess to know him.

2. Ambition is no less against the spirit of this command. It may be very low in its aims, yet if it rule a man it will ruin him. One may "aspire to be

a fool," he may aim at being esteemed rough, or unpolished; or he may aim high, and desire to subject thousands to his belief, or influence, or government. He may be ready to wade through rivers of blood and build a throne on human skulls. The deadly nature of this passion is often concealed under plausible names. It is called *spirit*, *energy*, *laudable emulation*, &c. But in its gratification, men often destroy soul and body, and become unjust enemies of those who favour not their selfish aims. To such, how clear is the word of God: "Seekest thou great things for thyself? seek them not." Jer. xlv. 5. The higher the ambitious rise, the greater is their peril and the more tremendous will be their fall.

3. Nor is envy less contrary to this commandment. It often destroys life. It is "a rottenness of the bones." Prov. xiv. 30.

> "What makes the man of envy what he is
> Is worth in others, vileness in himself,
> A lust of praise, with undeserving deeds,
> And conscious poverty of soul."

How some hearts sicken at rising merit, and growing worth, and increasing credit in others! How embittered is rivalry! The unsanctified heart dies within it at the advance of a competitor. The hollow-hearted professor of religion sickens at the moral grandeur of a church not of his sect. How envy detracts from the worth of good men. How it wastes its subject. "Wrath is cruel, and anger is outrageous, but who can stand before envy?" Prov. xxvii. 4. It directly leads to murder. 1 John iii. 12. And yet how common it is. James iv. 5. "The shadow doth not more naturally attend the sun than envy doth favour." Boston: "Envy is the devil's two edged sword drawn to slay two at once; the envious himself, Prov. xiv. 30, for he is like a serpent gnawing its own tail, Job v. 2; and the party envied. Prov. xxvii. 4."

4. Revenge is another malignant exercise of the heart. Some of the more devilish exhibitions of it will be considered hereafter. It manifests itself in the rencontres of public assemblies. But often it works secretly, where all seems fair and kind. It clandestinely attacks property, liberty, or reputation. Possibly it becomes open, and indulges in innuendo, invective or scurrility; or it delights in the envenomed retort, and with keen irony, biting sarcasm, or scornful ridicule, assaults its object. "Dearly beloved, avenge not yourselves, but rather give place unto wrath; for it is written, Vengeance is mine, I will repay, saith the Lord. Therefore, if thine enemy hunger, feed him," &c. Rom. xii. 19, 20.

5. Sinful anger is also contrary to the sixth commandment. All anger is not wicked. Jesus Christ himself was angry. Mark iii. 5. We are bound to express hearty and decided displeasure at wrongs committed against ourselves or others. But anger is sinful when it becomes outrageous, Prov. xxvii. 4; when we give way to passion, so that reason is virtually dethroned; or when it is without just cause, Matt. v. 22; or when it is of long continuance, Eph. iv. 26; or when it is accompanied with ill-will. It is not easy, yet it is possible to "be angry and sin not." Anger may rise in the bosom of a wise man, but it *rests* only *in the bosom of fools*. "Let all bitterness, and wrath, and anger, and clamour, and evil-

speaking, be put away from you with all malice." Eph. iv. 31. It is peculiarly sinful to bring our angry feelings into religion. "The wrath of man worketh not the righteousness of God." Secker: "He that would be angry and sin not, must not be angry with any thing but sin." James i. 20. "He that is slow to wrath, is of great understanding; but he that is hasty of spirit exalteth folly." Prov. xiv. 29. See also Prov. xvi. 32.

6. Hatred of our fellow-men, in any degree and in every shape, is sinful. It is essentially ill-will. Very properly does the apostle put it in the catalogue of works of the flesh. Gal. v. 19–21. "He that saith he is in the light and hateth his brother is in darkness even until now." 1 John ii. 9. "Whosoever hateth his brother is a murderer, and ye know that no murderer hath eternal life abiding in him." 1 John iii. 15. "If a man say I love God, and hateth his brother, he is a liar." 1 John iv. 20. These Scriptures settle the question. Hatred leads to actual murder, because it "stirreth up strifes." Prov. x. 12.

7. Rancour is hatred of long standing, known in Scripture by the epithets *old hatred* and *perpetual hatred.* Ezek. xxv. 15, xxxv. 5. Rancour is of course inveterate and exceedingly stubborn. It shows itself in shyness and coolness of manner, in grudges and in heart-burnings. Where such a sentiment possesses the heart, holiness cannot dwell. Left to himself, the subject of such an affection will soon be prepared for any deed of violence.

8. One of the strongest exhibitions of depravity is the spirit of unmercifulness. The Lord said,

"Blessed are the merciful; for they shall obtain mercy." Matt. v. 7. The same principle is asserted throughout the Scriptures. Yet behold the wretched. ness of our race.

> "And man, whose heaven-erected face
>     The smiles of love adorn,
> Man's inhumanity to man
>     Makes countless thousands mourn."

How often does the creditor take the debtor by the throat, and sternly say, "Pay me that thou owest." The poor man cries, "Have patience with me, and I will pay thee all." But the greedy monster wields all his power to distress even friends, that in some way he may extort the amount of his claims. Everywhere are found marks of this evil spirit. Oh how will the injured, and abused, and wronged of the race arise and clank their chains and show their scars, and pour abundant shame on the inhuman wretches, who made their lives a burden!

> "There's no flesh in man's obdurate heart,
> It cannot feel for man."

What would a tyrant monarch, a tyrant governor, a tyrant husband, a tyrant father, a tyrant master, a tyrant creditor, a tyrant officer do in heaven, where all is gentleness and love? Ah, without repentance he shall never see that holy, happy place. "He shall have judgment without mercy, who hath showed no mercy." James ii. 13.

9. An unforgiving temper is no less clearly sinful. The Lord says, "If ye forgive not men their trespasses, neither will your Father forgive your trespasses." Matt. vi. 15. To pretend to forgive, only

because we cannot otherwise be forgiven; and to forgive but not forget, is not what the Lord requires. He, who cherishes a sense of wrongs with an intention to requite them as soon as occasion offers, can never truly pray, "Forgive us our debts as we forgive our debtors." When such an one reads that we must forgive a brother seventy times seven, he does not even attempt conformity to this law.

10. Contempt is a sentiment not to be cherished. Commonly its chief ingredients are haughtiness and scorn. It forgets that God hath made of one blood all nations of men, that we are all sinners before God, and that the Almighty is no respecter of persons. *Haughty scorner* is the designation of a bad man.

11. Sometimes malice shows itself at the downfall of others. But "he that is glad at calamities shall not be unpunished." Prov. xvii. 5. None but devils and those who are of their father the devil will exult because evil has come on a fellow-worm.

12. Any unkind feeling to men is sinful, and strictly forbidden by the spirit of the sixth commandment. "Be ye kindly affectioned one to another."

13. Nor is ingratitude an uncommon sin. An ancient heathen said, "If ingratitude were actionable, there would not be courts enough in the world to try the causes." Another said, "Call me ungrateful, and after that you can say no more evil of me." How many are annually carried to the grave through the ingratitude of those from whom better things might have been expected!

14. Of all the dispositions of the mind, perhaps

none leads to more frequent violations of the sixth commandment than pride. Leighton: "Pride is the spring of malice and desire of revenge, and of rash anger and contention." Tully was proud of his humble origin, and boasted that he was "the first of his family." Others find fuel for this passion in the ancient respectability of their households. Diogenes was proud of the meanness of his circumstances; whilst many are lifted up with their wealth. The disposition, which makes one man put on purple and fine linen, makes another assume the roughness of a voluntary humility. Men are proud of their parents, of their children, of their brothers and sisters, of their companions, of their correspondents, of their acquaintance, of their learning, of their ignorance, of their talents, of their persons, of their success, of their education, or of their want of it, of their virtues, and even of their crimes. Even a little gauze, or a little tiffany makes some proud. Yea, a man may be proud of his humility. This pride fills men with self-conceit; it causes them to speak in assumptive tones; it makes them stubborn, heady, untractable; it fills them with the spirit of dictation; it kindles up fearful strife. "Only by pride cometh contention." Prov. xiii. 10. The proud condescends to mix with others only by the force of some reason like this: "A sunbeam contracts no pollution by shining on a dung-hill." Pride fills our courts with litigants. It leads to broils, disputes, and murders. Like salamanders, the proud live in fire. Like Nabal, they are such sons of Belial that a man cannot speak to them, without incurring their displeasure. They expect all others to be humble; for pride in their fellow-men is very offensive to the proud. At times indeed when overawed, the proud will cringe, and truckle, and show real meanness of spirit. The Scriptures set themselves everywhere against pride. "The proud and all that do wickedly shall be burned up." Mal. iv. 1. "A proud heart is sin." Prov. xxi. 4. "Every one that is proud in heart is abomination to the Lord." Prov. xvi. 5. "God resisteth the proud, but giveth grace unto the humble." James iv. 6.

## II. WRONG WORDS.

Another way of violating this commandment is by sinful language. "Grievous words stir up anger." Prov. xv. 1. "There is that speaketh like the piercings of a sword." Prov. xii. 18. David complained, "My soul is among lions: and I lie even among them that are set on fire, even the sons of men, whose teeth are spears and arrows, and their tongue a sharp sword." And again: "Behold they belch out with their mouth; swords are in their lips." Again: "They whet their tongue like a sword, and bend their bows to shoot their arrows, even bitter words." Ps. lvii. 4; lix. 7; lxiv. 3. In interpreting this precept, our Lord warned men against saying *Raca*, which means *vain fellow*. Michal, David's wife, violated this commandment when she scornfully said, "How glorious was the King of Israel to-day, who uncovered himself to-day in the eyes of the handmaids of his servants, as one of the vain fellows shamelessly uncovereth himself." 2 Sam. vi. 20. The Lord also forbade us to apply to men in any provoking way, the epithet *fool*, which signified not only that one is far from wisdom, but also that he is wicked and ungodly. He that swears away the life of a fellow creature is himself a murderer. Prov. vi. 16–19; xix. 5. He that suborns others to do the same is a murderer. Acts vi. 13. He who passes unjust sentence of death is a murderer, Prov. xvii. 15; 1 Kings xxi. 9–14. He who rewards the righteous according to the work of the wicked is a murderer. Isa. v. 23. He who sees a fellow-creature in danger, and warns him not, lies under blood-guiltiness. Lev. xix. 17; Isa. lviii. 1. He who utters even the truth maliciously is in the same condemnation. 1 Sam. xxii. 9, 10; Ps. lii. 1. He who speaks slightingly of justice, and is regardless of truth, does what he can to spread the spirit of murder. Isa. lix. 4. He who perverts the sayings of his fellow-men, Matt. xxvi. 60, 61; Ps. lvi. 5; he who by falsehood afflicts his neighbour, Ps. l. 20; he who backbites with his tongue, Ps. xv. 3; he who speaks evil of his neighbour, Titus iii. 2; he who turns tale-bearer, Lev. xix. 16; he who disturbs the peace of society by whispering, Rom. i. 29; by mocking, Isa. xxviii. 22; by reviling, 1 Cor. vi. 10; in short, he who, by any form of speech annoys his fellow-men, breaks up the peace of families, and fills upright men with anxiety and sorrow, violates the spirit of this commandment.

### III. WICKED PLOTS.

Men are not free from the guilt of breaking this precept, when they command or contrive the death of others; as when Saul bid Doeg kill the Lord's priests; or when David told Joab to put Uriah in the front of the battle; or when they counsel and advise the ruin of moral character, as did Jonadab, 2 Sam. xiii. 1–29;

or when men stand by and consent to outrages against others, Acts viii. 1; or by failing to give faithful warning, Ezek. iii. 18; or by giving their voice to put men in offices which they are not capable of filling, and from their incompetency sad evils result, 1 Tim. v. 22.

### IV. QUARRELLING.

Perhaps no form of social evil is more degrading, or leads to more misery than low quarelling. It makes a hell upon earth. See Gal. v. 15.

### V. WRONG ACTS.

All expressions of the evil passions already spoken of are acts contrary to this commandment. Of this kind are all looks and gestures of a menacing, malignant, revengeful, violent, irritating, spiteful or tormenting character, all oppression, Isa. iii. 15, smiting, maiming and wounding, Num. xxxv. 16, 21, Prov. xxviii. 17, or doing anything which tends to the destruction of human life, Ex. xxi. 18–36.

Some things suggested by this commandment require a more particular consideration. Let us therefore inquire,

### VI. IS SUICIDE CRIMINAL?

It cannot be denied that the value set upon our own lives is in many cases very small. Mr. Hume, of the eighteenth century, wrote in favour of suicide; and since his time societies for the encouragement of self-destruction have been formed in many parts of Europe. Their baneful influence has also been extended to America. Mr. Hume's reasoning is truly shocking to pious minds. He says: "In the sight of God every event is alike important; and the life of a man is of no greater importance to the universe than that of an oyster." This sounds well in the ears of profane men. Yet every man *knows* that there is no truth in it. Though lessons may be learned from the lowest of God's works, yet Infinite Wisdom has never given to the world the history of an oyster for its instruction. But God has inspired many men to write the lives of others, and has preserved them to us in the canon of Scripture. The reckless question of Mr. Hume: "Where is the crime of turning a few ounces of blood out of their channel?" is as applicable to murder as to suicide; and what further license can the murderer possibly ask than to be allowed to plead at the tribunal of public justice that he has committed no crime by turning a few ounces of blood out of their course?

With all his acuteness, Mr. Hume terribly confounds the plainest distinctions. He says: "When I fall upon my own sword, I receive my death equally from the hands of the Deity, as if it had proceeded from a lion, a precipice, or a fever." If this sentence has any meaning, it is that the wilful, deliberate taking of our own lives is the same as dying by the providence of God, when he permits us to fall under the influence of pestilence, or of wild beasts. And if that is true, then we are no more criminal for killing a man than we are for seeing him die of a fever.

The whole argument in favour of suicide goes on the supposition of the truth of these principles which are clearly false. 1, That man has a right to dispose of his own life; whereas none but the Author of our existence can lawfully do so; 2, that we are competent judges of the question whether we have lived long enough or not; whereas a large proportion of mankind have been very useful after they supposed they could do no more good; 3, that we owe no obligations to parents, or children, or others, who may be dependent upon our exertions; whereas we may entail upon them untold miseries by taking our own lives; 4, that God has not legislated on the subject; whereas the sixth commandment clearly forbids it; 5, that salvation is not an object worth seeking; whereas it is the only thing claiming our supreme attention; 6, that it is heroic to sink under distress or play the coward in suffering wrong; whereas a large part of the best moral lessons, taught by example, has been delivered to mankind in the depths of affliction.

It is not necessary to use any harsh language respecting the entire class of persons, who may be left to take their own lives. In some cases, no doubt, reason is dethroned before the fatal act is committed. While we may charitably hope that this is so, it is an appalling fact that the Scriptures do not mention a single instance of any good man committing this sin. Three cases are given in Holy Scripture. One is that of Saul, a man of violent passions, who sought to compass the death of his own son, Jonathan, and of his son-in-law and deliverer, David; an open transgressor of the divine will, who, before the close of life, committed crimes which he knew ought to be punished with death. Another is that of Ahithophel, a wily statesman, a man of unusual political sagacity, but wholly unprincipled, and a traitor against King

David. The third was that of Judas Iscariot, for years a thief, consummating his crimes by betraying his Redeemer. There can be no hope of the salvation of a man who in the exercise of his reason commits this crime.

It is fatal to all claim of inspiration to the Book of 2 Maccabees, that it vindicates suicide, as being something noble, in Razis. 2 Mac. xiv. 41–46. So unmanly is suicide that even Aristotle has condemned it: "For a man to die merely that he may avoid poverty or trials is not courage, but sheer cowardice. It declares that he wants fortitude to encounter them." Of the self-destroyer a poet says:

> "He thought, but thought amiss, that of himself
> He was entire proprietor; and so,
> When he was tired of time, with his own hand,
> He oped the portals of eternity,
> And sooner than the devils hoped, arrived
> In hell."

### VII. THE DUEL.

The duel is a combat with deadly weapons between two persons agreeably to previous arrangements. It differs from a boxing match, because in that no weapons are used. It differs from a rencounter, because that is a sudden combat without premeditation. These may be as immoral and as fatal in their consequences as the duel. But neither of them is so called.

1. The modern duel is maintained to avenge personal or family insults. It can in no way be justified. "*Thou shalt not kill,*" is the plain command of him that made us. No acumen can reconcile duelling with this prohibition. The law is clear. No exception is made in other parts of the divine code. The

contrariety betwixt this practice and the law of God is manifest. The statute is unrepealed.

2. The duel includes in it also the guilt of suicide. As man has no right to take his own life, so he has no right wantonly to expose it to destruction. He who without any call of Providence knowingly puts himself in needless peril, contracts the guilt of suicide. Nor can we plead for duellists as in some cases we may for suicides, that they are insane. Duellists themselves admit that it would be murder to call to the field any unfortunate fellow-creature, whose reason had fallen from its throne. The duellist is mad in no other sense than that the sorcery of sin has bewitched him. His blood, if shed, is, in a fearful sense, on himself. Even if from the first, he intends to fire his own weapon into the air, yet if he exposes his body to the fire of an antagonist, he is in heart a self-murderer. If he dies in the duel, he has done what the law of nature and the word of God forbid, and incurred the heinous guilt of dying in an act which admits of neither reparation nor repentance. "No murderer has eternal life abiding in him." This is as true of him who kills himself as of any other murderer. Before his conversion, J. A. Haldane fought a duel, and as he raised the pistol, he prayed, "Father, into thy hands I commit my spirit," Life of Haldane, p. 61. Such prayers are vain and are commonly admitted to be so. They are hypocritical.

3. Moreover duelling is in its very nature murderous. The weapons chosen are the weapons of death. The efforts of each party are almost without exception for the destruction of his antagonist's life. The fact of a malignant *animus* is proven by all the cir-

cumstances attending duels. The deliberate aim of a deadly weapon at the person of a fellow-creature determines the act to be murderous in design, and if life is taken, to be murder in fact. This is indeed strong but not rash language. Sir Matthew Hale says, "This is a plain case, and without any question. If one kill another in fight, even upon the provocation of him that is killed, this is murder." Judge Foster says, "Deliberate duelling, if death ensue, is, in the eye of the law, murder." Sir Edward Coke says, "Single combat between any of the king's subjects is strictly prohibited by the laws of the realm, and on this principle, that in states governed by law, no man, in consequence of any injury whatever, ought to indulge the principle of private revenge." Blackstone, supported by Coke, says: "Murder is when a person of sound memory and discretion, unlawfully killeth any reasonable creature in being, and under the king's peace, with malice aforethought, either express or implied." The applicability of this definition to the crime of killing in a duel, will be granted by all, except so much as relates to *malice aforethought*. Even a part of this will not be denied, viz. that if there be *malice* at all, it is *aforethought*. Is there malice at all? The forbidden act of shooting with intent to kill is clearly malice implied. Is it not also malice expressed? The authority last cited says, "This malice aforethought is the grand criterion which now distinguishes murder from other killing; and this malice prepense is not so properly spite or malevolence to the deceased in particular, as any evil design in general; the dictate of a wicked, depraved, and malignant heart; and it may be either express or implied in law. Express malice is when one with a sedate, deliberate mind and formed design, doth kill another, which formed design is evidenced by external circumstances discerning that inward intention; as lying in wait, antecedent menaces, former grudges, and concerted schemes to do some bodily harm. This takes in the case of deliberate duelling, where both parties meet avowedly with an intent to murder; thinking it their duty as gentlemen and claiming it as their right, to wanton with their own lives and those of their fellow-creatures; without any authority or warrant from any power either human or divine, but in direct contradiction to the laws both of God and man."

These statements of principles are clear. They are made by lawyers and judges, not by divines and moralists. Their authors cannot be suspected of any wild, religious fervour, or of any foolish devotion to a fine-spun theory in ethics.

Killing in a duel, then, is murder; intent to kill in a duel, is intent to commit murder. Milder terms ought not to be employed.

4. Both human and divine laws properly guard the life of man with much caution. Blackstone says: "If any man in a populous town throws carelessly from a house-top any tile or timber, and gives no notice to the crowd that is usually passing below, though he may see no one, yet if one thereby be killed, it is not merely man-slaughter, but it is murder, and the law assigns the reason that such conduct is an expression of malignity against all mankind; and even if he give loud warning, and yet it be in a place where many persons usually pass, and one be killed, it is man-slaughter, and is punishable by the laws."

The same principle was incorporated into the law of Moses, Ex. xxi. 29. It is right.

If these things be so, by what principle is he turned loose unpunished, who not only is careless about human life, but who trains himself to the skilful use of deadly weapons that he may destroy it, meets a fellow-creature by arrangement and takes away his life? Divine law is no less loud and clear in its demands for the punishment of blood-shedding. This point will be argued at length in a succeeding section.

### PLEAS FOR DUELLING.

In defence of duelling, it is sometimes pleaded that the practice is in accordance with a body of rules fit for the government of gentlemen, commonly called *The Code of Honour*.

Whenever a code is mentioned, we naturally ask for the enacting power. Who made the code of honour? God did not. All its principles are repugnant to his revealed will. Nor has any competent authority sanctioned them. Nearly all legislatures have condemned them. Yet some are so bold as to dignify them with the name of *The Commandments*, thus adding profaneness to other sins.

Two of these Digests of the laws of crime are before us. A statement of even half their provisions would show their absurdity, their cruelty, and their wantonness. They are sufficiently bloody to satisfy the most diabolical malice. Even in America, some of their leading principles are these: Some insults cannot be compromised or settled without fighting. Words do not satisfy words, nor blows, blows. Seconds go armed to the field, first to shoot the adversary of his principal, if he shall take any advantage; and secondly, to keep the other second in order. If principals will not fight, seconds are to pronounce them cowards, and abandon them on the field. You are not bound to fight a minor, unless you have made a companion of him. You are bound to fight a respectable stranger. Seconds have absolute control after a challenge is given and accepted. Time may always be claimed to make a will.

A code with such provisions is shockingly immoral. It violates all the charities of life. It tramples on the laws of God. It defies the statutes of the land. It reputes forbearance a weakness, and forgiveness a meanness. It exalts diabolical passions to a seat among the highest virtues. It puts revenge and murder above meekness and patience.

It is also full of absurdities. It places the aggressor and the aggrieved upon the same footing; or if the former be the best shot or the smallest mark, it gives him the advantage. If a man be injured and complain, by this code he may be compelled to lose his life and to write his wife a widow and his children fatherless. There is hardly an end to the absurdities which may be fairly drawn from its rules.

This code is useless. It elicits no truth. It determines not who is innocent, and who is guilty. By common consent it proves no man brave; it seldom proves him a coward. It does not even prove one a good marksman or a good swordsman. In 1815, the English almost invariably killed the French officers with the sword. Yet the former were unskilled and the latter were experts in its use. Very often in our own land, the less skilful in the use of weapons has killed his adversary.

This code is very bloody, not only in its laws, but also in its results. During the first eighteen years of the reign of Henry the Fourth, *four thousand* gentlemen perished by duels in France alone. In *one hundred and seventy-two* consecutive duels, *sixty-three* persons were killed, and *ninety-six* wounded—*forty-eight* of them desperately. This latter statement is made on the faith of an official paper prepared in England. A few years ago, *four* persons were killed in *four* successive duels in the same vicinity. This code smells horribly of blood. Why will men worship this modern Moloch?

Some plead for the code of honour that it maintains courage among men. True courage is indeed an enviable quality. But what is it? Is it recklessness of life? Does it delight in blood? No man has true courage except so far as he is a good man. "The righteous are as bold as a lion, but the wicked flee when no man pursueth." Burke: "The only real courage is generated by the fear of God. He who fears God, fears nothing else." Addison: "Courage is that heroic spirit inspired by the conviction that our cause being just, God will protect us in its prosecution." Seneca: "Courage is properly the contempt of hazards *according to reason;* but to run into danger from *mere* passion is rather a daring and brutal fierceness than an honourable courage." Pages from similar sources and to the like effect might be cited. The Duke of Sully, speaking of duels, says, "That which arms us against our friends or countrymen, in contempt of all laws, as well divine as human, is but a brutal fierceness, madness, and real pusillanimity." True courage is calm, just, mild, firm, reasonable. To such a quality, good men do reverent obeisance. It is truth and justice sitting on a throne of virtue. It has no malignity. It never thirsts for vengeance.

But is the duellist brave after his bloody work? Is he not timid, nervous, melancholy? Does he not often seem to anticipate the pains of hell? A dreadful sound is in his ears. A good writer says, "How fares it with him in the court of conscience? Is he able to keep off the grim arrests of that? Can he drown the cry of blood, and bribe his own thoughts to let him alone? Can he fray off the vulture from his heart, that night and day is gnawing his heart, and wounding it with ghastly and amazing reflections?"

Shall we award to such a system the meed of *honour?* The demand can never be granted. Humanity and God forbid it. Honour is a sacred thing. Honour is not lawless, is not cruel, delights in the approbation of the good, and abhors the infliction of misery. Honour is humane, generous, tenderhearted. Honour casts from her even her own rights, when insisting on them does a great wrong to others. Honour never willingly mingles the tears of widows and orphans with the blood of husbands and fathers. Honour looks at the things of others, bows to the majesty of law, listens to the conclusions of reason, and obeys the voice of God.

Can any thing be done to arrest this evil? Yes! Public sentiment can rectify it. Good laws can be enacted. Good men can execute them. A few years since, the Justices of the Supreme Court of the United States were invited by a committee of the House of Representatives to attend the funeral of one of that body. "After mature deliberation" they adopted the following:

"*Resolved*, That the Justices of the Supreme Court entertain a high respect for the character of the deceased, sincerely deplore his untimely death, and sympathize with his bereaved family in the heavy affliction which has fallen upon them.

"*Resolved*, That with every desire to manifest their respect for the House of Representatives, and the Committee of the House, by whom they have been invited, and for the memory of the lamented deceased, the Justices of the Supreme Court cannot, consistently with the duties they owe to the public, attend in their official characters the funeral of one who has fallen in a duel.

"*Ordered*, That these proceedings be entered on the minutes of the Court, and that the Chief Justice enclose a copy to the chairman of the committee of the House of Representatives."

If all good men and all public functionaries would show like mildness and firmness, like sympathy for the suffering, and like determination not to swerve from duty, there would soon be a change.

Let mothers teach their sons that killing in a duel is murder. Let wives soothe their irritated husbands and assert their rights not to be left mourning widows. Let young ladies discountenance the gallants who come into their society reeking with blood. Let the press and the pulpit utter just and solemn notes of remonstrance.

Is any tempted to commit this sin? Here are good answers, any one of which is sufficient to justify him in declining.

THOU SHALT NOT KILL. *The Almighty.*

IT IS THE GLORY OF A MAN TO PASS OVER A TRANSGRESSION. *Solomon.*

I AM NOT AFRAID OF FIGHTING, BUT I AM AFRAID OF SINNING. *Colonel Gardiner.*

I NEITHER AM, NOR WISH TO BE A MURDERER.
*A Modern Gentleman.*

'Tis hard, indeed, if nothing will defend
Mankind from quarrels but their fatal end;
That now and then a hero must decease,
That the surviving world may live in peace.
Perhaps at last close scrutiny may show
The practice dastardly, and mean, and low;
That men engage in it, compell'd by force,
And fear, not courage, is its proper source;
The fear of tyrant custom, and the fear
Lest fops should censure us, and fools should sneer,
While yet we trample on our Maker's laws,
And hazard life for any or no cause. COWPER.

## VIII. MURDER.

All men admit murder to be a crime. Nor do they doubt that it is a fearful crime, even when attended with the fewest aggravations. None but the divine Lawgiver is competent to decide on the heinousness of any sin as against himself. No mortal is capable of telling all the bearings of any sin in a moral government that has no end. But murder is an offence so obviously atrocious that man can judge somewhat of its mischievous effects in this life. It is the strongest expression of malignity against our fellow-creatures. It is commonly the result of pride, or cruelty, or avarice, and always of impiety. It supposes a long process of hardening the heart and indulging wicked passions.

But even the temporal consequences of murder are fully known to God only. Every man sustains relations to his family, his country, and the universe, which no finite mind can gauge. Then every life is worth untold millions to its possessor. Both in Hebrew and Greek the same word is rendered *life* and *soul.* And, indeed, the connection between them is such that the loss of the former may be the loss of the latter. The murder of an unregenerate man, for ever puts him beyond the reach of renewing grace and pardoning mercy.

In speaking of duelling, murder has been sufficiently defined.

Within the last half century, unusual opposition to the capital punishment of murder has been manifested in many quarters. Against it forms of expression full of railing and bitterness are frequently employed. One cries out against the orthodox Christian world: "The gallows and the gospel, Christ and the hangman." Those who deny eternal punishment seem particularly anxious to have the death penalty abolished. An ex-president of the United States, some years since, declared for the abolition of capital punishments. Some legislatures have fallen in with the popular error.

HAS GOD SETTLED THIS QUESTION? Our appeal is to his word. "Whoso sheddeth man's blood, by man shall his blood be shed." Gen. ix. 6. This command was not given to the Jews, but to Noah, the second universal father of the human race. It is limited to no time or nation. It has never been repealed. A wholesome law ought to continue while the *reason* for it continues. That is given in these words: "For in the image of God made he man." So that killing man is a very different thing from killing any other creature. It is a despising of God, whose natural image every man bears. To murder a man is to blot out this image of God. This interpretation of this law is agreed upon by Rivet, Le Clerc, Selden, Grotius, Michaelis, Rosenmuller and numerous other eminent scholars.

Nor is this the only instance in which God has expressed his will. The command to Noah was given sixteen hundred and fifty-seven years after the creation. Nine hundred and fifty-six years later, God ordained judicial regulations for the Jewish commonwealth. Into that code he incorporated these explicit teachings. "He that smiteth a man so that he die, shall surely be put to death." And to show that no refuge was to be allowed him, God adds, "Thou shalt take him from my altar that he may die." Ex. xxi. 12, 14. A year afterwards, God said again to Moses, "He that killeth any man shall surely be put to death." Lev. xxiv. 17. Thirty-eight years later, God gave minutely the law of murder and manslaughter, provided for the trial of all charged with either crime, gave particular rules according to which sentence was to be given, repeatedly stated that murderers should be put to death. This law is the basis of the laws of most Christian countries on this subject. It reads thus: "If a man smite any person with an instrument of iron, so that he die; he is a murderer: the murderer shall surely be put to death. And if he smite him with throwing a stone, wherewith he may die, and he die; he is a murderer: the murderer shall surely be put to death. Or if he smite him with a hand-weapon of wood, wherewith he may die, and he die; he is a murderer: the murderer shall surely be put to death. The revenger of blood himself shall slay the murderer; when he meeteth him, he shall slay him. And if he thrust him of hatred, or hurl at him by lying of wait, that he die; or in enmity smite him with his hand, that he die: he that smote him shall surely be put to death: for he is a murderer: the revenger of blood shall slay the murderer, when he meeteth him. Whoso killeth any person, the murderer shall be put to death by the mouth of witnesses: but one witness shall not testify against any person to cause him to die. Moreover ye shall take no satisfaction for the life of a murderer, who is guilty of death: but he shall be surely put to death. And ye shall take no satisfaction for him that has fled to the city of his refuge, that he should come again to dwell in the land, until the death of the priest. So ye shall not pollute the land wherein ye are: for blood it defileth the land; and the land cannot be cleansed of the blood, that is shed therein, but by the blood of him that shed it. Defile not therefore the land which ye shall inhabit, wherein I dwell: for I the LORD dwell among the children of Israel." Num. xxxv. 16–34. A clearer revelation of God's mind and will could not be made. Nor is this any ceremonial regulation. It is the wisdom of God expressed to a famous people for the guidance of their conduct in criminal proceedings. These laws given by God were carefully executed by the best kings, that ruled over that people. By the command of Solomon, Joab was put to death, even while holding fast to the horns of the altar; for he had killed two innocent men, "more righteous and better than he." 1 Kings ii. 28–34. This case is the more remarkable as Joab had rendered eminent military services to the country.

Again, God expressly says, "A man that doeth violence to the blood of any person shall flee to the pit; let no man stay him." Prov. xxviii. 17. The same doctrine is taught by Christ: "All they that take the sword shall perish with the sword." Matt. xxvi. 52. This saying was a proverb among the Jews. Its import was precisely the same with that of the words: "Whoso sheddeth man's blood, by man shall his blood be shed." The meaning is, he who, under a government of laws, takes the sword into his own hand, for private revenge, and slays a man, shall himself be put to death by the sword of public justice.

The same is taught by Paul. Of the civil magistrate, he says: "He is the minister of God to thee for good. But if thou do that which is evil, be afraid; for he beareth not the sword in vain; for he is the minister of God, the revenger to execute wrath upon him that doeth evil." Rom. xiii. 4. It is true that this passage does not confine capital punishment to the case of murder. But none will deny that if the death penalty should be inflicted on any, it should be on the wilful murderer. The sword in this passage clearly points to death, as it was used for beheading.

The apostle admitted the correctness of the same doctrine, in his argument before Festus. "If I be an offender, or have committed anything worthy of death, I refuse not to die," Acts xxv. 11; thus clearly implying that there were crimes properly punished with death; and that, if proven on the apostle, he would admit the justice of the death penalty against himself.

And in the very last book of Scripture, we have the same doctrine taught: "He that killeth with the sword, must be killed with the sword." Rev. xiii. 10. It is true this passage is not a precept, but a prediction respecting the doom of bloody persecutors, who are wholesale murderers. Yet it is a prophecy which Jehovah has caused and will ever cause to be wonderfully fulfilled. Let bloody tyrants beware how they shed the blood of innocent men; for He that is higher than the highest regardeth. With an awful vengeance, even in this life, he commonly marks so heinous sin. Often in providence does "the Lord come out of his place to punish the inhabitants of the earth for their iniquity; the earth also shall disclose her blood, and shall no more cover her slain." Isa. xxvi. 21. Thus speak the Scriptures.

The general consent of mankind in all ages and under all dispensations since the flood, would lead to the same conclusion. Blackstone: "Murder is a crime at which human nature starts, and which is, I believe, punished almost universally throughout the world with death." (L. 4, ch. 14.) The consent of mankind approaches as near universality on this as on any other subject. Perhaps as few men have held that murder should not be punished with death, as have professed their belief that there was no God. The force of the argument is this: When men in every variety of circumstances, civilized and uncivilized, rude and refined, Jews, Mohammedans, Christians and Pagans, have generally agreed to any principle and acted upon it, its propriety is manifest. There has never been a mistake amongst mankind of all descriptions, on any moral subject so wide-spreading as the opinion that murder should be punished with death.

The experiment of sparing the lives of murderers has been fully tried. The world is now considerably less than six thousand years old. Yet for the first sixteen centuries and a half, capital punishment was not inflicted. In his adorable sovereignty, God made a great experiment, beginning in the family of Adam. The first man ever born was a murderer—the murderer of his own brother. He was constantly apprehensive of death. "It shall come to pass that every one that findeth me shall slay me." Gen. iv. 14. But God sacredly guarded his life, and threatened dreadful vengeance on any who should touch him. Gen. iv. 15. His punishment was expulsion from the visible church, expressed by the words, "He went out from the presence of the Lord," Gen. iv. 16; together with his own reflections and the remorse of his conscience. Did his mental anguish and expulsion from the congregation of the righteous deter men from murder? No. Lamech soon followed his example, saying to his wives: "I have slain a man to my wounding, and a young man to my hurt. If Cain shall be avenged seven fold, truly Lamech seventy and seven fold." Gen. iv. 23, 24. Nor did the thing stop here. Men went from bad to worse, until "*the earth was filled with violence.*" Gen. vi. 11. The wickedness of man grew so rapidly that God swept from the face of the earth every breathing thing; those saved in the ark alone excepted. And no sooner had Noah come out of the ark, and become heir of the new world, than God enacted that henceforth murder should be capitally punished.

Nor do the lessons of history stop here. The Jewish commonwealth, in some form or other, existed for more than fifteen hundred years. Whenever, in the kingdom of Judea, the magistrates were faithful in punishing murder with death, peace and prosperity succeeded. But whenever they became remiss in this matter, the nation groaned in misery.

One of the States of America, (Michigan) about the middle of the nineteenth century, abolished capital punishment. The Grand Jury at Detroit, in 1852, under the solemnities of an oath said: "The increase of the crimes of murder and manslaughter, since the abolition of capital punishment, not only among us, but throughout our State, has become most manifest and alarming. The records of the courts of this County show that at each of the four terms, there has been at least one aggravated case of murder—and at one term two cases. Whereas, previously to the existing law, no conviction of murder had ever been had by any of the courts of the State. These facts we regard as a proof of an alarming disrespect for, and undervaluing of human life, legitimately referable to a change of the legislation upon this subject."

However men may fortify themselves with plausible arguments in favour of a sickly philanthropy, yet so exceedingly outrageous and shocking are some of the crimes which are committed, that it requires, not an ardent love of truth and commendable firmness, but an obstinacy of temper to stand up and say, they ought not to be punished with death. For a crime of deep dye, a man was sentenced to confinement, in a penitentiary, for a term of years. His treatment was mild. His tasks were moderate, and yet in cold blood he killed a kind and faithful officer. What would sickly philanthropists do in this case? Would they have him sentenced to the penitentiary? He was already there. Would they sentence him for life? How many faithful keepers might he kill before the law would assert its majesty in behalf of the lives of turnkeys and wardens? Abolish the penalty of death, and trustworthy men could not be found to keep our prisons. Abolish capital punishments, and mankind will return to the old practice of avenging blood.

Some have argued respecting capital punishment upon entirely false principles. Some assert that punishment can be justified only upon the ground of the right acquired by society, when men enter into that state, to prevent an evil-disposed person from repeating an offence. Others say that the only justification of punishment is found in the hope that the criminal may thereby be reformed. Others say that the right to punish is based upon the obligation of society to deter those, who have not yet offended, by exhibiting examples of the misery of criminals. Yet others contend that all punishment is merely for reparation, and should be of such a kind as to gain that end. Some have laid down all these as the foundations of punishment. Let us look at these statements.

It is admitted that some of the fore-mentioned things are occasionally gained by punishment. But neither severally nor jointly are they the ground on which it proceeds. If the right to punish is based upon the obligation of society to prevent an evil-disposed person from repeating an offence, none w l deny that capital punishment gains that end, and puts it quite out of the power of the culprit again to di -turb society. So that the mere admission of this principle would be no argument for the total abolition of the death penalty. But this statement of the matter does not furnish a principle sufficiently broad to cover every case of punishment. Some sentences are but light and temporary. They bear no proportion to the strength of men's passions for doing wrong. Yet severer penalties would by all enlightened men be esteemed excessive. But the great objection to this principle is, that it makes a man suffer, not for what he has done, but for fear he will hereafter do something wrong. He asks his country, "Why do you restrain my liberty?" The reply is, "We are afraid you will injure men if you are allowed to go at large." This reply suits the case of a man restrained under a writ of lunacy, or subjected to quarantine, no less than that of the culprit. He sees no justice in the case. He asks if society is not afraid that some men, going at large, will commit as great offences as himself; and the community must be very small, in which men could not be found, of whose future good conduct there was as little guaranty as of his. *Some* of the worst men in every country are going at large. Mere prevention therefore is not the basis of punishment.

Nor is the reformation of the criminal the ground of punishment. Incidentally it may sometimes be effected; and if in crimes of a lower grade one mode of punishment is found more conducive to reformation than another, and the ends of government can all be secured, that mode should be preferred. But who gave society a right to imprison men in order to reform them? No such grant of power is anywhere found. Surely God never gave it. When he would rescue men from vice and sin, it is by his blessed gospel. Besides, if society punishes only that she may reform bad men, then as soon as they are reformed they ought to be discharged. Would this be proper? And if reformation be the ground of punishment, then all penal sentences ought to be indefinite as to time, and the punishment should last until the reformation is effected. Universalists urge this point with great zeal. Their chief argument is, that all suffering, under the government of God, is for the good of the sufferer, and that therefore the same principles should obtain in human society. But the argument is false. All suffering under God's government is NOT for the good of the sufferer. What benefit have the fallen angels ever reaped from their chains of darkness? What blessing has ever come on the Sodomites for their suffering the vengeance of eternal fire? When Paul says that "all things work together for good," he limits the statement to "them that love God, to them who are the called according to his purpose." To such it is a glorious truth that their afflictions do them eternal good. But where is the like declared concerning them that hate God and are ordained to a fiery condemnation?

And even if reformation were the ground of punishment, no man, before the judgment-day, can certainly know that capital punishments for high crimes are not preceded by as many conversions to God and thorough reformations as any other modes of punishment whatever. We have inspired authority for believing that one man publicly executed for his crimes was truly penitent. Doubtless there have been others. But do not our wisest men confess that our *penitentiaries* are seldom, if ever, places of *penitence?*

Neither is the utility of example to others any ground for punishing a man. Punishment may deter some men from crimes; but it may be seriously questioned whether even this influence is not greatly overestimated. It has become proverbial, that punishments so inflicted as to afford a spectacle, have in many cases a hardening effect. Be this as it may, when did society acquire the right of punishing one man for the good of others? If it has such a right, why may it not exhibit the innocent in a posture of shame and under false accusation, for the benefit of the public?

Nor is reparation the ground of punishment. If in cases purely civil, where no felony is charged, this is the great end of punishment, yet in the case of murder, reparation is wholly and absolutely impossible. No tears, no repentance, no toils, no sacrifice of worldly goods can restore life to the murdered man, or the husband and father to his bereaved family.

The true ground of punishment is JUSTICE. The penalty of law is to be inflicted because it is *right*. If the murderer *deserves* death; if his guilt is so enormous that no other punishment is adequate; if God has pronounced death the proper penalty; if criminals themselves, whenever their consciences are awakened and enlightened, do acknowledge the justice of their sentence; then we have a sure foundation on which to vindicate our laws. *Justice, eternal inflexible justice is the sole ground of the right of punishment.* And it is ground enough. "WHOSO SHEDDETH MAN'S BLOOD, BY MAN SHALL HIS BLOOD BE SHED."

### IX. INTEMPERANCE.

Modern usage has almost confined the word intemperance, unless otherwise explained by the connection, to the excessive use of intoxicating drinks. In this sense let us consider it for a little while.

No form of vice is more contrary to the true spirit of the sixth commandment, and none brings more misery on society. Its sweep is wide and fearful. Every profession and every community have furnished victims to this destroyer. The annals of this miserable vice are written in blood. Its statistics rise high and tell us of hundreds of thousands of drunkards and of hundreds of thousands more reduced to pauperism or seduced to crime by intemperance. They tell us of millions of gallons of intoxicating drink annually consumed. For every hour in the year it is calculated that at least one drunkard passes to the retributions of eternity.

Nor is intemperance in any case a slight evil. To its subjects it brings complicated forms of disease, and pains of the most excruciating character. "Who hath woe? who hath sorrow? who hath contentions? who hath babbling? who hath wounds without cause?

who hath redness of eyes? They that tarry long at the wine; they that go to seek mixed wine." Prov. xxiii. 29, 30.

Loss of integrity frequently attends intemperance. Little by little the inebriate loses his once sacred regard to truth, to contracts, to promises and all engagements. At the same time, the fatal stab is given to the best and kindliest sentiments of the heart. Petulance and irritability supplant love and tenderness. Self-respect commonly dies early in this career, and the inebriate begins to herd with the degraded. Reputation cannot long stand such assaults, and by degrees public esteem and confidence are withdrawn. In his sober moments, the drunkard's bosom will be wrung with anguish. Shame, remorse, and the darkness of guilt are followed by the perishing of hope. He deplores his dreadful captivity, but has neither courage, nor expectation of bursting its bonds. Loss of property commonly follows close on the heels of other evils. While intemperance does not *always* lead its victims to the commission of crimes, yet more than three-fourths of all the felonies in the land are traceable to this source.

The worst thing attending intemperance is its direct and invariable tendency to destroy both soul and body in hell. "Be not deceived; neither fornicators, nor idolaters, nor adulterers, nor effeminate, nor abusers of themselves with mankind, nor thieves, nor covetous, nor drunkards, nor revilers, nor extortioners, shall inherit the kingdom of God." 1 Cor. vi. 9, 10. For the impenitent, unreformed drunkard, there is no salvation. God has determined that matter already. True, the context of the passage just cited shows that drunkards may be converted: "Such were some of you," says Paul to the Corinthians. But how seldom does the drunkard turn to God. When the direct tendency of a sin is to make the whole man sottish and even less than a man, how feeble is the hope we can entertain that he will turn and live. The case of the drunkard is very discouraging. It is hard to convince him either of his sin or his danger. He is full of confidence in his own strength. He is persuaded that the meltings of nature, which he sometimes feels, are a sign that all is not lost. His conscience is seared; his understanding is terribly darkened. Numbers of such die, giving fearful evidence to the last that they were wholly impenitent.

Nor are the evils of this sin confined to him who drinks. Others come in for a large share. The father, who had begun to recline on his son; the mother, who "thought that she had borne a man;" the wife, who had dreams of earthly happiness; the sisters, who had once been proud as they saw his manly bearing, all now find that honour is forsaking him, and that their hopes must soon perish. His children and servants are often filled with terror at his approach. He is no longer the kind and judicious friend of the poor, the widow and the orphan. He is a pest to his neighbourhood. His will might read thus: "I give and bequeath to society a ruined character, a wretched example, and a memory that shall rot. I give and bequeath to my parents, shame, sorrow and (so far as I am concerned) a childless old age. I give and bequeath to my brothers and sisters, deep mortification at the mention of my name. I give and bequeath to my wife, a broken heart, an early widowhood, a shattered constitution, poverty and an early grave. I give and bequeath to each of my children, penury, ignorance, and the remembrance that they had an unnatural father."

Multiply all these evils by hundreds of thousands and you will have something like the true result. But there are other evils of a general nature connected with intemperance. Time is wasted. Prisons are multiplied. Taxation is greatly increased. Property is destroyed; the elective franchise bought and sold; justice perverted; idleness fostered; riots encouraged; life jeoparded; and morality and religion made to bleed. Hell follows in its train. He who indulges in wine and strong drink shall find that "at the last it biteth like the serpent, and stingeth like the adder:" yea, "he shall be as one that lieth down in the midst of the sea, or as he that lieth upon the top of a mast," Prov. xxiii. 32, 34.

Where the population is crowded, the statistics of this sin are most appalling. When London had a population of 2,350,000 souls, it had a total of 471,000 persons steeped in crime, demoralization and vice; of whom 180,000 were habitual hard drinkers. The vices of the rest were akin to this.

All these evils are quite unnecessary. Strong drink laid aside, all the affairs of life would move on better than they do. The strongest man noted in history never tasted such stimulants.

In certain cases alcoholic drinks are proper for medicinal purposes. "Give strong drink unto him that is ready to perish, and wine unto those that be of heavy hearts." "Drink no longer water, but use a little wine for thy stomach's sake and thine often infirmities," Prov. xxxi. 6; 1 Tim. v. 23. Medical skill, or our knowledge of our own constitutions must determine when we need such aid to our health. In all other cases, the consciences of men are left free to abstain if they choose. The principle of voluntary abstinence is not new. By solemn vows, the Nazarites were bound to it. John the Baptist never drank wine. For thousands of years the Rechabites have been wholly abstinent. Every generation furnishes such cases.

It is said, on good authority, that one of the petty kingdoms of Africa has never permitted the introduction of intoxicating drinks, and while surrounding kingdoms are torn with intestine wars, and are sinking under the power of many evils, among which are the usual attendants of intemperance, this kingdom remains quiet, industrious and prosperous. Kidnapping and the slave-trade are unknown.

The Scriptures give very awful warnings against seducing men into this vice. "Woe to him that buildeth a town with blood. Woe unto him that giveth his neighbour drink, that puttest thy bottle to him, and makest him drunken also, that thou mayest look on their nakedness. . . . The cup of the Lord's right hand shall be turned unto thee, and shameful spewing shall be on thy glory." Hab. ii. 12, 15, 16. "Woe to him that coveteth an evil covetousness to his house, that he may set his nest on high, that he may be delivered from the power of evil! Thou hast consulted shame to thy house by cutting off many people, and hast sinned against thy soul. For the stone shall cry out of the wall, and the beam out of the timber shall answer it," Hab. ii. 9–11.

X. THE LOW ESTIMATE OF HUMAN LIFE.

Perhaps there never was a century in which mankind have been more disposed to think, and speak, and act, as if human life were a trifle, than the present. This remark is fearfully true of the country in which this volume is likely to be most read. In his Thanksgiving sermon, preached Nov. 24, 1853, Rev. H. A. Boardman, D. D., says: "It is scarcely a figure to say that the history of many a steamboat and rail road line, in the Union, has been written in blood. The statistics would probably show, that a greater number of travellers perish by these agencies in our country, than in all the rest of the civilized world combined. An accident which destroys a single human being, or three or four, is nothing thought of. Even those which involve the destruction of scores of lives produce but a temporary ripple in the current of public feeling, and are presently forgotten. Men are allowed to erect buildings which may tumble down of their own frailty, and bury a crowd of inmates beneath their ruins. Steamboats of such fragile construction are permitted to navigate our tempestuous lakes and dangerous sea-coast, that there is less to wonder at when we hear that they have gone down into the abyss, with a load of passengers, than when they survive a storm of ordinary violence. Conductors and engineers may whirl their crowded trains into other trains, down precipices, and into drawbridges; and superintendents and boards of management may so frame their arrangements as almost to insure the frequent recurrence of these disasters, without exposing themselves to any adequate penalties. Homicides are rapidly multiplying; but, with occasional exceptions, justice is slow in securing the murderers, and slower still in convicting and punishing them. Society has so far reverted towards its primitive condition, that even in our older States, the practice has become common of carrying deadly weapons, and avenging affronts, real or imaginary, with instant death. The generation of young men now coming forward in our cities, seem to think it manly to wear dirks and pistols, and to use them on the slightest provocation. Approximating to savages in their equipments, they resemble them no less in the value they put upon human life. And if matters proceed much further in this direction, the shooting of a man will soon come to be looked upon as very little more than the shooting of a beast. If these practices were properly rebuked—if the force of law or of public sentiment were adequately employed to repress them—it might be inapposite to cite them in this connexion. But they meet with a degree of tolerance which indicates any thing but a just appreciation of their enormity on the part of the community.

"As the natural result of these things, the feeling of personal insecurity has become very general. The unavoidable hazards of travelling are so multiplied, that a journey is a source of incessant anxiety, from its commencement to its close, both to travellers themselves, and their friends and families. Even in traversing the streets of a metropolis, people feel that they are liable to plunge, inadvertently, into some unprotected pitfall, or to be crushed by having building-materials or bales of merchandise precipitated upon them from above. Nor can thoughtful parents rid themselves of solicitude for the safety of their sons, lest they may some day be brought home to them 'in their blood,' victims to that fashionable code which makes every man the avenger of his own wrongs, and converts into a 'wrong' every hasty utterance or passionate gesture.

"That this insensibility to the true value of life, is a mark of our *imperfect civilization*, is a humiliating truth which it were quite useless to deny. If there is any gauge by which the progress of a people from barbarism to refinement can be tested, it lies in THE ESTIMATE THEY ATTACH TO HUMAN LIFE, and the pains which are taken to preserve and prolong it. If a nation fails in this point, the defect is one which admits of no compensation. It is idle to talk of its arts and arms, its literature and religion, its wise laws, its schools, its contented and thriving populations,—if it holds human life at a cheap rate, the less it boasts of its cultivation the better. Other nations, certainly, will concede to it nothing beyond a second or third rate type of civilization, while it is disfigured by one of the radical characteristics of barbarism."

This witness is true. Much innocent blood is shed. Violent deeds abound. One terrible tragedy follows another with rapidity. Lately seventeen murderers were executed in one day. Rencounters, assassinations, duels, suicides, and deliberate murders for revenge or for money, are reported with an alarming frequency. The cause of this deplorable state of things is to be found in human depravity. But why should this depravity now manifest itself, in so unusual a degree, in this particular form? The following answers may not include all that should be said, but they point to some leading influences which have a fearful potency for evil.

1. One fruitful source of crime has been the expectation of impunity. Many have argued, some have legislated, and more have practised on the belief that no crime ought to be capitally punished. This has increased the hope of impunity, so that some have declared their belief that death would follow no crime.

2. The country has been and is still flooded with books which mightily stir up all the principles of wickedness. Novels or narratives of fact have dressed up the burglar, the robber, the assassin, the duellist, the murderer, in gay colours, and held him forth to the youthful mind as a hero to be admired. These books are exceedingly common, are offered for sale in almost every train of cars, and are filling the pockets of thousands who never read any book suited to improve their morals.

3. Very corrupt religious doctrines extensively pervade portions of the lower classes; among them are Universalism, Deism, Spiritualism, and other infidel delusions. One who has for a long time visited prisoners in jails and penitentiaries, declares his belief that nine-tenths of our convicts disclaim the doctrine of eternal punishment. These maintain their doctrines with just such arguments as are heard from Universalist pulpits and infidel club-houses.

4. The intemperate use of intoxicating drinks is terribly on the increase, especially among the classes

who commit these bloody crimes. The liquors drunk are often terribly drugged. Reason is frequently dethroned. At all times the blood is overheated, or the temper roused, and so the poor victim of strong drink is kept ready for any thing.

5. Gambling in its worst forms is also fearfully prevalent. It fosters the worst passions, and hardens the heart beyond almost all other vices. It has its schools and "hells" almost everywhere. Its leaders are among the most desperate men in the world.

6. The practice of wearing side-arms, now so common, is a great provocative of blood-shedding. It makes men familiar with the instruments of death, and so diminishes their horror of blood-shedding. It awakens apprehension that another is armed, and so leads to a speedy resort to these weapons in case of any difficulty.

7. Of all the causes of every species of crime, none is more prolific than Sabbath desecration. This has always been so. It must always be so in Christian countries; for the reason that it is a deliberate sin, preceded by thought and a conflict, in which the award is in favour of renouncing moral restraint. An under-sheriff of London lately bore the following testimony: "My office has enabled me to confirm the value of the Sabbath, there being scarcely a criminal, whether for death or minor punishment, who was not daily confessing to me in Newgate, that he considered his first fall, and subsequent misery, to be owing to the violation of that blessed day."

Other causes doubtless concur with those already

mentioned, but they would probably have little power, if those above named were removed. Let good men all over the land reflect, confer, pray, and act as duty requires in the present solemn crisis in the public morals.

### XI. INTOLERANCE AND PERSECUTION.

EVERY MAN HAS A POPE IN HIM—LUTHER.

Intolerance is the parent of persecution. It refuses to let others alone, if they differ from us in views or sentiments. It takes a very wide scope in this respect. Galileo was persecuted for his views on science. Whately well remarks that if his cotemporaries could have answered his arguments, they would not have persecuted his person. No little of this intolerance is still manifested even among some modern philosophers. To differ from them is to incur their scorn and their ill-will.

Another matter on which men are intolerant is the subject of politics. How often does the vehemence of partisans rise to vituperation and deadly malice. Men are proscribed for utterances which are as honest and as harmless as any held by their adversaries.

But religious doctrine and worship have for many ages furnished the ground of the bitterest intolerance. It ought exceedingly to warn those, who are inclined to be bitter towards others for difference of religious belief or practice, that there is no unerring judge of truth and error upon earth, and that none have more egregiously erred than those who have made the highest pretensions to ability to discriminate between truth and error. Gregory Nazianzen says that he never saw a good end of any council and declared that he was resolved never to attend another. Luther says of the first and best of General Synods that 'he understood not the Holy Ghost to speak in it.' Beza says that such was the "folly, ignorance, ambition, wickedness of many bishops in the best times, that you would suppose the devil to have been president in their assemblies." John Owen says, "I should acknowledge myself obliged to any man that would direct me to a council, since that mentioned in Acts xv., which I may not be free from the word of God to assert, that it, in something or other, went astray." The awful challenge of Scripture is, "Who art thou that judgest another man's servant? To his own master he standeth or falleth." Rom. xiv. 4. Who but God is competent to decide on the aims, hopes, fears, desires, convictions, failings, darkness, misapprehensions and invincible prejudices of men? Oh that men had the spirit of Salvian, when he said of some of his cotemporaries, "They are heretics, but know it not; heretics to us, but not to themselves: nay, they think themselves so catholic, that they judge us to be heretics; what they are to us, that are we to them: they err, but with a good mind, and for this cause God shows patience towards them."

One of the saddest things attending this spirit is that intolerance begets intolerance, and persecution, persecution.

No doubt this evil has existed from the first. But it comes to the Western World through Pagan Rome, which admitted no worship and no doctrine but such as was established and approved by those who claimed authority in such matters. This was the ground of that great clamour, made at Philippi respecting the preaching of Paul and Silas: "They teach customs which it is not lawful for us to receive, neither to observe, being Romans." Acts xvi. 21.

Nor has there been any thing new uttered for centuries in favour of intolerance. The defence of it, made as early as the time of Augustus Cæsar was, that "They, who introduced new deities draw many into innovations, from which arise conspiracies, seditions, conventicles, in no wise profitable for the commonwealth." The other great ground of defence of persecution was that the worship of new gods was a dishonour and a provocation to those already worshipped, and thus they sent calamities upon the people.

It is a fact worthy of note, that persecution has never been raised against any man or people, whose opinions or practices have been fairly dealt with by adversaries. This is illustrated on almost every page of the history of spiritual despotism. Owen says, "The course accounted so sovereign for the extirpation of error, was first invented for the extirpation of truth." The same author long since gave the challenge to the world in offering to prove that "in sundry Christian provinces more lives had been sacrificed to the one idol, *Hæreticidium*, of those who bear witness to the truth in the belief for which they suffered, than all the heretics properly so-called, that ever were slain in all the provinces of the world, by men professing the gospel." As much has been admitted by many. Even persecutors have at times admitted the faultless character of their victims. Louis XII., with all his bitterness against the people of Mirindol, said: "Let them be heretics, if you please, but assuredly they are better than I and my Catholics." Thus far in the history of persecution generally, the "punished have been far better than the punishers."

Nor has persecution checked the progress of any thing but truth. Many a time has it been confessed that so far from suppressing heresy by the sword and fagot, it has thereby been exceedingly spread and established. When a man's followers honour him in his life as a saint, they count him a martyr as soon as you shed his blood. The fact is, that where heresy in religion exists, it is a spiritual disease, and so ought to have a spiritual remedy. The Christian church, for more than three centuries after the ascension of her Lord, neither knew nor thought of the carnal weapons of intolerance for the extirpation of wrong opinions or wrong practices in religion. John fled the bath where Cerinthus was found; Marcion reproved a great errorist in strong terms; Irenæus says he would have no intercourse with heretics; Cyprian says, "Neither eat, nor talk, nor deal with them;" Ignatius says: "Count them enemies, and separate from them who hate God; but for beating or persecuting them, that is proper to the heathen who know not God, nor our Saviour; do not you so." Constantine said: "This is most certain, that this is conducing to the peace of the empire, that free option and choice of religion be left to all." How terribly God has followed persecutors with his sorest judgments, can be seen in Jortin's remarks on Church History, in the fifteenth volume of Owen's Works, p. 229, and indeed in many other writings.

One good, not sought by persecutors, has been brought out of their cruel practices. It has given God's people an opportunity to illustrate the true character of a Christian. What Cowper says of Bunyan is as true of some others.

> He loved the world that hated him; the tear
> That dropp'd upon his Bible was sincere;
> Assail'd by scandal and the tongue of strife
> His only answer was a blameless life;
> And he that forged, and he that threw the dart,
> Had each a brother's interest in his heart:
> Paul's love of Christ, and steadiness imbibed,
> Were copied close in him and well transcribed.
> He follow'd Paul; his zeal a kindled flame,
> His apostolic charity the same.

After pagan Rome lost its power, papal Rome took up the trade of intolerance and persecution in the most fearful manner. In the Apocalypse, John speaks of that corrupt communion thus: "I saw the woman drunken with the blood of the saints, and with the blood of the martyrs of Jesus." Rev. xvii. 6. That the Church of Rome is in her fixed principles and uniform practice intolerant and cruel, is as easily proved as any other proposition. The creed of Pope Pius IV., issued Dec. 1564, after the decrees of the Council of Trent, and sworn to by every clergyman in that communion, contains these sentences: "I acknowledge the holy catholic and apostolical Romish church, to be mother and *mistress* (Magistram) *of all churches;* and I promise and swear true obedience to the Roman Pontiff, successor of the blessed Peter, Prince of the Apostles, and Vicar of Jesus Christ.

"Also, all other things handed down, defined and declared by the sacred canons and general councils, and chiefly by the most holy of Trent, I undoubtingly receive, profess, and, at the same time, all things contrary, and all heresies whatever condemned, rejected, and anathematized, I, in like manner, condemn, reject, and anathematize. And this true Catholic faith, out of which no one can have salvation, which at present I voluntarily profess and truly hold, I, the said A. B., promise, vow, and swear," &c. Here we have a clear and full declaration that all protestants and their children sink down to perdition.

The oath taken by every Roman Catholic Bishop contains, among other things, this sentence: "Hæreticos, schismaticos, et rebelles, eidem domino nostro, vel successoribus prædictis pro posse persequar et impugnabo:" *i. e.*, "Heretics, schismatics, and rebels, to our said Lord, or his aforesaid successors, I will to my power persecute and oppose."

In the year 1582, there was published at Rheims, a copy of the New Testament, with various notes, &c. This work, in several editions, has been frequently approved, sanctioned and published, by various Romish bishops. Here are some of the notes: "The insufficient and pretended church service of England—being in schism and heresy, is not only unprofitable, but also damnable." "If the temple of the Jews was a den of thieves, because of profane and secular merchandize; how much more now, when the house appointed for the holy sacrifice and sacrament of the body of Christ is made a den for the ministers of Calvin's bread." "The prayers and services of heretics are not acceptable to God out of their mouths; yea, are no better than the howling of wolves." "A Christian is bound to burn and deface all heretical books." "The translators of the English Protestant Bible ought to be abhorred to the depths of hell." "Justice and vigorous punishment of sinners is not forbidden, nor the church, nor the Christian princes blamed for putting heretics to death." "There never was any heresy so absurd, but it would seem to have Scripture for it." "To say that an heretic, evidently known to die obstinately in heresy, is damned, is not forbidden." "Where heretics have unluckily been received for fear of troubling the state, they cannot be suddenly extirpated—the weeds must grow while the church obtains power, then eradicate them from the soil." "The zeal of a Catholic ought to be so great towards all heretics and their doctrines that he should give them the curse,—the execration,—the anathema, —though they were never so dear to him,—though they were his parents."

Dens and Liguori fully confirm the whole spirit of this teaching.

On the Thursday before Easter, in every mass-house in the world, where service is conducted, unless public sentiment restrains the priest, there is read the Papal Bull, entitled *In Cœna Domini.* The second clause of this Bull contains the excommunication of all Hussites, Wiclifites, Lutherans, Zuinglians, Calvinists, Huguenots, Anabaptists, Trinitarians, and other apostates from the faith; and all other heretics, by whatsoever name they are called, or of whatever sect they be," &c., &c.

The sixth paragraph utterly curses all the civil powers, who impose new taxes without the consent of the Roman court.

The twentieth begins thus: "We excommunicate

and anathematize all and every, the magistrates, judges, notaries, &c., who intrude themselves in capital or criminal causes against ecclesiastical persons, &c." A more shamelessly wicked, cruel, and malignant document was probably never sent forth to the world.

The phrase *anathema sit*—let him be accursed,—occurs more than one hundred and twenty times in the canons and acts of the council of Trent. Paul said, "Bless, and curse not," Rom. xii. 14. But Rome thunders forth her curses on all hands. She sends forth as bitter anathemas against those who do not believe all the falsehoods and absurdities found in the Apocrypha, as against those who reject the Gospels. She as horribly curses one, who does not believe marriage to be a sacrament, as one who does not believe baptism to be a sacrament. With her, every dogma is fundamental; every principle essential.

Here are some of the decisions of the canon law: "The Roman faith destroys all heresy and tolerates none." "The Roman church admits no heresy, for the Catholic religion must be kept without spot." "It is permitted neither to think nor to teach otherwise than the court of Rome directs." "He who is separated from the church can neither have his sins pardoned, nor can he enter the kingdom of heaven." "Heretics may be excommunicated after death." The object of this canon was the confiscation of property by the church. Many a time the bones of the dead have been exhumed and burned in fulfilment of this horrible doctrine. When jackals dig up the dead, it is to fulfil the law of their animal nature. "The property of heretics must be confiscated for the good of the church." "Advocates and notaries, who defend heretics, or assist them by writings or deeds, shall be adjudged infamous, and deprived of their office." "They who are bound to heretics are released from every obligation." "Statute laws of the civil power, by which inquisitors of heresy are impeded or prohibited are null and void." "Heretics shall not be interred in ecclesiastical ground."

How fearfully these wicked principles have been carried out, history records. At least two millions of Jews and fifty millions of Christians are supposed to have perished by the hand of this cruel power. The Duke of Alva, in a short time hanged and beheaded eighteen thousand Protestants, besides thousands put to death by his ruffian soldiery.

At the command of Pope Paul III., twenty-four villages were burnt to ashes, and thousands of persons, men, women and children murdered. It is supposed that not less than one million of Waldenses have suffered death to gratify Romish bigotry and cruelty. St. Bartholomew's day, in 1572, will be ever memorable in France. It was the time fixed for the indiscriminate butchery of Protestants. It swept away seventy thousand people in the space of a few hours. The Dublin University Magazine for June, 1842, contains an account of a copy of a medal ordered by the Pope to be struck in commemoration of this shocking wholesale murder. But enough of these horrible annals. Let all men express their detestation of all persecution and intolerance. God abhors them. 1 Cor. xiii. 1–8. Jesus Christ prayed for even his murderers.

### XII. HARD-HEARTEDNESS, &c., &c.

Besides the things already noticed, it is clear that this commandment in its spirit and scope forbids and condemns hard-heartedness to the suffering poor, Matt. xxv. 42, 43, Jas. ii. 15, 16; all immoderate passions, Jas. iv. 1; oppression of every kind, Isa. iii. 15; devotion to carnal pleasures, Eccl. xi. 9; overtaxing the bodily powers of ourselves or others, Eccl. iv. 8; Ex. ii. 23, 24; excess in food or drink, Luke xxi. 34; Prov. xxiii. 20, 21; in short all that tends to disturb the peace of persons, families or communities, Rom. xiv. 19; 2 Tim. ii. 22; or needlessly to shorten human life, Prov. xxviii. 17.

# CHAPTER XXI.

## THE SEVENTH COMMANDMENT.

### THOU SHALT NOT COMMIT ADULTERY.

IT is both man's crime and misery that he often acquires a habit of thinking lightly of the most weighty and serious things. Such levity is not reconcilable with wisdom towards ourselves, or duty towards God. It generates recklessness and impetuosity of character. It banishes those solemn and salutary thoughts which are essential to sound discretion. It is still worse when we learn so to think and speak of matters of great moment as that the introduction of them is a temptation to impurity of thought. The consequence is, that we often find sadness where we looked for joy, and wretchedness where we supposed peace had her abode.

These remarks apply with great force to almost all topics belonging to the seventh commandment. Such is the state of the public mind that it is exceedingly difficult to write or speak on any of them without giving offence to some, or occasion of evil thoughts to others. Still here stands this great commandment. A right understanding of it is essential to the welfare of society. If any one shall be injured in his nicest feelings by the discussion proposed, it shall be his own fault.

It is convenient to the plan of discussion proposed to begin with considering the subject of

### MARRIAGE.

True, many smile and some lose sobriety of mind, whenever they think, or hear, or speak on this subject. But surely the matter is solemn, and deserves our gravest thoughts. It is not indeed a melancholy theme, a doleful matter ; and so we may bring to the study of it all our vivaciousness, as well as great earnestness.

I. The first thing which claims our attention is the nature of the institution.

Marriage is a solemn and perpetual covenant between one man and one woman to live together in the most affectionate and endearing state of social existence known upon earth. 1. It is a *covenant.* Such is the language used respecting it in nearly all the Christian forms of its solemnization, as well as in Holy Scripture, Prov. ii. 17. 2. It is a *solemn* covenant. With the exception of the engagements by which a man binds his soul to the service of God, there is no other covenant of more solemnity. 3. This covenant is of *perpetual obligation,* as long as the parties live. Exceptions to this remark will be stated hereafter. Other covenants may be set aside, sometimes by mutual consent, sometimes by the payment of a specified penalty, and sometimes by casualties, rendering fulfilment impossible ; but this cannot even be weakened, much less destroyed in this manner. Without a high crime, in one party subverting the very design of marriage, death only can release the other party. Whoever lawfully and properly enters the state of marriage intends that it shall be for life. 4. This covenant is between *one* man and *one* woman. All good laws insist upon this. This was the form of the institution in Paradise. Jesus Christ has taught us that the law of Eden is still of binding force, Matt. xix. 3–9. The laws of the land wisely enforce the same principle. Bigamy and polygamy deserve to be severely punished, as high immoralities, tending to the rapid destruction of society and of the commonwealth. 5. This covenant binds the parties to *live in the most affectionate and endearing state of social existence known upon earth.* All other relationships give place to this. It takes precedence of the tie of parent and child. So that from the first, the infallible rule of marriage required a man to forsake father and mother, and to cleave unto his wife. By parity of reason, the woman is to forsake her parents and cleave to her husband. Both human and divine laws regard husband and wife as in an important sense one. Blackstone says, they "are one person in law, so that the very being and existence of the woman is suspended during the coverture, or entirely merged, or incorporated in that of the husband." Dr. Johnson says: "Marriage is the strictest tie of perpetual friendship, and there can be no friendship without confidence, and no confidence without integrity; and he must expect to be wretched, who pays to beauty, riches, or politeness, that regard which only virtue and piety can claim." The divine lawgiver settles the question in a few words: "They shall be one flesh."

Some persons far removed from all sickly sensibility never witness the solemnization of a marriage without strong emotion. Behold that noble, generous young man, full of energy, courage and magnanimity. He has sincerely plighted his troth. He would not hesitate a moment to step in between his loved one and the stroke of death, and thus save her from all harm. By his side stands "a lovely female clothed in all the freshness of youth, and surpassing beauty. . . . In the trusting, the heroic devotion, which impels her to leave country, parents, for a comparative stranger, she has launched her frail bark upon a wide and stormy sea. She has handed over her happiness and doom for this world, to another's keeping. But she has done it fearlessly, for love whispers to her, that her chosen guardian and protector bears a manly and a noble heart. Oh woe to him that forgets his oath and his manliness We have all read the story of the husband who in a moment of hasty wrath said to her who had but a few months before united her fate to his,—"If you are not satisfied with my conduct, go, return to your friends and your happiness." "Can you give me back that which I brought to you?" asked the despairing wife. "Yes," he replied, "all your wealth shall go with you; I covet it not." "Alas," she answered, "I thought not of my wealth —I spoke of my devoted love; can you give that back to me?" "No!" said the man, as he flung himself at her feet. "No! I cannot restore that, but I will do more—I will keep it unsullied and untainted; —I will cherish it through my life, and in my death; and never again will I forget that I have sworn to protect and cherish her, who gave up to me all she held most dear."

II. The marriage state is honourable. For ages the wise and good of all countries have bestowed upon it high commendations. Hooker says: "The bond of wedlock hath been always, more or less, esteemed of as a thing religious and sacred. The title, which the very heathen themselves do thereunto oftentimes give, is, *holy*." Dr. Johnson: "Marriage is the best state for man in general, and every man is a worse man, in proportion as he is unfit for the marriage state." Addison: "Two persons, who have chosen each other out of all the species, with design to be each other's mutual comfort and entertainment, have in that action bound themselves to be good-humoured, affable, discreet, forgiving, patient and joyful with respect to each other's frailties and imperfections to the end of their lives." John Newton says: "Marriage has been, and is, to me, the best and dearest of temporal blessings. . . . Long experience and much observation have convinced me, that the marriage state, when properly formed and prudently conducted, affords the nearest approach to happiness, (of a merely temporal kind) that can be attained in this uncertain world, and which will best abide the test of sober reflection."

Our Creator has dignified this state by legislating upon it under every dispensation of his government over men. In Eden—before man was a sinner—in the Hebrew commonwealth as organized by Moses, and under the reign of Messiah, marriage has been regulated, guarded and honoured by solemn enactments, the whole tenor of which was to raise it high in the esteem of men. When Christ was upon earth, he wrought his first miracle at a marriage in Cana of Galilee, which he graced with his presence. Lest there should remain a shadow of a doubt in the human mind, God has declared by an inspired apostle that "MARRIAGE IS HONOURABLE IN ALL." Heb. xiii. 4. On this clear, unequivocal teaching of inspiration, we may rest the defence of the honourableness of marriage in all classes and conditions of life, high and low, lay and clerical.

III. Yet this institution has long been assaulted by ignorant and wicked men. Various apostates from the truth of God have made war upon it. Christ's apostles predicted the appearance of men who should "depart from the faith, giving heed to seducing spirits, and doctrines of devils, speaking lies in hypocrisy, having their conscience seared with a hot iron, *forbidding to marry*, &c." 1 Tim. iv. 1–3. Accordingly, there early arose men, who exerted all their power against this great bulwark of virtue. Irenæus tells us that Saturninus and Marcion led the way in this unholy assault. These were followed by the sect of the Encratites, founded by Tatian. They openly taught, as Epiphanius informs us, that "marriage was the work of the devil." Augustine says, these errorists "would admit no married person into their society." The Apostolici, or Apotactici, held the same views, and arrogantly denied all hope of salvation to such as were married, or would not grant a community of goods. Augustine tells us that the Manichees also condemned marriage and prohibited it as far as they could. "The Severians and Archontici held the same views. Some of their teachings were cruel and brutal. They said that "woman herself was the work of the devil." After these arose Hierax, whose followers took their name from him. He taught that marriage belonged only to the Old Testament institutions; since the coming of Christ it was no longer lawful; and that no married person could obtain the heavenly kingdom. Augustine says that they "admitted none but monks and nuns, and such as were unmarried into their communion" Still later arose Eustathius, bishop of Sebastia, who said that "no one who lived in a married state could have any hope in God." This man had many followers. Since his time we have had hosts of errorists, who have held that there was a holier state than that of virtuous wedlock. So confident and plausible have been these empirics, that in almost every age they have had some followers, male and female.

It is one of the gross inconsistencies of Popery that while, contrary to Scripture, it elevates marriage to the grade of a sacrament, it also, in the teeth of God's word, enjoins universal celibacy upon the clergy, and builds its prisons all over the world, where it locks up free-born females, white and black, who, under the force of superstitious fears and hopes, have been induced to take the vow of single life. But for all this there is not one word of divine authority. By the constitution of the Jewish commonwealth, the tribe of Levi was placed under the law of marriage just as were the other tribes. The son succeeded the father in his sacred functions. Nor was the doctrine of universal celibacy of the clergy known among the apostles. Both during and subsequently to our Lord's residence on the earth, Peter was the husband of one wife. The evangelists tell us that Peter's wife's mother lay sick of a fever, Matt. viii. 14; Mark i. 30; Luke iv. 38. Many years after Christ's ascension, Paul says, "Have we not power to lead about a sister, a wife, as well as other apostles, and as the brethren of the Lord, and Cephas?" 1 Cor. ix. 5. Peter and others of the apostles were married men. The evidence is clear. Paul also gives us the law respecting the marriage of pastors: "A bishop then must be blameless, the husband of one wife, one that ruleth well his own house, having his children in subjection with all gravity." 1 Tim. iii. 2, 4. The Greek church interprets this phrase so strictly that she requires all her pastors to be married men, and she allows them to be married but once during life. And if the wife die, the pastor ceases to exercise any function in the church. The Romish church interprets it only by contradicting it. She allows none of her pastors to have even one wife. The Protestant doctrine is that this passage permits pastors to be married, but not to practise polygamy. This is doubtless the sense of this Scripture.

There have arisen various founders of infidel communities, which have attacked this institution. The history of Robert Dale Owen of Lanark, of Frances Wright, and of their compeers and imitators, is before the world, illustrating, as all such attempts must do, the truth that material dishonour to marriage, as ordained by God, will subvert any community, and make life wholly undesirable.

An eminent patriot, philosopher, statesman and divine of this country, who signed the Declaration of Independence, has said: "Nothing can be more contrary to reason or public utility than the conversation of those who turn matrimony into ridicule. Such act in direct and deliberate opposition to the order of Providence, and to the constitution of the society of which they are members. The true reason why they are borne with so patiently is, that their wicked attempts are unavailing. But if we are to estimate the malignity of a man's conduct or sentiments, not from their effect, but from their native tendency and his inward disposition, it is not easy to imagine anything more criminal than an attempt to bring marriage into disesteem."

If men will indulge in satire, let them select some ridiculous or mischievous opinion or practice as a theme for merriment. But let them not amuse themselves by attempting to desecrate or destroy one of the best institutions Heaven has given to mortals.

IV. Marriage is the source of many blessings. These may be divided into three classes. The first relate to the parties themselves; the second to the church of God; and the third to mankind in general. 1. Marriage is of great value to the parties themselves. It is an old saying that "marriage sobers even the soberest." Whatever cures men's antics and frivolities is so far useful. Marriage greatly diminishes the sorrows and augments the enjoyments of those who are fitly united. This is a world of much unhappiness. Human life is possessed only at the cost of many pains and sorrows. It is true that in deep affliction God alone can give *efficient* help and succour. Blessed be his name! His ear is ever open to the cry of the humble. But in nearly all our woes, it is an unspeakable relief to have an earthly friend, to whom, in the sacredness of confidence, and with the perfect assurance of sympathy, we may unbosom our griefs. The Son of God himself, when in tribulation, did not disdain to call for sympathy. To his disciples he said, "What, could ye not watch with me one hour?" Matt. xxvi. 40. There is no human being so elevated in character, so independent in resources, as not to need the confidence and sympathy of some of the race. Most men admit that in her feebleness, timidity and delicate sensibility, woman, like the ivy, needs a support, that she may not be tossed about by every adverse wind, nor trodden down by the rude and the strong around her. A little reflection will convince us that the rougher sex also needs soothing and sympathy. Man spends most of his waking hours in severe studies, in exhausting toils, in grappling with great difficulties, and in enduring the asperities of many coarse and malignant persons. To him, how consoling it is to know that there is one spot, his own fireside, and one sanctuary, the heart of his faithful wife, where all is calm and kind. Every virtuous husband, who has a virtuous wife, has often returned home, pressed down, almost beyond endurance, with cares and anxieties, dreading an almost sleepless night. Yet in an hour, the love of his wife and the prattle of his little ones have made him blithe, and reassured him before he was again called to buffet the storms of life. In accordance with this view, Jehovah said: "It is not good that the *man* should be alone; I will make *him* an help meet for *him*." Gen. ii. 18. While wives need the care and even the caresses of husbands, they are themselves invaluable helps to their partners.

The married pair in many ways help each other They give mutual counsel in perplexity; they afford to each other the best and safest society; they are the surest guardians of each other's interests; and they rejoice in each other in a manner unknown in any other relation of life.

We are here met by the fact often alleged that some marriages are not happy, and that here and there the parties are very miserable. It would be worse than idle to deny that some husbands and some wives are extremely unhappy on account of their matrimonial relations. But does not candour require the admission that many *unmarried* persons are extremely unhappy? Besides, some matches are made merely for the purpose of securing a fortune, or some family distinction. In this case the person married is taken as a means to an end. The object is to make an acquisition of name or money. Could the same end be gained free from any incumbrance, it would be much preferred. Others in the choice of a wife regard only personal beauty. That beauty is a desirable quality no man of sense or taste will deny. But that in value it is not comparable to intelligence, good temper, industry, truthfulness, or any of the virtues, is clear to all except the silly. It should also not be forgotten that as some very beautiful flowers have thorns, so it is with some beautiful women. The flattery heaped on handsome women often greatly injures their dispositions. Besides, beauty is a flower that fades, in many cases early, and so all that was loved vanishes away. No one need be surprised at such marriages ending in misery. Erasmus: "Love that has nothing but beauty to keep it in good health, is short-lived, and apt to have ague fits."

In other cases there is a total dissimilarity of taste, habit, sentiment, and even principle. The man is refined and his wife coarse. Some say that a lady may love a man quite inferior in breeding, because she may improve him. But a gentleman cannot love one whose tastes are much inferior to his own. And the wife is so much secluded that commonly she cannot after marriage materially improve her mind or manners. What chance of permanent solid happiness is there for husband and wife, where one loves the ball-room, and the other the sanctuary? or one is ever seeking society, and the other loves home? "How can two walk together except they be agreed?" *Some* points of dissimilarity do not impair the happiness of a marriage; but where the substantial elements of character are diverse, there cannot be connubial bliss. Under the Jewish law an ass and a heifer might not be put to work at the same plough. Utter unsuitableness is a sure foundation for matrimonial misery. Another bane of married life is found in intemperance, not always confined to the stronger sex. It is utterly impossible that any virtuous woman should be happy with a drunken husband. Her very love will torment her.

It may be said that most unhappy marriages are brought about either by rashness, by refusing good counsel, by marrying to please some third party, by being actuated by wrong motives, or by being moved by senseless impulses and fancies, or by failing to look to God in humble supplication for heavenly guidance. Revelation well says: "A prudent wife is from the Lord." How many look every or anywhere else but to the Lord in such matters!

The subject of unhappy marriages has claimed the attention of many writers. Witherspoon says that the number of unhappy marriages is greatly overestimated; and that we do but deceive ourselves when we suppose others unhappy, because we should be so, if placed in their circumstances. This remark is entitled to great weight.

Dean Swift assigns another reason for unhappy marriages, viz. the want of the stronger and more enduring excellences in some females. He says: "The reason why so few marriages are happy, is because young ladies spend their time in making nets, not in making cages." Dr. Johnson says: "When we see the avaricious and crafty taking companions to their tables, and their beds, without any inquiry but after farms and money; or the giddy and thoughtless uniting themselves for life to those whom they have only seen by the light of tapers; when parents make articles for children without inquiring after their consent; when some marry for heirs to disappoint their brothers; and others throw themselves into the arms of those whom they do not love, because they have found themselves rejected where they were more solicitous to please; when some marry because their servants cheat them; some because they squander their own money; some because their houses are pestered with company; some because they will live like other people; and some because they are sick of themselves, we are not so much inclined to wonder that marriage is sometimes unhappy, as that it appears so little loaded with calamity; and cannot but conclude, that society has something in itself eminently agreeable to human nature, when we find its pleasures so great that even the ill choice of a companion can hardly overbalance them. Those, therefore, of the above description, that should rail against matrimony, should be informed, that they are neither to wonder, or repine, that a contract begun on such principles has ended in disappointment." This may suffice for the unhappiness of marriages.

2. Marriage is eminently conducive to the interests of the church of God. When properly regulated by Christian laws and when properly entered into and regarded, it shuts out many and nameless evils, evils everywhere condemned in Scripture, evils always subversive of thrift, good order, quietness and harmony in society. The name of these evils is Legion, for they are many. They are secret and they are open—they torment man and they provoke God. They are insidious and they are impudent. Some of them lead to the utter subversion of States, and all of them impair both bodily and mental energy—waste the health—deprave morals—pollute the mind and banish religion, pure and undefiled, from any community where they obtain a footing. So that an attempt to introduce the gospel among a people where such things prevail would be as discouraging as to preach the gospel with the worst forms of idolatry and the iron laws of Hindoo caste to oppose its progress. But the prevention of these dire evils is not nearly all the good done to the cause of religion by marriage. For it is only in communities where marriage is properly regarded, that we find ourselves able to make many of the most solemn

and moving appeals in behalf of virtue and piety. Who has ever listened to the calls given by the ministers of the gospel to husbands and wives, to parents and children, to brothers and sisters to pray and labour for each other's salvation, or to come, and go with the pious members of their own families to their promised inheritance, and has not felt that here was a chord that might be made to vibrate in such a way that all, who were not "past feeling," must know its power? Moreover, where there is no marriage, there is no family religion. Children in all such cases grow up without proper education. They are not carried to the house of God and by the mild authority, kind instruction, and good example of both the parents, taught to revere the name and ordinances of Jehovah. The longer I live, and the more I see the operation of moral causes, the more am I convinced that next to the pulpit, if not before it, God designs to perpetuate his church and renovate the world by family religion, in the broad sense of that term. But where the institution and Christian law of marriage are despised and rejected, the domestic altar is never raised, except to sacrifice to devils. Indeed, according to Scripture, the great design of preserving marriage pure, between one man and one woman, was the propagation of true religion throughout the earth. So says the last of the Old Testament prophets. "Did he not make one? . . . . . And wherefore one? That he might seek a godly seed. Therefore take heed to your spirit, and let none deal treacherously against the wife of his youth." Mal. ii. 15.

3. The state, no less than the church, comes in for

inestimable blessings flowing from this institution. If marriage is not properly guarded, population itself will dwindle away, even under the most favourable circumstances of soil, climate, and commerce. The fairest fields and the most thronged cities would in a very few generations become desolate and without inhabitants, if it were not for marriage. Carelessness of the health and lives of children, whose parents are not lawfully married, is so well established and so generally confessed, that it is enough to allude to it. Nor is this all. The real prosperity and solid wealth and resistless power of a nation do not depend upon splendid edifices and glittering crowns for the few; but upon the industry, frugality, and thrift of the component parts of an empire. Families make empires. And where are the domestic and social virtues successfully taught and practised except in families, constituted by lawful marriage? Visit our almshouses, our work-houses, our jails, our prisons of every description, yea, inquire into the history of the strolling beggars of the land, and what do you find? Here and there is a case of virtuous misfortune. Here and there are the offspring of virtuous parentage; but in an appalling number of cases, the persons are themselves those who have in some gross manner violated the law of marriage, or are the offspring of parents who have forgotten or failed to obey it.

All men are born with an irksomeness under restraint and government. Men by nature are averse to the controlling of their desires. Government is an artificial state, and yet with the present or any conceivable condition of society, it is necessary to man's well-being. The sooner he learns to obey just authority the better for him, the better for his country. Where then are the first and most useful lessons of obedience learned? Not in the public assembly, not in the camp, not in the counting-room, not in the neighbourhood school, but in the family—the well-ordered family, where the joint and just authority of an honest father and mother subdue the will, and teach important lessons of self-denial. Nor can the state, in the absence of marriage, ever make adequate provision for educating the minds and manners of the young in any way promising much good. Hirelings have neither the patience, nor the tact requisite to develop in an advantageous manner the mental energies of the young, as virtuous parents have. In short, look at this subject as we may, and we find the state deeply concerned to do all in its power to make marriage honourable, as God has made it, to guard it from all abuses, to keep the burdens of government light upon the lower classes, so that the industrious poor may not be prevented from entering the state of marriage at a proper time of life, and, above all, to punish with just severity every infraction of the wholesome laws made to defend the institution from perversion, contempt, or neglect.

V. Let us dwell a little on the duties growing out of this relation. Love is the fulfilling of the law. This remark is peculiarly just in regard to the law of marriage. This love must be the result, not of ecstasies produced by a fervid imagination, but of the warm pulsations of an honest heart. Hooker never spoke more wisely of man than when he said: "That kind of love, which is the perfectest ground of wedlock, is seldom able to yield any reason of itself."

It must be founded in solid esteem. For this there is no substitute. The cares and sorrows of life are so numerous, the trials of temper so many, and the calls for forbearance so frequent, that unless there be ardent, and strong, and mutual affection, life will soon be a weariness. This love must not only be a sentiment, it must be a principle. Then it will be abiding. It must not only be a principle, it must be a sentiment. Then it will be warm and generous. It must be,

> "A friendship that like love is warm,
> A love like friendship steady."

It is, therefore, an act of great cruelty in parents and friends to urge others to the formation of marriages, when there is wanting this fervent love. Nothing can make amends for deficiencies here. This is the root from which, under the divine blessing, grows up that tree of domestic happiness under whose shade myriads of households rejoice, and whose fruit is better than apples of gold. Prov. xv. 17. Love counts not its sacrifices. It gives all and would give more if it had more to give. This duty is often insisted on in Scripture. "Husbands, love your wives, and be not bitter against them." "Men ought to love their wives as their own bodies. He that loveth his wife loveth himself." "Husbands, love your wives even as Christ also loved the church and gave himself for it." Eph. v. 25, 28; Col. iii. 19. Compare Eccl. ix. 9. Paul says that one of the duties incumbent on aged pious females is to "teach the young women to love their husbands." Tit. ii. 4.

As the parties mutually owe to each other love, so do they fidelity in its highest sense. They are bound sacredly and tenderly to regard each others' rights, and peace, and happiness. 1 Cor. vii. 5. Moreover, the husband owes to his wife protection to her person, reputation, health, and comfort. He never fulfils the duties of a husband, who leaves his wife to contend with the adversities of life and steps not forth with the whole strength of his arm to shield her.

On the other hand, the wife owes to her husband reverence and obedience. On these the Bible insists. Eph. v. 22; Col. iii. 18; 1 Pet. iii. 1. And whether they were openly promised or not at marriage, they are enjoined by God and it is a sin to withhold them. The reverence and obedience required are not those of a servant, nor even those of a child, but of a companion, who is yet the weaker vessel. The woman is not the head of the man but the man of the woman. Adam was *first* formed, then Eve.

Husbands and wives owe each other honour in their respective stations. No churl can be a good husband; and no shrew, a good wife. 1 Sam. xxv. 17; Prov. xxi. 19, xxv. 24. When respect ceases, love and peace generally depart. Husbands and wives, who at all do their duties, are an honour to each other in fact. Prov. xii. 14, xxxi. 23; 1 Cor. xi. 7. But they are both commanded to aim at giving honour to each other. 1 Pet. iii. 6, 7.

They should also endeavour in all lawful ways to please each other. 1 Cor. vii. 33, 34.

Husbands and wives should tenderly sympathize with each other, and plead for each other, 1 Sam. i. 8, xxv. 18–28. The husband should cultivate tenderness.

BE GENTLE TO THY WIFE.

"Be gentle, for you little know
  How many trials rise;
Although to thee they may be small,
  To her of giant size.

"Be gentle, though perchance that lip
  May speak a murmuring tone,
The heart may speak with kindness ye
  And joy to be thy own.

"Be gentle; weary hours of pain
  'Tis woman's lot to bear;
Then yield her what support thou canst,
  And all her sorrows share.

"Be gentle; for the noblest hearts
  At times must have some grief,
And even in a pettish word
  May seek to find relief.

"Be gentle; none are perfect here;
  Thou'rt dearer far than life;
Then husband, bear, and still forbear;—
  Be gentle to thy wife."

And the wife should not be cold, but hearty in her endeavours to soothe and please. "It must be the best woman's lot in the world to bind up for the dearest on earth the wounds which men have inflicted."

VI. It is pleasing and not uninstructive to see how men of very diverse characters have felt their happiness increased by marriage. Calvin says of his wife, she was a *woman of rare example.* After her earthly career had closed, in lamenting her loss, he said of her: "I am separated from the best of companions, who if anything harder could have happened to me, would willingly have been my companion, not only in exile and in want, but also in death. While she lived, she was a true help to me in the duties of my office. I have never experienced from her any hindrance, even the smallest."

The following letters passed between Mr. Winthrop, the first Governor of Massachusetts, and his wife, in 1628. The reader will demand no apology for their insertion here. The wife writes first:

"My most sweet husband: How dearly welcome thy kind letter was to me, I am not able to express. The sweetness of it did much to refresh me. What can be more pleasing to a wife than to hear of her best beloved, and how he is pleased with her poor endeavours? I blush to hear myself commended, knowing my own wants. But it is your love that conceives the best, and makes all things seem better than they are. I wish that I might please thee, and that those comforts we have in each other may be daily increased, as far as they may be pleasing to God. I will use the speech to thee that Abigail did to David: 'I will be a servant to wash thy feet, my lord.' I will do any service wherein I may please my good husband. I confess I cannot do enough for thee, but thou art pleased to accept the will for the deed, and rest contented.

"I have many reasons to make me love thee, whereof I will now name thee two. First, because thou lovest God; and secondly, because thou lovest me. If these two were wanting, all the rest would be eclipsed. But I must leave this discourse and go about my household affairs. I am a bad housewife to remain so long away from them; but I must needs borrow a little time to talk with thee a little, my sweetheart. I hope thy business draws to an end. It will be but two or three weeks before I see thee, though they be long ones. God will bring us together in his good time, for which time I shall pray. Farewell, my good husband, the Lord keep thee. Your obedient wife, MARGARET WINTHROP."

THE HUSBAND ANSWERS.

"My good wife: Although I wrote thee but last week, yet having so fit an opportunity, I must write to thee again; for I do esteem one little short letter of thine (such as the last one was) to be worthy two or three from me.

"I began this letter yesterday at two o'clock; thinking to have been at large, but was so taken up with company and business as I could but get hither this morning. It grieves me that I have not liberty to make expressions of my love to thee, who art more dear to me than all earthly things; but I will endeavour that my prayers may supply the place of my pen, which will be of use to us both, inasmuch as the favour and blessing of God are better than all things beside.

"I know that thou lookest for troubles here, and when one affliction is over to meet with another; but remember our Saviour tells us, 'Be of good comfort, I have overcome the world;' therefore, my sweet wife, raise up thy heart, and be not dismayed with the crosses thou meetest in family affairs, or otherwise, but still fly to Him who will take up thy burden for thee. Go then on cheerfully in obedience to His will in the course He has set thee—peace shall come. I commend thee and all to the gracious protection of the Lord.

"Farewell, my good wife, I kiss and love thee, with the kindest affection, and rest thy faithful husband,

JOHN WINTHROP."

Sir James McIntosh thus describes his deceased wife in a letter to a friend:

"Allow me, in justice to her memory, to tell you what she was, and what I owed her. I was guided in my choice only by the blind affection of my youth. I found an intelligent companion, and a tender friend, a prudent monitress, the most faithful of wives, and a mother as tender as children ever had the misfortune to lose. I met a woman who by the tender management of my weaknesses gradually corrected the most pernicious of them. She became prudent from affection; and though of the most generous nature, she was taught frugality and economy by her love to me. During the most critical period of my life, she preserved order in my affairs, from the care of which she relieved me. She gently reclaimed me from dissipation; she prompted my weak and irresolute nature; she urged my indolence to all the exertions that have been useful or creditable to me, and she was perpetually at hand to admonish my heedlessness and improvidence. To her I owe whatever I am; and to her whatever I shall be. In her solicitude for my interest, she never for a moment forgot my feelings or my character. Even in her occasional resentment, for which I but too often gave her cause (would to God I could recall those moments,) she had no sullenness nor acrimony. Her feelings were warm and impetuous, but she was placable, tender and constant. Such was she whom I have lost, and I have lost her when her excellent natural sense was improving, after eight years of struggle and distress had bound us fast to each other—when a knowledge of her worth had refined my youthful love into friendship, before age had deprived it of much of its original ardour,—I lost her alas! (the choice of my youth, and the partner of my misfortunes) at a moment when I had a prospect of her sharing my better days."

The following description was written by Burke and presented to Mrs. Burke on the morning of an anniversary of their marriage. It was evidently intended as a description of his wife. It was headed

"The Character of Mrs. ——."

"I mean to give you my idea of a woman. If it at all answers an original, I shall be pleased; for if such a person really exists, she must be far superior to my description, and such as I must love too well to be able to paint as I ought.

"She is handsome, but it is beauty not arising from features, from complexion, or from shape; she has all three in a high degree, but it is not from these she touches the heart; it is all that sweetness of temper, benevolence, innocence, and sensibility, which a face cannot express, that forms her beauty.

"She has a face that just raises your attention at first sight; it grows on you every moment, and you wonder it did no more than raise your attention at first.

"Her eyes have a mild light, but they awe you when she pleases; they command, like a good man out of office, not by authority, but by virtue.

"Her features are not exactly regular; that sort of exactness is more to be praised than loved, for it is never animated.

"Her stature is not tall; she is made to be the admiration of everybody, but the happiness of one.

"She has all the firmness that does not exclude delicacy; she has all the softness that does not imply weakness.

"There is often more of the coquette shown in an affected plainness than in tawdry finery. She is always clean without preciseness or affectation. Her gravity is a gentle thoughtfulness that softens the features without discomposing them. She is usually grave.

"Her smiles are inexpressible.

"Her voice is a low, soft music; not formed to rule in public assemblies, but to charm those who can distinguish a company from a crowd; it has this advantage, you must come close to hear it.

"To describe her body, describes her mind; one is the transcript of the other. Her understanding is not shown in the variety of matters it exerts itself on, but in the goodness of the choice she makes. She does not display it so much in saying or doing striking things, as in avoiding such as she ought not to say or do.

"She discovers the right or wrong of things not by reasoning, but sagacity; most women, and many good ones, have a closeness and something selfish in their dispositions; she has a true generosity of temper; the most extravagant cannot be more unbounded in their liberality, the most cautious in their distribution.

"No person of so few years can know the world better; no person was ever less corrupted by that knowledge.

"Her politeness seems rather to flow from a disposition to oblige than from any rules on that subject, and therefore never fails to strike those who understand good breeding and those who do not.

"She does not run with a girlish eagerness into new friendships, which, as they have no foundation in reason, serve only to multiply and embitter disputes; it is long before she chooses, but then it is fixed for ever, and the hours of romantic friendship are not warmer than hers after the lapse of years.

"As she never disgraces her good nature by severe reflections on anybody, so she never degrades her judgment by immoderate or ill praises, for every thing violent is contrary to her gentleness of disposition, and the evenness of her virtue.

"She has a steady and firm mind, which takes no more from the female character than the solidity of marble does from its polish and lustre.

"She has such virtue as makes us value the truly great of our own sex; she has all the winning graces that make us love even the faults we see in the weak and beautiful of hers."

Even the severe and scathing Reviewer, Lord Jeffrey, felt the softening, cheering power of a wife's love and presence. A few days after the death of his wife, he wrote to his brother thus:

"EDINBURGH, *August* 15, 1805.

"MY DEAR JOHN: I am at this moment of all men the most miserable and disconsolate. It is just a week to-day since my sweet Kitty died in my arms, and left me without joy, or hope, or comfort in this world. Her health had been long very delicate, and during this summer rather more disordered than usual; but we thought it not serious, and looked forward to her complete restoration. She was finally seized with the most excruciating headaches, which ended in an effusion of water on the brain, and sank her into a lamentable stupor, which terminated in death.

"It is impossible for me to describe to you the feeling of lonely and hopeless misery with which I have since been oppressed. I doted upon her, I believed, more than man ever did on a woman before; and after four years of marriage, was more tenderly attached to her than on the day which made her mine. I took no interest in anything which had not some reference to her, and had no enjoyment away from her, except in thinking what I should have to tell or to show her on my return; and I have never returned to her after half a day's absence, without feeling my heart throb, and my eye brighten, with all the ardour and anxiety of a youthful passion. All the exertions I ever made in the world were for her sake entirely. You know how indolent I was by nature, and how regardless of reputation and fortune. But it was a delight to me to lay these things at the feet of my darling, and to invest her with some portion of the distinction she deserved, and to increase the pride and the vanity she felt for her husband, by accumulating these public tests of his merit. She had so lively a relish for life too, and so unquenchable and unbroken a hope in the midst of protracted illness and languor, that the stroke which cut it off for ever appears equally cruel and unnatural. Though familiar with sickness, she seemed to have nothing to do with death. She always recovered so rapidly, and was so cheerful and affectionate, and playful, that it scarcely entered into my imagination that there could be one sickness from which she would not recover. We had arranged several little projects of amusement for the autumn, and she talked of them, poor thing, with unabated confidence and delight, as long as she was able to talk coherently at all. I have the consolation to think that the short time she passed with me was as happy as love and hope could make it. In spite of her precarious health, she has often assured me that she was the happiest of women, and would not change her condition with any human creature. Indeed we lived in a delightful progress of every thing that could contribute to our felicity. Everything was opening and brightening before us. Our circumstances, our society, were rapidly improving, our understandings were expanding, and even our love and confidence in each other increasing from day to day. Now, I have no interest in anything, and no object or motive for being in the world.

"I wish you had known my Kitty, for I cannot describe her to you, and nobody else knows enough of her. The most peculiar and ennobling part of her character was a high principle of honour, integrity, and generosity, that would have been remarkable in a man, and which I never met with in a woman before. She had no conception of prevaricating, shuffling, or disguising. There was a clear transparency in her soul, without affectation or reserve, which won your implicit confidence, and commanded your respect. Then she was the simplest and most cheerful of human beings; the most unassuming, easy, and affectionate; dignified in her deportment, but affable and engaging in conversation. Her sweetness and cheerfulness in sickness won the hearts of all who came near her. She was adored by her servants, and has been wept for by her physicians, by the chairman who used to carry her, and the tradesmen with whom she dealt. O! my dear John, my heart is very cold and heavy, and my prospect of life every way gloomy and deplorable. I had long been accustomed to place all my notions of happiness in domestic life; and I had found it there, so pure, perfect, and entire, that I can never look for it any where else, or hope for it in any other form. Heaven protect you from the agony it has imposed upon me. Write me soon to say that you are happy, and that you and your Susan will love me. My heart is shut at this time to every thing but sorrow, but I think it must soon open to affection. All your friends here are well. I shall write you again soon.

Ever, my dear John, most affectionately yours,"

F. J.

The late lamented Abel P. Upshur, Secretary of State of the United States, thus wrote to the sister of his first wife, then recently deceased:

"If there be truth in the promises of Jesus, I do confidently believe that she is an angel in heaven. What kindness were it to withdraw such a being from a scene in which all is peace, and confidence, and joy, to involve her again in the cares, the anxieties, the idle contests and frivolous activity of the world? I can truly say that I derive much comfort from this reflection; other considerations contribute to calm me, but this alone brings with it a sensible consolation. We are assured that in a future state the good and pious will receive an infinitely more exalted happiness than any this world can afford, and surely none that ever lived can with more confidence claim that reward than she for whom we are mourning. When I analyze my feelings in this affliction, I find that it is for myself that I mourn, and not for her, that I am bewailing the comforts of her society, the cheering light of her countenance, the warm pulse of joy which throbbed for her so actively. Is it not selfishness which makes me regret to surrender these joys as the price of her infinite happiness? On earth I would have given all I possessed to purchase her one hour's exemption from pain, yet I envy her the joys she has taken from me, although they form her passport to endless happiness. Surely I ought to reproach myself that I yield up, even with reluctant consent, the imperfect pleasures of the few years I have to live, when I know that their surrender is necessary to her everlasting good. Besides, Madam, it is true though trite, that she is but removed to a little distance from us, and we are already on the road to meet her again. I am not afraid of this reflection; it is mingled with melancholy, but it is a melancholy of a soothing character. It is certain we are approaching her by daily journeys, nor can we tell how soon the last day's journey shall be performed. In the meantime, we should persevere with constancy and with cheerful hopes, relying that when we meet her again it will be in a far different scene, that we shall find her happy beyond our natures to imagine how perfectly, that this happiness will be subject to no accident to render it less complete, and that we also may seize hold on it with the strong confidence that it will last for ever. Have we not the greatest reason to rejoice and to be grateful that we are permitted to entertain these consoling hopes? How different would be our feelings if we dared not to look beyond the grave, or if in looking beyond it, we were forbidden to contemplate any thing but its horrors. I am sure I could not believe without distraction that all that I loved is gone from me for ever, that all my life to come must be a contest with despair. And how full of horror would be our feelings if in contemplating this eternity, we could even doubt that she whom we so tenderly loved is enjoying its best rewards. We have certainly much reason to rejoice in the light which has broken in upon the tomb, that in our anguish we are not abandoned to the imperfect consolations of this life that fall surely to her, whose steps never erred. The grave is but the passage to endless felicity. If she had been less good, these hopes would have presented themselves to us with less strength and fewer consolations, so that in fact, those very excellencies which make us regret her so much afford us the strongest motives for being reconciled to her loss. It is possible that at another time death would have found her less prepared to receive him. As it is, he has set his everlasting seal upon her character, the living will love and revere her memory, and those to whom she was most dear have the consoling consciousness that her summons came before the cares of the world had alienated her from God.

"It appears to my mind that we ought to derive much strength from these reflections. At all events we must not forget that resignation to the will of Heaven is a duty which none shall be excused from neglecting. To command and to submit is the only reasoning between the Creator and his creatures. Nor, if we consider the matter aright, is resignation as difficult a duty as in our agony we may think it. It is extremely presumptuous in us, who cannot penetrate the issues of one moment that is to come, to question the correctness of His doings, whose eye is over the universe, whose glance is through eternity, and whose goodness is without bounds. If it were not good, would the God of goodness do it? If it were not right, would the God of justice bring it to pass? In the decrees of that Being there can be no caprice, in his ordinances there can be no mutability. He acts by settled laws, which are hid from human scrutiny, but we have the fullest assurance that they are right, and that human wisdom could not alter one of them for the better. We would have ordered this thing differently, and yet, if we could have lifted the veil which hides us from the future, it is perfectly certain that we should have shuddered at the consequences of our weak interference.

"There are some afflictions which come upon us like a torrent, which bears down and breaks in pieces all the barriers which reason, philosophy and even religion can set up against it. Yet the torrent passes away and imparts in its progress strength and healthy fertility to the soil. It is only in such a soil that the seeds of religious consolation can flourish. To a mind at ease and rejoicing in the world it would be useless to address arguments drawn from beyond the grave. Those only who need such consolations are capable of feeling their force, and it is certain that the heart which has been truly wrung, will find all other consolations a feather in the storm.

"As long as I looked no further than the grave, I saw nothing before me but despair. I have seen the necessity of drawing my consolation from a purer and more exalted source, and I am sincerely grateful to God that he gave me, even for a little while, an example by which I can profit in the day of my distress. While she lived it was habitual with me to refer all my actions to the standard of her judgment and goodness, and if even in secret an impure thought rose in my bosom, her image was present to rebuke me. Madam, she was a being not fitted for this world, and she has taken a flight to a better. Still, however, her example remains with us, and in my bereavement I shall not forget it. It shall be my endeavour so to conduct myself in my affliction as I think will be acceptable, if it be permitted her to bend her regards from heaven on my conduct on earth, to act as far as my less perfect nature will permit me as I think she would have acted under the circumstances."

Solomon has given us the following portraiture of a good wife: "Who can find a virtuous woman? for her price is far above rubies. The heart of her husband doth safely trust in her, so that he shall have no need of spoil. She will do him good and not evil all the days of her life. She seeketh wool, and flax, and worketh willingly with her hands. She is like the merchants' ships; she bringeth her food from afar. She riseth also while it is yet night, and giveth meat to her household, and a portion to her maidens. She considereth a field, and buyeth it: with the fruit of her hands she planteth a vineyard. She girdeth her loins with strength, and strengtheneth her arms. She perceiveth that her merchandise is good: her candle goeth not out by night. She layeth her hands to the spindle, and her hands hold the distaff. She stretcheth out her hand to the poor: yea, she reacheth forth her hands to the needy. She is not afraid of the snow for her household: for all her household are clothed with scarlet. She maketh herself coverings of tapestry: her clothing is silk and purple. Her husband is known in the gates, when he sitteth among the elders of the land. She maketh fine linen, and selleth it; and delivereth girdles unto the merchant. Strength and honour are her clothing; and she shall rejoice in time to come. She openeth her mouth with wisdom; and in her tongue is the law of kindness. She looketh well to the ways of her household, and eateth not the bread of idleness. Her children rise up and call her blessed; her husband also, and he praiseth her. Many daughters have done virtuously, but thou excellest them all. Favour is deceitful, and beauty is vain: but a woman that feareth the Lord, she shall be praised. Give her of the fruit of her hands; and let her own works praise her in the gates."

Others must judge what proportion of our modern *fashionable* ladies can be said to be up to Solomon's standard. Have you found many of them seeking wool and flax and working willingly with their hands? Do they rise while it is yet night? How many of them have planted a vineyard with the fruit of their hands? If their candles go not out by night, is it not because they slept most of the day before, or expect to sleep most of the day afterwards? And as to the spindle and the distaff, how few would know these articles if they were to see them. Many cannot show webs spun and woven at home;* but they can show hands as soft and white as lilies; for like the lilies they toil not, neither do they spin. They never make nor sell fine linen, though they buy a good deal of the article with money, to procure which father or husband was expatriated for years, or was obliged to give a mortgage on real estate. They are often highly sentimental over poverty or distress *in a novel,* but seldom stretch out the hand to the poor and needy. They love to be praised in the gates, even if husband and father are left at home to shift as best they may. Who would not commend Solomon's portraiture to all his country-women?

Although the Bible does not draw at length the character of a good husband, (or house-bard as the word signifies,) yet in many places it tells us how he should behave towards the wife of his bosom. His character might be thus sketched.

However he may appear to others, to his wife he is generous and confiding. While he commands respect, he abhors tyranny, and never breathes the spirit of domination. He does not love to make any one feel his power, but he rules his house with such gentleness that all, and especially his wife, deplore his occasional absence. His duties may call him abroad, but his own fireside is the chief seat of his delight. He is courteous and benevolent to all, but loves his family with unfailing tenderness. His manners may be rough, but his warm affection takes from them all that is unseemly except awkwardness. While he loves the company of his wife, he remem-

* The word *wife* belongs to the same family as *weove, woof web.*

bers that human life cannot subsist on doting fondness. He therefore resolutely toils and labours for the comforts required for our frail natures. He knows his own business, yet he is not such a son of Belial that his wife cannot speak to him about any of his affairs. While he encroaches not on her department, he is yet ready to give counsel and aid in any matter that occupies the mind of his partner in life. He bears his full share of domestic cares. He is neither demure, nor frivolous, morose, nor petulant. He may be neither wit, nor humourist, yet he does not dictate, nor dogmatize. He knows when to weep, and when to rejoice. His temper is far removed from suspiciousness. He is not blind to the faults of his wife, but his conjugal affection covers them all from sight. He suggests improvements and labours to effect them, but not by means of rage or passion. He exemplifies the difference between cold civility, and solid respect. His means may be limited, but he rejoices to have his wife share with him the pleasure of befriending the needy, and advancing the welfare of his race. In all good things he seconds her efforts. He goes with her to the house of God, and often implores Heaven's blessings on her. When she is pleased, he rejoices. In her days of nervous timidity, he neither laughs at her idle fears, nor makes a jest of her sorrows. If he is a king in her eyes, she is a queen in his. However rugged his nature, he is alarmed when first he sees the hectic flush, or other sign of danger; and when he finds she must die, he is more nearly unmanned than ever before. And when she dies, divine cordials are necessary to sustain him. Or, if he dies first, his greatest grief is at leaving her to meet the storms of life alone, and he says, as a great man [Dr. Archibald Alexander] lately fallen in Israel, with great tenderness said to his wife, just before his death: "My dear, one of my last prayers will be that you may have as serene and painless a departure as mine."

Are you a happy husband or wife, give thanks to Him who has made you so. Put not on yourself or any mortal the crown which belongs to God alone. "Whoso findeth a wife, findeth a good thing, and obtaineth favour of the Lord." Prov. xviii. 22.

VII. It is the obvious duty of all men to use their best endeavours to maintain good laws on the subject of marriage. In some places they are already enacted; let them be enforced. As a civil institution, marriage is subject to municipal regulations. As appointed by God, it is subject to divine laws.

Among the influences exceedingly unfriendly to the right observance of the seventh commandment may be named

### I. THEATRICAL ENTERTAINMENTS.

It is generally conceded that these lead to expensive habits. The very constitution of the whole system demands large sums of money. The price of tickets of admission declares how this matter stands. All persons know how fascinating these exhibitions are. He who has acquired a zest for them will forego the luxury of relieving even the widow and the fatherless; yea, he will neglect his business, often deprive himself of the means of paying his just debts, and in some cases, consent to subject himself and his family to a scanty mode of living, rather than fail of these entertainments. It is also a well-known fact, that young men, in our large cities, when once brought within the suction of this mighty vortex, will not flee from it, even though, in many cases, their only pecuniary means for gratifying their fondness for a favourite amusement, must be money taken from the chests of their employers. At first they fully intend to return it; but the means of restitution not coming into their possession, and the desire for amusement continually gaining strength, they finally go further, and take money without either the purpose or prospect of refunding it. Thus many young men commence thieves. Of nine young men and lads found guilty of felony, five stole to get the means of going to the theatre. Of seven others, two purloined money to buy lottery tickets, and three to buy tickets to attend the circus.

Theatrical entertainments also tempt to dissipation and intemperance. These vices are known to be exceedingly expensive; but we wish to speak of them in other respects. In the first place, a very frequent preparation for attendance at theatres and such places, is indulgence, to some degree in stimulating drink. Then, these places of resort, almost without exception, are supplied with one or more bars, at which liquors of every tempting variety are sold; and what is more common, after the excitement of a protracted sitting at the theatre, than a certain sensation of lassitude and exhaustion, tempting to the use of additional stimulus?

This leads to the remark, that the company which a man finds at these places, is tempting; and he who goes into it is in danger of ruin. All observation unites with revelation in declaring, that he who walketh with wise men shall be wise, but the companion of fools shall be destroyed. By common consent, in all Christian communities, ministers of the gospel, and professors of serious godliness, venture not to these entertainments, on pain of witnessing all that they deem sacred exposed to the ribaldry of the profane. It will also cost all that the fairest female reputation is worth, for its possessor to be seen, even for one minute, in the gallery of a theatre; and yet it does not remain unvisited by the sons, and brothers, and husbands, and fathers, of many an humble, and pious, and modest female. In this career of crime, the first step is to the theatre, the next to the bar, the next to that lewd company in the gallery, the next to the brothel, the next to disease, the next to death, and the last to HELL.

Attendance at the theatre is also a great waste of time. How much time is taken up first in thinking and talking about it! how much in attending it! and how much in thoughts and remarks upon what has been seen and heard! If "minutes make the years," how soon will he have consumed years of time, who wastes hundreds of minutes nightly at the place of amusement! Allowing a man to spend but six hours in each week at the theatre, for ten years, he will thus consume, of waking hours, one hundred and thirty days, equal, at least, to two hundred days of ordinary time, a period long enough to pay a visit to London and Paris, and spend sixty-five days in each; and this, too, at a cost of money sufficient to pay one's expenses in performing the tour of Europe.

Neither must it be forgotten that the theatre is not under the control of play-writers, nor of play-actors, nor of the refined and chaste part of the audience.

The exhibitions of the stage are such as to familiarize and even encourage vicious and sinful inclinations and dispositions, and entirely to leave unsung the praises of sobriety, temperance, Christian watchfulness, gospel humility, evangelical penitence, self-denial, heavenly-mindedness, and indeed every Christian virtue. Let me here present the thoughts of a writer in the Port-Royal in France. The author is supposed to be the Prince of Conti. He says: "It is so true that plays are almost always a representation of vicious passions, that the most part of Christian virtues are incapable of appearing on the stage. Silence, patience, moderation, wisdom, poverty, repentance, are no virtues the representation of which can divert the spectators; and, above all, we never hear humility spoken of, and the bearing of injuries. There must be something great and renowned, according to men, or at least something lively and animated which is not met with in Christian gravity and wisdom; and therefore those who have been desirous to introduce holy men and women upon the stage, have been forced to make them appear proud, and to make them utter discourses more proper for the ancient Roman heroes, than for saints and martyrs. Their devotion upon the stage ought also to be always a little extraordinary." Now, when we place ourselves in such circumstances as continually to fill our minds with images of viciousness, must we not be tempted first to endure, then to admire, then to imitate? Does not all experience corroborate this view? The pious Psalmist said: "I will set no wicked thing before mine eyes: I hate the work of them that turn aside." Psal. ci. 3. Another scripture declares that "the thought of foolishness is sin." Prov. xxiv. 9. Shall frequenters of theatrical entertainments then be innocent? Another portion of scripture speaks of "vain imaginations" as marks of a wicked character. Rom. i. 21. Are not theatres and such places the very nurseries of vain imaginations? "Lead us not into temptation."

Another passage of scripture requires us to avoid all "filthiness and foolish talking and jesting, which are not convenient," or becoming virtuous character. Eph. v. 4. How any frequenter of theatres, circuses, &c., can avoid oft-repeated violations or powerful inducements to violations of this precept, requires more ingenuity to discover than any mortal has ever yet manifested. Indeed this precept forms no part of the moral code of devotees of theatrical diversions and amusements.

These general views derive considerable strength from the general impression, that attendance on these amusements is *tempting* to *some* people. For the young and inexperienced to go without some special safe-guard is generally confessed to be unsafe. Men show their candid and real judgments on this subject, when their apprentices, clerks and wards acquire a passion for this amusement.

That the foregoing views are not confined to any one person or age, it is very easy to show by a reference to the views expressed by historians, biographers, philosophers, poets, moralists and religionists, of almost every nation and grade. We shall quote them as witnesses, whose conspiring testimony, mightily strengthened and confirmed by their discordance on almost every other subject, is conclusive proof of their correctness on this.

At Athens, where the stage was first known, both tragedy and comedy were soon abolished by public authority because judged injurious to the state. The Greek philosophers speak the same language. Plato says: "Plays raise the passions, and pervert the use of them: and, of consequence are dangerous to morality." Aristotle says: "The seeing of comedies ought to be forbidden to young people, until age and discipline have made them proof against debauchery." It is thought in our day that there are some *old* men who are not proof against debauchery. Ought not they to stay away from the theatre? The Romans did to a limited extent allow of theatres, yet did they so much dread their prevalence that no public theatre was allowed to remain standing more than a certain number of days. Even the great theatre erected by M. Scaurus, which cost more than four and a half millions of dollars, was speedily taken down. Pompey the Great was the first who had influence sufficient to continue a theatre. Tacitus, the great Roman historian, says: "The German women were guarded against danger and preserved their purity by having no play-houses among them." Ovid, in a grave work addressed to Augustus, advises the suppression of theatrical amusements as a grand source of corruption. Indeed, Guevara says, that a virtuous prince or emperor was known by his banishing from his presence players, jesters and jugglers; and that a vicious prince was known by his retaining such. Many of even the Roman emperors declared the scenes of the stage to be "unbecoming exercises and effeminate arts which very much corrupted and disgraced the state, and were seminaries of all vices and intolerable mischiefs in the commonwealth." Seneca, the moralist, says: "Nothing is so destructive (damnosum) of good manners or morals as attendance on the stage." Titus Livy, the accomplished Roman historian, in his history thrice mentions the theatre. In the first instance he says: "It commenced with the purpose of aiding in the worship of the gods," i. e. the devils. In the next instance he calls it a "folly, which had grown to an intolerable height of madness." In the third instance he says the stage had its origin in purposes of superstitious devotions. St. Augustine agrees with Livy in making the same statement of its origin. Juvenal says that in his time "a man could not find one chaste woman whom he might safely love as his wife in all the play-house, and that all who frequent stage-plays are infamous, and forfeit their good names." That Christians ought not, in the judgment of good men of past days, to attend theatres, is very clear. One to whom America is vastly indebted said many years ago: "For many ages there was no debate on it at all. There were players, but they did not pretend to be Christians themselves, and they had neither countenance nor support from any who did." In the Apostolic Constitutions, stage-players and actors are enumerated among those who are not to be admitted to baptism. All the ancient forms of baptism, written after the Apostolic Constitutions, required a renunciation of all such things. Individual writers have also from the early ages of Christianity borne a decided testimony on this subject. Cyprian says: "The Scripture hath everlastingly condemned all sorts of such spectacles and stage-plays." In another place he styles theatres "the stews of public chastity, the mastership of obscenity, which teach those sins in public. It is not lawful for faithful Christians, yea, it is altogether unlawful to be present at these plays." Elsewhere he says: "She that perchance comes a chaste woman to the play, goes away with stained chastity." Tertullian says that "the heathen did chiefly discern who were infidels and who Christians, by the latter abandoning all stage-plays." In another place he says: "We (Christians) renounce your spectacles and stage-plays—we have nothing at all to do with the fury of your circus, and the dishonesty of the theatre—we come not to your plays." In another place he says: "We who compute our nobility not by blood, but by our manners, do with good reason renounce your sinful pleasures, pomps and spectacles, whose original with respect to their sacredness, and whose pernicious allurements to sin, we both alike condemn. For in your *Circensian* games, who can but abhor the madness of the people clamoring on different sides? And as for your *gladiatorian* diversions, who can sit with ease in that school of murder? And for your theatres, there also the extravagance is not less, but the lewdness longer. For one while the mimic either recites adulteries or exhibits them; another while the lascivious actor plays the gallant and kindles the passion he feigns. He likewise vilifies your gods by personating their rapes, sighs and discords. And so by well-dissembled sorrow and hypo critical gestures, he sets you a crying to the life. Thus are you mad upon murder in good earnest, and yet, forsooth, cannot bear it in fable without a tear." Clemens Alexandrinus calls "stage-plays, comedies, and amorous songs, teachers of adulteries and defilers of men's ears with fornications;" and says: "Not only the use, the sight, the hearing, but the very memory of stage plays should be abolished." In another place he directs Christian youths "not to permit their pedagogues to lead them to plays or theatres, because they are the occasion of lewdness, and wicked counsel is plotted at them." How much like the modern theatre. "Wicked counsel is plotted there," such as is peculiarly dangerous to young men! Origen says: "Christians must not lift up their eyes to stage-plays, the pleasurable delights of polluted eyes." Lactantius says: "These interludes with which men are delighted, and which they willingly attend, are wholly to be abolished from among us, because they are the greatest instigations to vice, and the most powerful instruments to corrupt men's minds." Gregory Nazianzen calls "stage-players the servants of lewdness, and stage-plays the dishonourable, unseemly instructions of lascivious men, who repute nothing filthy but modesty." He also calls "play-houses the lascivious shops of all filthiness and impurity." Ambrose calls "stage-plays spectacles of vanity," and exhorts "Christians to turn away from them." Augustine says that "stage-plays are the subverters of goodness and honesty, the destroyers of all modesty and chastity, the arts of mischievous villanies which even modest pagans did blush to behold." In another place he calls them "the cages of uncleanness, the public profession of wickedness." Epiphanius says, "that the catholic and apostolic church doth reprobate and forbid all theatres, stage-plays, and all such like heathenish practices." Chrysostom says: "I wish the theatres and play-houses were all thrown down, though as to us (Christians) they lay desolate and ruined long ago." "Nothing," says he, "brings the oracles and ordinances of God into such contempt as admiring and attending stage-plays. Neither sacraments nor other ordinances of God, will do a man any good, so long as he frequents stage-plays." Bernard says: "All true soldiers of Jesus Christ abominate and reject all dicing and stage-plays, as vanities and false frenzies." These testimonies of individuals are fully corroborated by the ancient synods or councils, which did often prohibit, condemn and reprobate, all sorts of stage-plays; and appoint to excommunication from the visible church all who attended them. The Eliberine council in Spain, in A. D. 305, the council at Arles in France, in A. D. 314, the council held in the same place, in A. D. 326, the third council of Carthage, in A. D. 397, the council of Hippo, in A. D. 393, the great African council in A. D. 408, the great council at Constantinople, in A. D. 680, and the great council in the same place, in A. D. 692, did severally and solemnly condemn every thing belonging to theatrical exhibitions of every description.

Modern divines and synods have been as little divided on this matter as on any other subject of Christian practice. Let a few men speak for themselves. Archbishop Ussher says: "Stage-plays offend against the seventh commandment in many ways together—in the abuse of apparel, tongue, eyes, countenance, gestures, and almost all parts of the body; therefore they that go to see such sights, and hear such words, show their neglect of Christian duty, and their carelessness in sinning, whereas they willingly commit themselves to the snare of the devil." Bishop Collier says: "Nothing has done more to debauch the age in which we live than the stage-poets and the play-house." Archbishop Tillotson says: "The play-house is the *devil's chapel*, a *nursery* of *licentiousness* and *vice;* a recreation which ought not to be allowed among a civilized, much less a Christian people." Andrew Fuller says: "The introduction of so large a portion of heathen mythology into the songs and other entertainments of the stage, sufficiently shows the bias of people's hearts. The house of God gives them no pleasure; but the resurrection of the obscenities, intrigues and bacchanalian revels of the old heathens, affords them exquisite delight." The Synod held at Rochelle, in A. D. 1571, unanimously voted that "Congregations shall be admonished by their ministers seriously to reprehend and suppress all dances, mummeries and interludes; and it shall not be lawful for any Christian to act or be present at any comedies, tragedies, plays, interludes, or any other such sports, either in public or in private chambers, considering that they have always been opposed, condemned and suppressed, in and by the church, as bringing along with them the corruption of good manners, especially when the Holy Scripture is profaned, which is not delivered to be acted or played, but only to be preached." The Westminster Assembly numbers among the violations of the seventh commandment "all unclean imaginations, thoughts, purposes, and affections, all corrupt or filthy communications, or listening thereto, immodest apparel, unchaste company, lascivious songs, books, pictures, dancings, stage-plays, and all other provocations to, or acts of uncleanness, either in ourselves or others." But not only have the ancient heathens and the divines and councils of the church in every age condemned these things. All classes of moderns have borne their testimony in the same way. Dymond says: "The night of a play is the harvest time of iniquity, where the profligate and the sensual put in their sickles and reap." Sir John Hawkins, the biographer of Dr. Johnson, and an infidel, observes: "Although it is said of plays that they teach morality; and of the stage that it is the mirror of human life, these assertions are mere declamation, and have no foundation in truth or experience. On the contrary, a play-house and the regions about it are the very hot-beds of vice." Lord Kaimes, a skeptic, says: "It requires not time nor much thought to discover the poisonous influence of such plays, where the chief characters are decked out with every vice in fashion, however gross, and where their deformities are carefully disguised under the embellishments of wit, sprightliness and good humour." Dr. Johnson, speaking of Collier's view of the immorality and profaneness of the English stage, says: "The wise and the pious caught the alarm, and the nation wondered that it had suffered irreligion and licentiousness to be openly taught at the public charge." Dryden, a Catholic, acknowledged the propriety of Collier's remarks, and published his repentance for the licentiousness with which he himself had written. Rousseau, the infidel, has said some things I would not dare to say, viz: "It is impossible that an establishment (a theatre at Geneva) so contrary to our ancient manners can be generally applauded. How many generous citizens will see with indignation this monument of luxury and effeminacy raise itself upon our ancient simplicity! Where is the imprudent mother that would dare to carry her daughter to this dangerous school? And what respectable woman would not think herself dishonoured in going there?"

"What the stage might be," says Mrs. Hannah More, "under another, and an imaginary state of things, it is not very easy for us to know, and therefore not very important to inquire. Nor is it, indeed, the soundest logic to argue on the possible goodness of a thing, which in the present circumstances of society is doing positive evil, from the imagined good that thing might be conjectured to produce in a supposed state of unattainable improvement."

That there is nothing in theatrical entertainments inconsistent with the wildest excesses was abundantly illustrated in the French Revolution, near the close of the 18th century. Speaking of the state of things in Paris, Edmund Burke says:

"While courts of justice were thrust out by Jacobin tribunals, and silent churches were only the funeral monuments of departed religion, there were no fewer than *twenty-eight theatres*, great and small, most of them kept open at the public expense, and all of them crowded every night. Among the gaunt, haggard forms of famine and nakedness; amidst the yells of murder, the tears of affliction, and the cries of despair; the song and the dance, the mimic scene and the buffoon laughter went on as regularly as in the gay hour of festive peace.

"Even under the scaffold of judicial murder, and the gaping planks that poured down blood upon the spectators, the space was hired out for a show of dancing dogs.' The society of Paris was like a den of outlaws upon a doubtful frontier, a lewd tavern for the revels and debauches of banditti, assassins and paramours,—filled with licentious and blasphemous songs, proper to their brutal and hardened course of life."

And will not every American heed the following testimony?

In Congress, October 12th, 1778: "Whereas, true religion and good morals are the only solid foundation of public liberty and happiness: *Resolved*, that it be, and is hereby earnestly recommended to the several States to take the most effectual means for the encouragement thereof, and for the suppressing of *Theatrical entertainments*, horse-racing, gaming, and such other diversions, as are productive of idleness, dissipation, and a general depravity of principles and manners."

"*Extract from the Minutes.*

(Signed) CHAS. THOMSON, *Sect.*"

But let us look at the effect of stage-plays upon those who are most affected by them. Reference is had to the players themselves. Tertullian says: "The heathens themselves marked actors and stage-players with infamy, and excluded them from all honours and dignity." Augustine says: "Men reject from the advantages of good society, and from all honours, the actors of the poetic fables and stage-players." Rousseau says: "In all countries the profession of a player is dishonourable, and those who exercise it are everywhere contemned." Witherspoon says: "Even those who are fondest of theatrical amusements, do yet notwithstanding esteem the employment of players a mean and sordid profession. Their character has been infamous in all ages, just a living copy of that vanity, obscenity and impiety, which is to be found in the pieces which they represent." Thus also a French writer of some note during the reign of wickedness in that land, near the close of the last century, says: "It must appear very surprising, that even down to the expiration of the French monarchy, there was a character of disgrace affixed to the profession of a player, especially when compared with the kindred profession of preacher or pleader." This same language was used in lamentation by one of our oldest journals forty years ago. A modern writer asks a question which each man can answer or not at his pleasure: "Is there any family of rank or high standing that would not feel degraded by a marriage alliance with a stage-player?" Wilberforce says: "It is an undeniable fact, for the truth of which we may safely appeal to every age and nation, that the situation of the performers, particularly those of the female sex, is remarkably unfavourable to the maintenance and growth of the religious and moral principle, and of course highly dangerous to their eternal interests." Dymond says: "If I take my seat in the theatre, I have paid three or four shillings as an inducement to a number of persons to subject their principles to extreme danger—and the defence which I make is, that I am amused by it. Now we affirm that this defence is invalid." Even the famous Mrs. Frances Ann Butler—known as Miss Fanny Kemble—says, in her journal: "Acting is the very lowest of the arts" . . . "I acted like a wretch of course; how could I do otherwise" . . . "What a mass of wretched mumming mimickry acting is" . . . "How I do loathe my most impotent and unpoetical craft." Surely a late poet was fully justified when he said:

> "The theatre was, from the very first,
> The favourite haunt of sin, though honest men,
> Some very honest, wise and worthy men,
> Maintained it might be turned to good account:
> And so perhaps it might, but never was.
> From first to last it was an evil place."

All these testimonies, gathered from pagans, infidels, Christians, laity, clergy, poets, statesmen, historians, philosophers, councils, and our national congress, have been presented for the purpose of showing what these entertainments have been in every age, as they have been regularly handed down to us, and for the purpose of developing in a satisfactory manner the peculiar vices which are thus nourished.

No man can properly object to the testimonies cited, because, be his views what they may in morals, here is evidence that the theatre is an "evil place."

There is no method by which the force of these testimonies could be destroyed, except by showing that the theatre is *now* in an improved condition—

that it is really *reformed*. Yet that it has NOT changed for the better, is manifest from the complaints made in the journals of the day—the very journals that are crowded with advertisements and notices respecting plays, and therefore cannot be suspected of being righteous overmuch.

## II. DIVORCE.

The subject of divorce claims increasing attention. In this age and country, we are inclined to too great readiness to legal separation of husband and wife. Let us beware that we do not follow the sad example of revolutionary France in this matter. The Abbé Gregoire, speaking of the statute of divorce said: "This law will soon ruin the whole nation." And yet it is a great mistake to suppose that we uphold virtue by adopting rules on this subject more strict than those laid down in Scripture. Our Lord explicitly states that infidelity to the marriage vow is a sufficient cause of a divorce. Matt. v. 31, 32. This case is perfectly clear.

Another case clearly settled by the apostle according to the general understanding of the Christian world is that of wilful desertion; where one party or the other persistently refuses to perform the duties of the relation. 1 Cor. vii. 15.

Some years ago, a youthful lady was married to a man considerably older than herself. He had property; she had none. She told her friends that she married him for his money; but to him she was complaisant. Very soon after marriage, she attempted to pour melted lead into his ear while he was asleep. His petition for a legal separation was promptly granted. Perhaps few intelligent persons will doubt the morality of that divorce. A wilful and deliberate attempt at murder is surely a crime of as high a grade as either of the others mentioned. The mode of reasoning on this subject is this: If for a minor offence, utterly subverting the design of marriage, a divorce is lawful, surely it is so for a greater offence against the same person.

### III. INCEST.

This unnatural sin may be committed even under the forms of law. It is not proposed here to discuss it at length; but to state that the understanding of the Christian world has long been that the law of incest laid down in the 18th chapter of Leviticus is still binding. The only other hint of any rule directing us on this subject is found in 1 Cor. v. 1, where without marriage, incest was committed. Of late years there has been manifested a disposition to set aside the law of incest, given in Lev. xviii. But let men remember that if the rules there given be not binding, the whole world is left at large, without any law of God prohibiting even brother and sister from marrying.

### IV. THIS PRECEPT IS COMPREHENSIVE.

This commandment, like all the rest, is spiritual, and extends to the thoughts of the heart. Our Saviour put this point beyond all doubt in his sermon on the Mount. Matt. v. 28. We must therefore maintain purity in body and behaviour, in mind, in feeling, in words and in conduct. 1 Thess. iv. 4, 5, Eph. iv. 29; Col. iv. 6. This precept forbids unchaste looks, unchaste company, and immodest apparel. Job xxxi. 1; 1 Cor. v. 9; 1 Tim. ii. 9; 2 Pet. ii. 14. It requires us studiously to avoid whatever may lead to impurity of affection or of life. Prov. v. 8.

The venerable Thomas Scott, writing on this commandment, says, "Under the word *lasciviousness*, various transgressions are denoted, which cannot be mentioned without offence; and everything, which does not comport with the spirit of marriage, though sanctioned by that name, violates the spiritual meaning of the prohibition. All impure conversation, imaginations, or desires, are likewise condemned by this law. 'He that looketh on a woman to lust after her, hath committed adultery with her already in his heart.' Writing, reading, publishing, vending, or circulating obscene books; exposing to view indecent pictures or statues, or whatever else may excite men's passions, must partake of the same guilt: and wit, elegance, and ingenuity only increase the mischief, wherever the specious poison is administered. All the arts of dress, motion, or demeanour, which form temptations to heedless youth; with all those blandishments, insinuations, amorous looks and words, which subserve seduction, fall under the same censure. In short, the commandment requires the utmost purity, both of body and soul, in secret as well as before men; with a holy indifference to animal indulgences, and the strictest government of all the appetites, senses, and passions; and it enjoins the desire and endeavour of preserving the same disposition and behaviour in all others, as far as we have it in our power."

The following things are clear.

1. The language of Scripture concerning the breaches of this commandment is exceedingly well-suited to alarm any guilty soul. It says, "This is an heinous crime; yea, it is an iniquity to be punished by the judges. For it is a fire that consumeth to destruction." Job xxxi. 11, 12.

2. All uncleanness, even of mind, is contrary to God. "This is the will of God, even your sanctification, that ye should abstain from fornication: that every one of you should know how to possess his vessel in sanctification and honour; not in the lust of concupiscence, even as the Gentiles which know not God." 1 Thess. iv. 3–5.

3. All impurity is entirely contrary to the Christian profession. "God hath not called us unto uncleanness, but unto holiness." 1 Thess. iv. 7. "Fornication and all uncleanness, or covetousness, let it not be once named among you, as becometh saints; neither filthiness, nor foolish talking, nor jesting, which are not convenient." Eph. v. 3, 4.

4. All violations of this commandment are signs of a depraved nature. "Now the works of the flesh are manifest, which are these; Adultery, fornication, uncleanness, lasciviousness, &c." Gal. v. 19.

5. God calls upon us to put to death all vile affections. "Mortify your members which are upon the earth; fornication, uncleanness, inordinate affection, evil concupiscence, &c., &c." Col. iii. 5.

6. The Scriptures tell us of the debasing and ruining effects of this sin on those who fall under its power. "Whoso committeth adultery with a woman lacketh understanding: he that doeth it destroyeth his own soul. A wound and dishonour shall he get;

and his reproach shall not be wiped away." Prov. vi 32, 33. Compare Prov. vii. 22.

7. They further declare that it leads to general irreligion. "Whoredom and wine and new wine take away the heart." Hos. iv. 11; Eph. iv. 18, 19.

8. Good writers have dwelt much on the heinousness of those acts which transgress this commandment. They especially notice the fact that two souls are murdered at once. Hopkins says: "Suppose that God should vouchsafe thee repentance unto life; yet art thou sure that his justice and severity will not harden the other in this sin, to which thou hast been the author and persuader?"

9. Everywhere the Scriptures declare the reigning power of this sin to be an infallible token of coming perdition. "This ye know, that no whoremonger, nor unclean person, nor covetous man who is an idolater, hath any inheritance in the kingdom of Christ and of God." Eph. v. 5. Compare Heb. xiii. 4; Rev. xxi. 8, xxii. 15. There is no room for doubting that he who dies impenitent for violations of the *seventh* commandment goes to an undone eternity.

### V. BEWARE OF SINS AGAINST THIS PRECEPT.

The following thoughts may suggest rules and motives that may be helpful in enabling us to avoid violations of this precept.

1. The time is short, and eternity is near. The Judge standeth before the door. Let every man remember that he is mortal. Let those that have wives be as though they had none; and those that rejoice as those that rejoiced not; for the fashion of this world passeth away.

2. In all things endeavour to be temperate and moderate. Ask yourself, will I approve of my present conduct, when called to give up my last account?

3. Remember that the Lord is omniscient. "Thou God seest me," is a good motto for all occasions.

4. Remember that no mortal ever had exaggerated views of the evil of sin. It burns to the lowest hell. The sweeter the unlawful indulgence to our carnal nature the bitterer will be the cup of repentance or of indignation put into our hands.

5. Let each one remember his own weakness. None but God can preserve any man from falling into the worst of sins. Our strength is nothing. All human resolutions unsupported by divine grace, are like fences of snow before a burning sun. When temptation comes, they soon melt away.

6. Our great business should be to obtain thorough renewal of nature. Without this, we have no guaranty that we may not be overcome at any moment. Let every man cry, "Create in me a clean heart, O God, and renew a right spirit within me." Augustine found regeneration the only remedy for his wickedness, and so have millions of others.

7. Let each one continually set before him the bright and blessed example of our Lord Jesus Christ, and let us dwell much on his amazing sufferings in our behalf. If our sins are ever effectually mortified, we must nail them to the cross of Christ.

# CHAPTER XXII.

## THE EIGHTH COMMANDMENT.

### THOU SHALT NOT STEAL.

THE honour of religion is deeply involved in the course men pursue concerning this commandment, which regulates our labour, our buying, our selling, our expenditures, and our entire civil conduct. We are bound to "provide things honest in the sight of all men." Rom. xii. 17. We are not at liberty to live in needless poverty and wretchedness, nor to let our dependents suffer. "If any provide not for his own, and specially for those of his own household, he hath denied the faith, and is worse than an infidel." 1 Tim. v. 8. Compare Eph. iv. 28. This is wholesome doctrine. No religious teacher may keep silent concerning it. The church that disregards it is ruined.

Yet we may "not make provision for the flesh, to fulfil the lusts thereof." Rom. xiii. 14. Our attention to our temporal affairs must not minister to our pride, our sloth, our vanity, our sensuality, our love of the world. 1 John ii. 16; Prov. xxi. 25; Eph. iv. 17, &c. Although man's absolute wants, to be supplied by his personal industry, are not very numerous, nor of long duration; yet they are more than some suppose. And while we ought to be content, yes, and thankful for food and raiment of a simple kind; yet it is lawful, and when practicable it is obligatory on men to secure the comforts of life. Paul exhorts his converts to "do your own business, and to work with your own hands, as we commanded you; that ye may walk honestly towards them that are without, and that ye may have lack of nothing." 1 Thess. iv. 11, 12. One of the great obstacles to be overcome in some heathen nations is found in the fact that masses of the people feel their wants to be so few, and so easily supplied, that they spend most of their time in idleness, in gambling, in sauntering about, in listening to foolish songs and stories, in witnessing the feats of jugglers, and in attending on vain processions. The same is true of Roman Catholic countries in the south of Europe. There are so many saints' days, that the labouring classes have not time to earn enough to secure the comforts of life. They become discouraged in the attempt, and extreme poverty and squalid wretchedness are perpetuated from generation to generation. Everywhere in Scripture indolence is condemned, and industry commended. Of the virtuous housewife, Solomon says, "She eateth not the bread of idleness." "By much slothfulness, the building decayeth; and through idleness of the hands the house droppeth through." Eccles. x. 18. "Pride, fulness of bread, and abundance of idleness," were among the causes of the ruin of Sodom and the other cities of the plain. Ezek. xvi. 49. These sins fostered others which provoked the wrath of Heaven beyond forbearance. It is a remarkable fact that

Paul himself once addressed a congregation of idlers, who "spent their time in nothing else, but either to tell, or to hear some new thing." Acts xvii. 21. But so far as we know, not one of them received any spiritual benefit. For "when they heard of the resurrection of the dead, some mocked: and others said, We will hear thee again of this matter." Acts xvii. 32. The only persons mentioned by name among those who profited by his preaching were a member of the chief court of the city and a woman named Damaris. Man was not allowed to be idle even in Paradise; and when he apostatized from God, the sentence to which it is wise ever to submit, was, "In the sweat of thy face shalt thou eat thy bread, till thou return unto the ground." Gen. iii. 19.

Let us consider

### THE LAW OF HONESTY.

There is hardly a word of more varied classical meaning than the word *Honesty;* and the Latin word *Honestas* from which it is derived. The same remark is true of the Greek word rendered *honesty.* In all these the range of meaning is very extended. But when applied to civil affairs, there are two ideas connected with the word, which we may not pass over in silence. One is that of JUSTICE. That which is unjust can never be honest. All injustice ought to be avoided, and is clearly condemned by Scripture. However refined, or countenanced by society or custom, it is still contrary to God's word and will. No human conscience ever aproved of a clear and decided case of injustice. The other idea inseparably connected with the word honesty, when applied to civil affairs, is that of HONOUR, or good repute. Any dishonourable conduct in temporal affairs is not honest. For a Christian to receive a bribe to do what was his obvious duty, or to refuse to do his duty without reward, is dishonest. So, for one to consent to do an odious thing (for instance, to act as hangman, not because his office required it of him, but because he loved gain,) would be dishonourable and so dishonest. A good man must keep his eye on the things that are lovely and of good report, if he would avoid a stain upon his escutcheon, and a wound on his conscience. All the ordinary and necessary avocations of life, the culture of the soil, the practice of the learned professions, trade, and the useful and ornamental arts, are honest. That it is not enough barely to satisfy one's own conscience of the honesty of a course, or even to meet the demands of the mere letter of God's word respecting rigid justice, is manifest in many ways. The Scripture abounds in proof: "Provide things honest in the *sight of all men*,"—not merely honest in the sight of God, in the sight of yourself, in the sight of some men—your partial friends and neighbours, or those who practise the same things—but in THE SIGHT OF ALL MEN. Let your probity be above all doubt and suspicion in the eyes of men, who understand what your conduct is. The apostle laid down no more rigid rule for others than he was willing to be governed by himself. He says that he and his coadjutors provided for honest things, not only in the sight of the Lord, but in the sight of all men. 2 Cor. viii. 21. Selden says: "They that cry down moral honesty, cry down that which is a great part of religion—my duty toward

God and my duty toward men. What care I to see a man run after a sermon, if he cozen and cheat as soon as he comes home? On the other side, morality must not be without religion; for if so, it may change as I see convenient. Religion must govern it. He that has no religion to govern his morality, is not better than my mastiff dog; so long as you stroke him and please him, and do not pinch him, he will play with you, as finely as may be; he is a very good, moral master; but if you hurt him, he will fly in your face."

Let us then look at the great principle of honesty, as it ought to enter into our affairs, and see how it may be and often is violated.

I. All robbery, theft, receiving stolen goods, forgery, embezzling, swindling, obtaining goods under false pretences, and cheating in every shape are contrary to the eighth commandment. Ps. lxii. 10; Eph. iv. 28; Ps. l. 18; Prov. xxix. 24; 1 Thess. iv. 6; Prov. xi. 1, xx. 10; Amos viii. 5. These things are more near akin to each other than some suppose. Mark x. 19. As this part of the subject is generally well-understood, and warmly entertained by most who will read this book, it is not necessary to dwell upon it. A few observations, however, will not be amiss. One is, that the law of honesty makes no extenuation of these or like sins, because they are practised against *the rich.* It is as dishonest unrighteously to possess the goods of one class as of another. True, in taking unjustly from the poor, we commonly add oppression to dishonesty, and thus perpetrate two crimes. But we are not to grade dishonesty by the worldly estate of him whom we defraud. What if a man is able to bear the loss? If all men should treat him fraudulently, he would soon have nothing. Our sin is against the law of God chiefly and primarily, and not against the man.

Another remark is, that the avails of our dishonesty are not to regulate our ideas of its criminality. He that unjustly holds a farthing, is as truly dishonest as he who has amassed a fortune by fraud. To pant after the dust of the earth on the heads of the poor, is as strictly forbidden as to covet thrones and empires not our own, Amos ii. 7. Ahab was as really wicked and unjust in covetously desiring and violently obtaining Naboth's vineyard, as if he had marched an army against the king of Syria, and taken his possessions from him. Our offence cannot be measured by the amount unjustly secured. With one sentence our Saviour for ever settled this principle. "He that is faithful in that which is least, is faithful also in much; and he that is unjust in the least, is unjust also in much," Luke xvi. 10. Compare Matt. xxv. 21; Luke xix. 17.

Another remark is, that corporations and the government of the country in which we reside, sustain to us, in the matter of honesty, the same relations as individuals. He that will cheat a body of men, or his government, is as guilty as if he defrauded his neighbour. He who wrongs a corporation, not knowing or caring who may be thereby affected, shows a wicked principle in general, a malignity against his race. He who will not render unto Cæsar the things which are Cæsar's, who will not pay custom to whom custom is due, is not likely to render unto God the things that are God's. All peculation, smuggling, false invoices, and unauthorized perquisites of office, making the government odious, are thus condemned by this precept.

Another remark is, that no man can merge his individual moral responsibility in a corporation. It is sometimes said that "corporations have no souls," and there is painful evidence that some corporators have no consciences, or bad consciences, and do things acting jointly with others, which they would not dare to do acting alone. Such should not forget that he that goeth with a multitude to do evil, shall go with a multitude to suffer punishment, Prov. xi. 21.

II. All persons are bound to regard the law of honesty in making bargains, or contracts. To be a sharper is to have an unenviable distinction. It is wholly inconsistent with Christian principle. The rule of some, That we may buy as cheap as we can and sell as dear as we can, is liable to so many exceptions, and must receive so many explanations before it ceases to conceal immorality, that it ought not to be received. We may not sell as dear as we can, nor buy as cheap as we can, when we deal with the ignorant, who are no judges of the quality or value of the articles bought or sold. It would make any one infamous, were it known that he cheated a little child out of his pennies by giving him not half what he should have done. In any such case, one acts as dishonest a part as if he had taken a ten-dollar note from one who cannot read and who supposes it is of a less denomination, and had given him only the change which he expected. Many who wish to buy or sell know almost nothing of the value of the commodity in trade, and are dependent on the superior knowledge of their merchants. To deceive them is dishonest. One cannot say, Their eyes were open; for on this subject they were without eyes and so were blind. The same exception holds in regard to the credulous, who are children in understanding. They are easily persuaded to buy or to sell at the price others may fix. To take advantage of their feeble minds or sanguine temperaments, is fraud.

Nor may we buy as cheap, nor sell as dear as we can, when we deal with those who are in distress. The pressing want of another does not make our goods any more valuable in fact. To avail ourselves of his necessity, therefore, is to rejoice in his calamity, because it may be profitable to us. Such conduct shall not go unpunished, Prov. xvii. 5. To a drowning man, the end of a rope might be worth a whole estate. Shall one therefore sordidly bargain for a great reward before he extends assistance? Prov. xxiv. 11, 12. One may say, I put him not in the water; I brought him not into his present distress. But this alters not the case. The same is as true of the man who is hard pressed in his worldly affairs.

Nor may we buy as cheap nor sell as dear as we can, when by heightening the defects of what we would buy, or by magnifying the value of what we would sell, we lead others into error. Such artifices are as old as trade among men, and are condemned in the Bible. "It is naught, it is naught, saith the buyer; but when he is gone his way, then he boasteth," Prov. xx. 14. This practice is not only odious, but soon ceases to gain its end. A. B. is a respectable Christian man. He is worth a handsome estate.

He lives in a small city. Not a shop-keeper is ignorant that he never gives what is first asked by his merchant. The consequence is, that when he prices an article, every one asks more than he is willing to take. But the very entrance of this good man into a shop awakens significant hints and looks.

It sometimes occurs even in free governments that a state of things very much like a monopoly exists, putting much in the power of one man or of a few men. A fire, a drought, a storm, or a war, may leave one man, or a few men, in possession of an article of no great value in itself, yet much needed by their neighbours or others. Then to sell as dear as we can is dishonest. "He that witholdeth corn, the people shall curse him; but blessing shall be upon the head of him that selleth it," Prov. xi. 26.

Nor is it honest to buy as cheap or sell as dear as we can when threats or deceitful promises, or flattery, or any such art is employed to influence the minds of those with whom we deal.

Here it may be observed that in trading generally, men are apt to use too many words. They say more than is good. They do not fix their prices or make their offers at what is right or fair, and then abide by it. There is a great deal of lying in the world in the driving of bargains.

Self-interest is in all ages the most powerful principle at work in the commercial world. From the influence of it even good men are not wholly free. If one feels doubtful, therefore, let his neighbour have the benefit of his doubts; for the uncertainty probably arises from a conflict between selfishness on the one hand and conscience on the other. Let every man keep fairly and unquestionably within the bounds of justice and honour.

Sometimes it occurs with the poor that in making bargains, they habitually or with indecent frequency and urgency plead their poverty, in favour of terms advantageous to themselves. Such seldom succeed for a long time, and even then with the loss of character. Such a practice is unmanly and so is dishonest. If any really needs charity, let him ask charity; but in trade, let justice and honour hold the scale.

III. As but few things have any real intrinsic value in trade, we still want a rule, by which to be governed. Perhaps this is as safe a maxim as any other. In all buying and selling, a fair equivalent according to the general and regular tenor of things ought always to be given or received. There is a fair market price for every thing in common use. Men having no interest in the purchase or sale, and knowing the facts in the case would seldom disagree respecting it. Articles of a rare quality, intended merely for luxury or ornament, and obtained at very great risk of loss, may be unsettled in value, and more scope may be left for the exercise of a general discretion. But of most things bought and sold, it is possible for us to ascertain the fair market price, and that ought to be given or received, no more and no less. It is true that in merchandizing, on some things there will necessarily be loss. This ought to be met by increased profit on others. But then no price should be unconscionable. All extortion is forbidden, Ezek. xxii. 12; Matt. xxiii. 25. It is also true that he who sells only for an equivalent in hand, may sell cheaper than he who runs the risk and incurs the delay of a credit. But to charge two prices to him who has not the means of ready payment, but who may reasonably expect to have them in possession, is unjust, and so is dishonest. If he who buys on credit knew how much more he was charged than his neighbour who buys for cash, he would deal no more there. "Do unto others as ye would that they do unto you."

IV. When bargains contain promissory engagements, let every man adhere to his word, cost what it may. One description of a good man is, that "he sweareth to his own hurt and changeth not." Ps. xv. 4. Domat: "In all sorts of engagements, whether voluntary or involuntary, it is forbidden to use any infidelity, double dealing, deceit, knavery, and all other ways of doing hurt or wrong." "The getting of treasures by a lying tongue is a vanity tossed to and fro of them that seek death." Prov. xxi. 6. Is there not a lamentable want of veracity manifested in many contracts? What could more painfully afflict a virtuous mind, than the ten thousand rash promises made respecting the fulfilment of contracts?

V. The Bible opposes the system of debt and credit, at least when carried to such lengths as we sometimes see. "Owe no man any thing, but to love one another." Rom. xiii. 8. If the debtor is honest, he is to a painful extent servant to the creditor. The spirit of many a man is crushed out by a sense of his indebtedness to others. His goods are distrained for rent; the peace of his mind or of his family is impaired; he finds himself avoiding particular walks lest he should meet the man to whom he owes money. Every dun puts him in anguish or irritates his mind. We have no reason to believe that Paul ever resorted to borrowing as a means of relieving his wants. In fact, we do know that when he was destitute of means, he went to tent-making. Acts xviii. 3, xx. 34. An honest mechanic or labourer may sleep sweetly and walk abroad composedly. But what is social position worth, when appearances are preserved only in the face of most painful facts respecting one's worldly estate?

Debts may not be honestly contracted under the following circumstances. 1. When we have no reasonable prospect of paying them. In such cases it is swindling and robbery to take another man's property out of his hands. This is remarkably the case when the commodity received is of a perishable nature and is likely to be consumed before the day of payment arrives. A *reasonable* prospect of payment is something not very precarious, something better than the prospect of a prize in a lottery, or of profit from a daring speculation. 2. He who is so careless of the condition of his own affairs as not to know how they stand, and yet goes forward and contracts new responsibilities, violates the law of honesty. No man has a right to live in such ignorance of his worldly estate as not to be sure, when he receives a neighbour's goods, that he will in the ordinary and regular course of business be able to pay him; and that too, 3. At the time agreed upon. Many, who are in the main upright men, and on the whole sustain a fair reputation, are always so far behind their engagements as to require the most charitable construction of their conduct by friends and foes, to keep them from falling into disrepute. A delay in payment, especially to the poor, and often to the rich, is as real, if not as great an injury as absolute failure to pay. It was a part of the code of Moses that the sun should not go down upon the hire of the labourer. Compare Deut. xxiv. 14, 15. 4. The Scriptures give no countenance to the practice of those who go on heedlessly and recklessly in their affairs, until insolvency ensues, and then compound with their creditors for five or ten shillings in the pound; and even if able afterwards, do not pay the full sum due. Voluntary relinquishment of creditors in order to give further opportunity to acquire the means of payment may be accepted. But if ever the whole can be paid, let the *bonâ fide* offer be made, with money in hand. Once a debt always a debt unless freely forgiven, is a sound maxim. Rom. xiii. 8. If we had honest debtors and merciful creditors, we should need no bankrupt laws.

VI. On the whole subject of our business affairs, these maxims, duly regarded, would save a world of trouble.

1. Never engage in a business you do not understand, however inviting the prospect of gain. Prov. xiv. 8.

2. Let not young men, who are in the way of acquiring a thorough knowledge of business, be hasty in setting up for themselves. Let them be patient.

3. Avoid all highly hazardous speculations, even in a lawful business, except where they involve no more than you are able to lose without injury to your creditors or your family. You may not needlessly jeopard in wild adventures the rights of others.

4. Always prefer a regular business to any new and striking scheme of making money. The latter

may beget many beautiful dreams. The former is sustained by the usual course of divine providence. "The hand of the diligent maketh rich." Prov. x. 4. "Seest thou a man diligent in his business? He shall stand before kings; he shall not stand before mean men." Prov. xxii. 29.

5. Be not anxious to grow rich all of a sudden. "He that maketh haste to be rich shall not be innocent." Prov. xxviii. 20.

6. Beware whom you admit as partners in business. Say not A confederacy, to all them that say A confederacy to you. Of plausible men the world is full. Safe men are scarce. Partners ought to have a congeniality in views, in temper, and in all the leading principles of business. Prov. xxii. 24; Amos iii. 3.

7. If you have any regard for your peace and comfort, avoid all suretyships, which exceed the amount you are able and willing to lose for your friend. "He that is surety for a stranger shall smart for it: and he that hateth suretyship is sure." Prov. xi. 15. It may be safely said that he is the only man that is sure. "Be not thou one of them that strike hands, or of them that are sureties for debts. If thou hast nothing to pay, why should he take away thy bed from under thee?" Prov. xxii. 26, 27. See also, Prov. vi. 1, xvii. 18, xx. 16, xxvii. 13.

8. Practise no deceptions. Let "no man go beyond and defraud his brother in any matter; because that the Lord is the avenger of all such, as we also have forewarned you and testified." 1 Thess. iv. 6. Never resort to false weights and measures. They are an abomination to God. Lev. xix. 36; Deut.

xxv. 13; Prov. xvi. 11, xx. 10, 23; Hos. xii. 7 Amos viii. 5; Micah vi. 11. Never adulterate goods. Always send the precise quality that was sold. Beware of all *filthy lucre*, that is, of all gain obtained in any manner dishonourable.

9. Never buy any thing because it is cheap. What you do not need is dear at any price.

VII. Are you already involved in debt? Inquire whether you cannot in some important respects retrench your usual expenses. Scorn to live in luxury, to roll in affluence or glitter in splendour, while you are unable to pay your debts. Your wife, if a prudent and honourable woman, will cheerfully submit to great self-denial. You will also find it useful to ascertain precisely how much you owe, and to keep the matter continually before you in memorandum. Be not afraid to know the state of your own affairs. Never avoid a creditor. Go to him with the manliness and fearlessness of uprightness. Tell him precisely how the case stands. Do not deceive him by plausible statements and fair promises. Tell him your real prospects, and how you are labouring to meet your liabilities. Remember that your charities ought not to be bountiful, while you are in debt; because in giving away, you rather dispose of the goods of others than of your own. Yet, be not hard-hearted. Without money, you may do a little to help the deserving poor. Also settle it in your mind that you will never make over your estate to some who will hold it for your benefit or that of your family, in order to keep your creditors from getting it. NEVER ASK YOUR WIFE TO RELINQUISH HER RIGHTS OF PROPERTY, WHICH WAS HERS BEFORE YOUR INDEBTEDNESS. Never begin the ruinous practice of paying usurious interest. Exercise rigid economy. Work day and night at your lawful and honest calling. Observe with regularity seasons of devotion in secret, in the family, and in the house of God. Never suffer your mind to be annoyed with worldly affairs on the Lord's day. Maintain a cheerful and inflexible resolution to bear up like a man and a Christian under your great afflictions. Resist melancholy. As you acquire even a little, hand it over to your creditors. Beware of needlessly expending small sums. Cry to God for deliverance. Think not that he will scorn your humble, fervent petitions.

To a young man in debt, Dr. Franklin gave the following advice: "Make a full estimate of all you owe, and of all that is owing to you. Reduce the same to note. As fast as you can collect, pay over to those you owe. If you cannot, renew your note every year, and get the best security you can.—Go to business diligently and be industrious; waste no idle moments; be very economical in all things; discard all pride; be faithful in your duty to God, by regular and hearty prayer morning and night; attend church and meeting regularly every Sunday; and do unto all men as you would that they should do unto you. If you are too needy in circumstances to give to the poor, do whatever else is in your power for them cheerfully, but if you can, help the poor and unfortunate. Pursue this course diligently and sincerely for seven years, and if you are not happy, comfortable and independent in your circumstances, come to me and I will pay your debts."

VIII. In matters of trust, observe the utmost

exactness. Are you a treasurer of any institution? You cannot be too careful in your accounts, nor too cautious in the disposition of funds. Are you an agent, and so entrusted with money? Never spend it for your own convenience or comfort. Many a man has gone to his grave with a wounded reputation and an aching heart, because he had spent money that did not belong to him. He hoped indeed soon to replace it; but his expectation was like the *mirage* of the desert. Paul's example in this behalf is worthy of close imitation. He raised many collections and distributed them. But he tells us that he "avoided this, that no man should blame us in this abundance which is administered by us." 2 Cor. viii. 20. Are you a guardian of such as are not able in law to represent themselves? The courts of the land will very properly hold you to a strict account. Carelessness and mismanagement will almost certainly bring terrible exposure and anguish. But the sin of such conduct is worse than the shame. It is in the teeth of the eighth commandment. In all fiduciary matters, keep your behaviour on the highest key of morality.

The class of offences against this precept entitled *breaches of trust* is very numerous. Many have expressed wonder that they are not punished as felonies.

IX. Not a little sin is committed in borrowing. Sometimes indeed it is necessary. "From him that would borrow of thee, turn not thou away." Matt. v. 42. But as little borrowing as possible ought to be resorted to. For, 1. "The borrower is servant to the lender." 2. Men are often tempted not to return, at least with promptness, what they have borrowed. Some yield to this temptation. Ps. xxxvii. 21. 3.

That which we borrow may be lost, and we may be unable to replace it; and then our position is truly distressing. 2 Kings vi. 5. The law of Scripture is, "If a man borrow aught of his neighbour, and it be hurt, or die, the owner thereof being not with it, he shall surely make it good," Ex. xxii. 14, and this sometimes he is quite unable to do. Then hard thoughts and speeches are apt to ensue, and the peace of the neighbourhood is broken.

Some have attempted to justify borrowing without any intention of returning, (if they think they have been injured) by citing the case of the Israelites' borrowing jewels from the Egyptians. Ex. xii. 35, 36. In that passage, the words *borrowed* and *lent* are found; and the original words may be so rendered. But it is now generally conceded that the translation is wrong. It would be better, and the Hebrew would bear it, to render the words *asked* and *gave;* for this is doubtless the sense. The text confirms this view, by saying that *God gave the people favour in the sight of the Egyptians*, that is, for a little while, being crushed by plagues and having their hearts touched by God's Spirit, a sense of justice and of kindness prevailed. Josephus expresses it; "They honoured them with gifts." So that this passage gives no countenance to the bad morals taught in some books of Romish Theology, that a servant may defraud his master to the amount of what he supposes is his due. Borrowing may be and often is so conducted as to be in effect the same as theft. When it is proper to lend, it should be done heartily and freely. Deut. xxiii. 20; Luke vi. 35. Many a time the best charity is not a gift, but a loan without interest.

X. We may never steal. There is an impression among some that dependent persons, or the poor, may take that which belongs not to them, provided it is merely to satisfy the demands of hunger or to meet necessary wants. Even Solomon says, "Men do not despise a thief, if he steal to satisfy his soul when he is hungry." Prov. vi. 30. And Agur prayed that he might not be poor, lest he should steal. Prov. xxx. 9. But all such taking what belongs to others is dishonest. Man's standard of ethics, especially when drawn from his appetite, is very low. The word of God makes no such allowance. In this very case it says, "If the thief be found, he shall restore seven-fold; he shall give all the substance of his house." Prov. vi. 31. Hopkins: "Though his necessity and hunger may take off somewhat from the shame, yet it shall not from the punishment of his offence, but he shall restore that which he hath stolen seven-fold. Not that the restitution should be seven times as much as the theft, for the utmost that the law requires was but a five-fold restitution, Ex. xxii. 1; but as the word *seven-fold* is most frequently used in Scripture to signify that which is complete and perfect, so is it here, 'he shall restore seven-fold,' that is, he shall make a full and satisfactory restitution."

XI. Restitution. The closing remark of the preceding paragraph suggests this important matter. Why should not men restore that which they have wrongfully withheld or taken away, or that which they may not longer lawfully hold? Common justice demands it. The law of Moses required it. David's sentence against him that took the poor man's lamb, was this: "The man that hath done this thing shall surely die; and he shall restore the lamb four-fold, because he did this thing, and because he had no pity." 2 Sam. xii. 5, 6. Zaccheus understood that he lived under the same law. "If I have taken any thing from any man by false accusation, I restore him four-fold." Luke xix. 8. Domat: "It is a natural law, that he who has been the author of my damage ought to repair it." "Unjust possession is a continued and prolonged theft, and certainly repentance can never be true, nor sincere, while we continue in the sin of which we seem to repent; and thy repentance not being true, pardon will never be granted thee." God's word is very explicit: "If the wicked restore the pledge, give again that he had robbed, walk in the statutes of life without committing iniquity; he shall surely live, he shall not die." Ezek. xxxiii. 15. And if the person to whom restitution was at first due, is dead, payment can be made to his heirs. But if neither he nor they can be found, then it is to be made to the LORD. Num. v. 6–8. Surely the law of good neighbourhood requires us no less to restore that which has strayed from its owner or has been lost by him. Deut. xxii. 1–3. Nor would high-toned honour consent to receive a reward for returning that which had been lost, unless time or money had been expended for its recovery. The law of Moses very fitly required that a man who injured another in a fight, if he did not die, should pay him for the loss of his time, and cause him to be thoroughly healed. Ex. xxi. 19.

XII. BEGGING. This is a sad evil in many parts of the world. In some portions of Europe and in the large cities of America, it is a great sore on the body politic. What legislation can do in the matter, statesmen must decide. But let the conscience of each one settle it that beggars who could get employment, and who are able to work for a livelihood, ought not to be countenanced. The law of Scripture and the law of nature are clear upon this point. "In the sweat of thy face shalt thou eat thy bread." Gen. iii. 19. "Even when we were with you, this we commanded you, that if any would not work, neither should he eat." 2 Thess. iii. 10. Compare verses 11, 12. Every man ought to set his face steadfastly against a system of mendicity. Everywhere the Scriptures pronounce against the slothful. Prov. xii. 27, xv. 19, xviii. 9, xix. 24; Rom. xii. 11. So far, therefore, as beggary is the result of indolence persisted in, the duty of those who have means is to refuse assistance.

XIII. FRUGALITY consists in avoiding needless expenditures which we are not able to afford. "Frugality may be termed the daughter of Prudence, the sister of Temperance, and the parent of Liberty." It is essential to the peace of our lives. The want of it brings on a world of wretchedness; while its exercise greatly conduces to our happiness. Prov. xxi. 20.

XIV. POVERTY. There may be virtuous poverty, though often we find vicious poverty. Poverty is a disgrace when it is the result of indolence, slothfulness, carelessness, or extravagance. Prov. vi. 10, 11. But it is no discredit to any man when he was born poor; or when he has made himself poor for the benefit of others; or when after careful industry and all lawful exertion and prudence, God leaves him without ample means. In that case, we should be content with those things we have. Heb. xiii. 5.

Abject poverty is a great misery and a source of much temptation. Prov. xxx. 9. Yet God may have great ends to answer in the world by keeping some of his best people in great straits. The poor are in danger of hardening their hearts against one another. No less than the rich they ought to believe that "*it is more blessed to give than to receive.*" No man has ever practised on this precept without finding it true. It is as true now as ever, that "he that hath pity upon the poor lendeth unto the Lord; and that which he hath given will he pay him again." No man is in the end a loser for any willing sacrifice or self-denial practised for the good of others. He enjoys life far better than the selfish man. He has a vast storehouse of good laid up for him. To him the promises are many and wonderful. "The Lord will preserve him and keep him alive; and he shall be blessed upon the earth: and thou wilt not deliver him to the will of his enemies. The Lord will strengthen him upon the bed of languishing: thou wilt make all his bed in his sickness."

Nor should any one regard himself as too poor to do something. The reason why the small gift of the poor woman was greater than that of all the rich was, that she gave "all her living," and they did not. She had to practise self-denial to give any thing. They only cast in of their abundance. He that shall finally reward the giving of a cup of cold water, will not be unfaithful to forget any work of faith or labour of love. In Stevenson's Exposition of the twenty-third Psalm, we have this little narrative:

"The long-tried and consistent piety of the wife of a poor labourer had attracted the regard of her wealthier neighbours. She was one of those happy Christians whose holy cheerfulness of manner adorns their profession of the gospel. She 'rejoiced and wrought righteousness,' and 'remembered the Lord in his ways.' She had gained the esteem of all who knew her, and now that a slow but sure decline rendered her incapable of contributing to her own support, some pious friends agreed together to provide her regularly with those little comforts which were so necessary to her sinking condition. The Lord thus met her necessity by their instrumentality. But she knew not that he had awakened this thought within the hearts of any of them. Her own heart was stayed upon the heart of her God. As she stood one afternoon in her humble doorway to breathe the balmy air, she observed three objects of misery soliciting alms in the street. Her heart pitied the famished mother and her two tattered children, but all the money that she possessed was her last and only sixpence. Every article of provision in the house had been already consumed. Without delay or hesitation, however, she drew from her pocket the little coin which was needed for her own necessities, and freely bestowed it on the widow and the fatherless. She considered that all her own wants for the day had been supplied, and that she ought not to be distrustful for the morrow. 'I have a heavenly Friend,' she said within herself, 'to provide for me, and perhaps this poor woman does not know the God that is above. I have no one to think of; she has these two children to struggle for. I know my own need, but they are more needy than I.' That very evening the individual deputed by her unknown friends visited her dwelling to inform her of their kind determination; and great was her astonishment and gratitude to hear that a sum double the amount she had that day given to the poor wanderers, was to be her daily allowance during the remainder of her life. It pleased the Lord to spare her two years, as she declared, 'in plenty and comfort.'"

So in every case God will be as good as his word, as gracious as he has promised to be. All the promises are yea and amen.

XV. MONEY. The Bible says nothing against money. It admits that it is *a defence*, and *answers all things*, Eccles. vii. 12, x. 19. After Job's restoration to prosperity, "every man gave him a piece of money," Job xlii. 11. What the Scriptures warn us against is the abuse of that which is good. 1. We must not set our hearts upon it; nor be distracted with the care of it. "The love of money is the root of all evil," 1 Tim. vi. 10; Matt. vi. 21. 2. We must not employ it for purposes of sinning, Acts viii. 20. 3. We must not rely upon it, 1 Tim. vi. 17. 4. We must not hoard it up with greediness, James v. 1–3. 5. We must not use it to make ourselves wanton in life, James v. 5. 6. We must not needlessly squander it, Isa. lv. 2. 7. We must not use it for purposes of oppression, Lev. xxv. 37; Deut. xxiii. 19; Ps. xv. 5. 8. We must not be led by a regard to it to disobey any of God's commands, 2 Chron. xxv. 9. 9. We must give to the poor, and thus lay up treasure in heaven, Luke xii. 33, 34. And we ought to give for conscience' sake, because we thus desire to honour God, Prov. iii. 9. Our alms ought to be cheerful and according to our ability, 1 Cor. xvi. 2; 2 Cor. ix. 7. Our liberality ought also to be unostentatious. Our Lord settled this matter in his Sermon on the Mount, Matt. vi. 2–4. All the reasons of this command we may not know; but we do know two reasons, either of which is sufficient. 1. We ought, as far as possible, to save the feelings of those who are profited by our kindness, Ruth ii. 16. 2. All vanity in religion is very disgusting to well-balanced and well-instructed minds. Our liberality should be abundant towards the truly needy. In particular they should never be forgotten in days of unusual gladness, Neh. viii. 10. Our liberality should be out of our own funds. Eccl. xi. 1; 1 John iii. 17. Durham tells us the story of "Selymus, the Turkish emperor, a most bloody man, that when he was a dying, one of his Bashaws desiring him to build a hospital for relief of the poor with the wealth taken from the Persian merchants, he replied thus, "Wouldst thou, Pyrrhus, that I should bestow other men's goods, wrongfully taken from them, on works of charity and devotion, for mine own vain-glory and praise? assuredly I will never do it; nay, rather that they be bestowed on the right owners again; which was accordingly done."

XVI. When God gives us good things richly, it is that *we may enjoy them.* 1 Tim. vi. 17. It is a great reproach to religion when God opens his hand liberally and supplies our wants, that we should stingily withhold them from ourselves and our dependents. "He hath made every thing beautiful in his time. . . . I know that there is no good in them, but for a man to rejoice, and to do good in his life. And also that every man should eat and drink, and enjoy the good of all his labour; it is the gift of God." Eccles. iii. 11–13. Compare Eccles. iv. 8, vi. 1, 2.

XVII. One species of sin against this commandment is common in all ages and countries. It relates to boundary lines between neighbours. The forms in which this sin is committed are exceedingly numerous, but they are all forbidden under the general prohibition to alter land-marks. Deut. xix. 14, xxvii. 17; Job xxiv. 2; Prov. xxii. 28, xxiii. 10.

XVIII. A sin kindred to the last mentioned is greed for land beyond our necessities, and a desire to hold it for its own sake. There is no little of this spirit in some parts of the world; and yet there is no mode of violating this commandment more strictly forbidden. "Woe unto them that join house to house, that lay field to field, till there be no place, that they may be placed alone in the midst of the earth." Isa. v. 8. Compare Micah ii. 2.

XIX. The Scriptures do not require a COMMUNITY OF GOODS. "The Most High has divided to the nations their inheritance." Deut. xxxii. 8. He divided to the tribes of Israel and to each family in every tribe a separate portion. He taketh also the desolate and setteth him in families. It is true indeed that when the church was in her infant state in Jerusalem, and had great numbers of poor and suffering members, God poured out a spirit of liberality, according to the exigencies of the case, and "all that believed were together, and had all things common; and sold their possessions and goods, and parted them to all men, as every man had need." Acts ii. 44, 45. But this was wholly a voluntary and temporary arrangement. In addressing Ananias, Peter expressly said, that there was no law on the subject binding any man, "While it remained, was it not thine own? and after it was sold, was it not in thine own power?" Acts v. 4.

XX. What shall we say of LAW-SUITS? It is very clear that litigiousness is contrary to the spirit of the gospel. Our Saviour said, "If any man will sue thee at the law, and take away thy coat, let him have thy cloak also." Matt. v. 40. This passage has been uniformly understood as a call upon us to repress that natural desire for insisting upon our legal rights before courts. Paul also warns his Corinthians to abstain from all litigation before *heathen* magistrates. 1 Cor. vi. 1–7. Let no man go to law for a mere trifle, involving no principle. "A bad settlement is better than a good law-suit." Avoid a law-suit, if you can, without wrong to some one.

XXI. Perhaps one of the most common errors respecting property is THE NEGLECT OF HEARTY PRAYER to God on that subject. "Then shalt thou remember the LORD thy God: for it is he that giveth thee power to get wealth." Deut. viii. 18. "Feed me with food convenient for me." Prov. xxx. 8. "In all thy ways acknowledge him." Prov. iii. 6. "Give us this day our daily bread." Matt. vi. 11.

XXII. Sometimes theft and robbery are committed directly against God. He is the rightful proprietor of all things. Whatever therefore he claims as proper for his worship, our time, the time of our servants, our property and our affections, should be sincerely rendered to him. "Will a man rob God? Yet ye have robbed me. But ye say, Wherein have we robbed thee? In tithes and offerings. Ye are cursed with a curse: for ye have robbed me, even this whole nation." Mal. iii. 8, 9. Compare John x. 1. Sacrilege is a heinous sin. "It is a snare to the man who devoureth that which is holy." Prov. xx. 25. The sin that filled up the measure of the iniquity of the haughty monarch of Babylon was taking the vessels of God's house, and thus lifting himself up against the Lord of heaven. Dan. v. 23.

XXIII. It should greatly deter us from any and every violation of this precept that God visits awful judgments upon those who transgress it. "The robbery of the wicked shall destroy them." Prov. xxi. 7. "As the partridge sitteth on eggs, and hatcheth them not, so he that getteth riches, and not by right, shall leave them in the midst of his days, and at his end shall be a fool." Jer. xvii. 11. Compare Ps. lv. 23; Prov. xxii. 23; Hab. ii. 6–13; Zeh. v. 3, 4; 1 Cor. vi. 10; James v. 1–6.

XXIV. On the other hand an exceedingly rich blessing is surely promised to those who obey this commandment. "A little that a righteous man hath is better than the riches of many wicked." Ps. xxxvii. 16. Compare Prov. xvi. 8; Matt. vi. 9–34; Matt. xxv. 31–44; 1 Tim. vi. 17–19.

## CONCLUSION.

Never in any wise be an instrument of sowing the seeds of enmity between the rich and the poor.

If you are poor, beware of envying the rich. If

you knew their crosses and their miseries, you would probably think them heavier than your own. James v. 9; Ecc. v. 12.

If you are rich, beware of despising the poor. In so doing you reproach your Maker. Prov. xvii. 5.

# CHAPTER XXIII.

## THE NINTH COMMANDMENT.

### THOU SHALT NOT BEAR FALSE WITNESS AGAINST THY NEIGHBOUR.

THE tongue is, at the same time, the best part of man, and his worst: with good government, none is more useful; and without it, none is more mischievous.—*Anacharsis.*

A wound from a tongue is worse than a wound from the sword.—*Pythagoras.*

There is nothing so delightful as the hearing or speaking of truth.—*Plato.*

Truth is the object of our understanding, as good is of our will; and the understanding can no more be delighted with a lie, than the will can choose apparent evil.—*Dryden.*

There are but ten precepts of the law of God, and two of them, so far as concerns the outward organ and vent of the sins there forbidden, are bestowed *on the tongue* (one in the first table, and the other in the second table,) as though it were ready to fly out, both against God and man, if not thus bridled.—*Leighton.*

Truth, like light, travels only in straight lines.—*Colton.*

Truth will be uppermost, one time or other, like cork, though kept down in the water.—*Sir William Temple.*

Truth is the foundation of all knowledge and the cement of all societies.—*Casaubon.*

Truth and Falsehood, travelling one warm day, met at a well, and both went in to bathe at the same place. Falsehood coming first out of the water, took his companion's clothes, leaving his own vile raiment, and went on his way. Truth, coming out of the water sought in vain for his own proper dress—disdaining to wear the garb of Falsehood. Truth started, all naked, in pursuit of the thief, but not being so swift of foot, has never overtaken the fugitive, and has ever since been known as naked truth. —*Anon.*

"Let us remember that not our *actions* only, but the *fruits of our lips* are to be brought into the solemn account, which we must give to the great Judge of all the earth; and that the day is coming when all our idle and unprofitable talk which has proceeded from the evil treasure of a depraved heart, will undergo a strict examination. . . . And if foolish and wicked speeches are to be accounted for in the day of judgment, let us set a watch on the door of our lips to prevent them, and labour daily to use our tongue so that it may indeed be, as it is in Scripture called, our *glory.*"—*Doddridge.*

"Tale-bearing is as bad an office as a man can put himself into, to be the publisher of every man's faults, divulging what was secret, aggravating crimes, and making the worst of everything that was amiss, with a design to blast and ruin men's reputation, and to sow discord among neighbours. The word used for a tale-bearer signifies a *pedler* or *petty chapman*, the in terlopers of trade; for tale-bearers pick up ill-natured stories at one house, and utter them at another, and commonly barter slander by way of exchange."—*M. Henry.*

"When we are not able wholly to separate from the wicked, we should double our watchfulness, and especially impose a strict restraint upon our tongues, lest we should be betrayed into boasting, reviling, slandering, flattering, or trifling conversation; remembering that they will criticise every expression, and turn it, if they can, to our disadvantage, and to the discredit of religion. Sometimes it may be necessary to keep silence even from good words, when they are likely to excite profane contempt or rage; yet in general we run into an extreme when we are backward to engage in edifying discourse."—*T. Scott.*

He said, surely they are my people, children that will not lie: so he was their Saviour.—*Isaiah.*

Speak ye every man the truth to his neighbour.—*Zechariah.*

Perhaps on no one point of morals has so much been written or spoken as on the use of the tongue. Ancients and moderns, heathen and Christians, have alike said many excellent things.

The pen is subject to the same laws as the tongue. It is an artificial tongue, speaking to those at a distance in time or place. What a man may not speak, he should not write. Indeed, writing evil things often does more harm than speaking them. Sir T. Brown: "Scholars are men of peace; they bear no arms, but their tongues are sharper than Actius' razor; their pens carry further, and give a louder report than thunder. I had rather stand in the shock of a basilisk, than in the fury of a merciless pen."

We may sin not only by the words used, but also by the tones with which they are spoken, and by looks and gestures. The language of pantomime is universal, vigorous, and easily perverted. "A naughty person, a wicked man, walketh with a froward mouth. He winketh with his eyes, he speaketh with his feet, he teacheth with his fingers." Prov. vi. 12, 13.

In many ways we may sin with our tongues. Laurentius enumerates as many sins of the tongue as there are letters in the alphabet. In his Christian Directory, Richard Baxter gives a list of thirty sins of speech, beginning with blasphemy. In expounding the *third* and *ninth* commandments, the Westminster Assembly makes the number still larger. There is, therefore, no want of matter on such a theme.

Some speak too fast. Merely rapid articulation is not here intended. But statements made without reflection, though not designed to mislead, are a great evil. "Seest thou a man hasty in his words? There is more hope of a fool than of him." Prov. xxix. 20. The intellect of such is in a state unfriendly to accuracy of knowledge or statement. He seldom improves in mind or manners. He jumps at conclusions, and wishes others to do the same.

Others speak too often. When awake and in company they are seldom silent. "From morn to night the ceaseless larum rings." In the absence of things weighty, wise or true; trifles, folly, or falsehood serve their turn. It is a mark of intolerable self-conceit to be continually offering unsolicited opinions. Even the oracles of the heathen were sometimes silent, though paid for speaking.

Others say too much. Not content with stating what is called for, they proceed to tiresome and sinful lengths. They are neither "swift to hear," nor "slow to speak."

Others speak too soon. They do not inquire, listen and consider, but are ready to deliver their views at all times, and often in dashing style. "A wise man regardeth time and judgment," but they disregard both. "He that answereth a matter before he heareth it. it is folly and shame unto him." Prov. xviii. 13.

As "there is a time to speak," so "there is a time to keep silence." Eccles. iii. 7. One of these times is when you have nothing pertinent to say. Another is, when others are speaking. Did any family ever come to much good, where the young were not taught to be silent when the old were speaking, or where all the children were allowed to speak at once? Another such time is when we first visit a friend overwhelmed with affliction. Some sympathies are best expressed by silence. Thus, Job's friends "sat down with him upon the ground seven days and seven nights, and none spake a word unto him; for they saw that his grief was very great." Job ii. 13. When others are greatly heated by passion, it is usually best to be silent. A very good man wrote down this rule, "I will never talk *to* an angry man."

In general, men probably speak too much. The Scriptures warn us on this point. "A fool's voice is known by multitude of words." Eccles. v. 3. "A fool also is full of words." Eccles. x. 14. "In the multitude of words there wanteth not sin." Prov. x. 19. Garrulity is not always innocent. Even good and wise men censure it. One of our proverbs is, "The fool's tongue is long enough to cut his own throat." Babblers were never held in high esteem among a virtuous people. "Surely the serpent will bite without enchantment; and a babbler is no better." Eccles. x. 11. This odious character is often more or less acquired by those who suppose themselves unsuspected of it. Of many a man it is said, "He is not worth minding, he is always talking." This is a sign that all is not right. One may plead that he is a licensed character, and that he was always allowed to say just what he pleased. But it may be asked, Who signed and gave the license? Can it be produced? It never came from God, and good men would not dare to sanction what God condemns. If any man has such license, he forged it. By excessive talking professors of religion make sad the hearts of their brethren, and all men are less esteemed for it. The judgment of mankind is with Solomon, that "a fool uttereth all his mind; but a wise man keepeth it in till afterwards," Prov. xxix. 11; and that "even a fool, when he holdeth his peace, is counted wise; and he that shutteth his lips is esteemed a man of understanding." Prov. xvii. 28. Some one has well said: "He is not a fool that hath unwise thoughts, but he that utters them." Quarles: "A word unspoken is, like the sword in the scabbard, thine. If vented, thy sword is in another's hand. If thou desire to be held wise, be so wise as to hold thy tongue." It is much to be lamented that some can never be cured of the folly of much speaking. To them silence is torture. Like one of the ancients they might say, "If I hold my tongue, I shall give up the ghost." Job xiii. 19. They know little of the peace and quiet of one who follows them not. "Whoso keepeth his mouth and his tongue, keepeth his soul from troubles." Prov. xxi. 23. The troubles brought on by an unbridled tongue in this life are but a prelude to far worse in the next.

Excessive talking is frequently attended by loud speaking. The former betrays self-conceit; the latter impudence One feature of as bad a character as is sketched in Scripture is that "she is loud." Prov. vii. 11. "A foolish woman is clamorous; she is simple, and knoweth nothing." Prov. ix. 13. It was a bright ornament of the character of the divine Redeemer that he was gentle and quiet, and did "not cry, nor lift up, nor cause his voice to be heard in the street." Isa. xlii. 2. He was not a clamorous person, but meek and lowly.

Is the following a fancy sketch? When others were speaking, he was restless, and if ruled to entire silence, he was miserable. Ordinarily he seemed to have some amiable traits, but when others had the good sense to listen to his wit or wisdom, he was in a specially good temper. The more you attended to him, the louder and more emphatic he was. On nearly *all* subjects he knew something; on *many*, he knew much; on *some*, he was an oracle in his own esteem. When doomed to spend some time with those whose dignity restrained him, he might well have adopted the words of one who bears a part in the oldest epic poem extant. "I am full of matter, the spirit within constraineth me. Behold my belly is as wine, which hath no vent; it is ready to burst like new bottles. I will speak that I may be refreshed." Job xxxii. 18–20. Our hero wished to pass for a benevolent man. He was great at a public meeting. He commonly said something, and was full of promises in aid of the cause. To fulfil them was far from him. His children caught his spirit, though in his presence they were sometimes forced to keep silence. But when they had a chance, they lost no time. Even on his death-bed the same propensity was sometimes manifest, and he left the world without seeming to know that he bore the character of a babbler.

One of his townsmen was little like him. He was a man of few words. When he did speak he was heard with marked respect. If others were impatient, it was because he was slow to utter his mind. His maxim, was, "The fewer words, the less sin." He thought much and weighed his words well. Far removed from sourness, he was given to self-communion. His prayers were brief, but fervent and comprehensive. His words were well ordered. He was not hasty to utter any thing, especially before God. His sincerity was apparent. His word was as good as his bond or his oath. He was rarely required to explain or retract any of his statements; but if he had been mistaken, he frankly said so. His children, though sprightly and joyous, were neither pert nor impudent. They honoured gray hairs. In him "the effect of righteousness was quietness and assurance for ever." Isa. xxxii. 17. His end was peace. Survivors generally mentioned his name with honour. His family never blushed to own him as their former guide and head.

Would it not be wise for every man to say with a servant of God of the *seventeenth* century, "I am resolved, by the grace of God, never to speak much, lest I often speak too much, and not to speak at all, rather than to no purpose."

Our words should also be pure and chaste. How many narratives, anecdotes, songs, riddles, and questions are indelicate, and therefore unchristian! How many hints, allusions, innuendos, insinuations, and surmises are of this description! Nearly every thing in the form of *double entendre* falls under the same condemnation. Whatever pollutes the mind is wicked, and never without necessity to be repeated. This class of evils is vastly sustained by the stage, by works of wit and fiction, and by many popular ballads. Tradition also shows both fidelity and industry in transmitting impure sayings from age to age. Those who thus sin sometimes excuse their conduct by saying that "unto the pure all things are pure," but they seem to forget that "unto them that are defiled and unbelieving is nothing pure; but even their mind and conscience is defiled." Tit. i. 15. This latter class constitutes no small portion of mankind. The sow washes more frequently than the sheep, and yet is not clean. The nature of the flock is to avoid the mire. Shun those who are foul-mouthed. Never smile at their impurity. Never imitate them. "Let no corrupt communication proceed out of your mouth, but that which is good to the use of edifying, that it may minister grace unto the hearers." Eph. iv. 29. "But now ye also put off all these; anger, wrath, malice, blasphemy, *filthy communication* out of your mouth." Col. iii. 8. "Be not deceived, evil communications corrupt good manners." 1 Cor. xv. 33. Many who greatly offend against these laws of speech, would be both surprised and displeased if their sin was charged upon them.

Another grievous sin of the tongue is flattery, which consists in undue or unseasonable praise. Few things are more ensnaring. Riches, talents, family, office, person, attainments, deeds of distinction, and even vices furnish occasions for it. Husbands flatter their wives, and wives their husbands; parents their children, and children their parents; ministers their people, and people their ministers, and all under the pretence of manifesting esteem. The poor flatter the rich, and demagogues the people. Yet all commendation is not flattery; but that which exceeds the truth is always sinful, and untimely praise, even when true, disgusts wise men and puffs up the minds of the simple. It was a good purpose of Bishop Beveridge, "I am resolved, by the grace of God, to speak of other men's sins only before their faces, and of their virtues only behind their backs." The only exception to this rule is that of necessity. Properly observed, it would banish a large part of social misery. Flattery is always an unkindness. "A man that flattereth his neighbour, spreadeth a net for his feet." Prov. xxix. 5. Those are good words of Elihu—"Let me not accept any man's person, neither let me give flattering titles unto man. For I know not to give flattering titles; in so doing my Maker would soon take me away." Job xxxii. 21, 22, Paul says,—"Neither at any time used we flattering words." 1 Thess. ii. 5. Courtly manners may require such words, but the truth, even bluntly spoken, is more pleasing to God. Almost all flatterers have some wicked design in view. "Discretion shall preserve thee from the stranger, that flattereth with her words." Prov. ii. 16.

Nor is the sin or danger of flattery diminished when it is directed to ourselves. Indeed this is sometimes the worst of all. Plutarch said, "Every man is his own greatest flatterer." The undue commendation of others would harm us but little, if we were honest with our own hearts. "It is not good to eat much honey: so for men to search their own glory is not glory." Prov. xxv. 27. "Let another man praise thee and not thine own mouth; a stranger, and not thine own lips.' Prov. xxvii. 2. The only thing that can justify speaking in our own praise is the necessary defence of ourselves or our offices. John viii. 49. 2 Cor. xii. 11–18. But let no man put upon himself a lower estimate than the truth requires. Ex. iv. 10–14; Rom. xii. 3.

This is a great evil under the sun. Kings have their courtiers, and few are sunk so low as not at times to have their sycophants. Yet if a man is really displeased with flattery, it will seldom be offered. To be pleased with it is to become a candidate for shame, perhaps for ruin. Every human being is entitled to some respect. Even the guilty felon on his way to execution should not be mocked or rudely gazed at. Every well-meaning person is entitled to such treatment as will express approbation of his good character. But fawning servility is due to no mortal. "The Lord shall cut off all flattering lips." Ps. xii. 3. Among some "to be agreeable" is to be adulatory. This sin is one of the most degrading to him who practises it, and tempting to him who is flattered. It greatly hinders the proper giving and receiving of reproof. One who was famous in his day said, "I will do my best to cross any man in his sins; if I have not thanks of him, yet I shall of my own conscience."

Flatterers are quite sure to be backbiters. This is neither conjecture, nor the mere fruit of observation. The Bible so teaches. "He that goeth about as a tale-bearer, revealeth secrets; therefore meddle not with him that flattereth with his lips." Prov. xx. 19. A defeated flatterer is a malicious slanderer. His principles are bad. He who will lie in your favour will upon a turn lie against you. He who will unduly praise, will unduly censure. Flattery and slander are branches of the same trade, and are carried on by the same people. Those called in the Bible, "whisperers," belong to the same class. They go about their work by stealth. They often enjoin secrecy on their dupes. To them an evil report is music. They are often very cunning in avoiding responsibility before men, but God knows the filthiness of their hearts. Their career is sometimes long, but generally ends in open shame. They have sometimes poisoned the minds of many with their falsehoods. They often speak well of a man to his friends, but evil of him to his enemies. "He that uttereth a slander, is a fool." Prov. x. 18. A heathen once said, "the most dangerous of wild beasts is a slanderer; of tame ones, a flatterer."

Men sometimes pretend to know some great evil of another, but will not tell what it is. They know that the human imagination, appealed to mysteriously, can soon outrun any common scale of enormity, and so they set it to work. That such conduct is mean, cruel, and indefensible, few will deny. Yet how many practise it! And if, instead of going abroad with such or other charges against their neighbours, men would go directly to them, how much evil would be prevented. "Debate thy cause with thy neighbour himself, and discover not a secret to another, lest he that heareth it put thee to shame, and thine infamy turn not away." Prov. xxv. 9, 10.

The law of love to man may be violated in speech without uttering a word that is not true. That no man is any better than he ought to be, is literally true, yet to say as much of any particular person is often slanderous in its effect, and may tear a good name to pieces.

Tale-bearing and news-carrying are species of slander, and are very mischievous. In this more than in most ways, one man may produce deep and extensive distress. Like the incendiary, who has fired a city and fled to an eminence to ravish his eyes with the progress of the ruin he has wrought, the talebearer loves to embroil families and communities, and then, if possible, escape unnoticed and unhurt. Often he is found out in time to receive the frowns of the virtuous, but commonly not till he has engendered strife. Paul says such persons were found in his day, "And withal they learn to be idle, wandering about from house to house; and not only idle, but tattlers also and busy-bodies, speaking things which they ought not." 1 Tim. v. 13. Hopkins says that Paul here gives "a true description of giddy flies in our times, that are always roving from house to house, and skipping about, now to this man's ear, and by and by to that, and buzzing reports of what ill they have heard or observed of others." In the law of Moses is this statute, "Thou shalt not go up and down as a tale-bearer among thy people." Lev. xix. 16. "A tale-bearer revealeth secrets; but he that is of a faithful spirit concealeth the matter." Prov. xi. 13. Every man, family, and firm have secrets, which it does not concern others to know. If by accident, or in confidence, they come to your knowledge, reveal them not. To be a spy upon your neighbour is a low occupation, and he to whom confidence is not sacred, is truly debased. None but the imprudent are in the habit of telling their secrets. "If you would teach secrecy to others, begin with yourself. How can you expect another to keep a secret when you yourself cannot?" It was a wise determination of a good man of the last generation, "In general, I will deal in secrets as little as possible."

Much social misery is owing to tale-bearing. "Where no wood is, the fire goeth out; so where there is no tale-bearer, the strife ceaseth." Prov. xxvi. 20. The dreadful effects of this vile practice are clearly stated in Scripture. "The words of a tale-bearer are as wounds; and they go down into the innermost parts of the belly." Prov. xviii. 8. Among the seven abominations which the Lord hates, four of them are, "a lying tongue, feet that be swift in running to mischief, a false witness that speaketh lies, and he that soweth discord among brethren." Prov vi. 17–19. Compare Prov. xi. 9. Lying in some form is a common attendant on tale-bearing. Useless strife always follows it. It argues a low mind, and a meddlesome disposition. And "he that passeth by and meddleth with strife not belonging to him, is like one that taketh a dog by the ears." Prov. xxvi. 17. To others he gives trouble, while he has a large share himself. Very few men openly declare themselves candidates for contempt, but tale-bearers gain it without direct seeking.

If such persons met with no encouragement, they would cease their evil work. If none will dance, they will not pipe. Pity it is that they are not made ashamed of their evil course. He who listens to them is partaker of their sins. A good man "taketh not up a reproach against his neighbour." Prov. xv. 3. Tale-hearing is twin sister to tale-bearing. "Where the carcass is, there the eagles will be gathered together." And where evil report is rifest, there will gather foul birds, which prey upon ruined character. How court-houses are crowded by this sort of persons, when matters of a scandalous nature are to be investigated! Their dolorous notes of regret do not even conceal their hypocrisy. Like sepulchres, their memories are full of dead men's bones and all corruption. If none would hear evil reports, none would be made. "The north-wind driveth away rain; so doth an angry countenance a backbiting tongue." Prov. xxv. 23. Compare Jer. xx. 10; Neh. vi. 6. "It is not the lie that passeth through the mind, but the lie that sticketh in and settleth in the mind, that doth the hurt." Cowper says:

"Whoever keeps an open ear
For tattlers, will be sure to hear
The trumpet of contention;
Aspersion is the babbler's trade,
To listen is to lend him aid,
And rush into dissension."

Bishop Hall says, "As 'there would be no thieves, if there were no receivers,' so there would not be so many open mouths to detract and slander if there were not so many open ears to entertain them. If I cannot stop other men's mouths from speaking ill, I will either open my mouth to reprove it, or else I will stop my ears from hearing it; and let him see in my face that he hath no room in my heart."

"A good name is better than precious ointment." Eccles. vii. 1. Yea, "a good name is rather to be chosen than great riches." Prov. xxii. 1. Character is all the estate many have. To any man it is of great value. Hopkins: "Indeed a good name is so excellent a blessing that there is but one thing to be preferred before it, and that is a good conscience." Everywhere and always human happiness much depends upon it. Compared with it, other possessions are paltry:

> "Who steals my purse steals trash, 'tis something, nothing;
> 'Twas mine, 'tis his, and has been slave to thousands;
> But he that filches from me my good name,
> Robs me of that which not enriches him,
> But makes me poor indeed."

Who is the gainer by tattling or slander? He who utters either is greatly polluted. He who listens to either is an "eater of calumnies," as the Syriac calls Satan. He of whom either is uttered, does not thereby lose a good conscience, but he sometimes loses his temper, which is the source of much of his enjoyment; and sometimes he loses his good name, which is the best legacy he can leave his children. Both tattling and slander are commonly malignant, and always wanton. Nor is any one safe from these robbers. No lock and key, no armed sentinel, no life of usefulness, no solid worth can secure a good name from their attacks.

> "No might, nor greatness in mortality,
> Can censure 'scape; back-wounding calumny
> The whitest virtue strikes. What king so strong
> Can tie the gall up in the slanderous tongue?"

Well does the word of God describe such: "Their throat is an open sepulchre; with their tongues they have used deceit; the poison of asps is under their lips." Rom. iii. 13. "There is that speaketh like the piercings of a sword." Prov. xii. 18. One asked a Spartan if his sword was sharp. He replied, "Sharper than calumny." The good of all ages have testified against these sins. One said, "The most abandoned and sordid minds have the least abhorrence of calumny. He who is but moderately wicked, dares not venture upon it. He who has the least particle of ingenuousness in his nature disdains it." Another said, "The malice of ill tongues cast upon a good man is only like a mouthful of smoke blown upon a diamond, which, though it clouds its beauty for the present, yet it is easily rubbed off, and the gem restored with little trouble to its owner." Were this the proper place, it might be well to consider at length how we should behave under such wrongs. One said, "The sparks of calumny will be presently extinct of themselves unless you blow them." In some cases this is true, but in all cases imitate Christ, and commit yourself to Him that judgeth righteously.

Detraction is a species of slander. It consists in taking away *something* from the character of another. It denies not *all* his merits, but it puts in many abatements, exceptions, and insinuations. It is a common sin with rivals, sectaries, and partisans. Sallust explains to us the motives of such; "By casting down others, they hope to rise to honour." But to prove that one man is base will not prove another noble or virtuous.

One of the meanest ways of sinning with the tongue is so to attack character that no fair defence can be made. Some will give no names, others will avoid all particulars, but yet both will so describe things as to give cruel thrusts. If called to an account, they meanly enough put you to the proof of their having said aught against you, and show the cunning of a fox in eluding a pursuit which is becoming hot.

The great difficulty in all evil speaking is that so soon as a man utters it, his pride and self-love pledge him to make it good. Unless compelled, he seldom retracts. To injure a man is the surest way to hate him, and to wish to have ground of justification in such a case is quite natural. Passion, once enlisted, is blind and obstinate. Most of the hard and cruel things said, would, but for this cause, be taken back. Detraction is seldom followed by retraction.

A fondness for the strange and marvellous is one of the sins of every age, and shows itself in speech. To forge a chain out of a gossamer film, to make a mountain out of a mole-hill, and to abound in the wonderful may make fools gape, but will cause wise men to fear. When such men speak soberly, they fail of gaining credit. Some of the most painful scenes witnessed in social intercourse arise from the love of big stories. Asseverations, and even oaths, do not secure belief in them. He who duly fears God, will take care neither to invent, retail, nor even listen to them. It is to be regretted that superlatives are so commonly in use. How many speak of others as the meanest, the cleverest, the wisest, or the kindest people they ever knew! How often do we hear such expressions as these: "This is the hottest, or the coldest, or the darkest day I ever saw!" Perhaps these very people have said the same things oftentimes, and do not really mean what they say. They may not so much wish to deceive as to be impressive. True, all hyperbole is not unlawful. John xxi. 25. But this habitual use of it is out of place, weakens respect for our sobriety of mind, if not for our love of truth, and utterly fails of any good object. Exaggeration is said to run in some families. In giving solemn testimony there is often no little lying of this kind. President Edwards, the elder, wisely "*resolved*, in narrations, never to speak any thing but the pure and simple verity."

The spirit which leads men to the marvellous, often guides them to boasting. As formerly, so now, "most men will proclaim every one his own goodness." Prov. xx. 6. So they boast of their exploits, property, influence, talents, charity, family, friends, and correspondents. Those "whose glory is in their shame," go further, and proudly tell of things which should crimson their cheeks. They seem to have one pleasure in committing a sin, and two in speaking of it. Men sometimes unwittingly let others know that they are knaves. "It is naught, it is naught, saith the buyer; but when he is gone his way, then he boasteth." Prov. xx. 14. Perhaps there are commonly too many words used in buying and selling. Many assert their large possession of qualities, of which they have little or none. And "whoso boasteth himself of a false gift, is like clouds and wind without rain." Prov. xxv. 14. Such a man is sometimes said to be *windy*, and he is a mere puff. "All such boasting is evil." James iv. 16. "Boasters" do not bear a high character for truth in other respects, and Paul enrols them among backbiters, haters of God, inventors of evil things, blasphemers, and such like vicious characters. Rom. i. 30, and 2 Tim. iii. 2.

It is very important that we should avoid the extremes of excessive confidence or doubtfulness in our statements. Some men *conjecture*, *think*, *suppose*, *presume*, *guess*, *are not sure but* that things are or were thus and so, when they know it. On the other hand some *know*, *aver*, *declare most positively*, *are ready to make oath* about trifles and things in their nature doubtful. The first class is certain of nothing; the latter, of every thing. The one by seeming doubtful of plain facts well known to them, would hang an innocent man; the other would bring about the same result by speaking so confidently of things doubtful as to destroy their own credibility in other things. The rule is, obtain correct views, if you can, and express them modestly, but clearly; but if there is room for rational doubt be not positive. If you know a thing, say so; if you know it not, say so.

There is much sin committed respecting promises. Some promises are wicked, and should be neither made nor kept. If made, they are to be repented of.

Some are rash, yet not wicked; such are to be kept. Rashness is always a folly and commonly a sin, and so should be mourned over. But "he that sweareth to his own hurt and changeth not," is the man that shall never be moved. Ps. xv. 4, 5. But even in lawful and prudent promises, what slackness of fulfilment! How few men keep all their engagements! How little punctuality and promptness do we see! If a man would be confided in by none, let him promise much, and perform little. There is no surer mark of general corruption than want of fidelity. "When the Son of man cometh, shall he find faith on the earth?"

For remarks on blasphemy, see above on the third commandment, pp. 262–266.

For remarks on the sin of perjury, see exposition of the third commandment, pp. 266–269.

On profane swearing, see above, pp. 269–282.

Following the usual course of theologians, Boston says, "Lies are of four sorts:

"1. Jesting lies, that is, when a person speaks that which is contrary to the known truth, in a jesting or ludicrous way; and embellishes his discourse with his own fictions, designing thereby to impose on others. See Hos. vii. 3.

"2. Officious lies, that is, when one speaks that which is contrary to the truth, and the dictates of his conscience, to do good to himself or others thereby. Job xiii. 7; Rom. iii. 8.

"3. Pernicious lies, that is, when a person raises and spreads a false report, with a design to do mischief to another.

"4. Rash lies, that is, when a person utters that

which is false through surprise, inadvertency, and customary looseness." 2 Sam. xiii. 30.

Perhaps of all the sins that men commit, none is more difficult to be cured than lying. Hateful as it is, it adheres to men with great tenacity.

Montaigne: "After a tongue has once got the knack of lying, 'tis not to be imagined how impossible it is almost to reclaim it." This is felt in churches formed in heathen countries at this day. The same difficulty was experienced by Paul and Titus, at least in reference to the churches in Crete. Paul says, "One of themselves, even a prophet of their own, said, The Cretians are alway liars, evil beasts, slow bellies. This witness is true: wherefore rebuke them sharply," &c., &c. Titus i. 12, 13.

It is not necessary to be able to classify every kind of lying. The essence of the sin consists in an intention to deceive where we are under obligation to speak. If any thing is spoken, it should be the truth. Of every species of this sin the old saying is true: "A liar should have a good memory." Montaigne expresses it thus: "He who has not a good memory should never take upon him the trade of lying." Tillotson's illustration of this idea has been often quoted: "Truth and reality have all the advantages of appearance and many more. If the show of any thing be good for any thing, I am sure sincerity is better: for why does any man dissemble, or seem to be that which he is not, but because he thinks it good to have such a quality as he pretends to? for to counterfeit and dissemble is to put on the appearance of some real excellency. Now, the best way in the world for a man to seem to be any thing, is really to be what he would seem to be. Besides, that it is many times as troublesome to make good the pretence of a good quality, as to have it; and if a man have it not, it is ten to one but he is discovered to want it, and then all his pains and labour to seem to have it are lost. There is something unnatural in painting, which a skilful eye will easily discern from native beauty and complexion.

"It is hard to personate and act a part long; for where truth is not at the bottom, nature will always be endeavouring to return, and will press out and betray herself one time or other. Therefore, if any man think it convenient to seem good, let him be so indeed, and then his goodness will appear to every body's satisfaction; so that, upon all accounts, sincerity is true wisdom. Particularly as to the affairs of this world, integrity hath many advantages over all the fine and artificial ways of dissimulation and deceit; it is much the plainer and easier, much the safer and more secure way of dealing in the world; it has less of trouble and difficulty, of entanglement and perplexity, of danger and hazard in it; it is the shortest and nearest way to our end, carrying us thither in a straight line, and will hold out and last longest. The arts of deceit and cunning do continually grow weaker, and less effectual and serviceable to them that use them; whereas integrity gains strength by use; and the more and longer any man practiseth it, the greater service it does him, by confirming his reputation, and encouraging those with whom he hath to do to repose the greatest trust and confidence in him, which is an unspeakable advantage in the business and affairs of life. Truth is always consistent with itself, and needs nothing to help it out; it is always near at hand, and sits upon our lips, and is ready to drop out before we are aware; whereas a lie is troublesome, and sets a man's invention upon the rack, and one trick needs a great many more to make it good."

The reason why lying is so hard to be cured is that it is seated in sin itself. Men go astray from the womb, speaking lies. How few there are, even in boyhood, who possess the entire confidence of their play-mates in matters of veracity. Once in a while, such a case is observed and always attracts attention. Thomas —— was never known to tell a lie. He would sometimes do wrong, but when asked about it, his chin would curl up, and his lip quiver, and out would come the truth. When he was eight or ten years old, bad boys, who wished to do any mischief, would not ask him to go with them; often they would not let him go with them; for they said, "he will be sure to tell all about it, if he is asked." In this way he kept out of much sin and sorrow too.

Yet when the boys were playing ball and a dispute arose, it was pleasing to see how they would all agree to leave it to Thomas. Everybody knew that he would tell the truth. If any boy was not willing to take the word of Thomas, it was thought that he must wish to cheat.

When Thomas was quite a young man, he was called into court to give his evidence under oath, and he told a modest plain story. One of the lawyers told the jury that the young man behaved very well, but he was so young that they ought not to give much weight to what he said. But the judge told the jury that there was no better witness, old or young, than Thomas. So he was honoured there before all the people.

Thomas lived to be an old man, and was much respected. He was always a man of truth. When he died there were many sad faces.

Perhaps very few have known more than one or two persons, whose character for veracity was like that of Thomas ——.

One thing in this sin should not be forgotten. It is exceedingly daring. "A liar is brave towards God, and a coward towards man." "A lie has no legs," and so cannot stand. Blessed is the man "that speaketh the truth in his heart," Ps. xv. 2. Compare Prov. xii. 19. Downright lying, without an object, is perhaps not very common, though some such cases do appear. But equivocation, prevarication, Gen. xx. 9–16, wresting men's words, Ps. lvi. 5, and Matt. xxvi. 60, 61, disparagement of others, Luke xviii. 11, undue praise of others, Acts xii. 22, 23, untrue commendation of ourselves, Luke xviii. 11, denying our own gifts, Exodus iv. 10, 14, exaggerating the faults of others, and making "a man an offender for a word," Isa. xxix. 20, 21, are kinds of falsehood, always having some guilt in them. In short, whatever is contrary to candour, fairness, and sincerity, should be avoided. It is to the great reproach of human nature that there should so often seem to be manifest pleasure in falsehood. "All liars shall have their part in the lake which burneth with fire and brimstone, which is the second death," Rev. xxi. 8. Compare Rev. xxii. 15.

Not a little injustice is done, not a little sin is committed by a class of men, who denominate themselves critics

> "A simple race of men who had
> One only art, which taught them still to say,
> Whate'er was done might have been better done."

These few words complete the account of them.

Some time ago a minister quoted the words "we be all dead men." A young coxcomb walking home, said that he was astonished at the minister's ignorance of grammar, and so occupied the attention of others and flattered his own vanity by his silly criticism. A large body of this class of men may properly be denominated *professional fault-finders*. Stowell: "There is more surmising, insinuating, censuring of what is dishonourable, inconsistent, or iniquitous, than expressed approbation of what is pure and just." Such have no patience with the principle laid down by Bunyan in the Preface to "Grace Abounding." Speaking of that work he says: "He that liketh it, let him receive it; and he that doth not, let him produce a better." A certain class of critics have no heart and no talent to produce a better work; and yet they delight in showing how poor is the production of another far their superior.

One of the most worthy men of his day, was the Rev. Job Orton. He lived in troublous times. He has left some valuable writings. They begin to be inquired after anew. This good man often disclaimed all participation in politics. On one occasion he says: "I have nothing to say about politics, but well remember the saying of Synesius, 'What hath a bishop to do with politics?'" Yet this same good man forgot himself exceedingly—he says: "Whatever the principles of the Americans may be, the spirit they show, is malignant, rebellious and wicked." How sweeping this charge against two millions of Christian freemen! Soon after he says: "I wish the London ministers would leave politics to statesmen, and give themselves wholly to their ministry." Yet it is certain that all the London ministers, who espoused the cause of America, said far less in the pulpit on politics than those who differed from them. Many have noticed that when a minister's politics suit a man, he seldom finds fault with a mild, seasonable and firm expression of them, in private or at the ballot-box; but if he is on the other side, he is all wrong, he is a meddler, violent, rash.

In another place, Orton speaking of Jonathan Edwards on the Will, says: "I never read it and I suppose I never will." He adds: "I bought and read his tract upon Religious Affections, which I did not understand." This is certainly short metre and sufficiently dashing; but soon after he says: "I scarcely know a worse writer, as to style and manner, than Davies of Virginia. His language is various; sometimes highly poetical, and seems to be verse run mad; sometimes he is in the clouds, and common readers cannot understand him; at other times he is not only plain, as every sermon-writer should be, but even low."

One is ready to ask, how could a man of Mr. Orton's piety and good sense pronounce so sententiously and unfavourably upon two of the brightest lights of the last century?

It cannot be denied that under the name of criticism, the very worst feelings and meanest passions of the heart often give vent to themselves. This is often confessed in high life as well as low. More than one critic, in "attempting to commit murder has committed suicide." A man is as accountable for his temper as a critic, as in any other respect.

One of the worst misapplications of criticism is to preaching; it seems to destroy nearly all prospect of doing good to those who indulge it. One such critic may infect a whole people with his hateful spirit; such hearers can hardly be profited—they are self-constituted judges; they are hardly hearers of the word—much less are they commonly doers of it; they go not to the house of God in a mood to be profited. If such would see divine light, they must first put out their own candle. It is a great fault in some that they relish discourses entirely beyond their comprehension. With many to be plain and low is the same thing. The loss to one of such a temper is great; he loses both enjoyment and edification; he feeds on wind. If he knows himself he must feel sad at his own leanness. Nor can he be much profited until there is a change in him—happy will he be, if that change be speedy and thorough.

Passing judgment before hearing evidence or argument, is a common sin. "All are not thieves that the dogs bark at." Many an innocent man is clamorously and falsely accused. To come out against the innocent or for the guilty is a great sin. "He that justifieth the wicked, and he that condemneth the just, even they both are abomination to the Lord." Prov. xvii. 15. A tumult or an uproar for or against a man is no proof. Nor are we innocent in justifying, when we should condemn ourselves. Luke xvi. 15. Confessions of sin in prayer, if not true, are very shocking to pious ears, and must be offensive to God. Making merry with the miseries of others is a great sin of the tongue and heart. "He that is glad at calamities shall not be unpunished." Prov. xvii. 5. We should be sorry both at the sorrows and sins even of our worst foe. "Rejoice not when thine enemy falleth, and let not thine heart be glad when he stumbleth; lest the Lord see it, and it displease him, and he turn away his wrath from him." Prov. xxiv. 17, 18. None but men of fiendish dispositions allow the violation of this law.

Railing, reviling, and scornful words are also condemned in Scripture. "Render not railing for railing." 1 Pet. iii. 9. If another reviles you, set him an example of patience. Paul puts "railers" among "fornicators, covetous, idolaters, drunkards, and extortioners." 1 Cor. v. 11. When Jesus "was reviled, he reviled not again." 1 Pet. ii. 23; Gal. iv. 29. Of the early Christians Paul says, "being reviled we bless." In reading Heb. xi. 33–39, John Blair Smith once said, of all the things mentioned in this catalogue of trials, perhaps the hardest to be borne were these "*cruel mockings.*" Hopkins: "As Nero for his barbarous sport wrapped up the Christians in beasts' skins and then set dogs to worry them; so these disguise their brethren in false and antic shapes, and then fall upon them and beat them." Our Saviour condemned the use of the scornful titles *Raca* and *Thou fool;* surely then we are not at liberty to call men *Liars;* "for a liar loseth all credit and reputation amongst men." Whoever has a right sense of honour would prefer death rather than a life in gooc society where he was justly esteemed a liar. 1 Cor. iv. 12. Our rulers in church and in state are to be spoken of respectfully. We read of some who "are not afraid to speak evil of dignities. Whereas angels, which are greater in power and might, bring not railing accusation against them before the Lord." 2 Pet. ii. 10, 11. Even "Michael, the archangel, when contending with the devil, he disputed about the body of Moses, durst not bring against him a railing accusation, but said, The Lord rebuke thee." Jude 9. Let those who indulge in scornful language consider well the import of Matt. v. 22. "A soft tongue breaketh the bone." Prov. xxv. 15. "A soft answer turneth away wrath: but grievous words stir up anger." Prov. xv. 1. Quarrelling is one of the lowest vices, and "recrimination is the last resort of guilt." The late Dr. Ebenezer Porter entered it among his solemn purposes, "When I am angry I will never speak, till I have taken at least as much time for reflection as Athenodorus prescribed to Cæsar." This was, "Always repeat the twenty-four letters of the alphabet before you give way to the impulse of anger."

Scolding is a kind of threatening without the power, or at least without the intention, of punishing. It is finding fault in a surly manner. It is one of the most unamiable of domestic vices. It banishes peace, spoils the temper, and makes many a house the miniature of hell. Many "hard speeches" are uttered in this way. The effect on children and servants is so discouraging that they often become desperate, thinking it is of no use to try to please. Any unnecessary exposure and repetition of the faults of others is a sin. Prov. xvii. 9. It was a resolution of one of the greatest men of his day, "Never to say any thing at all against anybody, but when it is perfectly agreeable to the highest degree of Christian honour, and love to mankind, agreeable to the lowest humility, and sense of my own faults and failings, and agreeable to the golden rule; and when I have said any thing against any one, to bring it to, and try it strictly by the test of this resolution."

"Foolish talking and jesting are not convenient." Eph. v. 4. That is, they do not become Christians. "Every idle word that men shall speak, they shall give account thereof in the day of judgment." Matt. xii. 36. "Idle words" are words without effect, and are "frothy, unsavoury stuff, tending to no purpose, nor good at all." When Latimer, on his first examination, heard the pen of the notary who was writing behind a curtain, he was careful what he said, because he knew it might be brought against him at his trial. All our words will meet us at the tribunal of Christ.

The question is often asked, What rules should guide us in the use of pleasantry, humour, wit, satire, irony, sarcasm, and ridicule? The following seem to cover all cases:

1. It is certain that all use of these things is not unlawful. The examples of Elijah, David, and Isaiah prove this. 1 Kings xviii. 27; Ps. cxv. 4–8; and Isa. xliv. 9–17.

2. Yet they are dangerous talents. They are edge-tools, and sometimes cut terribly. "Wit is folly unless a wise man has the keeping of it." It is, therefore, better to err in making a spare rather than

a free use of them. To make a trade of any of them is contemptible.

3. They should never be employed to effect malignant or mischievous purposes, nor to put down truth, nor to defeat justice, nor to uphold wickedness. They should never be wielded against the serious misfortunes or afflictions of men, nor against the good name of any, nor on sacred subjects.

4. They should not be used unseasonably. To some minds they are always unpleasant. Unfitly employed, they sunder friendships. "He is not a wise man who will lose his friend for his wit; but he is less a wise man who will lose his friend for another man's wit." Discretion is better than a *bon mot;* and friendship is more valuable than fun.

5. In this, as in all things, "love is the fulfilling of the law." Whatever is not benevolent is not wise or right.

6. Their chief use should be to enliven the mind, to promote cheerfulness, to expose absurdities, to lash popular vices, to reprove self-conceit, and to show the enemies of God's word that these things are not solid tests of truth and righteousness.

7. "The wisdom of man lies not in satirizing the vices and follies of others, but in correcting his own." A deep sense of our true characters will commonly prevent us from too much severity against others, and from allowing our pleasantries to sink into buffoonery.

The Scriptures also condemn undue and untimely conversation on worldly affairs, John iii. 31, and Isa. lviii. 13; all ill-natured, censorious remarks, though they be but surmises, Matt. vii. 1, 2; Rom. xiv. 4–13;

and 1 Tim. vi. 4; all fiery, bitter wars of words, Prov. xviii. 6; Rom. xiv. 1; Phil. ii. 14; 1 Tim. vi. 4, 5; and 2 Tim. ii. 23–26. "The wrath of man worketh not the righteousness of God." James i. 20. They also forbid all murmurings and complainings against God, Num. xiv. 27, and 1 Cor. x. 10; all seductive, tempting speeches, Rom. xvi. 18; all defence and propagation of false doctrine, Matt. v. 19; xxiii. 16; Isa. ix. 14–16; Ezek. xiii. 18; Col. ii. 8, 18, 22; 1 Tim. iv. 1–6; 2 Tim. ii. 18; iii. 6, 8, 13; Tit. i. 10; Rev. xviii. 19; and all scoffing at sacred things. 2 Pet. iii. 3.

But there may be sinful silence as well as sinful speaking. A dumb devil is an evil possession. Ambrose says, "As we must render an account of every idle word, so must we likewise of our idle silence." Another says, "Strange is the disorder that sin has brought into the world; as in the tongue, which is often going when it should be quiet, and often quiet when it should speak. Our tongues are our glory; but they are often found wrapt up in a dark cloud of silence, when they should be shining forth."

Our tongues should be used in acknowledging, adoring, praising, thanking, blessing, extolling, justifying, and supplicating God. We should honour him with our tongues in prayer, in sacred songs, in solemn vows, in humble confessions of sin, in solemn oaths judicially administered, and in professing the true religion. On all these points the Bible is full and clear.

We should also use our vocal powers in giving honour to whom it is due, Rom. xiii. 7; in charitable expressions concerning others, Heb. vi. 9; in readily acknowledging their good qualities, Rom. i. 8; 1 Cor. i. 4–7, and 2 Tim. i. 5, 6; in hearty and timely expressions of sorrow for the sins and infirmities of others, 2 Cor. xii. 21; 1 Cor. xiii. 7; in giving proper warning to the erring, Ezek. iii. 17–21; Col. i. 28; in pleading the cause of the poor and needy, Prov. xxxi. 9; 1 Sam. xxii. 14; in advocating truth, Jer. ix. 3; in speaking truth, Eph. iv. 25; in speaking the whole truth when properly called to do it, Jer. xlii. 4; Acts xx. 20; and in confessing our sins and errors known to men, or committed against them, James v. 16.

Self is a poor theme of conversation, yet indifference to character is no fruit of piety. If unjustly accused we may, like Job, David, Jeremiah, Paul and Christ, defend ourselves, John viii. 49; 2 Cor. xii. 11–18. But no wise man says much of himself unless compelled, and then with modesty and a sacred regard to truth.

According to our station, it is also our duty to give reproof, admonition, rebuke, and advice, Prov. xvii. 10; Ps. cxli. 5. True, every man is not to be reproved. "He that reproveth a scorner, getteth to himself shame; and he that rebuketh a wicked man, getteth himself a blot. Reprove not a scorner lest he hate thee," Prov. ix. 7, 8. Silence is often the best reproof, and the only wisdom. "I will keep my mouth with a bridle, while the wicked is before me. I was dumb with silence. I held my peace even from good," Ps. xxxix. 1, 2.

The most essential quality in a reprover is meekness; next to this are love and humility. Even "sin may be sinfully reproved." Advice is often the best charity; yet "to advise much is a sign that we need advice." In giving advice, do not try to please, but to do real good. An adviser fills a very responsible post. "The greatest trust between man and man is the trust of giving counsel." Beware of the vanity of affecting to know things beyond your reach. Admonition and rebuke must not be untimely, unjust, severe, or bitter. "To him that is afflicted pity should be shewed from his friend," Job vi. 14. "A word fitly spoken is like apples of gold in pictures of silver," Prov. xxv. 11.

And can any thing be more important than that our speech be such as to please God? "By thy words thou shalt be justified, and by thy words thou shalt be condemned," Matt. xii. 37. "What shall be given unto thee? or what shall be done unto thee, thou false tongue? Sharp arrows of the mighty, with coals of juniper," Ps. cxx. 3, 4. "A wholesome tongue is a tree of life, but perverseness therein is a breach in the spirit," Prov. xv. 4. "Death and life are in the power of the tongue," Prov. xviii. 21. "Heaviness in the heart of man maketh it stoop; but a good word maketh it glad," Prov. xii. 25. "A man hath joy by the answer of his mouth; and a word spoken in due season, how good is it," Prov. xv. 23. "As an ear-ring of gold, and an ornament of fine gold, so is a wise reprover upon an obedient ear," Prov. xxv. 12. One of the heathen said, "Tongues cut deeper than swords, because they reach even to the soul." A religion which leaves the tongue uncontrolled is mere pretence. "If any man among you seem to be religious, and bridleth not his tongue, but deceiveth his own heart, this man's religion is vain," James i. 26. After such representations, where is anything to be added to convince men that here is a most weighty matter? If men will not be moved by arguments drawn from human happiness and human misery on earth, from the august scenes of the last day, from the miseries of future punishment, and the rewards of a life of piety, their case is beyond the reach of human skill.

Thus we get some just views of the number and heinousness of our sins, and of the necessity of divine grace both to pardon and to reform us. Left to ourselves we are undone and helpless. "If any man offend not in word, the same is a perfect man, and able also to bridle the whole body. Behold we put bits in the horses' mouths, that they may obey us; and we turn about their whole body. Behold also the ships, which, though they be so great, and are driven of fierce winds, yet are they turned about with a very small helm, whithersover the governor listeth. Even so the tongue is a little member, and boasteth great things. Behold how great a matter a little fire kindleth! And the tongue is a fire, a world of iniquity; so is the tongue among our members, that it defileth the whole body, and setteth on fire the course of nature; and it is set on fire of hell. For every kind of beasts, and of birds, and of serpents, and of things in the sea, is tamed, and hath been tamed of mankind; but the tongue can no man tame; it is an unruly evil, full of deadly poison. Therewith bless we God, even the Father; and therewith curse we men, which are made after the similitude of God. Out of the same mouth proceedeth blessing and cursing. My brethren, these things ought not so to be," James iii. 2–10. He, who thinks he needs not amazing mercy to blot out the sins of his tongue, is indeed blind; and he, who thinks he shall easily cease to sin by word, knows nothing of the strength of an evil nature, confirmed by evil habits. If we have nothing else to repent of, surely our lips may well abase us. If we have nothing else to confess and bewail, surely each of us has reason to say with Isaiah, "I am undone, for I am a man of unclean lips." If in nothing else we are called to make restitution, have we wronged no one in words? If we can reform nothing else, can we not amend our habits of speech?

Yet, as Archbishop Leighton says, the conquest of these evils of the tongue "must be done in the heart; otherwise it will be but a mountebank cure, a false imagined conquest. The weights and wheels are *there*, and the clock strikes according to their motion. Even he that speaks contrary to what is within him, guilefully contrary to his inward convictions and knowledge, yet speaks conformably to what is within him in temper and frame of his heart, which is double, *a heart and a heart*, as the Psalmist hath it. Ps. xii. 2. A guileful heart makes guileful tongue and lips. It is the workhouse, where is the forge of deceits and slanders, and other evil speakings; and the tongue is only the outer shop where they are vended, and the lips the door of it; so that such ware as is made within, such and no other can be set out. From evil thoughts, evil speakings; from a profane heart, profane words; and from a malicious heart, bitter or calumnious words; and from a deceitful heart, guileful words, well varnished, but lined with rottenness. And so in general, *from the abundance of the heart the mouth speaketh*, as our Saviour teaches. That which the heart is full of, runs over by the tongue; if the heart be full of God, the tongue will delight to speak of him; much of heavenly things within will sweetly breathe forth something of their smell by the mouth; and if nothing but earth is there, all that man's discourse will have an earthly smell; and if nothing but wind, vanity, and folly, the speech will be airy, and vain, and purposeless. *The mouth of the righteous speaketh wisdom; the law of his God is in his heart.*" Ps. xxxvii. 30, 31.

Nor is it possible for us to effect a thorough change without diligence, watchfulness, and prayer. An unguarded mouth will pour forth folly and wickedness. Therefore after all David's resolutions and efforts he comes to God in earnest prayer, and cries, "Set a watch, O Lord, before my mouth; keep the door of my lips." Ps. cxli. 3.

If you go on sinning with your lips, you either *will* repent or *not*. If you shall repent, you will have more anguish than all the vile pleasure of sin is worth. If you never shall truly repent, how sad your state for ever! And are we not all guilty enough already? Are not our iniquities fearfully multiplied? They are more than the hairs of our head. We cannot answer for one of a thousand of our offences. Even now our only hope is in the infinite mercy of God. How sweet are the words of Scripture to those who rightly feel their sinfulness! "If any man sin, we have an advocate with the Father, Jesus Christ the righteous." "The blood of Jesus Christ, his Son, cleanseth us from all sin."

Wonderful, wonderful are the compassions of the Lord. Oh that we may no longer abuse them, but by them be won to God, to love, to holiness in thought, word, and deed!

Would it not, therefore, be right for you to make these solemn resolutions?

1. I will steadily keep in view my latter end, and remember that soon I must stand before my Judge. I would not live a day or an hour in forgetfulness of the truth that all my thoughts, *words* and deeds are to undergo the scrutiny of Him, who is so holy as to hate all sin, and so great as to know all things, and so just as never to clear the guilty.

2. I will endeavour often to ask myself, How would Jesus Christ speak were he in my circumstances? He has left me an example that I should follow his steps. His life is the law of God put in practice. If I walk in his steps I shall not err.

3. I will rely more and more on the grace of the Lord Jesus Christ to preserve me from sins of the tongue. I have too much relied on the strength of my own virtue and perseverance, and so I have failed. "O Lord, undertake for me."

4. I will constantly strive to have a deep sense of the importance of making a right use of my tongue. I will endeavour to avoid levity of mind, and so escape levity of speech and behaviour. By God's grace I will be serious.

5. I will often call myself to an account for my words during the day, and when I have erred, I will not spare myself from these severe, yet salutary answers, which my sins deserve. I will not justify, excuse or extenuate the sins of my lips.

6. I will labour to have my mind stored with valuable information and reflections, that I may not be tempted to deal in gossip, and scandal, and idle news, and that my words may be instructive to those with whom I mingle.

7. I will endeavour to be more impressed with a sense of the amazing grace and mercy of God to me a sinner, in bidding me hope for his favour, notwithstanding all my offences. Thus I shall have alacrity and joy in resisting evil and seeking holiness.

8. I will labour to have a proper view, not only of the meanness, mischief, and troubles of a loose tongue, but also of its great sinfulness in the sight of God. As an unbridled speech is a wickedness, I would avoid it, even if it brought me no temporal evil.

9. Above all things, I will seek to be thoroughly renewed by the power of the Holy Ghost. If he will make his abode with me, I shall be able to resist all sin, and overcome all evil habits. To change my nature is beyond my power, but not beyond the power of the Sanctifier. My power is but another name for feebleness: his energy is irresistible.

10. I will strive to practise the wise rules which Dr. Watts so well suggests in his version of the xxxix. Psalm.

Thus I resolved before the Lord,
  Now will I watch my tongue,
Lest I let slip one sinful word,
  Or do my neighbour wrong.

Whene'er constrained a while to stay
  With men of lives profane,
I'll set a double watch that day,
  Nor let my talk be vain.

I'll scarce allow my lips to speak
  The pious thoughts I feel,
Lest scoffers should occasion take
  To mock my holy zeal.

Yet if some proper hour appear,
  I'll not be overawed,
But let the scoffing sinner hear
  That I can speak for God.

# CHAPTER XXIV.

## THE TENTH COMMANDMENT.

THOU SHALT NOT COVET THY NEIGHBOUR'S HOUSE, THOU SHALT NOT COVET THY NEIGHBOUR'S WIFE, NOR HIS MAN-SERVANT, NOR HIS MAID-SERVANT, NOR HIS OX, NOR HIS ASS, NOR ANY THING THAT IS THY NEIGHBOUR'S.

THIS precept was the key that unlocked the mystery of iniquity in the mind of Paul. He says, "I had not known lust, except the law said, Thou shalt not covet," that is, he would not have known that the thought of foolishness, the secret desire of evil was wicked, but for this precept. It served to show him the nature of all the commandments. Charnock: "Paul thought himself a righteous person till he came to measure himself by the exact and spiritual image of the law. His head and the law were acquainted, and then he thought himself a living person: but when his *heart* and the law came to be acquainted, there he found himself dead, and his high opinion of himself fell to the ground."

It is clear, therefore, that this commandment directs attention immediately to the state of the heart. White-washing the sepulchre will do no good, while it is full of dead men's bones. The heart must be purified. There is no substitute for a thorough renewal of nature. Calvin: "Since it is the will of God that our whole souls should be under the influence of love, every desire inconsistent with charity ought to be expelled from our minds." Stowell: "This closing commandment is of great importance in two distinct points of view—first, as exhibiting the spirit of all the previous commandments, and secondly, as laying the foundation for just and consistent views of all the doctrines of the gospel."

Some have undertaken to trace the progress of concupiscence in the soul, showing its various stages. Perhaps something may be done that way; but there is an inscrutable mystery in iniquity. No man can understand his errors. Ps. xix. 12. The growth of iniquity is like the diffusion of leaven. It is very rapid, and soon changes the whole lump. The more full the consent of the soul to any sin, the more defiled it is. This command clearly settles the point that the seat of the divine government in man is the human heart. When that is right, all is right. When that is wrong, all is wrong. Let us look at this precept in regard to

### WEALTH.

The Scriptures say that "the ransom of a man's life are his riches;" that the "crown of the wise is their riches;" and that "house and riches are the inheritance of fathers." Prov. xiii. 8, xiv. 24, xix. 14. So that God's word admits the lawfulness of possessing riches, and of setting a right value upon them. Although man does not live by bread alone, but by every word that proceedeth out of the mouth of God: yet by worldly goods we ordinarily maintain our natural life, support our families, help the poor, and aid in strengthening the cause of Christ. If all men were perfectly holy, riches would, in every case and in every sense, be a blessing.

But sin perverts every thing. It takes that which was ordained to life, and causes it to be unto death. By reason of sin, riches are ordinarily tempting, seductive, dangerous and ruinous. Our Saviour announced this in strong language. "It is easier for a camel to go through the eye of a needle, than for a rich man to enter into the kingdom of God." Matt. xix. 24. A right view of the perils of wealth would, with the divine blessing, have a mighty efficacy in curing our covetousness and discontent, and in causing us to cease improperly to love what we have, or sinfully to desire that which belongs to others. Why should we enhance the obstacles to our reaching the kingdom of God?

1. He that increaseth riches, commonly increaseth cares. Should these cares become engrossing, salvation is not possible. If we would be saved, religion must command our attention, so as nothing else does. If our minds are eagerly turned to gold and silver, to farms and merchandize, to debts and demands, to gains and losses, religion can take but a slight hold of us, and yet its first call is, "*Give me thy heart.*" If we sit in the house of God with our minds reeking with worldly cares, the best preaching will probably make very slight impression on our minds. Or, if we should be somewhat affected, the service will hardly be over, till worldly thoughts and anxieties

rush in like an armed man, and carry us captive. "He that received seed among the thorns, is he that heareth the word: and the care of this world, and the deceitfulness of riches choke the word, and he becometh unfruitful." Matt. xiii. 22. This is a short but sad account of the whole matter. The hope of expelling cares by increasing wealth is as vain as the hope of banishing ravenous birds by multiplying the carcases on which they prey. He is not wise, "who imagines that the chief power of wealth is to *supply* wants. In ninety-nine cases out of a hundred, it *creates* more wants than it supplies." If even in public worship, we cannot "attend upon the Lord without distraction," how much more difficult it is to do so in private. And if the spirit of devotion is wholly wanting, our religion is vain. What a testimony was borne to the terrible power of worldly care by the late Mr. Stephen Girard, of Philadelphia. "As to myself, I live like a galley slave, constantly occupied, and often passing the night without sleeping. I am wrapped in a labyrinth of affairs, and worn out with care. I do not value fortune. The love of labour is my highest emotion. When I rise in the morning, my only effort is to labour so hard during the day, that when the night comes I may be able to sleep soundly." Is there not great danger that one thus pressed with care will neglect his soul? Jesus Christ answers that question.

2. But one may so arrange and invest his property that necessary attentions to it will not demand much of his time. Yet it is not found that this state of things generally exempts men from care. Their thoughts are as busy as ever. If their investments

are good, they wish they were better; or if they should be freed from care, then new dangers arise. The heart is led to idolize a state of secure and independent wealth; or idleness, luxury and practical atheism imperil salvation. When one says: Soul, thou hast much goods laid up for many years; take thine ease, eat, drink and be merry," Luke xii. 19, destruction is already at the door. No state of mind is more opposite to the spirit of the gospel than that of slothfulness, high living, banqueting, and carnal mirth. Ezek. xvi. 49. Wantonness and luxury, sloth and corruption usually go together. The great nourisher of these is wealth. Neale: "The million covet wealth, but how few dream of its perils! Few are aware of the extent to which it ministers to the baser passions of our nature: of the selfishness it engenders; the arrogance, which it feeds; the self-security which it inspires; the damage which it does to all the nobler feelings and holier aspirations of the heart."

3. Riches have also a mighty tendency to fill the heart with pride. Than this, nothing is more hostile to the soul's best interests. Dominant pride is the forerunner of destruction. So says the Psalmist: "Their inward thought is, that their houses shall continue for ever, and their dwelling-places to all generations; they call their lands after their own names," Ps. xlix. 11. When men set their nest on high and pride revels in the soul, ruin comes on apace. Above pride, nothing more effectively opposes the reception of the gospel. Often did the Saviour say, "Whosoever exalteth himself shall be abased, and he that humbleth himself shall be exalted." The gospel message is: "Let the rich man rejoice in that he is

made low," James i. 10. No man can go on a more unwelcome errand than to disrobe his neighbour of the distinction and pleasing unction of a full coffer, and to invite him to sit down in sackcloth and ashes with the beggar and the true penitent. In the heart, the levelling of Christianity spares nothing. It abases whatsoever exalts itself against God. Jehovah will stain the pride of all glory. They that boast themselves in their riches, and trust in the abundance of their possessions, shall fall; the mouth of the Lord hath spoken it, Ps. xlix. 6; lii. 7; Prov. xi. 28. Nothing is more opposed to God than pride. Nothing more hinders salvation. How needful the apostolic exhortation: "Charge them that are rich in this world, that they be not high-minded, nor trust in uncertain riches, but in the living God," 1 Tim. vi. 17. Cecil: "We hear much of a decent pride, a becoming pride, a noble pride, a laudable pride. Can that be decent of which we ought to be ashamed? Can that be becoming, of which God has set forth the deformity? Can that be noble which God resists and has determined to abase? Can that be laudable which God calls abominable?" "Pride goeth before destruction, and a haughty spirit before a fall."

4. It is very difficult to possess wealth without loving it and desiring more of it. And "if any man love the world, the love of the Father is not in him," 1 John ii. 15. Compare Luke xiv. 26. "Covetousness is idolatry." It disowns Jehovah. It sets up gold to be worshipped. It brings man, like the serpent, to lick the dust. It sadly perverts God's mercies as well as all our own thoughts. It makes men "believe in no God but mammon, no devil but the

absence of gold, no damnation but being poor, and no hell but an empty purse."* How few rich men can say with Calvin in his poverty: "I confess, indeed, that I am not poor; for I desire nothing more than what I have." How few are ready to say with a moralist, "To be truly rich is not to have much, but to desire little." He who loves riches can never say either of these things. Each acquisition naturally adds fuel to the flame. Fire can never be extinguished by pouring oil upon it. The more a worldling possesses, the more he desires. Although for fear of losing what he has, he may cease to make ventures, yet his covetousness may take the sullen form of grasping like death what he possesses. He seeks no more because he dreads failure. To be greedy of gain is still in his heart; but fear deters him from attempts to acquire more. He sits down wickedly to dote on what he has. If he thought he could succeed in increasing his wealth, he would still sell the righteous for silver and the poor for a pair of shoes; for he still pants after the dust of the earth on the head of the poor, and turns aside the way of the meek, and drinks the wine of the condemned, Amos ii. 6–8. Oh that men would believe their final Judge, when he says, "Ye cannot serve God and mammon," Matt. vi. 24. Oh that they would believe his servant Paul, when he says: "They that will be rich fall into temptation and a snare, and into many foolish and hurtful lusts, which drown men in destruction and perdition. For the love of money is the root of all evil; which while some coveted after they have erred from the faith and pierced themselves through with many sorrows," 1 Tim. vi. 9, 10.

* South.

5. All that has been said is on the supposition that wealth has been acquired in a righteous and honorable way. But is it not often otherwise? How many estates are built up by fraud, by extortion, by usury, by unjust gain, by monopoly, by unconscionable prices, by wild and dangerous speculations, by imposing on the ignorant, by the triumph of one race of sharpers over another, by false weights and measures, by lying, by unfaithfulness in contracts, by oppression, by gaming, by wicked law-suits, by inveigling the unwary into suretyships, by stinginess and meanness towards ourselves and our dependents, and in general by undue eagerness for wealth. The curse of God is this day resting on many an estate because it was acquired in some sinful manner. "An inheritance may be got hastily at the beginning; but the end thereof shall not be blessed," Prov. xx. 21. "He that hasteth to be rich hath an evil eye, and considereth not that poverty shall come upon him," Prov. xxviii. 22. Better be poor by birth, by misfortune, by the villany of others, than be rich by any species of iniquity. The more wealth unjustly held, the more is the soul in peril.

6. To all men, the call to self-denial and mortification of the flesh is unwelcome; but to the rich it is peculiarly distasteful. To them self-denial is as necessary as to the poor. Yet commonly it is far more difficult. It is true of every class that if they live after the flesh, they shall die. The poor man is seldom tempted to gluttony; yet this sin is very prevalent among the rich, and if allowed to reign, it will be as fatal as theft or murder, Phil. iii. 19. How many too, waste life in idle and fashionable ceremonies, in pay-

ing calls on those whose absence is refreshing, in seeing sights, in feasting the ears with instruments of music, and in cultivating the arts of effeminacy. It is a great mercy that when for his sins Jehovah drove man from Paradise, he did not sentence him to a life of such senseless occupations as some members of almost every rich family voluntarily subject themselves to,—thus running a round of vanity, refusing the laws of self-mortification, and jeoparding the interests of the immortal soul.

7. So generally do pious men regard the case of the rich as discouraging, that commonly but few and faint efforts are directly made for their salvation. The poor and the middle classes, unless very vicious, usually receive kindly a visit from a minister of the gospel, or from a Christian friend, even if he shall faithfully speak to them of their soul's affairs. But the rich often discourage all such calls to life and mercy. So that there is danger that they will lose their souls by the neglect of their plain and humble neighbours, who get the impression that the rich despise close, pungent, personal appeals to themselves. We are forbidden to cast pearls before swine. "He that reproveth a scorner getteth to himself shame." Perhaps very few men can bear the elevation acquired by wealth, without adopting the belief that their talents, wisdom and intellect are equal to their fortune. This is not true. Very feeble-minded men often grow rich. Yet such self-conceit excludes the spirit of docility. Such scorn to learn from a man who never made a dollar by sagacious foresight in temporal affairs. They expect to be courted. Like Naaman, they look for some great thing to be done

for them. Such cases are not rare, though gain is no more a sign of wisdom than it is of godliness.

8. Sometimes wealth is accompanied by long continued exemption from sad reverses. Thus practical atheism is engendered. "Because they have no changes, therefore they fear not God." Ps. lv. 19. "They cry to-morrow shall be as this day and more abundant," and so they plunge on in sin.

9. On the other hand, the fear of change for the worse often agitates some rich men, and when sad reverses overtake them, they become sullen and desperate, and behave badly. In some cases their reason is dethroned, or their tempers soured, or they resort to the bottle, or seek refuge in suicide. How often do riches take wings and fly away as an eagle toward heaven. The torment and restlessness of dreaded change wear many a life away. Oftener do we see great reverses leading to misanthropy or melancholy. Speak to such of their souls and of eternity, and you will find them intensely occupied with the folly or wickedness, which robbed them of their earthly possessions, or crippled them for life. Very seldom do they cease to long after that which they once enjoyed, but which is now gone for ever.

10. Another difficulty in the way of the salvation of the rich is the flattery which they receive from the foolish or the designing around them. "Men will praise thee when thou doest well to thyself." Ps. xlix. 18. Who has not seen unprincipled men rise to wealth, and yet ere long one and another would say, Really we never knew till of late how great their merits were? Hosts of mean sycophants and of vain fools gather around them and flatter them with their

lips. Where rich men are entitled to a good name for integrity, still another class of flatterers appear, and the peril is increased. Where men have no gracious principles, such adulation is very seductive. By degrees the flattered rise to giddy heights of self-esteem. Many are even flattered out of their souls.

11. Almost all rich men are induced at times to give something to the poor, or to works of benevolence. Or, they make a feast, and invite to it those whose presence will honour them, or whose means will enable them to return the compliment. All this they may be able to do without self-denial, and for the sake of a good name with their neighbours, or for even baser motives. But there is danger lest those who do these things may infer that they are in favour with God. They forget that their motives are not holy, and that at the last day Jesus will say, *What have ye done unto* ME?

12. The rich seem to be so happy in their possessions, that it is often impossible to make them feel their need of the solace of religion, the comfort of love, and the supports of the Holy Spirit. Were they sure that death, disease or poverty would never disturb them, they would rather be let alone, than take any pains about salvation. Yet until one feels his *need* of religion to the completion of his happiness, he will not seek the favour of God, with any considerable zeal or earnestness.

13. Perhaps even more than the poor, the rich feel that true religion would put a strong and unwelcome restraint on their passions and appetites. All the sins that kennel in the bosom of wealth must die, no less than the hungry pack found in the haunts of

poverty. The Sabbath must be sanctified, God's law must be kept, the code of Christian morals must be obeyed, the Christian graces must be cultivated. All this looks unlovely to any natural man. To the rich sinner it is peculiarly so. To lead a Christian life is to give up one's idols. Oh how hard it is for the rich man to yield so much, to renounce self-will and self-righteousness; and to sit down like a little child at the feet of Jesus, and practically learn the lessons of salvation.

14. The very fact that men have great possessions here creates a presumption that they have nothing better hereafter. Jesus said: "Woe unto you that are rich! for ye have received your consolation. Woe unto you that are full! for ye shall hunger. Woe unto you that laugh now! for ye shall mourn and weep." Luke vi. 24, 25. In like terms did Abraham address the rich man in hell: "Son, remember that thou in thy lifetime receivedst thy good things and likewise Lazarus evil things: but now he is comforted and thou art tormented." Luke xvi. 25. David also speaks of "men of the world, which have their portion in this life." Ps. xvii. 14. So that a man may receive all his good things here. The last mercy ever extended to him is in the hour of his death. It is amazing that men who have great earthly prosperity are not alarmed lest they should wake up in eternity without one blessing in reserve for that endless state.

15. These fears may well be strong if our prosperity is accompanied by a disposition to hoard wealth. "Go to now, ye rich men, weep and howl for your miseries that shall come upon you. Your riches are corrupted, and your garments are moth-eaten. Your

gold and silver is cankered, and the rust of them shall be a witness against you, and shall eat your flesh as it were fire. Ye have heaped treasure together for the last days." James v. 1–3. This is indeed an awful account of things. And every act of oppression, of pride, of hard-heartedness, of covetousness, of ostentation, of insolence, or of selfishness does but give signs that when the eyes shall close on time, the last blessing will have been drained from the cup held to our lips by a merciful God.

With Solomon some believe there is a time to gather, but alas! they do not hold with him that there is a time to scatter. If men have so little fidelity to their engagements as was exhibited by Laban towards Jacob in changing his wages ten times, Gen. xxxi. 41, they cannot expect the divine blessing.

"Verily I say unto you, that a rich man shall hardly enter into the kingdom of heaven." Matt. xix. 23.

While all that has been said is true, let us not forget that it is *possible* for a rich man to be saved. The Bible does not say, Not any rich are called; but, *Not many rich are called.* Abraham, Job, Solomon, Joseph of Arimathea were all rich men saved by grace. Such cases are amazing. They show how God can take the camel through the eye of a needle. And where the piety of the rich is unquestionable, their exhibition of the Christian character is often very attractive. The faith, and love, and meekness, and charity of a rich believer gladden and surprise us. When their "horn of plenty overflows, and its droppings fall upon their fellow-men; fall like the droppings of honey in the wilderness, to cheer the faint and weary pilgrim;" we are ready to wish the world was full of such men. When we see a rich man exercising the humility of a cottager, the self-denial of a peasant, the love and faith of a martyr, and the bountifulness of a prince, we know that he must have higher aims and purer motives than those who are not born from above.

But if the obstacles to a rich man's salvation are so many and so great, his earnestness and carefulness must correspond to the opposition he meets. If all men must watch, and pray, and labour, and fight, and run, and faint not; how much more must he, whose cares, and temptations, and enemies are so terrible. And if all men find it hard to keep their hearts right, how much more he, whose personal and social position is a perpetual snare to his soul.

And let not the rich be offended when God's ministers, according to his word, "charge them . . . that they do good, that they be rich in good works, ready to distribute, willing to communicate; laying up in store for themselves a good foundation for the time to come, that they may lay hold on eternal life." 1 Tim. vi. 17–19. How much good might be done; how many poor relieved; how many useful institutions aided; how many churches built up; how many Bibles and good books scattered; how many ignorant children educated; and how many widows made to sing for joy, if the wealth that is in the world were freely and judiciously used! What a light would then shine upon the path of many, who now almost "choose strangling rather than life!"

"We live in deeds, not years; in thoughts, not breaths;
In feelings, not in figures on a dial.
We should count time by heart-throbs. He most lives
Who thinks most, feels the noblest, acts the best."

"If riches increase, set not your heart upon them. Ps. lxii. 10. Remember "that riches profit not in the day of wrath," Prov. xi. 4. They never make it easier to die. Many things are to be preferred to wealth. A good conscience, an unsullied honour, the friendship of the virtuous around us are incomparably better. Prov. xxii. 1. "Riches are not for ever." Prov. xxvii. 24. Your wealth must soon leave you, or you must soon leave it. "You brought nothing into this world, and it is certain you can carry nothing out." 1 Tim. vi. 7. "He, that will not permit his wealth to do good to others while he is living, prevents it from doing any good to himself when he is dead."

If you were once rich and are become poor, be not cast down with overmuch sorrow. Sanctified reverses are better than unsanctified prosperity. Leighton: "Certainly it is true in matter of estate, as of our garments, not that which is largest, but that which fits us best, is best for us." Remember Job in the midst of his poverty. Rather remember Christ, who "though he was rich, yet for our sakes became poor, that we through his poverty might be made rich." And if you never were rich in earthly things, neither was your Saviour. "Having food and raiment, let us be therewith content." 1 Tim. vi. 8. Carefully guard against all wilfulness in your desires. Ps. lxxxvii. 29–31; 1 Tim. vi. 9. Let us cheerfully take up our cross and follow Christ. Matt. xvi. 24. Let us sweetly submit to the will of God in all things. 1 Sam. iii. 18; Phil. iv. 11, 12. Let us learn to bear the yoke whenever God shall lay it upon us. Lam. iii. 27–29. Let us dismiss all tormenting solicitude, putting our trust in the unerring wisdom and gracious providence of God. Hab. iii. 17, 18; Phil. iv. 6. Let us by experience prove how God's grace can abound towards us in the greatest straits, and let us glory in our infirmities. 2 Cor. xii. 9. Let us never question the right of God to do what he will with his own; much less set up our wisdom against his. Job xxxiv. 33; Matt. xx. 15. Let us remember that our sins deserve far worse than we have ever received. Neh. ix. 16, 17; Micah vii. 9. Nor will our sufferings be long. They will last but for a little moment and be gone for ever. 2 Cor. iv. 17. Let us only believe and they will do us good. Rom. viii. 28.

Those parents are not wise, who live, and risk their own souls to heap up riches for their children. A good name is the best inheritance we can leave to posterity. When to that we add a good example, a good education, good counsel, and good principles, there is but little more that is valuable in an inheritance. At all events, it is God's blessing that maketh our children rich and addeth no sorrow. Let us commit them to him in hearty prayer, and be not over-anxious respecting their temporal wants. "The Lord will provide." "I have been young, and now am old, yet have I not seen the righteous forsaken, nor his seed begging bread."

And let not the poor envy the rich. When all is told, the latter have not many advantages. In eating and sleeping, they are frequently worse off than the poor. "The sleep of a labouring man is sweet, whether he eat little or much; but the abundance of the rich will not suffer him to sleep." Eccles. v. 12.

The rich can live no longer, can die no more easily, can fill no larger space in the grave, than the poor. What profit then has he of all his wealth? He works hard for years to amass a fortune. He spends the residue of his life in watching that fortune for his victuals and clothes. "What good is there to the owners of riches saving the beholding of them with their eyes." Eccles. v. 11.

Let all men seek the true riches. "Sell that ye have, and give alms: provide for yourselves bags which wax not old, a treasure in the heavens that faileth not, where no thief approacheth, neither moth corrupteth. For where your treasure is, there will your heart be also." Luke xii. 33, 34. If God has denied you great things here, seek the more diligently for glory, honour, immortality, and eternal life. Poverty is no virtue. Your poverty will not save you; but it ought to remind you of your greater wants, and to make you the more earnest in seeking the unsearchable riches of Christ.

But let us not forget that we are never out of danger till we reach our heavenly home. The way to heaven is like the way that Jonathan and his armour-bearer ascended. There is a sharp rock on one side, and there is a sharp rock on the other side. Leighton: "We pervert all: when we look below us, it raises our pride; and when above us, it casts us into discontent. Might we not as well, contrariwise, draw humility out of the one, and contentment out of the other?" "Dearly beloved, I beseech you as strangers and pilgrims, abstain from fleshly lusts, which war against the soul." 1 Pet. ii. 11.

Good writers have stated that this commandment

requires full contentment with our condition, and that it forbids ambition, envy, the inordinate love of what we possess, greediness after more, repining at providences and grieving at our neighbours' good. All these things have been noticed in previous pages of this book.

The great requisition of this command is fervent love, charity out of a pure heart towards our neighbour. This excellent grace is so fully explained in the New Testament, and especially by Paul in the 13th chapter of 1 Corinthians, and we have so many good popular treatises upon it, that the reader's time and attention will not be asked any longer to this subject.

## CHAPTER XXV.

### HOW MAY WE KNOW OUR SINS?

ONE of the most difficult attainments is such a knowledge of our own defects, errors and sins as shall lead us to right apprehensions of Christ and his salvation. Self-delusion is natural to man. He is wedded to self-righteousness. He naturally denies the charge of guilt. Like the Jews of old, men cry out, "What have we spoken and done so much against thee?" Even those who are somewhat enlightened from above, when they fall into error, are ready to say, "We are rich and increased in goods and have need of nothing," while they are poor, and miserable, and blind and naked. This self-justifying spirit keeps men from a knowledge of sin and from accepting Christ. It destroys tens of thousands. Those who indulge it reject mercy because they do not feel any need of mercy. Benjamin and all his brethren declared that none of them had the silver cup. They thought they were telling the truth. But they had not looked to see whether they had it or not. When they searched, they found it right in the mouth of Benjamin's sack. So if men would honestly search their lives and hearts by the light of the law, they would find out that they were undone. "By the law is the knowledge of sin."

Take these rules for knowing your own hearts. 1. Diligently compare them with the law of God. Study the letter of the law. Acquire a knowledge of its true spirit and scope. Let it be your daily business to go through the dark chambers of the soul with these ten lighted candles and see what is wrong.

2. Consider what your friends say of you. It is a pity that some convert a friend into a foe if he suggests that they are in error. Such must be let alone. They will probably work out their own destruction with greediness. When one is disposed to seek the truth, however, he may get useful hints and suggestions from pious and judicious friends. Ps. cxli. 5. And as friends are prejudiced in our favour, we may give full credit to what they say, unless we have positive proof that they are mistaken. David was bound to receive Nathan's reproof. Peter would have acted foolishly, if he had flared up against Paul for reproving him.

3. Weigh well what those say who are unfriendly to you. "It is lawful to learn from an enemy." Bitter enemies sometimes fabricate statements and frequently exaggerate and misrepresent. Sometimes they nearly hit the nail on the head, and sometimes they tell the plain truth, which others are afraid to speak. A shrewd enemy commonly attacks the weak points of character. What do your enemies say of you? Do they charge you with pride, or malignity, or covetousness, or vanity, or ingratitude, or hardness of heart? Improve what they say.

4. Observe what that is which always comes to your mind when inclined to pensiveness or melancholy. Some indeed are so beset with a sense of guilt that

they dare not reflect. They fly from scene to scene and from place to place. They avoid solitude, and seek merriment that their own thoughts may not disturb their peace. But even in the midst of laughter, their heart is sad.. If they would sit alone, and keep silence, and not call off their minds from sober reflection, they would soon get a profitable insight into their defects.

5. Notice your thoughts when you are sick or in peril of death. At such times the mind sometimes gets a ready insight into personal faults. Men generally are more disposed to be honest when they feel that their life is in danger. How did you regard your moral character when you were sick? Did no ghost of sin present itself to your view? Probably your alarm was well founded.

6. When you are in distress and inclined to think your affliction a judgment or a punishment for some sin, you may be pretty sure that there is guilt in that affair. When the web of distress had perfectly entangled the sons of Jacob, and one calamity but opened the door for another, they well said, "We are verily guilty concerning our brother, in that we saw the anguish of his soul, when he besought us, and we would not hear; therefore is this distress come upon us." And afterwards when in still greater distress, Judah as a mouth for the rest, said, "How shall we clear ourselves! God hath found out the iniquity of thy servants." Gen. xlii. 21, xliv. 16. So if you suspect that any distress is come on you for any particular sin, you may be quite sure that guilt attaches to you in that transaction.

7. When you suppose a preacher is personal, it is

pretty good evidence that you are guilty. No right-minded man under the influence of Christian feelings will hold up personal character to the scorn of an audience. Therefore if any thing seems especially to suit you, do not be offended; do not refuse to listen to the voice of warning. The fact that it suits you is reason enough for letting it come with all its force and edge.

8. When you are afraid that others suspect you of a sin, though they have said nothing, it is pretty good evidence that you are guilty. In their conversation some men are always fending and defending themselves. They feel that their conduct is liable to serious reprehension, and the chief aim of their lives is to keep others from finding them out. Why is this, if they are innocent?

9. When you do not like to hear a particular sin preached against, you may suspect that you are guilty of it. If it were chargeable only to others, you would probably not care how much it was reproved. The wicked themselves seldom object to rebukes administered to their neighbours.

10. When in conversation, a sin is spoken of and you would gladly change the subject, you are probably guilty on that point. When Paul reasoned of temperance, righteousness and judgment to come, Felix told him that he would hear him at another time. When Christ charged the woman of Samaria with wickedness in her marital relations, she immediately called his attention to an old controversy between the Jews and Samaritans.

11. When a sin is mentioned in general terms of disapprobation, and you begin to excuse it, or try to

make it appear small, then probably you are guilty in that matter.

12. So when in pleading exemption from any fault, you lose your temper and fall into passion, you are hardly innocent. Thus Hazael seems to have been quite vexed with the prophet. He said, "Is thy servant a dog, that he should do this great wickedness?" Yet as soon as he had the opportunity, he did it all. He knew not the depths of iniquity in his own heart.

13. When one is so sure of his innocence that he will not examine his own heart, he may be sure there is sin there. He is afraid to look, lest he should see frightful sights in his own bosom. His persuasions of innocence are not well founded, and he suspects as much.

14. We are guilty of a sin, when the prevailing tendency of our mind is towards that conclusion. Suspicion of guilt ought to awaken and alarm us, 1 John iii. 21.

15. We are chargeable with all the sins which the Bible imputes to the same class, to which we belong. If we are unconverted, then all that God's word alleges against such lies against us—as unbelief, impenitence, forgetfulness of God, enmity against the Most High, blindness of mind, ingratitude, destitution of holiness, &c.

Any right view of our case will make us see that we are undone. One who had studied the law with some care might use this soliloquy:

I am sick. O, I am very sick. I am sick at my very heart. I know I am sick. God's word says so. My own feelings declare as much. I have pain, and fever, and delirium, and restlessness, just like a madman. I am wretched. There is no soundness in me. There is a rottenness in my bones. Without relief I must die. Cannot I be saved? Must I linger on a while and then perish? Blessed be God, I need not die. There is a Physician. His name is Jesus Christ. He is able. He is willing. He is full of grace and truth. He is just such a friend as I need. Let us see.

He is very skilful. He never mistakes symptoms. He knows the malignancy of diseases. Flattering appearances never deceive him. He knows the difference between depression of spirits and a penitent heart; between natural frankness and godly sincerity; between the humility of Ahab and that of Paul; between the repentance of Judas and that of Peter. His skill is divine, because He is divine. He knows my case perfectly, because he knows all things perfectly. My case is not hidden from him in any particular.

He knows the remedies I need. He knows I cannot be sound without his blood and righteousness, his word and Spirit, his grace and power. If He will but undertake my case, I am sure it will be treated aright. I shall never perish, if I make Him my Physician.

He has been chosen of God; appointed and ordained to this very work. Whatever He has done has been by the choice and commandment of his Father. He was approved of God in all he did and in all he suffered. He had greater witness than that of John, for there came a voice from the excellent glory, saying: "This is my beloved Son; hear ye Him;" and the works which the Father gave Him to finish, the same did bear witness of Him. He was no impostor, or vain pretender. The seal of God was on His commission.

The great Physician is also very tender and loving. He was once hit by the archers himself. One object of his incarnation was that he might be a merciful and kind Saviour, and sympathize with us in all things. He was tempted as we are. He is the most gentle and most approachable being that ever walked this earth. He was often reviled, but he never resented it. He suffered, but he never threatened. He was mocked, but he never showed bitterness.

The great Physician cured the first case He ever undertook, and He has had great experience since. He has cured millions. The realms of glory are filled with the wonders of mercy which He has wrought. He never wounds where cordials are called for. He never heals slightly the hurt of his people. He probes deeply every imposthume. He loves his people too well to let them die rather than cut off the gangrene. He gives wine and oil to the faint and wounded. He gives no peace to those who add drunkenness to thirst.

To the truly penitent and godly Jesus is very tender and gracious. He never breaks the bruised reed, nor will he quench the smoking flax. He also goes where He is most needed and sought unto. Our poverty is nothing, for He does all without money and without price. Our wretchedness is nothing, for the first word of his ministry was, *Blessed.* Our unworthiness is nothing, for His merits are infinite. Our necessities may be great, but His riches are unsearchable. O wondrous Physician! To thee I submit my case, my whole case. I know nothing. I reserve nothing. I deserve nothing. I am nothing but a poor lost sinner. Unless Thou undertake, I shall be for ever undone. Saviour, be patient with me. Spare me. Heal my diseases. Then will I give thee glory for ever, and spread thy fame through heaven and earth.

# CHAPTER XXVI.

## CHRISTIAN LIBERTY.

FEW things are more commended or less understood than Christian liberty. Most men praise it; not many maintain it. The vile Antinomian boasts of it, and casts off the cords of the moral law. The bigot praises it, and counts you a fool because you do not adopt his whims. The superstitious lauds it, and makes himself a slave of some imposture. The openly profane struts, and swaggers, and is the servant of corruption.

What then is Christian liberty? The comfort and usefulness of many are destroyed by not understanding this matter.

1. The first element of Christian liberty is freedom from the ceremonial law of Moses. At this time the Christian world is undivided respecting this matter. This was not always so. The apostles had much trouble, and even Peter was involved in dissimulation on the subject.

2. Believers are free from the moral law as a covenant of works. "Ye are not under the law, but under grace," Rom. vi. 14. "Ye are become dead to the law by the body of Christ," Rom. vii. 4.

3. God's people are free from the penalty of the

moral law which we have all broken. "Christ hath redeemed us from the curse of the law, being made a curse for us," Gal. iii. 13. The Judge himself, by his own most precious blood, has opened the prison doors, and said to the prisoners, Go free.

4. Christ sets his people free from the torments of a guilty conscience. They are not crushed with a sense of terrible condemnation. He, who has a fearful looking for of judgment and fiery indignation, is indeed in a sad plight. He has a hell upon earth. But the blood of Jesus Christ speaks as perfect peace to the conscience as it does at the throne of God.

5. Christ sets his people free from the reigning power of sin. The unconverted are the slaves of lust, of pride, of malice and of all iniquity. They are led captive by the devil at his will. But to his people, Christ makes good the promise, "Sin shall not have dominion over you." He preaches deliverance to the captives and sets at liberty them that are bruised, Luke iv. 18.

6. Christ frees his people from the evil of afflictions, though not from afflictions themselves.

7. Jesus Christ also delivers his people, who, through the fear of death, were all their lifetime subject to bondage—a dreadful bondage indeed.

Such are the chief elements of Christian liberty taken in the broadest sense. But

8. The liberty of Christians, while it makes them Christ's freemen, and binds them in chains of love to his service, DELIVERS THEM FROM THE ORDINANCES AND COMMANDMENTS OF MEN IN ALL MATTERS OF FAITH, WORSHIP AND MORALS. This is the sense in which the term *Christian liberty* is now most commonly used.

If God has made no law in these matters, we can do as we please. If he is silent, man's word is of no force.

That God has set his people free from the commandments of men in matters of faith is very evident. Jesus Christ alike forbade his servants to be called Master, or to call others Master. He expressly said that even the apostles should not be lords over his heritage. The apostles disclaimed all dominion over the faith of Christians. Churches have no power to alter, amend, enlarge, or diminish the creed given us in Scripture.

Nor can any church give Scriptural authority for claiming the right of ordaining ceremonies, and imposing forms upon the consciences of people; so that non-conformity shall be esteemed schism. If some such things were commended as decent or expedient, they might be comparatively harmless; but when they are exacted, they are worse than *tolerable fooleries;* they are engines of wickedness and cruelty.

The same is true of morals. That, which is not made sin by God's word, can never become so by the legislation of men. That, which is not in Scripture prescribed as a part of duty, can never become such by the canons of church authorities. Sin is a violation of the law of God, or a want of conformity to a divine precept. Nothing else is sin. Men have often forbidden what the decalogue required, and as often required what it forbade.

The rules to be observed respecting all attempts to bind us in faith, worship or morals, by the commandments of men are such as these:

1. Never yield your liberty wherewith Christ hath

made you free. Whether the laws of men shall be permitted to set aside divine statutes ought never to be a question among men. To oblige another, Paul would yield up all but his honour and his conscience; but when there is an attempt to invade his rights under form of law, he exclaims, "I am a Roman citizen;" and when they put his life in jeopardy, he exclaims, "I appeal to Cæsar." Rather than offend prejudices or hinder the gospel, he circumcised Timothy because of the Jews, which were in those quarters. Acts xvi. 3. This he did uncommanded. But when an attempt was made to enforce circumcision, he "gave place by subjection, no, not for an hour; that the truth of the gospel might continue with" the churches. Gal. ii. 5. Wherever there is a clear attempt at domination, the rule of reason, of public spirit, and of Christian duty is one—*Obsta principiis*. Never yield an inch. Paul did not. Modern times afford no brighter example of magnanimity and resistance to lawless power than that of John Hampden. Of him Richard Baxter said, he "was one that friends and enemies acknowledged to be most eminent for prudence, piety, and peaceable counsels, having the most universal praise of any gentleman that I remember of that age." Contrary to the constitution of England, Charles I. demanded an illegal tax of his subjects. The share of the general assessment demanded of Hampden on account of some of his estates in Buckinghamshire was but twenty shillings. But "the payment of half twenty shillings, on the principle it was demanded, would have made Hampden a slave," said Burke. So felt that immortal man, and from the first he resisted. For so doing he has ever since had the gratitude and admiration of all Christian freemen. None but God knows how much the civil and religious liberties of mankind owe to that one assertion of right. For although a majority of the judges was against him, yet the moral effect was on the right side. Life is not desirable, when civil and religious despotism have the sway. To yield a point enforced by no command of God is to admit that there is more than one lawgiver. And to yield to civil wrongs, when the laws protect us, is to admit that the will of one man is above a free constitution.

2. We must never hypocritically plead our consciences, when in fact we are governed only by prejudice or passion. It is a great weakness, and a wickedness to raise doubts where duty is clear, or to wish a purpose defeated by a false plea. Let men never plead conscience where conscience is not involved.

3. Let no man use his liberty for a cloak of maliciousness. 1 Pet. ii. 16. Even if we are in fact right, and our brethren through weakness are in error, we may not be reckless of their spiritual interests. We must love them tenderly and seek their good.

4. Beware of lightly esteeming one, who through weakness does not use his liberty as he might. Paul gives the whole law on this subject in Rom. xiv. 1–4.

5. When a thing is lawful, or when it is not forbidden, and the only question relates to the expediency of a given course, the whole decision must be made by every man for himself. This is clearly taught by Paul in Rom. xiv. 10, 12. "Why dost

thou judge thy brother? or why dost thou set at nought thy brother? for we shall all stand before the judgment-seat of Christ. . . . So then every one of us shall give account of himself to God." The spiritual despotism of modern times shows itself in nothing more than in judging others, where God has left them free.

This whole subject came up repeatedly in the early history of Christianity, and Paul then clearly marked the distinction between the lawful and the expedient. "All things are lawful unto me, but all things are not expedient: all things are lawful for me, but I will not be brought under the power of any." "All things are lawful for me, but all things are not expedient: all things are lawful for me, but all things edify not." 1 Cor. vi. 12, x. 23. This distinction should be preserved. Considerable difficulty arose respecting things offered to idols. Beasts were slain, and their blood and fat used in idolatrous worship; but the meat was sold in the market. Libations of wine were also offered in heathen temples, and the priests sent to the wine-merchant what they did not wish for their own use. Some contended that it was in itself lawful to buy and eat any meat sold in the shambles, and to buy and drink any wine offered for sale. Of this class were Paul and other strong established Christians. But there were weak brethren who doubted the lawfulness of so doing. These were tempted to judge their stronger brethren, and their stronger brethren were tempted to despise them. Paul would not have the strong believe that to be wicked which was innocent. He would not have the strong to become weak. But he would not have the weak defile their consciences by doing anything, the lawfulness of which they doubted. This would be wicked. "To him that esteemeth any thing unclean, to him it is unclean." "Whatsoever is not of faith is sin." On the other hand, he would not encourage any to do that which would harden others in sin. "All things indeed are pure: but it is evil for that man who eateth with offence. It is good neither to eat flesh, nor to drink wine, nor anything whereby thy brother stumbleth, or is offended, or is made weak." Rom. xiv. 20, 21. A similar difficulty arose respecting days. One man esteemed one day above another; another esteemed every day alike. Rom. xiv. 5. Some wholly rejected the Jewish holy-days, while others as yet held on to them. It was not wicked to observe them, if it was done *to the Lord.* The question whether it was expedient to observe them was left to each man to decide for himself.

It is here noticeable that Paul directs us never to violate our consciences. If a man thinks an act wrong, nothing is more clear than that it is sinful for him to do it. To do what we are doubtful about is always sinful. But it is not always right to do what we think is right. Whatsoever is not of faith, is sin, but it doth not follow that whatsoever is of faith is holy. For Saul of Tarsus verily thought he ought to do many things contrary to the name of Jesus of Nazareth.

While, therefore, a weak brother has no right to require us to adopt his notions, our love to him and to Christ should make us tender of his feelings, careful not to tempt him to violate his conscience, and anxious to edify him. Thus an effectual stop is put to any attempt of minority or majority, weak or strong, to afflict their brethren, wound their feelings, or defile their consciences. Terms of communion in the church of God are never to be made more or less close than Christ has made them.

# CHAPTER XXVII.

## CONSCIENCE.

IN morals and religion, conscience holds a prominent place. Nice and curious questions on this subject are unprofitable. The practical views of the matter are far the most important.

The word *conscience* means joint or double knowledge. There is a knowledge of the law, which binds us, and a knowledge of the fact, that we have kept or broken the law. For present purposes it is sufficient to say that conscience is the judgment of a man concerning the moral character of his thoughts, words and deeds. Because its decisions are accompanied by peculiar sensations of approbation or remorse, it is often called the *moral sense.* It is the office of conscience to judge and decide on the morality of all our acts. Conscience is the soul of man sitting in judgment upon his moral conduct, condemning or justifying as the case may be. The decisions of conscience are never theoretical but always practical. It accuses, it excuses; it afflicts, it consoles; it terrifies, it gives joy. Nothing produces such consternation, nothing imparts such boldness.

As conscience determines the right or wrong of acts before they are committed, we speak of it as a light or a law. As it respects guilt or innocence in a given matter, we speak of it as a judge pronouncing, or a witness testifying. Its process is simple. It says: "The soul that sinneth it shall die." That is the law. "I have sinned." That is the fact. "I am therefore exposed to death." Or, "Thou shalt not covet any thing that is thy neighbour's." "I have coveted my neighbour's prosperity." Therefore I have broken the tenth commandment.

The rule by which the conscience is to be governed is the whole will of God, however made known. The heathen learn God's will by the law of nature. *Every man* knows that murder, theft and ingratitude are wicked. But in the Bible we have the whole will of God revealed for our guidance. There all is clear and plain. This binds the conscience. It obliges every one to obey its teachings. God alone is Lord of the conscience. He alone can bind it. Blindly to follow the teachings of any creature is an act of wickedness. It is giving to a worm a prerogative of God. To assert a right to control the conscience of another, except by reason and Scripture, is an atrocious offence. It is the foundation of all diabolical persecutions. In a sense conscience impels us to duty, that is, it is accompanied by a strong sense of moral obligation. Thus Paul says, "Woe is me if I preach not the gospel;" the meaning is, that he had so strong, so controlling a sense of duty that he knew he would be guilty if he kept silence. Conscience is a safe guide so far as it is informed of the will of God, and is not perverted by sin, error or ignorance.

Whatever falls short of supreme love to God, or equal love to our neighbour as to ourselves, whatever violates the letter or spirit of the commandments, burdens an enlightened conscience. Simple questions of morality are easily solved. It is on complex matters that we are most liable to err. We should therefore study with docility the whole word of God, and impartially scrutinize our own acts, ends and motives. The extreme evil of an erring conscience is, that it always involves us in guilt. If we follow it, we sin, as did Saul of Tarsus in persecuting the church. If we violate it, we are guilty of doing what we believe to be wrong. An erring conscience is almost invariably the result of a gross want of the love of truth. If your conscience is not clear, stand still. "Happy is he that condemneth not himself in that thing which he alloweth." The great duty of those having erring consciences is to seek for light.

A doubting conscience is one that is not clear respecting duty. Here too we must stand still, till we are resolved. It may be one's duty to preach the gospel, but not while he prevailingly doubts his call to the sacred office. "He that doubteth is damned (guilty) if he eat." But let not one with a doubting conscience be idle. Let him diligently seek to know the will of God in every matter of duty. A doubting conscience not enlightened and not resolved is very apt to end in

A scrupulous conscience. The habit of doubting in questions of morality grows by indulgence. Scrupulousness is evinced by doubts in clear cases, by a morbid fearfulness of doing wrong, and so life is wasted in considering vexed and vexatious questions. A scrupulous conscience is like a diseased eye, which weeps if air, or water, or light reaches it. It is very favourable to the temptations of the devil. Hearty prayer, an honest search after truth, holding fast great principles, and an earnest performance of all known duties are the chief remedies for a scrupulous conscience. It has been found very useful also to abound in acts of kindness to the poor and afflicted. Such a conscience is well called "weak," and it will probably be best strengthened by vigorous exercise in what it admits to be plain duty.

A conscience is said to be evil when it is guided by wrong principles, when it decides contrary to known truth, or when it is burdened with a load of guilt. Thus the consciences of all unregenerate men are greatly defiled. They do not give ready and hearty assent to the duty of loving God supremely, and their neighbour as themselves. They see not the iniquity or the danger of rejecting the Lord Jesus Christ, which is the greatest sin of the impenitent in Christian lands. Such have, indeed, misgivings, qualms, or even terrors, but these lead to no thorough amendment. Some consciences seem wholly blind. They call good evil and evil good. This darkness is followed by stupidity. If such hold the truth, it is in unrighteousness. Even the most pungent words of God do not properly move their affections. Their lives are unrestrained by the most sacred laws of Heaven. Their minds are inflated with delusive opinions of their own worth. If they have zeal in religion, it is not according to knowledge, or wisdom or meekness. Sometimes such a conscience whispers, all is not right; and sometimes it thunders. When a great calamity is feared or felt, when some truth is brought home with power, when death seems to be near, the anguish of such a conscience is often dreadful. The terrors of God then become consuming.

The most usual manifestations of an evil conscience among reputable people in Christian communities are obtuseness and dulness. Convince some men that a course is wholly agreeable to the will of God, and you have in effect done nothing towards their right behaviour. They may go as far as Agrippa, and say, "Almost thou persuadest me to be a Christian," or, like Saul, they may lift up the voice and weep and make some confession of sin, and then go and be as carnal, as sensual, as unbelieving, as abominable, yea, as devilish as ever. Their case is described by the prophet: "Moab hath been at ease from his youth, and he hath settled on his lees, and hath not been emptied from vessel to vessel, neither hath he gone into captivity; therefore his taste remained in him, and his scent is not changed." Jer. xlviii. 11. Carnal security is the ruin of most men, who lose their souls under the preaching of the gospel. The great source of such stupor is practical infidelity and the habit of sinning, which takes away a sense of guilt. Of all habits, that of sinning is the hardest to conquer. It is the only habit that hardens the heart.

A seared conscience is one that can be moved by nothing, not even by the most atrocious sins. It is commonly found in those, who have been much enlightened but have resisted the calls of mercy, and given themselves over to a wicked life. "What they know naturally, as brute beasts, in those things they corrupt themselves." He, whose conscience is seared, gives these signs of his sad state: he rejoices in iniquity; he has pleasure in others, who openly practise wickedness; he obstinately perseveres in doing evil, whatever may be God's dealings with him; and he gives himself up to what he knows to be sins.

An evil conscience, a conscience defiled, polluted, or seared, is the great source of heresy. As every man has a standard, he must either bring his life up to his standard, or bring his standard down to his life. The latter is much the more easy, and is therefore commonly done. Of such Paul says, that having put away a good conscience, concerning faith they have made shipwreck. Their lives being wrong, their creed soon becomes erroneous.

Henry Smith, a good writer who lived about the middle of the seventeenth century says, "There is a warning conscience, and a gnawing conscience. The warning conscience cometh before sin, and the gnawing conscience followeth after sin. The warning conscience is often lulled asleep; but the gnawing conscience wakeneth her again. If there be any hell in this world, they, who feel the worm of conscience gnaw upon their hearts, may truly say that they have felt the torments of hell. Who can express that man's anguish but himself? Nay, what horrors are there which he cannot but express himself? Sorrows are met in his soul as at a feast; and fear, thought, and anguish divide his soul between them. All the furies of hell leap upon his heart as on a stage. Thought calleth to fear; fear whistleth to horror; horror beckoneth to despair, and saith, 'Come and help me to torment this sinner.' One saith she cometh from this sin; and another saith that she cometh from that sin; and so he goeth through a thousand deaths, and yet he cannot die. Irons are laid upon his body like a prisoner. All his lights are put out at once. He hath no soul fit to be comforted. Thus he lies, as it were, upon the rack, and saith that he bears the world upon his shoulders, and that no man suffereth that which he suffereth. So let him lie, saith God, without ease, until he confess and repent, and call for mercy."

All this is the more striking when compared with

A good conscience. The properties of a good conscience are

1. It is enlightened. It knows the will of God, the entrance of whose word giveth light. A good conscience delights in knowing the whole mind of God. It hates darkness. It rejoices in the truth. It cometh to the light that its deeds may be reproved. It approves what God approves. It condemns what God condemns. It judges true judgment. It holds fast correct principles. It hates every lie.

2. It is firm and decided. It does not waver like a wave of the sea. It has stability in knowledge and principle. To it truth is not a *notion*, but a *law*. It is grounded and settled in the revealed will of God. He, who has it, is fully persuaded in his own mind. He will probably yield many of his own rights to serve and please others; but he will not yield a single claim of God. In his own cause he may show all amiable compliance. In his Master's cause, he dare not surrender any thing.

3. So far as any conscience is good, it is also tender. He who possesses it is ashamed to think before God what he would be ashamed to speak before men; and to meditate before God, what he would be afraid to do before the world. Sibbes: "All scanda-

lous breakings out are but thoughts at the first. Ill thoughts are as little thieves, which, creeping in at the window, open the door to greater; thoughts are seeds of actions." Thus the true Christian judges. No man ever had a good conscience, who did not hate vain thoughts, idle words, and little sins; for to a good man no sin is absolutely little.

A tender conscience is distinguished from a scrupulous conscience in this; that the former makes no difficulties where God makes none; whereas the latter perplexes itself with needless refinements and endless questions. An eye may be tender and delicate, may be stimulated by the least light, may perceive the nicest shades and faintest lines in a picture. This is a good eye. But to have an eye that is pained at the least light, or confused with much light so as not distinctly to see anything, is to have the visual organ in an unhealthy state. A good conscience is not a dull and stupid thing, but it is wakeful and lively. It has a ready perception, is of quick understanding, and the more plainly it sees the path of duty, the better it is pleased.

4. A good conscience is guileless and simple. It seeks not pretences, excuses and subterfuges. It abhors cunning, craftiness and delusive refinements. It delights in "simplicity and godly sincerity." It is not governed by "fleshly wisdom." It is fair, candid and truthful. To it subtilty and artifice are revolting. Wherever such a conscience is found, it is proof of a great change of character, for by nature the heart is deceitful above all things and desperately wicked. There never was sin without guile. The greater the sin, the more the deceit.

5. A good conscience is accompanied by the spirit of obedience. "We trust we have a good conscience, in all things willing to live honestly." Heb. xiii. 18. Where there are not right dispositions, honest intentions to do the will of God, there cannot be a good conscience. Wrong affections will soon disorder any conscience; and how can any conscience be good, if it has not power to direct the life and control the heart?

6. No conscience is good till it is sprinkled with the blood of Christ. It draws its sweetness from the cross of the Redeemer. A great defect of the law of sacrifices among the Jews was that it "could not make him that did the service perfect, as pertaining to the conscience." But "the blood of Christ, who through the eternal Spirit offered himself without spot to God, purges our consciences from dead works to serve the living God." "Those, who are thus purified from guilt, have no more conscience of sin." They therefore "draw near with a true heart, having their hearts sprinkled from an evil conscience, and their bodies washed with pure water." The most enlightened and burdened conscience demands no other atonement, no more perfect sacrifice than that of Christ. Its sufficiency is as completely satisfactory to him, who fully believes, as it is to God, whose law was broken. Nor can any man, with an enlightened mind, find ease for a troubled conscience any where else than in precious atoning blood.

7. God's Spirit is also poured upon all who believe, and their consciences are good in a very high sense. Speaking of the Gentiles, Peter said: "God, which knoweth the hearts, bare them witness, giving them the Holy Ghost, even as he did unto us." Acts xv.

8. To the Ephesians, Paul says: "After that ye believed, ye were sealed with that Holy Spirit of promise, which is the earnest of our inheritance until the redemption of the purchased possession, unto the praise of his glory." Eph. i. 13, 14.

In accordance with these views, Leighton says, "That conscience alone is good which is much busied in self-examination, which speaks much with itself, and much with God. This is both the sign that it is good, and the means to make it better. That soul will doubtless be very wary in its walk, which takes daily account of itself, and renders up that account unto God. It will not live by guess, but naturally examine each step beforehand, because it is resolved to examine all after; will consider well what it should do, because it means to ask over again what it hath done, and not only to answer itself, but to make a faithful report of all unto God; to lay all before him continually, upon trial made; to tell him what is in any measure well done, as his own work, and bless him for that; and tell him, too, all the slips and miscarriages of the day, as our own; complaining of ourselves in his presence, and still entreating free pardon, and more wisdom to walk more holily and exactly, and gaining, even by our failings, more humility and more watchfulness. If you would have your consciences answer well, they must inquire and question much beforehand. Whether is this I purpose and go about, agreeable to my Lord's will? Will it please him? Ask that more, and regard that more, than this, which the most follow. Will it please or profit myself? Fits that my own humour? And examine not only the bulk and substance of thy ways and actions, but the manner of them, how thy heart is set. So, think it not enough to go to church, or to pray, but take heed how ye hear; for, consider how pure He is, and how piercing his eye, whom thou servest."

He who is thus has a good conscience, and in it a source of unfailing gladness. "This is our rejoicing, the testimony of our conscience, that in simplicity and godly sincerity, not with fleshly wisdom, but by the grace of God, we have had our conversation in the world." This kind of a merry heart doeth good like a medicine. It is a continual feast. He who has it has so far terminated the fearful war within his own heart, that he has crucified his evil passions, has enthroned his conscience in his own bosom, and breathes benevolence towards men, and piety towards God. He rejoices in the mighty work of grace begun in him. He no longer shudders at a sight of himself. His designs are approved by the vicegerent of God in his soul. Harmony reigns in his bosom. He esteems God his Father. He no longer trembles at the thought of meeting his Maker. "*Quid in vita esset expers metus? Bias respondit, Bona conscientia. Et Socrates, quærenti quinam sine perturbatione viverent, regessit, Qui nullius peccati sibi conscii sunt.* "The righteous are as bold as a lion." There is no shield to repel sharp arrows like that of a good conscience.

Hic murus aheneus esto, nil conscire sibi. HOR.

Such a good conscience will be a passport and a stay in the severest trials. It will disarm death of its sting. It will give boldness in the day of judgment. All the wealth, honours and pleasures of earth are not to be compared to it. A man may be full of them, and yet full of misery. The more he has of them, the less of a man may he be. But with a good conscience a man is a man, yea, he is a great man under all the accumulated ills of life. Nothing can infect him with puerility or pusillanimity.

But how different it is with the wicked. They "flee when no man pursueth." "They come out against the righteous one way, and flee before them seven ways." "The wicked man travaileth with pain all his days. . . . A dreadful sound is in his ears. . . . He believeth not that he shall return out of darkness."

"*Degeneres animos timor arguit*"—VIRGIL.

So dreadful are the torments of an evil conscience that in many periods of human history, men, who knew not the evil of sin, have held that it was adequately punished in this life. The fears of the wicked, especially at times when it is peculiarly desirable to be unshaken, are oftentimes overwhelming.

"Conscience makes cowards of us all."

A heathen left this petition inscribed on a pillar in the temple of his god: "Save me from my enemies." One coming after him wrote: "Save me from my friends." It seems to have occurred to no one to write: "Save me from myself." Yet unless a man heartily offers such a prayer, and is rescued from his passions, his prejudices, his sinful desires, and the lashings of his guilty conscience, he is eternally undone. "There is no peace, saith my God, to the wicked." This is true in time. It is more fearfully true in eternity.

## DIRECTIONS FOR KEEPING A GOOD CONSCIENCE.

1. Put a high value upon such a blessing. Never be satisfied without it. It is worth more than all the kingdoms of the world and the glory of them.

2. Labour diligently to secure it. It comes not to the careless and indolent. Paul says: "Herein do I exercise myself, to have always a conscience void of offence toward God and toward men."

3. Especially maintain in your heart a strong and constant sense of the goodness, authority, majesty, and holiness of God. "Be thou in the fear of the LORD all the day long." "The fear of the LORD is a fountain of life to depart from the snares of death." "They, that fear God least, have reason to fear him most."

4. Meditate on God's law day and night. Study both tables with care and diligence. Let it dwell in you richly.

5. Set the Lord always before you. If you can honour and please him, that is enough.

6. As far as possible avoid confusion of mind respecting duty. Gurnall: "There are three kinds of straits, wherein Satan loves to entrap the believer; nice questions, obscure Scriptures and dark providences."

7. Beware of all tortuous ways of proceeding. When you find your course demanding cunning, be alarmed. Be honest and frank with yourself, with your neighbour, and with God.

8. Beware of the least sins. They are the little foxes that spoil the tender grapes. Avoid every form of evil.

9. Guard with all possible care against secret sins. You have no worse enemies.

10. Watch against the sins of the times. If there is great heat in the public temper, be doubly careful to keep cool. If all around you are eager or violent, let your moderation appear.

11. Ever watch against easily besetting sins, those to which your constitution, education, habits, or calling incline you. You cannot be too guarded against old sins.

12. Never venture on any course of doubtful propriety. "Let every man be fully persuaded in his own mind."

13. In all cases of doubt, decide against self-will, self-interest, and self-indulgence, against your passions, prejudices, and even preferences.

14. If overtaken in a fault, do not deny it, or excuse it before God or man, but ingenuously confess and forsake it. So shall you find mercy.

15. Fervently pray to God to keep you. Beg him not to take his Holy Spirit from you, and not to leave you to yourself. That was a good prayer of David: "Hold thou me up, and I shall be safe."

16. If you strongly suspect that you are wrong, you probably are wrong; and if conscience is against you, you may know that God is also against you. "If our heart condemn us, God is greater than our heart, and knoweth all things."

17. Be not afraid of knowing the worst of your case. Your discovery of your own vanity, imperfection and nothingness, so far from being a bad sign, will be a token for good, if it leads you to trust wholly in Christ.

18. Choose your company with care and in God's fear. "He that walketh with wise men shall be wise; but the companion of fools shall be destroyed." Loose companions, freely chosen, will give a loose conscience.

19. Die unto the world. Let its charms fade from your view. Freely consent to be a stranger and a pilgrim on the earth. Seek for heavenly-mindedness. Owen: "Unless we can arrive at a fixed judgment that all things here below are transitory and perishing, reaching only to the outward man, the body; and that the best of them have nothing substantial and abiding in them, . . . it is impossible but we must spend our lives in fears, sorrows, and distraction."

20. Be not faithless, but believing. Trust God in the darkest hour. He "will either keep his saints *from* temptations by his *preventing* mercy, or *in* temptations by his *supporting* mercy, or find a way for their escape *from* temptation by his *delivering* mercy." "He who loves you into sorrow, will love you through sorrow."

21. "Resist the devil and he shall flee from you." Give place to him, no, not for an hour. He is mighty, but he is not almighty. He is cunning, but he has no wisdom.

22. Beware of attempting to be wise above what is written, yet humbly pray to be taught up to what is written.

23. In every new enterprise undertaken for God's glory, look out for sharp trials. "My son, if thou comest to serve the Lord, prepare thyself for temptation." As our Lord himself entered on his public

ministry, he had long and fearful conflicts with the adversary.

24. When God is humbling you, try to humble yourself. "With the lowly is wisdom." "Be not high-minded, but fear." "He that is down needs fear no fall." Dyer: "He, that lives without fear, shall die without hope." "Pride goeth before a fall, and a haughty spirit before destruction."

25. If you have a great fight of afflictions, remember that "it is a worse sign to be without chastisement, than to be under chastisement; and that all you suffer is not hell, yet it is all the hell you shall suffer," provided your heart is right with God.

26. Often come to the fountain opened for sin and uncleanness, and wash away all guilt contracted in life. The blood of Christ is both the purifier and the preserver of a good conscience. Dyer: "Christ with his cross is better than the world with its crown. Study more how to adorn the cross than how to avoid it." Miller: "If God's people fall into sin, it is not while they are eyeing the perfection of Christ's righteousness, but when they lose sight of it."

27. Think often of death, judgment, heaven, hell, and eternity. Keep your latter end in view. "The time is short." "The Judge standeth before the door."

# INDEX.

## A.



## B.

## C.



## D.

## E.



## F.

## G.



## H.

## I.



## J.

## L.

## M.

## O.



## P.

## S.

54 *

## T.

## U.



## V.



## W.

THE END.

www.ingramcontent.com/pod-product-compliance
Lightning Source LLC
LaVergne TN
LVHW021057110826
845150LV00001B/99

* 9 7 8 1 4 2 5 5 6 6 7 6 0 *